WAR AND SOCIETY in the
AMERICAN REVOLUTION

War & SOCIETY in the American Revolution
MOBILIZATION and HOME FRONTS

John Resch and Walter Sargent, editors

Introduction by John Shy

NORTHERN ILLINOIS UNIVERSITY PRESS

DeKalb

Published by the Northern Illinois University Press, DeKalb, Illinois   60115
Manufactured in the United States using acid-free paper

Library of Congress Cataloging-in-Publication Data

War and society in the American Revolution : mobilization and home fronts /
edited by John Resch and Walter Sargent; introduction by John Shy.

p.   cm.

Includes bibliographical references and index.

ISBN-13: 978-0-87580-366-1 (library edition : alk. paper)

ISBN-10: 0-87580-366-0 (library edition : alk. paper)

ISBN-13: 978-0-87580-614-3 (pbk. : alk. paper)

ISBN-10: 0-87580-614-7 (pbk. : alk. paper)

1. United States—History—Revolution, 1775-1783—Social aspects. 2. United States—Militia—
History—18th century. 3. United States. Continental Army—Mobilization. 4. Soldiers—United
States—History—18th century. I. Resch, John Phillips. II. Sargent, Walter (Walter L.)

E209.W35 2006

973.3′1—dc22

2006014234

CONTENTS

WAR AND SOCIETY
IN THE AMERICAN REVOLUTION
Mobilization and Home Fronts

As the United States begins the twenty-first century, the public has again been intrigued by the American Revolution as measured by the popularity of new biographies of the Founders and rousing histories of great events, such as the battles at Lexington and Concord, Washington's daring crossing of the Delaware, and the struggle for Independence in 1776. In this volume, historians explore the Revolution from a different perspective. They view the Revolution as a total war that at some time during the eight-year conflict touched the lives of virtually all American families, slaves and free blacks, and Indian tribes. Ordinary men and women coped with the demands of mobilization, tribal leaders chose sides, families and communities fought against one another, and black veterans recalled their service with patriotic pride when they petitioned for pensions. They are the central actors in these essays.

This volume grew out of a vision of John Shy, who challenged historians in his 1976 volume, *A People Numerous and Armed,* to integrate the military history of the American Revolution into the social history of the American colonies. He invited scholars to consider war as a seminal social experience and to analyze Revolutionary society and more generally societies at war. Since then, several historians have responded to that challenge, but, especially in recent years, a growing cadre of historians has added new research linking social and military history. Shy's "Looking Backward, Looking Forward: War and Society in Revolutionary America," opens this anthology with reflections on fundamental issues of motivation and mobilization, an overview of this field of scholarship, an introduction to the ten essays, and thoughts on directions for future research.

In June 2000, following the Annual Meeting of the Omohundro Institute of Early American History and Culture, after delivering papers on mobilization, we thought it was time to create an anthology of original essays that would showcase recent scholarship. Our aim was a collection that would be interesting to general readers, useful in undergraduate and graduate courses, and encourage new research projects. This collection, by no means a complete sample, illustrates the variety and richness of recent research that is contributing new insights into the Revolution. Examining the experience of war in its social context provides the unifying theme of the essays in this volume. Each of these essays stands alone, but, taken together, they constitute more than the sum of the parts. One result is an expanded view of ordinary people who accomplished extraordinary feats under the most trying circumstances.

In the American Revolution, national mobilization relied upon a blend of congressional, state, and local initiatives interacting with the particular circumstances and motivations of families and individuals. Charles Neimeyer, Walter Sargent, and John Resch reveal some of the complexities of mobilization processes throughout various New England communities. Race and class also affected mobilization. Judith Van Buskirk explores the legacy of race through the memories of black veterans recorded in pension applications, as well as racism experienced as old soldiers. Michael McDonnell reveals a complex calculus of class relations in Virginia's mobilization.

Unlike America's later wars, the Revolution had no single home front because communities and societies within and among the American provinces were often disconnected, radically different, and variously touched by a war that shifted in site, intensity, and conduct—from formal naval and big army operations to guerrilla warfare—over eight years. Jim Piecuch and Karim Tiro offer views of the Revolution looking east from the backcountry: Piecuch sheds new light on the cauldron of shifting loyalties in the South Carolina backcountry and Tiro unravels the intricacies of the diplomacy of the Oneida Nation. Wayne Lee takes another approach to the experience of the Revolutionary War in his analysis of its effects in North Carolina on the cultural restraints that limit violence and restrict retribution. Joan Gundersen adds to her prior work by taking readers to the home fronts created by women who, displaced by marching armies, sustained themselves and their families in refugee communities. Holly Mayer expands her earlier work on women who accompanied the armies. She shows how they created a semblance of a home front around the campfires while performing critical service for the war effort.

As scholars, we all stand upon the shoulders of those who labored before us, and we owe our thanks to all who have paved our way. They are recognized throughout this volume in the many citations that bear witness to their scholarship and in acknowledgments by the authors. We wish to thank our contributors, our respective universities, and the libraries, archives, and institutions that have supported our work. In particular, we express our appreciation to Kevin Butterfield and Melody Herr, our editors at Northern Illinois University Press, who have made valuable suggestions that have improved this volume. We owe a special debt of gratitude to John Shy and Alfred Young for their invaluable advice and support.

John Resch and Walter Sargent

WAR AND SOCIETY in the
AMERICAN REVOLUTION

LOOKING BACKWARD, LOOKING FORWARD

War and Society in Revolutionary America

JOHN SHY

The beginning of a book of valuable contributions to our understanding of the American Revolution is a place to stop and think before going on with the individual chapters. The general subject seems clear: war and society in the Revolutionary era. But the two terms of that title—*war* and *society*—raise important questions. "Society" is hardly a precise term; rather, it is comprehensive and elastic, quotidian and somewhat vague, rightly suggesting that almost any human activity is "social," or has a social aspect. The variety of subjects represented in this volume suggests the inclusive nature of social history. "War," by contrast, is highly specific, focused on organized violence legitimated by a political agent and its agenda. However frequent warfare may be, most of those caught up in war find the experience bizarre, frightening, often surreal. Wars are exciting and well remembered, but they also sow death, misery, and loss—a social experience to be avoided if possible. Linking "normal" social existence to the harrowing activity of warfare makes good sense, in that the true engine of war is collective human action, but it is not easily done by any precise analytical scheme. Here too, the essays in this volume illustrate the point.

One way to bring some order to the complex and confusing relationship between war and society is to follow a few distinct lines of inquiry that have been pursued in studies of the American Revolution, as well of other wars, and that appear in the chapters that follow. These lines, or issues, may be described as concerning motivation, mobilization, and impact. Before following each line and finding the links between them, however, we need to consider the peculiar historiography of one of our terms—war.

Stories of battles, military campaigns, and military heroes, as well as leaders who blundered to defeat, exert a compelling popular fascination.

That fascination has long been a problem for historians of the American Revolution. In 1837 Peter Force defined the issue in the preface to the first volume of his monumental and never-completed documentary compilation of the Revolution, titled *American Archives:*

> By many superficial persons it is supposed that the *American* Revolution began with the battle of *Lexington,* and terminated with the evacuation by the *British* Troops of these *United States.* It seems to be the opinion of such, that the whole history of that Revolution is to be found in the narrative of the campaigns of that War.

However clearly Force defined the problem, his admonition did not solve it, but may instead have helped to make it more intractable. Although his *American Archives* is filled with military rosters and letters exchanged between military commanders, Force was expressing in the quoted passage a scholarly distaste for military history, and by extension the history of war, that became characteristic of the emerging historical profession even to this day. The reading public appears never to tire of the subject of war and notoriously buys books about it, but most academic historians themselves have regarded military history as beneath serious notice, as a nuisance and a distraction—a species of entertainment better left, if not alone, then to a few summary pages when the subject is otherwise unavoidable.

Force was devoted to the worthy cause of broadening our understanding of the American Revolution, a devotion shared by the editors and authors of this volume. But by dismissing the history of the war, and equating those who emphasized its importance with "superficial persons," he was joining a more general movement to make the causes and the outcome of the Revolution the principal subjects for serious study, leaving the war years as having had if anything too much attention. This shift of scholarly emphasis away from the violent processes of an eight-year war, 1775–1783, and on to the pre-1775 origins of the war and the post-1783 working out of the victorious Revolution, has continued to mark the historiography of the American Revolution. The great historians of the Revolution since George Bancroft (1800–1891), who did not flinch from military narrative, down to Bernard Bailyn, have heeded Force's call, leaving military historians to roam freely over the fields of battle and to record and debate every detail of what happened at Bunker Hill, Trenton, Saratoga, and Yorktown, while more consequential matters, far removed from the battlefield, were being deeply explored by those better qualified. There are exceptions: David Hackett Fischer, no military historian, has written two fine studies of Revolutionary warfare, each of which ably connects the military to the social.[1] Nevertheless, the overall pattern is clear; the military history of the American Revolution has followed its own line, while the general historiography of the Revolution has followed a distinctly different line. Even one of the most impressive efforts to present a comprehensive version, the Pulitzer-winning metanarrative of Gordon Wood's

Radicalism of the American Revolution (1992), spares only a few pages to discuss the effects of eight years of the Revolutionary War.

Motivation

To return, then, to our analytical categories for relating war to society in Revolutionary America: the question of the soldier's motivation has become an aspect of a much larger historiographical issue. Early in the twentieth century, American historians were attracted by the idea that perceived economic interest largely determines political behavior, and they used this idea to present the American Revolution as having been triggered and driven by clashing economic interests, not only between Britain and its colonies, but also between an affluent American elite and the mass of ordinary Americans. Although this behavioral model succumbed to its many critics soon after the end of the Second World War, it has survived to inform a contentious debate about why men joined—or did not join—the military struggle for American independence, 1775–1783. Another, much older idea provides the context for this ongoing debate—the idea that soldiers are recruited disproportionately from the marginal elements of any society, from among men who have no other options, attracting those who see the chance to be fed, clothed, and at least minimally paid as a genuine opportunity for a better life. Long before 1775, this model of every European army's rank and file was well known and widely accepted. The debate, as applied to the American Revolutionary War, centers on who actually fought for American independence.

No one has done more than Charles Royster to engage this argument. His *American Revolutionary People at War: The Continental Army and American National Character, 1775–1783,* appeared in 1979, when historians of the American Revolution had long since turned away from economic determinism to seek other theories explaining why there had been a revolution and what it had brought about. Royster described an aroused America—or, more accurately, an aroused New England—that in 1775 had freely sent its sons and fathers and husbands and brothers by the thousands to resist forcibly the British Army. Lexington, Concord, and Bunker Hill gave names to this massive resistance. That first year, when the British learned that the New England nut was too tough to crack, and decided to move their main operations southward and westward, to the so-called Middle Colonies, Royster calls the American *rage militaire,* when patriotism and enthusiasm reigned. Royster was writing a social history of the war, of the relationship between the American people and the Continental Army—that relatively small, semiprofessional force, led by Washington, whose survival in the end secured American victory. But Royster was also writing a particular kind of social history, a history devoid of statistical tables, a history of impressions and expressions, following the dictum of Virginia Woolf that "nothing has really happened until you have described it."[2] Using letters, diaries, and comparable evidence, Royster described a sharp decline by 1776 in the initial *rage militaire,* and during the middle and later years of the war a mutual, deepening estrangement between those Americans who supported the cause and the little army that did most of the actual fighting. Americans who had taken an active part in the first year of the war seemed to lose interest in signing up for the long enlistments required by Continental service, and in undergoing the severe hardships and predictable dangers of that service, while those few who did enlist were well aware of the many who were strenuously avoiding service in the Revolution's army.

Only at the end of his book, in a brief appendix (pp. 373–78), did Royster confront other historians who had done statistical work and from its results had concluded that an army of "poor, young men" confirmed the old idea that the Revolution was also an internal struggle between economic classes, and that Revolutionary soldiers were motivated more by immediate, personal need than by genuine commitment to the Revolutionary cause. Citing the pioneering studies of Edward Papenfuse, Gregory Stiverson, John R. Sellers, Mark Lender, and Robert Gross, who had used surviving military and civil records to identify individuals and count noses, Royster disputed their chief inference, which was that the relative poverty and youth of Continental soldiers after 1776 indicates they were unmotivated by Revolutionary idealism. Gross, in his influential study of Concord, Massachusetts, *The Minutemen and Their World* (1976), stated the case in question most succinctly:

> The demand for manpower [after 1776] was immense, but the town never failed to meet its quota, one way or another. In the process, though, the very character and social meaning of the war were transformed: from a voluntary struggle to a battle by conscripts and eventually from a community-wide effort to a poor man's fight. (p. 147)

And Gross went on to detail how Concord met its enlistment quota, by allowing men drafted to hire substitutes, even sending Concord's handful of slaves off to war. The implication was clear: motivation to perform active military service as a civic duty was virtually dead after 1776, and those who served from Concord did so because they had no better choice.

Drawing on his own kind of evidence as well as logic, Royster insisted that an army of impoverished mercenaries would never have been willing to endure what the Continental Army endured, and he cited the current best estimate of 25,000 deaths in Revolutionary military service through battle, disease, or captivity, making the Revolutionary War, with respect to population, second only to the Civil War as the bloodiest in national history. His strongest argument was also the simplest: that there is no reason to assume self-interest and idealism did not coexist in the heart and mind of a Continental soldier.

There is a further inference that Royster did *not* discuss in the appendix, perhaps because those who have presented economic models of Revolutionary soldiery rarely spell it out, but also because it lies very much at the heart of his own argument, an inference to the effect that, if the soldiers were young and poor, then more mature, more affluent Americans were by 1776 losing interest in actually fighting for their new republic. From his research, Royster had derived a shared ideal of virtuous republican warfare in which hardship and danger were to be shared equitably. An obvious and troubling deviation after 1776 from this republican ideal is what Royster's excellent book is about. From Washington on down, no one needed statistics to realize that Americans willing to enlist for arduous military service were in very short supply and that the republican ideal of equitably shared military service bore little relation to Revolutionary reality. So, on this issue of motivation, these two inferences have been in play: first, that if Continental soldiers were young and poor, their motives for joining and fighting must have been more like those of their hard-bitten, professional European counterparts than of the legendary minuteman who rushed instinctively to defend home, community, and liberty; and, second, that the Revolution's chronic shortage of soldiers must mean that most available men were willing to leave the fighting to those few thousands who could be enticed or coerced to do it. The inferences are related, but they are distinct from one another. Royster rebutted the first as unproved and implausible but conceded and built upon the validity of the second.

Attentive readers of Royster, or even of this bald summary, will notice some ambiguity in his position. Most Americans after 1776 avoided the most arduous and hazardous form of military service even as they expressed their belief that the goal of an independent republic demanded the burden of its creation being shared fairly among its citizens. Soldiers of the Continental Army were angry at being neglected by citizens and politicians who declined to do more to reinforce, pay, and supply them. Despite the agricultural riches and large population of the American colonies, the army never had the numbers or the financial and logistical support it so desperately needed.

So what do the following chapters contribute to the resolution of these issues? In their chapters, our editors, John Resch and Walter Sargent, attack both inferences directly, using cases from the rich wartime documentation of New England, Resch for New Hampshire and Sargent for Massachusetts. By changing the terms of the debate to include state and militia forces, they present data from military and town records to argue persuasively that active military service was widely shared and very extensive within the adult male population. Their conclusion is that the decline of martial zeal after 1776 has been exaggerated, maybe even by contemporaries, and that a remarkably large proportion of New England manpower, a true cross-section of society, took up arms for considerable periods of service during the eight-year war. From their impressively thorough research we see much of the old legend confirmed, of most Americans fighting for their independence, a legend well grounded in the historical record as presented in the opening chapter by Charles Neimeyer on the Massachusetts militia in 1775.

If all America were New England, the motivation debate would seem to have been settled. But the evidence presented by Michael McDonnell on Virginia is troubling for those who would reject the motivational inferences in question. At the outset it should be said that no state kept the full local and military records available to Resch and Sargent for New England, so it is not possible to replicate for anywhere west and south of Connecticut the kind of thorough, systematic research we have for New Hampshire and Massachusetts. County records for Virginia are sketchy, and McDonnell must rely on correspondence among the leadership and a few scattered recruiting lists. But, from this evidence, it is clear that, by 1780, when Virginia came under direct British attack, motivation in the state had faltered badly. To quote McDonnell, "most middling, independent farmers resisted any and all attempts to persuade, entice, or coerce them into service in the Continental Army." Virginia was the most populous of the new United States, and more than two of every five Virginians were African American, most of them enslaved. Many of the white "middling" farmers feared slave insurrection should they and their neighbors march off to war, but they also resented the ruling elite of Virginia, whose wealth derived from owning most of the slaves and whose white overseers were exempted by law from military service. McDonnell shows how these racial fears and economic class differences, themselves closely linked to the racial makeup of the society, played out in the effort to motivate Virginians to fight for American independence. Some slaves won their freedom by agreeing to serve in place of a white owner, but their numbers in relation to the total required were relatively small. Throughout the war, Virginia followed its own established tradition by recruiting for military service primarily among white men who lacked property and employment. It is hardly surprising that the question of motivation appears to have one answer for New England and a quite different answer in Virginia.

Wayne Lee, in his chapter on the war in the North Carolina backcountry, reminds us of yet another perspective on motivation: whatever may have motivated men to enlist, violence itself could become a great motivator, prompting victims to strike back in almost any way they could. Much of the debate about motivation in volunteer armies, like those in the Revolution and the Civil War, skirts this self-evident truth. After the First World War, with its horrific casualties, and major mutinies in the Russian and French armies, the question of the soldier's motivation received greater attention, and during the Second World War serious social-science research was devoted to the question. From that research came an answer that emphasized not military discipline and leadership or the impetus of patriotic idealism, but the role of what was called the "primary group"— the small group of comrades with whom each soldier lived and fought, the buddies who supported him and who in turn relied on him for support. These modern research findings harked back to one of the oldest myths of warfare—the crucial importance of comradeship. Note that this modern research was directed at conscript armies, in which the soldier's motivation to join is hardly an issue. On the other hand, many historians of the American Revolution, in which almost all military service may be said to be more or less voluntary, take this initial motivation to serve as the key question, ignoring the transformative effects of active military service and armed combat.[3] Lee's chapter is a valuable exception, in that he directs our attention back to the kind of motivation that emerges from the experience of war itself.

In the end, the question of motivation to serve and to fight may be seen as not an irresistible question, but an analytical swamp. Debates about motivation, deprived of direct evidence, tend toward conjectural polemics, with romantic idealism and behaviorist cynicism as competing extremes of the argument. Social identities (e.g., "poor" and "young") are rarely satisfactory inferential data for perhaps the most tangled problem of human existence, why we do what we do. The problem is particularly resistant to the kind of evidence history leaves behind, especially for individual decisions about an activity in which fear, confusion, and other powerful emotions are as prominent as they are in war. Memoirs lie, diaries conceal, and wartime correspondence rarely has time for this deeply personal question to which even the individual hardly knows the answer. We can hope to learn something from historical research about the intentions that underlie human decisions, but the real motives underlying the intentions remain impenetrably murky.

All the other chapters in this volume have some bearing on the question of what may have motivated the American Revolutionary soldier, particularly the soldier who agreed to serve for fairly long periods far from home, whether in the militia, state troops, or the Continental Army itself, but these other chapters may better be considered as bearing on our second and third issues: mobilization for war and war's social impact.

Mobilization

Mobilization is, of course, closely related to motivation—Resch uses the former word in the title of a chapter that deals extensively with the latter—but it is also a distinct issue. Whatever the quality and degree of individual motivation in a society, some collective process must harness and direct it, and that process is mobilization. What appears to be spontaneous action by large numbers of people almost always reveals, on close examination, preexisting organization and direction, and David Hackett Fischer's meticulous reconstruction in *Paul Revere's Ride* (1994) of the local response to violence at Lexington and Concord in April 1775 is a case in point. But compared to the more successful monarchies of Europe, American government was relatively weak, and its means for compelling people to act were very limited. Nevertheless, government, as represented in the Continental Congress and the newly independent states, was responsible for waging the war, legitimating what otherwise would have been criminal acts, and most Americans looked to government to organize, sustain, and lead the society's collective military effort. Not all Americans, it should be said, looked to these Revolutionary governments for leadership: an estimated one in five Americans refused to accept the majority's declaration of independence from British rule.[4] This dissident loyalist minority made the task of governmental mobilization all the more difficult.

Resch and Sargent offer the clearest picture of mobilization in action. From time to time each New England town received a quota, passed down from state through county government, of soldiers to be raised, either as recruits for the Continental Army or for another purpose, and it was the task of town officials—selectmen and militia officers—somehow to fill that quota. As the war went on, the methods used by the town to meet its quota were seldom models of republican justice, but the quota was usually met, in many instances at the cost of saddling the town and its citizens with a crushing postwar debt. The outright drafting of men was less a direct method of enlistment than a threat to goad the citizenry into finding another recruit somewhere, somehow. The town had nothing like a police force to compel obedience, but it seems clear that, in most cases, the whole body of the townspeople supported the collective effort of mobilizing military manpower, provided the effort did not fall blindly on just any man. Certain fathers, husbands, and sons were to be spared the worst. And there were exceptions and limits. Pockets of loyalist sentiment existed throughout New England, around the southeastern town of Marshfield for example, and in the towns of Barnstable and Sandwich on Cape Cod. And even a basically patriotic town could simply refuse; Resch tells us about Canterbury and Weare, New Hampshire, towns more scattered and less cohesive than others, divided before the war by parochial conflicts. Both towns had trouble recruiting after 1776. In 1777, Weare simply refused to meet its quota of sixteen men for the Continental Army because the financial and personal burdens were unfairly distributed. A committee of townsmen sorted out that crisis, but in 1779 the town balked again. There were other places like Canterbury and Weare, and much worse, all over Revolutionary America. But we can also see, even in Weare, a remarkable capacity and willingness throughout New England to send men off to war. Attitudes toward military service shifted after 1776, but collective behavior changed very little in this region. It was not top-down government that mobilized New England; rather, the effective mobilizing effort came from society itself, from dozens of communities cohesive enough to repress dissent and compel response.

Collective resistance had forced the British Army out of New England in March 1776, and thereafter the region was like a giant fortress, vulnerable to attack along its periphery but with its interior secure. British forces threatened New England repeatedly. In 1776, a British force occupied Newport, Rhode Island; in 1777, a large British army marching southward

LOOKING BACKWARD, LOOKING FORWARD **11**

from Canada endangered its western frontier, and a seaborne raid devastated parts of western Connecticut; in 1779, a small British force established a timbering outpost on Penobscot Bay, in Maine; and in 1781 Benedict Arnold led another seaborne raid that destroyed New London, Connecticut. These events kept New Englanders on edge, but never carried the war far inland.[5]

The main theater of military operations for two years after the British evacuation of Boston in early 1776 would be New York, New Jersey, and Pennsylvania. New York City was occupied for the rest of the war and Philadelphia for the year 1777–1778, the lower Hudson Valley became a military encampment and a no-man's-land for raiders from both sides, while elsewhere bands of armed loyalists and rebel militias contested sporadically for local control. No chapter in this volume deals with mobilization in these Mid-Atlantic states, but my own reading and research indicates that anything like the New England communitarian model of mobilization was rarely found in this region. To take one example, in the hills and valleys of modern Putnam County, then southern Dutchess County, east of the Hudson on the Connecticut border about forty miles north of Manhattan, the patriot militia had all it could to do to control the area, fighting a murderous little war against neighbors who rejected the glorious cause of American independence. From this area the British raised a whole regiment of loyalist American soldiers. Meeting regular quotas for Continental recruits was almost impossible for the hard-pressed precincts of south Dutchess. During the British occupation of Philadelphia, something like civil war raged around the city, not only between rebels and loyalists, but even between Continental troops and Pennsylvania militia who clashed in trying to stop the flow of foodstuffs from the countryside to the British garrison.[6]

As Michael McDonnell tells us, Virginia did not experience real war until very late, when the British shifted their operational focus southward after their defeat at Saratoga and the subsequent alliance between France and the United States in 1778. Perhaps the French alliance reduced American incentive to join the army, but McDonnell makes clear that even heroic measures, like the plan to offer slaves taken from wealthy Virginians to lure prospective recruits, yielded very little. Thomas Jefferson was blamed for being an ineffective governor in this critical period, but it is not easy to see what he might have done to mobilize his state. Most of Virginia's large population was concentrated in the fertile valleys of the Tidewater, with its high concentration of African American slaves, or it lived in scattered farmsteads throughout the Piedmont and into the mountain valleys. The contrast with contemporary New England is stunning. In New England, dispersed settlement had increased during the later colonial period, but the supply of good farmland was very limited, and almost every bit of the region was part of one township or another. Not much of the population was remote from local authority, and as part of its mobilization effort the town could take responsibility for supporting families who sent menfolk to the war. Nothing comparable existed in Virginia, and one can readily imagine the reluctance of a remote Virginia household to give up any of its men for distant service in the army. The same was true as well of the Carolinas, where the backcountry population had grown rapidly and scattered widely during the generation before 1775.

Somewhere between the social extremes of New England on the one hand, and of Virginia and the Carolinas on the other, lay the Mid-Atlantic states, whose small towns and numerous villages gave it a looser version of the New England community structure. But the mobilizing capacity of these middle-state communities seems often to have been undercut by the sectarian and ethnic divisions characteristic of New York and Pennsylvania. Quakers objected to military service on principle, while Germans tended to keep their heads down.

In her chapter on women with the army, Holly Mayer calls attention to what may be considered an aspect of mobilization. If communities failed to mobilize adequate manpower, allowing community to recreate itself within the army could serve as an inducement for men to serve. That, at least, was the way Sergeant John Hawkins described a Continental Army encampment in 1779. European armies of the time typically included some women—wives of noncommissioned officers, widows, and a few without a regular attachment. Cooking, cleaning, and nursing made these women valuable to the army, and a limited number for each regiment were authorized to draw rations for themselves and their children, if any. Women helped to civilize life in an uncivilized occupation, but they could also be a source of trouble and, for Americans, shame. Washington regarded women as an unavoidable nuisance, and more than once tried to conceal their presence from the American public. But they were there, and by performing work that would later be done by separate branches of the military, and at this writing is now being contracted out to civilian corporations, they added to the strength of an understrength army and no doubt something to its morale. A very few women served as soldiers, disguising their sex, and became, like Deborah Sampson, legendary, but the women who followed the troops and shared their hardships made by far the greater contribution.[7] The greatest contribution of all came from thousands of women who replaced soldiers who had left farms and shops for the army.

Americans were forced to recruit wherever men could be found, and even the estimated one in five who was opposed to the Revolution was not exempt. On more than one occasion loyalists were drafted into the militia as a cheap, simple means of keeping track of them. Prisoners of war, including loyalists, were sometimes given the option to join the Continental Army. Observers also noted a growing number of African American soldiers in the American forces as the war continued, and their numbers are reflected in Judith Van Buskirk's chapter on black veterans who applied for service pensions. Much of army life was hard labor—caring for animals, digging, hauling, and chopping. African Americans assigned to such roles could be rejected for pensions because they had not been "soldiers." Another minority, the Indians of eastern North America, numbering perhaps a hundred thousand in 1775, were especially important. Most Indians, if they could not remain neutral, supported the British because the real enemy was seen to be American settlers who coveted their land, and because the British government had made at least some effort to protect Indians from the settlers. There was not much hope of mobilizing any large body of Indians in the American cause, but even a few cooperative tribes or individuals, if strategically located, could strengthen highly vulnerable frontier defenses. The Oneida, part of the Iroquois Confederacy in upstate New York, was one such Indian group, and their valuable but ultimately tragic contribution to winning the war is well described in the chapter by Karim Michel Tiro.

Jim Piecuch describes the problems of mobilization in South Carolina, but as seen from the other side of the hill. The British were unable to find a way to draw on and meld their three main sources of potential strength: powerful Indian groups along the Appalachian frontier, a very large African American slave population concentrated near the coast but also increasingly spread through the interior, and a large minority of white Americans who were unhappy for whatever reason with the Revolution and promised to support a return of British rule. To maintain the support of these white loyalists, the British foreswore the active mobilization of Indian or African American fighters, but in the end the loyalists proved too weak to help bring about a pacified South Carolina. The British dilemma mirrored the American challenge. War with the Indians would bring all whites, loyalist and rebel, together, while the threat of a slave uprising worked in the same way. Yet, recruiting white soldiers was as difficult as it was everywhere outside New England. Taking the British viewpoint is instructive for our focus on mobilization.

Initially, British strategy in South Carolina was quite successful. Charleston, with its large American garrison, was forced to surrender in May 1780, and the remaining Continental forces were all but destroyed at the Battle of Camden in August. From that point on the British relied heavily on loyalist forces, militias primarily, to pacify the rebellion. During the year after Camden, 1780–1781, this strategy of pacification failed. The reasons for failure were various and debatable, but its social effects were spectacular. Relying on loyal Americans to suppress American rebels in effect meant fomenting a civil war. British strategy thus mobilized American resistance on a scale that would otherwise have been impossible, forcing some qualification of the earlier remark that mass action is rarely in fact spontaneous. Violent acts perpetrated by Tory militias triggered retaliatory violence in an escalating spiral, spreading through both Carolinas, recruiting neighbors in many cases to fight neighbors. Wherever the British had used loyalist militias or irregulars in earlier campaigns, the effects had been similar, notably in the area around New York City, but civil war in the Carolinas in 1780–1781 reached an intensity and a viciousness seen nowhere else. The South, until 1779, when the British made it an active theater of operations, had been relatively quiet, with the social and political system not tested by fairly low levels of mobilization and internal conflict. But when the British arrived in great force, with their plan to "Americanize" the war, all hell broke loose, and war itself became the great mobilizer.

A final word on mobilization is about numbers. Whatever the regional differences in the mobilization effort, whatever the degree of American reluctance or resistance to joining the army, and however strong the enduring popular image that only Washington and a few thousand Continental heroes saved the Republic while everyone else stayed home, the numbers are impressive. The Revolutionary War files for service pensions, which did not begin until 1818, contain data on about 70,000 veterans. Even allowing for some fraud and bureaucratic mistakes, that number would require as many as 200,000 soldiers serving at least the sum of six months in the militia or nine consecutive months in the Continental Army—the legal minimums for eligibility under the several laws—during the war, waged by these pensioners forty or more years earlier.[8] This belated enactment of Federal pensions for Revolutionary War service meant that many veterans would no longer have been alive to apply and collect. The population of the thirteen rebellious colonies in 1775 was about 2.5 million of all races, growing to about three million by the end of the war. A half million are estimated to be loyalist, and another half million were African American with limited opportunities for military service, leaving fewer than two million rebellious whites; half of these (say, a million) women, and at least half of the white male rebels (another half million) too old, too young, or otherwise incapable of serving, leaving a white military manpower pool of roughly half a million. If two in every five of this pool actually served six months or more as a soldier, it was indeed a huge social effort, accomplished with little in the way of formal coercive machinery. It is comparable to the mobilization of Americans in the Civil War and the Second World War. To call this mobilization of the American Revolution purely voluntary would be to ignore all its many complexities, but the sheer quantity must give pause to those who take a cynical view, like the British officer who opined that the American war was started by the descendants of Puritan regicides, and was fought mostly by Irish immigrants.

Impact

Dr. David Ramsay (1749–1815), a Princeton graduate, lived through the American Revolution, serving in both the Continental Congress and the South Carolina legislature. In 1789, Ramsay published one of the earliest and most valuable histories of the Revolution. In an appendix to his second volume, which dwelt heavily on the events of the war, he considered the "influence" of the Revolution "on the minds and morals of the Citizens."[9] Ramsay's is the first systematic effort to assess the impact of the Revolutionary War on American society. Conflating the Revolution with the war in the manner that Peter Force would later deplore as "superficial," Ramsay argued that the impact had been profound, for good and ill.

> When the war began, the Americans were a mass of husbandmen, merchants, mechanics and fishermen; but the necessities of the country gave a spring to the active powers of the inhabitants, and set them on thinking, speaking and acting in a line far beyond that to which they had been accustomed. . . . In the years 1775 and 1776 the country, . . . [was] suddenly thrown into a situation that needed the abilities of all its sons. . . . As they severally pursued their objects with ardor, a vast expansion of the human mind speedily followed. (630)

Before the war most Americans, living remote from one another, were unacquainted with people outside their locality, but the war had moved thousands of men in armies up and down the seaboard, and into the interior, fostering "principles of union among them." (631)

Geographical knowledge, medical arts, the science of government, and public speaking and writing, all had been greatly stimulated by the war, while leaders had learned how to involve the masses in this great venture:

> As the war was the people's war, and was carried on without funds, the exertions of the army would have been insufficient to effect the revolution, unless the great body of the people had been prepared for it. . . . To rouse and unite the inhabitants, and to persuade them to patience for several years, under present sufferings, . . . was a work of difficulty: This was effected in great measure by the tongues and pens of the well-informed citizens, and on it depended the success of military operations (633–34)

But the war had been corrupting as well:

> War never fails to injure the morals of the people engaged in it. The American war, in particular, had an unhappy influence of this kind. Being begun without funds or regular establishments, it could not be carried on without violating private rights; and in its progress, it involved a necessity for breaking solemn promises. (637)

And Ramsay concluded his survey on an ominous note:

> So great is the change for the worse [in American moral character], that friends of public order are fondly called upon to exert their utmost abilities, in extirpating the vicious principles and habits, which have taken deep root during the late convulsions. (638)

Among the many aspects of the war's impact, Joan Gundersen has focused on the thousands of women uprooted by war in Virginia. Her chapter reveals that many of these women were not driven from their homes by fear, but moved as a matter of political choice. Other women entered the state as the wives of British or German prisoners of war. Women driven from home by warfare soon returned to claim property and reestablish households, while others followed loyalist husbands into exile.

Even Cherokee women living along the western frontiers of the state appear capable of making political choices when war forced them to move, just as women in coastal Norfolk, on the bull's-eye for British operations early in the war, made comparable decisions, many of them staying when prudence indicated it was time to leave. African American women, fleeing slavery as well as the war, carried their children into British lines and what they hoped would be freedom. British seaborne raids on the Tidewater in 1779–1781 started a new wave of refugees—slaves seeking freedom, and women fleeing burning houses as the raiders swept through hastily. What in the end was the lasting impact? Refugees from both the coast and the frontier strained the resources of Piedmont farmsteads, where food was already in short supply. The blow to slavery in Virginia was severe, though doubtless exaggerated by slaveowners claiming compensation. Property was destroyed, but quickly replaced. Most refugee women appear to have acted in a way to sustain their marital ties. Perhaps most lasting would be the memory of flight.

Another lasting memory of war is explored by Judith Van Buskirk in her original chapter on African American veterans who applied when the first pension law for Revolutionary War service was passed in 1818. These were fairly old men, survivors of not only the war, but also the other hazards of life in the four decades since the war. Poor, as the pension law required, but free, by their military service if not previously so, their affidavits and supporting documentation offer a moving testament to a point made by Ramsay: that the upheaval of war had caused the first faint cracks in the institution of slavery. An interesting sidelight on this body of evidence is that these men had served in military units more racially integrated than were any American units until the latter twentieth century. Surprising to me was the author's finding that early applicants from 1818 often had warm support from white comrades and received treatment from the War Department bureaucracy that appears to be free of blatant racial discrimination. But with the passage of a new law in 1832, making militia service eligible for a pension, a law administered when Andrew Jackson was president, the situation changed. Because militia records were lacking in the federal archives, applicants were required to tell the full story of their military service, and to make the story plausible by including names, dates, and other details that might be checked. Whether it was the problem of narration, or the advent of Southerners on the War Department staff, a disproportionate number of African

American applicants began to be rejected. The year 1832 is a long time after the Revolutionary War to be tracing its impact, but the trace is apparent, whatever its significance.

One aspect of "impact" in this or any war is its reciprocal nature; society has an impact on warfare. That much is made clear by the stark differences between the regions of Revolutionary America, from the fairly compact settlements of New England to the more polyglot and dispersed populations of the Mid-Atlantic and Southern states, as if two or three altogether different wars were fought in America between 1775 and 1783. But Wayne Lee's chapter on North Carolina points to a more subtle effect of society—some would call it culture—on warfare. As has been noted, war in the western areas of North Carolina became very ugly in its latter stages, but Lee discerns a cultural factor that served to mitigate and ultimately to quench a cycle of retaliatory violence. People on both sides killed without mercy, with the grisly execution of loyalist prisoners after the Battle of King's Mountain in late 1780 the most memorable instance. But many more prisoners were spared than were killed, and these men were allowed to return home and survived the war. Lee sees a pattern in retaliatory violence, a pattern informed by a shared cultural understanding of what justified retaliation and what forbade it.

There may be a larger significance in Lee's highly original finding. The best estimate is that about a half a million Americans refused to support the Revolution and even resisted it, at least 30,000 of them in arms. At the end of the war, less than 100,000 loyalists emigrated to Canada, England, or elsewhere. So what happened to some 400,000 loyalists who remained? Somehow they were able to reintegrate themselves into American society, perhaps by changing residence or just by being quiet. Unlike other revolutionary wars, America saw little or nothing like a postwar reign of terror, with victorious bullies harassing and cracking the skulls of the losers.

Conclusion

This volume points a way forward. Perhaps the impossible question of motivation should be put to rest, at least for a while. The magnitude of the collective American effort in the war suggests that an emphasis on class conflict does not promise much in the way of general understanding. Although such conflicts surely existed and influenced events at particular times and places—interior Virginia, or towns like Weare, New Hampshire—the high level of popular support for the political objective reduces to lesser importance the inevitable wartime squabbling over who should make the greater sacrifice to achieve that objective. At the same time, microcosmic studies, like that of Gross on Concord, remain valuable to qualify and challenge the kind of sweeping generalizations of which this introduction is not free.

Our third issue, the impact of the war, remains a fair ground for further research, but it is also a minefield. The very idea of "impact" assumes that, without an eight-year war of attrition and popular resistance, certain changes in American society would not have taken place. Would a new American national unity and the unleashing of popular energy and talent, so lyrically described by Ramsay as results of the war, have taken place if Britain had been wise enough to grant the American colonies their independence in 1776 without a long, costly war? It is impossible to know. A few things about impact are clear. War certainly led directly to chaos in the monetary situation of the immediate postwar period, a chaos that had major political repercussions. But other questions about war's impact demand that imagination be tempered by very careful consideration of the causes pushing major changes and a recognition that the general question of "impact" makes historians susceptible to flights of fancy derived from our own situation, experience, and personal inclination. Ramsay was a both a conservative and a nationalist, and his brief but fascinating account of the impact of the war reflects those aspects of his personal bias. Closer to home, my own attempt to depict the war as a politicizing and democratizing force was sternly countered a few years later by my friend Sung Bok Kim, whose personal and family experience in the Korean War, as well as his own historical research on the lower Hudson Valley in the Revolution, led him to think that people caught in the middle of war were likely to grow cynical about politics and to hunger for order more than democracy.[10] Those who would resolve this issue for the American Revolutionary War will need to proceed with caution and self-criticism as well as bold imagination.

Notes

1. David Hackett Fischer, *Paul Revere's Ride* (New York: Oxford University Press, 1994), and *Washington's Crossing* (New York: Oxford University Press, 2004).

2. Margalit Fox, Obituary of Nigel Nicolson, *New York Times,* September 25, 2004, p. B-13.

3. A useful review of the literature, and the debate among military social scientists, is Elliot P. Chodoff, "Ideology and Primary Groups," *Armed Forces and Society* 9 (1983): 569–93, especially pp. 576–91, with notes, distinguishing between ideology and primary groups as motivating factors, and between precombat and in-combat motivation.

4. Paul H. Smith, "The American Loyalists: Notes on their Organization and Numerical Strength," *William and Mary Quarterly,* 3rd ser., 25 (April 1968): 259–77.

5. The pioneering work by Richard Buel, Jr., *Dear Liberty: Connecticut's Mobilization for the Revolutionary War* (Middletown, Conn.: Wesleyan University Press, 1980), is important to our overall understanding.

6. Wayne Bodle, *The Valley Forge Winter: Civilians and Soldiers in War* (University Park: Pennsylvania State University Press, 2002).

7. Alfred F. Young, *Masquerade: The Life and Times of Deborah Sampson, Continental Soldier* (New York: Alfred A. Knopf, 2004).

8. John Resch, *Suffering Soldiers: Revolutionary War Veterans, Moral Sentiment, and Political Culture in the Early Republic* (Amherst: University of Massachusetts Press, 1999), p. 261, n.22, seems to accept the estimate of 200,000, but Daniel Scott Smith, of the University of Illinois at Chicago, thinks this estimate may be too high. No one, apparently, has used pension records and actuarial tables to project back to the number of potential applicants, 1775–1783.

9. The most convenient edition is David Ramsay, *The History of the American Revolution,* 2 vols., ed. Lester H. Cohen (Indianapolis: Liberty Fund, 1990). The appendix is in vol. 2, pp. 625–38.

10. Compare my conjecture in *A People Numerous and Armed: Reflections on the Military Struggle for American Independence,* rev. ed. (Ann Arbor: University of Michigan Press, 1990), especially pp. 242–44, with Sung Bok Kim, "The Limits of Politicization in the American Revolution: The Experience of Westchester County, New York," *Journal of American History* 80 (1993): 868–89. I have made another attempt, with an altered focus, in "Logistical Crisis and the American Revolution: A Hypothesis," in John A. Lynn, ed., *Feeding Mars: Logistics in Western Warfare from the Middle Ages to the Present* (Boulder, Colo.: Westview Press, 1993), pp. 161–79.

Part I

SOLDIERS

Motivation and Mobilization

1

"TOWN BORN, TURN OUT"

Town Militias, Tories, and the Struggle for Control of the Massachusetts Backcountry

CHARLES NEIMEYER

What avails Prudence, Wisdom, Policy, Fortitude, Integrity without Power, without Legions?[1]

In the early morning hours of September 1, 1774, specially selected British regular soldiers of the 4th (Kings Own) Foot were rowed across the harbor to the Mystic River to seize what remained of the "provincial reserve" of gunpowder then located in the "windowless stone tower" in what today is Somerville, Massachusetts. Patiently waiting for the morning light, for fear of an explosion if lanterns were used, the redcoats quickly carted away 250 half-barrels of the precious powder and later seized two brass field pieces near Cambridge. The soldiers had pulled off what amounted to a near-perfectly executed raid and, "by noon, the munitions were deposited in Castle William, and the men were back in their barracks."[2]

Extremely satisfied with the discipline and efficiency of his men and the military results of his raid, General Thomas Gage, military governor of Massachusetts and commander in chief of His Majesty's forces in North America, was not prepared for the colonial reaction that followed. The very next day, "4000 angry men gathered on Cambridge Common, mostly farmers of towns between Sudbury and Boston." But instead of taking out their ire on the redcoats or perhaps even Gage himself, the mass of men, "armed only with wooden cudgels, marched to 'Tory Row' in Cambridge" and immediately threatened the lives of arch-Tory militia commanders like the wealthy Brigadier General William Brattle and Sheriff David Phips, who himself was a colonel in the militia. The mob then moved on to the home of the lieutenant governor, Thomas Oliver, a Tory who also held a high commission in the militia, and forced him in writing to "resign his seat on Gage's new Royal Council."

To add fuel to the fire, in a particularly ill-timed moment, customs offi- cial Benjamin Hallowell appeared on the scene in his elegant carriage complete with a liveried servant. A local wag approached him and screamed, "Damn you, how do you like us now, you Tory son of a bitch"? Frightened out of his wits, Hallowell grabbed his servant's horse and galloped away toward Boston with the mob in full pursuit.[3]

Jonathan Brigham, a militiaman from Marlborough, Massachusetts, was evidently one of those who showed up at the home of the lieutenant governor. Brigham had joined the town minute company in April 1774 and, in his application for a pension many years after the war, stated that about twenty-five members of his company had been ordered by their commanding officer, Colonel Cyprian How, to find Oliver and determine why the powder had been taken from the magazine. Knocking at the front door of Oliver's home in Cambridge and getting no answer, Brigham and his mates went around to the back door and knocked. This time Oliver an- grily poked his head out of a chamber window and "demanded their busi- ness." Brigham's militiamen informed the lieutenant governor that they meant him no harm but had come to inquire about the status of the pow- der. Brigham noted that Oliver "then came out, marched with uncovered head through the company, and then signed the written pledge that he would not in the future interfere or intermeddle with any of the town stores and would remain quietly and peaceably at home."[4] An interesting turn of events, since it was clear by Brigham's deposition that he believed the Marlborough militia had been the means of Oliver's "political conver- sion." Furthermore, forcing someone to walk hatless through a military formation was an important symbol of subservience and obedience in the eighteenth century, and this point was certainly not lost to the militiamen then present.

Long confronted with a restive population, Gage was faced with a real dilemma. On the one hand, he firmly believed that he needed to appear strong and decisive in the face of growing colonial insults against the pre- rogatives of the Crown and his office as royal governor. Yet, on the other, he felt he needed to "treat the inhabitants on all occasions, with lenity, moderation and justice." Gage, however, also observed that "lenient measures, and the cautious and legal exertion of the coercive powers of government, have served only to render [the Massachusetts Whigs] more daring and licentious."[5] So he settled on a strategy whereby he would seize the means of colonial resistance—their finite stock of munitions, and especially gunpowder. He decided he would accomplish this task through a series of bold but secretive raids into the Massachusetts coun- tryside that surrounded the epicenter of rebellious activity in Boston proper. Unfortunately for him, the actual result of his strategy, along with other political errors both he and the Crown made in the months leading up to the Lexington and Concord fight was to militarize the Massachusetts countryside rapidly.

Fig. 1-1. *General Thomas Gage,* by John Singleton Copley, circa 1768. General Gage was the acting royal governor of Massachusetts, replacing the much-reviled Thomas Hutchinson in early 1774. His appointment placed in the minds of many Bostonians that their colony was under a state of military rule. (Yale Center for British Art, Paul Mellon Collection.)

In anticipation that Gage might try to seize the powder stores of the provincial militia, all summer long, in town after town in Middlesex County, the citizenry had been quietly removing their supplies from various powder magazines and dispersing them throughout the countryside. Indeed, the towns had much to be worried about. Writing to the Tory commander of the Massachusetts militia, Brigadier General William Brattle, Gage asked, "Sir, as I am informed there are several Military Stores in your Charge at Cambridge, I beg the favor of you to send me a Return [report] of them as fast as convenient, specifying the different sorts of each."[6]

But Brattle was not worried about only powder supplies. He was more concerned about the loyalty of the militias ostensibly still under his command. He warned Gage in a letter that the towns were forming "special" militia companies able "to meet at one minute's warning equipt with arms and ammunition" as a possible further insurance against what they deemed was illegal activity by the royal governor. Unfortunately for the loyal Brattle, this letter was either stolen or lost by Gage and fell into the hands of his political enemies, who had it immediately published in the Boston newspapers.[7] Forced to flee his estate in Cambridge on the day of the powder raid, Brattle was never again to return to his home. With the Whig press mockingly calling him "Brigadier Paunch," he eventually became an object of public scorn.[8] This scorn and belittlement of a heretofore respected member of the community should not be seen as a small matter. As we shall see, it was clearly part of a larger process to transform the militia into a patriot-minded tool of resistance and drive out those who might favor the Crown.

Gage was absolutely astounded at the colonial reaction to his powder raid. It had been a tremendous political and military mistake. Canceling a planned subsequent strike against more distant Worcester, Massachusetts, Gage instead began to "think defensively" and informed London that "the whole country was in arms and motion." Instead of following up his success on the Somerville magazine, he began hectoring the colonial secretary for reinforcements. "If you think ten thousand men sufficient [to subdue Massachusetts] send twenty." Soon Gage's demands began to be seen by officials in London, and even the king, as "absurd" and "even hysterical."[9]

The truth be told, the patriots had been caught by surprise. Tories with militia connections had provided Gage with key intelligence concerning the amount and location of powder, and Tory guides helped royal troops to and from their objective. Even the local sheriff, Colonel David Phips, had willingly provided the redcoats with the keys to the door. So it became abundantly clear in the last months of 1774 that more would have to be done politically, socially, and militarily to prevent the Crown from winning their point in the battle for the hearts and minds of Middlesex County. And it quickly became evident that the tool for patriot success devolved on what heretofore had been a relatively moribund and Tory-ridden institution—the New England militia.

Indeed, prior to 1774 and earlier, Tory-minded officers, at least at the higher echelons of command, abounded. Now, patriot leaders saw replacing militia commanders with those more politically reliable as extremely crucial to their cause. One of the more sensational cases of this happening revolved around Brigadier General Timothy Ruggles, a senior militia commander who had won some notoriety during the French and Indian War. Settling in the backcountry near Worcester, Massachusetts, he had recently been appointed as a judge of the inferior court by Thomas Gage. Moreover, Ruggles "fought tooth and nail against changes in the militia, especially the dismissing of the old officer corps, and as a result he was among the first swept out. When he continued to object, his cattle were poisoned, his horse painted garishly, and he was driven from his hometown of Hardwick and forced to take refuge in Boston."[10] In fact, it may have been threats directed against Ruggles that prompted Gage to consider taking some sort of military action against the town of Worcester. Prior plans had been drawn up by Gage's officers for a raid on the order of the one that had earlier taken place in Somerville. Writing to Lord Dartmouth a few days before the Somerville raid, the usually "reserved" Gage angrily stated that "in Worcester they keep no terms; openly threaten resistance by arms; have been purchasing arms; preparing them; casting balls; and providing powder; and threaten to attack any troops who oppose them. Mr. Ruggles, of the new council, is afraid to take his seat as judge of the inferior court, which sits at Worcester on the 6th of next month; and I apprehend, that I shall soon be obliged to march a body of troops into that township, and perhaps into others, as occasions happen, to preserve the peace."[11] The fact that Gage ultimately did not carry out his threat was not lost to the patriot leadership in the towns.

Nonetheless, Ruggles was hounded wherever he went. Attacked by a mob in Dartmouth, Massachusetts, in late August 1774 (the place where they painted his horse), Ruggles sought refuge in the home of Colonel Gilbert (himself a former militia commander under the old regime). In an unidentified extract of a letter from Taunton, Massachusetts, dated August 24, 1774, the writer noted that about "two to three thousand men"—most likely militiamen of various towns of Bristol County—were on their way to Gilbert's house in Freetown (Fall River, Massachusetts) to encourage him to "not accept the office of High Sheriff, under the present administration of the new laws, and that if he should, he must abide the consequences; also to desire Brigadier Ruggles to depart this county immediately. They [the militia companies of Bristol County] seem to be quite awake, and to have awoke in a passion. It is more dangerous being a tory here than at Boston, even if no troops were there."[12] Gilbert was not treated any better. Patriots had put glass under the saddle of his horse. When he attempted to ride to Boston for his own safety and sat down in his saddle, the glass broke and the horse threw him "and the Colonel lighted on his head, and remained senseless for some time, to the infinite joy and amusement of the rebels." In fact, nearly the entire high command of former militia officers were turned out of office either because they also chose to accept simultaneous positions as one of Gage's new governmental officials or because they had already expressed Tory sentiments.[13]

The trend for exposing Tory militia officers and men and replacing them with more "politically reliable" Whigs can be seen in town after town throughout the politically charged months leading up to Lexington and Concord.[14] In the minutes of the Lynn, Massachusetts, town meeting, it was noted that "agreeably to the advice of the respectable Provincial Congress, the training band company in Lynn, north parish, being part of the first regiment in the county of Essex, formerly commanded by William Brown, politically deceased of a pestilent and mortal disorder, and now buried in the ignominious ruins, met on Monday, 15th inst. (November 1774)." This was the same William Browne who had been arrested in 1769 for his participation in the infamous coffeehouse brawl involving James Otis, Jr. The town went on to elect new Whig-minded officers for its militia.[15]

The growing militarization of the Massachusetts towns continued into the winter of 1774–1775. Perhaps emboldened by Gage's failure to carry out his plan to support Ruggles and company in Worcester, the county convention, in conformance with other county conventions, remodeled its militia system. This system "would serve as the pilot model for the minutemen and the basis for the creation of the new militia system throughout the province. The convention first required that all field officers of the militia resign immediately and publish their resignations in the Boston newspapers." Then they voted to choose new officers and to "enlist one third of the men of their respective towns, between sixteen and sixty years of age, to be ready to act at a minute's warning; and to choose a sufficient number of men as a committee to supply and support those troops that shall move on an emergency."[16] The Worcester sentiments were "echoed in the next few weeks by the assemblies in Suffolk, Essex, and Middlesex counties." A citizen of Boston, John Andrews noted that "this day a deputation of twelve came to town with a very spirited remonstrance from the body of Worcester county, which consists of five and forty towns: where they have incorporated seven regiments consisting of 1,000 men each, chose their officers, and turn out twice a week to perfect themselves in the military art which are called minute men."[17] Again, the purpose of this action was to cleanse militia establishments of Tories and replace them with "right-thinking" and politically reliable patriots.

Not only were the towns preparing militarily but political appointments also took on a decided military cast. For example, of the members appointed from the county of Middlesex to the "extralegal" Provincial Congress in the fall of 1774, nineteen of seventy-four appointees (or more than one in four) had military rank attached to their names (signifying past or present affiliation with their respective town militias)—all held the rank of captain. The fact that they were captains also meant that they were considered leaders in their respective towns, because the tradition of the New England militia was to directly elect their officers. "Militia leaders [in Salem, Massachusetts,] also comprised 66 percent of the Boycott Committee in 1770 and 55 percent of the Committee of Correspondence. In

1774 militia officers made up 63 percent of the delegates to the Essex County Convention and provided both of Salem's representatives to the Provincial Congress in the same year." In a letter that welcomed the arrival of General Gage as the new governor of Massachusetts only "8 of the 48 signatures belonged to militia officers, 3 of whom soon after [publicly] apologized for this mistake."[18]

Town after town met in the fall of 1774 to approve the Suffolk Resolves (largely authored by Joseph Warren). The resolves urged the citizens of Massachusetts to reject the "Intolerable Acts" and to organize and recognize only their own provincial government. Included was an admonishment for Massachusetts to look to its own defense and organize its militia to accomplish this mission as soon as possible.[19] Most other counties in Massachusetts published similar "Resolves." All sought to repudiate the new government created by the Intolerable Acts. All decried the arbitrariness of the new Gage-led government. All believed that the establishment of a robust militia to prevent the enforcement of the Intolerable Acts was justified. "The adoption of the Middlesex County resolves by a vote of 146 to 4" was a clear "indication the unanimity of sentiment in the towns."[20] In a letter to her husband John, then in attendance at Congress, Abigail Adams remarked that "the first of September, or the month of September, perhaps, may be of as much importance to Great Britain as the Ides of March were to Caesar."[21]

Gage's first powder raid deserves to be given a much greater historical role in creating and inspiring Revolutionary activity than has heretofore been acknowledged. Paul Revere certainly thought so. Writing to his friend, John Lamb, in New York soon after the raid, he noted,

> Dear Sir,
>
> I embrace the opportunity to inform you, that we are in Spirits, tho' in a garrison; the Spirit of Liberty was never higher than at present, the troops have the horrors amazingly. By reason of some late movements of our friends in the Country, our new fangled Councellors are resigning their places every day; our Justices of the courts, who now hold their commissions during the pleasure of his Majesty, or the Governor, cannot git a jury to act with them, in short the Tories are giving way everywhere in our Province.[22]

The reaction to the powder raid and the passage of the Resolves were crucial for another important reason. They plainly declared that Gage's military preparations on Boston Neck needed to be met with force and essentially nullified his ability to enforce laws or protect Tories in the backcountry. Thus, the power to govern the province naturally and directly fell back upon the towns, and the one viable institution in each Massachusetts town was the various rejuvenated militia and its political organs, the town meetings—nearly all of which, by late winter of 1775, had replaced or run off any citizens of Tory inclination from participating in militia drills and service. Since the towns supported the Suffolk Resolves, the various militia formations were expected to conform as well. There would be no more turning over of the powder house keys to royal officials. In sum, the Resolves clearly repudiated the legitimacy of any functioning organs of Gage's post–Intolerable Acts government.

John Andrews wrote a letter to William Barrell stating that "the present temper of the People throughout the Province is such, that they wont suffer a tory to remain any where among 'em without making an ample recantation of his principles."[23] As was the case with Thomas Oliver following the Somerville raid, militia forced other Tory-minded citizens like Concord physician Joseph Lee to apologize profusely in writing for allegedly attempting to warn a friend on the evening of September 1, 1774, that the militia was headed into Cambridge to exact some retribution for Gage's powder seizure. Lee eventually fled to Boston. The wealthy and powerful Israel Williams of Hatfield was stuffed inside a small room in a house and was literally "smoked" by the militia, who had stuffed up the chimney and blocked the doors and windows for several hours until Williams was nearly dead from smoke inhalation. He, too, was forced to sign a recantation similar to Lee's. The elderly militia colonel Elisha Jones of Weston was forced by three hundred militia, who "made his Mightiness walk through their Ranks with his Hat off and express his Sorrow for past Offences, and promise not to be Guilty of the like for the future."[24]

Contrast for a moment the attitude of the backcountry towns following the September 1 powder raid to an earlier proposed boycott of British goods known as the "Solemn League and Covenant." Whereas the Solemn League was more rigorous and wide-reaching than any earlier proposed non-consumption agreements, it had little support in the county towns. "Of the 260 towns and districts in Massachusetts, only 7 entered the Solemn League and Covenant, and even 2 of these believed it was divisive." The Middlesex County town of Billerica, one of the few towns to actually sign on to the Solemn League, "pledged to adhere to it only as long as the Continental Congress saw fit, and it wholly excluded any method of ostracizing offenders against the agreement." Although it was clear that Massachusetts citizens were still generally enraged over the implementation of the Intolerable Acts, most believed that any direct action at this particular moment was premature. Most towns (at that earlier moment) still strongly preferred internal town unity above an immediate and potentially divisive boycott and "were generally conscious of the fundamental necessity of coordinating their own resistance with that of other colonies."[25]

By contrast, just six days after the Somerville raid, an estimated six thousand citizens of Worcester stood ready to defend themselves. When it became evident that Gage had canceled a not so secretive raid against the town in support of Ruggles and company, the Worcester militia forced forty-three Tories and justices of the county "who had signed [an earlier] loyalty address to General Gage, to march between parallel lines of the armed assemblage, their principals reading the recantations they signed." Shortly after that, "an important convention was held for the radical reorganization of the county militia, when all commissions were to be resigned." The town of Needham dissolved its company of royal militia and created three new units, including a "minute" company.[26] During this same time frame, the towns of Southborough and Stoughton also reorganized their militias. In March 1775, in the Stoughton town meeting, it was voted to "raise about one fourth of the town's militia as minutemen. It also voted to pay one shilling for half a day's training and the militia was to train two half days a week." Drillmasters were chosen from among loyal patriot leaders. On August 24, 1774, the town of Bridgewater "voted unanimously" to relieve Colonel Josiah Edson as militia regimental commander. Edson was forced to flee to the British in Boston.[27]

During this period, paying militia for training had become a fairly standardized procedure throughout the colonies. Most Massachusetts towns had been asked by the Provincial Congress to create, equip, and train about one-quarter of their available militia force as minutemen. Because they drilled more, the associated cost to the towns also increased. Perhaps owing to the high cost of these "minute" formations, the town of Medford capped their minute company at only twenty-five men.

Following the powder raid, the town of Wareham engaged in some unique Revolutionary activity. A group of townsmen led by Noah Fearing, John Gibbs, Nathan Briggs, and Salathiel Bumpus organized a "Body of the People March," and on September 26, 1774, they "converged upon the courthouse in Barnstable" and forced the judges to sign pledges not to support the royal government in Boston. On January 16, 1775, Wareham then organized its own minute company. By April 19, 1775, the Wareham militia, now led by Noah Fearing—the same person who had earlier organized the "Body of the People" event—marched with his men, including Nathan Briggs, eighty miles to Marshfield on an erroneous rumor that the British were plundering that particular town. He and his men received four-days pay for their efforts.[28] The town of Marblehead followed suit and desired that its men "be trained two hours a day, four days a week."[29] Later, on January 10, 1775, at a town meeting, "the people of Marblehead" stated that it was necessary that they should be instructed in the art of war and that "a committee of fifteen be appointed to attend to the conduct of the ministerial tools and Jacobites" in their town so that "effectual measures may be taken to silence them in the future, or expel them from the community."[30]

Gage began to believe that the country towns were becoming more militant and threatening than even the Boston Committee of Correspondence. One Boston patriot noted that the countryside was "continually sending Committees down [to Boston] upon one errand or another—which caused the Governor to say, that he can do very well with Boston Selectmen, but the damn'd country committees plague his soul out, as they are very obstinate and hard to be satisfied." Dr. Benjamin Church—who at the time was still ostensibly loyal to the Whigs—warned Samuel Adams on September 29, 1774, that "the Country [meaning the towns outside Boston] are very uneasy . . . long they cannot be restrained they urge us & threaten to compel us to desert the Town, they swear the Troops shall not continue unmolested . . . the utmost extent of their forbearance is limited to the rising of the Congress."[31]

As the spring of 1775 approached, both sides were clearly headed for a collision in the backcountry. During the preceding months, Gage had ordered in reinforcements in the form of the "10th and 52nd Regiments of Foot from Quebec, along with the 18th and 47th from New York and the two detached companies of the 65th from Newfoundland, bringing that regiment up to strength." Yet, despite the ramp up of British military manpower, Gage had little to show for it, and, as his failed powder raids suggest, he had little control beyond the confines of Boston. Moreover, with "the General Court dissolved, the Crown-appointed judges unable to act, the militia—stripped of reliable loyalist officers—turned against him, and the Provincial Congress [now] governing the colony," Gage had little to be optimistic about.[32] Desertions were up, the water and food inside Boston was growing foul, and Welsh Fusilier Frederick MacKenzie noted a rising number of incidents between the Boston town watch, "yankee pedlars," and officers as the calendar approached April. To keep his men fit and active and to perhaps provide a modicum of operational security to future and as yet unplanned munitions raids, Gage had taken to cleverly ordering out regiments on marches into the countryside throughout the winter and early spring of 1775. Using his own officers as not very efficient spies, Gage quickly recognized the importance of Concord and vicinity as a supply depot for the provincial militia forces then feverishly training to resist any future powder raids.

The early spring of 1775 had been renowned for its "mild, wet weather." By March 1775, the town of Sudbury, the largest settlement in Middlesex County, had already established five militia companies to include two minute companies—one each for its east and west sides of town and a troop of horse. In all, by early 1775, Sudbury could claim to have around 350 militiamen in training for possible use against the British. An analysis of the town muster rolls revealed that at least 302 of them served on April 19, 1775. Although much detailed data is lacking on the economic background of these men, preliminary research makes it clear that they were men of some standing and, with a few notable exceptions, were most likely engaged in some sort of agriculture-related profession. The average age of the town participants in the action of April 19, 1775, was thirty years. Even accounting for later marriage ages of most New England men by this time, this number is still significant for the militia cohort clearly represents established and active members of the town and signified that a large proportion of the town younger than sixty years of age served in their local militia units.[33] Moreover, Sudbury's participation rate is very high. In 1775, Sudbury had a population of 2,160, with about 500 adult males above the age of twenty-one. Nearly 70 percent of the adult males had been organized into some sort of military command.[34]

Whereas Sudbury participation levels were significant, the same cannot be said of their actual military readiness. Town records from March 27, 1775, indicated, in a military return just three weeks before the Lexington and Concord fight, that most of Sudbury's militia companies were still claiming serious shortages in military hardware. Captain Moses Stone, who commanded the South Sudbury militia company, reported that of his ninety-two men, eighteen (or about 20 percent) were without weapons. Of the weapons that they did have, he noted, "at Least one third part ye fire-locks unfit for Sarvice, otherwise un a quipt." While Captain Aaron Haynes's North Sudbury militia company was well situated for firearms and "most of them Provided with Bayonets and hatchets," only "a boute one quarter Part [had] Cartridge Boxes." Captain Joseph Smith, command-ing the East Sudbury militia company, reported that he had "75 able Bod-ied men, forty well a quipt, twenty Promise to find and a quip themselves Emedetly, fifteen no guns and otherwise un a quipt." Earlier records from the fall of 1774 show Captain Ezekiel How, who on April 19, 1775, would be promoted to lieutenant colonel and command the Sudbury men at Concord, was feverishly endeavoring to buy guns, bayonets, lead, and flints for his men. It is clear that, by March, he was still relatively unsuc-cessful.[35] Thus, one might question the old saw that all the minutemen owned their own weapons.

The muster rolls of Captain John Nixon's minute company revealed that few men missed drill. Records show that they gathered for training once a week. This was a bit less frequent than the Provincial Congress had recommended for minute companies. Most likely this was because the town of Sudbury only authorized a payment of "one shilling six pence for training one half day in a week." Notably, by October 1775, the minute-men still had not been paid for their spring services.[36]

Nixon's men were a minute company, but their training was something less than desired and they had only been at it for a little more than five weeks when fighting broke out at Lexington. They did, however, reli-giously attend their scheduled drill sessions. Of the six drill days where records exist, only six men of sixty missed a single drill, and only Hosea Brigham missed two sessions. Militiamen who missed a drill without per-mission, however, were heavily fined, so this practice may explain their military diligence as much as anything else.

Nonetheless, the desire to serve in a military company of some sort was so great in this town that, according to the town records, "the men that were freed by Age from doing Military Duty formed themselves into a Company Called the Alarm Company Commanded by Captain Jabez Puffer. Training were as often as once a week the full three months, in the winter Not so often. The young Men in the Winter months made a Practis of calling on their officers Evenings and going through the Manual Exercise in Barn Flours. I have exercised many a Night With my Mittens on."[37] Such meetings also provided a very convenient method for the officers to inculcate their men with the Whig political agenda and ensure that all would be solidly "educated" toward the patriot cause.

Although no equipment returns can be found for the minute companies, it can be surmised, because of their requirement to maintain a higher state of readiness, that they did not face the same shortages as the standard militia. Town records indicate that, on the morning of the Lexington and Concord fight, one of the minute companies issued each man "about a pound of powder and two pounds of balls."[38]

Town records show that Sudbury received warning of the April 19, 1775, British raid against Concord at 4:00 a.m. A rider made his way to the home of minute company commander Captain Nixon and allegedly stated, "Up, up! The Redcoats are up as far as Concord!" Nixon immediately went to join his company then gathering near the west-side meeting house. All five companies marched toward Concord that morning. The north militia, under Aaron Haynes, and Nixon's minute company were supposed to reach Concord via its south bridge. These two formations were clearly the most ready of the entire Sudbury contingent, according to the aforementioned readiness reports. The other companies were directed to approach on a more circuitous route through the town of Lincoln. Upon arrival, Nixon and Haynes found that British troops were holding the south bridge in force. Colonel James Barrett's son, Stephen, directed them toward other companies then beginning to gather on Punkatasset Hill just beyond the north bridge in Concord. They arrived there most likely just after the initial shots had been exchanged between Colonel Barrett's ad hoc militia regiment and another British company holding the north bridge. During the British retreat through Concord and Lexington, it is likely they ran into the East Sudbury companies near Meriam's Corner and Hardy Hill. During the entire fight, the town militia recorded two men killed and one wounded. Of the two killed, one was Deacon Josiah Haynes, who was either seventy-nine or eighty years old (several accounts differ as to his actual age). He was shot down near Lexington, earning him the distinction of being the oldest militiaman killed that day. Haynes is not listed on any specific company muster roll but was most likely part of Jabez Puffer's Alarm company of old men and boys who got caught up in the spirit of the day. The other casualty was Ashahel Reed, of Nixon's minute company. Joshua Haynes, also of Nixon's company, was wounded.[39]

Military preparation and militia activity took on a similar cast in the town of Concord. For months, Concord had taken on the look of what today's commentators might refer to as a "strategic hamlet." Selected as an arms depot and occasional location for the extralegal Provincial Congress,

Concord was appreciated for its central geographic importance. Consequently, like other Middlesex towns, on September 26, 1774, Concord voted "that there be one or more Companys Raised in this Town by Enlistment and that they Chuse their officers out of the Body So Inlisted and that Said Company or Companies Stand at a minutes warning in Case of an alarm."[40] Like its sister town, Sudbury, however, Concord did not get around to actually enlisting men into its new minute companies until January 1775. Their first attempt at a training day, January 12, was singularly unsuccessful. "Another muster, two days later, netted only 50 or 60 men." Most likely, their problem was the low pay allotted them for drill. Whereas laborers could easily earn two shillings a day, the town was only willing to pay its minutemen "one shilling, 8 pence for drilling two half days a week."[41]

By early February, Concord was finally able to field 104 men for its two minute companies. An examination of this group of men revealed that fifteen men were without any arms. The town voted to supply them. Captain David Brown commanded the men who formed the company generally from the north quarter of town. Captain Charles Miles commanded the other with men principally from the southern part of town. In all, in the early spring of 1775, Concord would provide a total of four militia companies (two standard and two minute companies). As was the case with Sudbury, the town also formed an alarm company of old men and boys.[42]

A review of all the four Concord militia companies took place on March 13, 1774. Meanwhile arms, munitions, and equipment poured into the village. Colonel James Barrett was appointed by the Provincial Congress "to have the care of all the military stores." In an effort to spread out some of the equipment, stores were also directed toward the town of Worcester. In view of just how important gunpowder was to both sides, it is noteworthy that Colonel Jeremiah Lee, of Marblehead, forwarded to Concord in December 1774 "6 hogsheads, containing 35 half-barrels of powder." This powder was later spread out to a variety of safe houses within the town. In an accompanying letter, however, Lee warned, "Don't so much as mention the name of powder, lest our enemies should take advantage of it." In fact, on March 29, "a report circulated that the British troops were coming to Concord, which produced a considerable alarm." The false alarm caused the minute companies to begin carrying their arms with them at all times.[43]

On the morning of April 19, 1775, the Concord militia had been alerted by Dr. Samuel Prescott, who had eluded capture by British scouts earlier that evening, that the regulars were on their march from Boston and intended to seize the military stores in Concord. At daylight, the militia companies had gathered in the center of town, at Wright's Tavern. Hearing reports of fighting taking place at Lexington, Captain David Brown advanced his company of minutemen toward Meriam's Corner, about a mile outside of town on the Lexington Road. Seeing the British

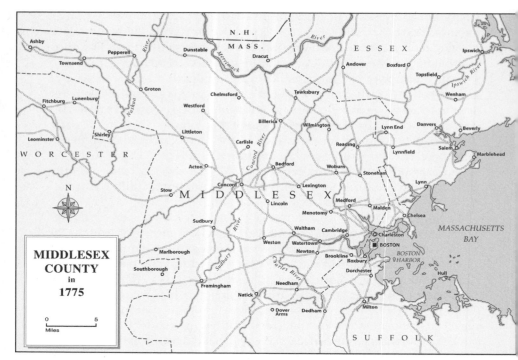

Map 1-1. Map of Boston Vicinity in 1775. (Map by Tom Willcockson, Mapcraft, Inc.)

column headed directly for them, Brown ordered the company to face about and marched about a hundred rods in front of the British force. The other men of the town, however, were most likely busily engaged in attempting to further hide the precious military stores everyone assumed the British were after. Colonel Barrett ordered the Concord companies to join the others who were assembling on Punkatasset Hill, just beyond the north bridge. Further, Concord was not an arms depot by chance. The town was the "geographical center around which the county regiments were located, every one of them containing at least one company raised in Concord or in a town bordering on Concord. These regiments alone totaled 6000 men."[44]

Concord personnel casualties that day were exceptionally light—most likely because they did not chase the retreating Redcoats too far beyond the town limits. Minuteman Jonas Brown, "the twenty-two year old nephew of Captain David Brown," was grazed by a musket ball near the north bridge. Alarm rider Adel Prescott, Jr., was wounded in the side. Three captains of militia—Nathan Barrett, Charles Miles, and George Minot—were slightly wounded as the British retreated toward Charlestown. The Concord militia had the honor of capturing Major Pitcairn's horse that had bolted from him during the retreat. The "animal was awarded to the Reverend William Emerson" for his services that day.[45]

Consider for a moment the backcountry town's lukewarm reception of the Solemn League and Covenant just ten months earlier and contrast it with their reaction to Gage's raid on Concord. Their newfound belligerence is nothing short of remarkable. It is also clear that the town militia structure and the repeated powder raids of the previous months were major factors in their political conversion. Today we can imagine militia captains like John Nixon, Isaac Davis, and David Brown conversing in frozen barns on cold winter nights "with their mittens on" about their worsening situation with the military occupiers of Boston. And the data clearly reveal that the militia captains were recruiting most of the men of military age. Few were left out. Although many of the militia companies were not as well equipped or trained as the towns desired, their sheer willingness to respond with force is significant. They were also organized. Their presence on the field that day was not a spontaneous reaction. It was a planned one. Moreover, as John Galvin has noted, the minuteman concept in New England did not end on April 19, 1775. More research is necessary on the "Lexington/Concord" army that formed that day. Which officers and men ended up in the Continental army (and for how long)? Who stayed home (and why)? Who continued their service in the militia? Who saw service in both components? Again, by focusing on a group of patriot-minded soldiers who found themselves staring down British regulars at Concord's north bridge or at Meriam's Crossroads and tracing their military careers throughout the rest of the war, a better determination can be made about who actually served from this region and in what particular capacity during the eight years of war that followed.

In sum, the militia system used by the colonists in 1775, coupled with an effective intelligence and alarm network, worked well enough to defeat Gage's powder-seizure strategy. It was also clear that participation in the militia was widespread—at least at this point in the conflict—especially after the Tory commanders had been so unceremoniously dumped in 1774. Although much research remains to be done on the militia of individual towns, several conclusions can be drawn from the social structure of these organizations. First and foremost, the members of the various companies comprised the bulk of each community, with patriot community leaders rising to replace former Tory-minded leaders. Recent research on the background of John Parker's Lexington militia revealed that nearly all these men were small landowners.[46] The same can also be said of the Sudbury and Concord militias. "Of the 68 militiamen who could be identified on the 1771 Lexington tax list, 58 were landowners in the town. Only 5 owned no land. The largest holding was assessed at 19 pounds annual worth, a comfortable but modest estate."[47]

The age of the militiamen from both Sudbury and Concord was relatively high for a military formation. The average age of a Concord militiaman was twenty-nine. In Sudbury it was thirty. Lexington was even higher, at thirty-two. Most minute companies—because of the requirement for them to be instantaneously ready—were generally younger than the "standard" militia formations of the towns. Alarm companies were usually comprised of much older and consequently less mobile men. Age and kinship matter in these Massachusetts towns. It is clear that the militiamen of both Sudbury and Concord were young, but not too young. As older Tory-minded leaders like Timothy Ruggles, William Browne, and William Brattle were turned out of office, they were replaced by a younger cohort of Revolution-minded officers. William Pencak has long argued that "age accounts for differences between Massachusetts' Revolutionaries and loyalists more than class." Indeed, we see the old guard being turned out in town after town, especially following Gage's first powder raid. "The average loyalist was 60 years old in 1775; the typical revolutionary, 46."[48]

An analysis of the muster rolls from the towns of Sudbury and Concord also reveal a strong pattern of kinship. Gordon Wood has noted that "the minutemen of the towns were held together less by chains of command than by familial loyalties. The 3,047 Massachusetts soldiers who served in the Seven Years' War had only 1,443 family names. Over one-quarter of the Lexington militiamen mustered by Captain John Parker on 19 April 1775 were related to him by blood or marriage." In Captain David Brown's Concord minute company, of fifty-two listed men, there were seven Buttricks, five Browns, four Flints, and three Barretts. Not listed were Major John Buttrick and Colonel James Barrett, both senior militia officers at the Concord fight. Thus, 37 percent of the entire company was related to just four families, two of whom in turn were related to the senior officers on the field that day. This trend takes place in company muster roll after muster roll in a variety of Middlesex towns.[49]

Moreover, a review of the 1790 heads-of-household census reveals that many of these men remained in the community long after the war. For example, an analysis of both east-side and west-side Sudbury minute companies reveals that, of a total of ninety-two men who served in these two companies, 63 percent were still living in these towns in 1790. When one considers Sudbury's south, east, and north standard militia companies and the troop of horse, the trend is much the same. Again, the vast majority of the men, or an amazing total of 75 percent, were found still living in Sudbury in 1790. The lower percentage of long-term town residents for the minute companies may be due to the fact that younger, more-mobile, less-established men were typically steered toward these particular outfits, whereas the standard militia most likely contained slightly older men. The Sudbury south militia company had the highest single percentage, with 80 percent of its men being listed as an in-town heads of households in 1790.

In Concord, the story is a bit different than at Sudbury. Although there are extant muster records for only two of the four companies engaged on April 19, 1775, the data reveal that, though the town of Concord was slightly less prosperous and less populous than Sudbury, only about half of the minutemen of 1775 were listed on the heads-of-households census. Research by Robert Gross indicates that, by 1775, "Concord was a community in decline. The economy was stagnant, the land worn out, and the town was losing its young." Nonetheless, most Concord minutemen (75 percent) came from households whose gross valuation placed them in the top or middle levels of wealth in the community.[50]

Finally, we need to see the town militias of Middlesex County in a new light. The remodeling of the militia served more to "infuse popular support into the patriot cause" and made membership "an expression of [one's] patriotic sympathies." It could also serve, as John Shy has noted, as a form of personal insurance from harassment and as a loyalty test. In 1775, since "the colonial rebellion still aimed only at redressing grievances with the crown, committees of safety and provincial assemblies throughout the colonies linked the reconstituted militia with the return of political stability and constitutional balance." Thus, participation becomes more important than military effectiveness because of the crucial political role played by the militia organization itself. Indeed, at a time when the government of Massachusetts was dissolved and, as Patrick Henry had decried soon after the imposition of the Intolerable Acts, "we are now in a state of nature, sir," town government backed up by its self-manned militia seemed to be the one combined institution that could provide order and stability in such troubling times and be an effective counterweight against Gage's powder schemes and the imposition of royal authority in the countryside.[51]

The revitalized town militias had certainly caught General Gage by surprise. Familiar perhaps only with less-capable provincial troops that he encountered during the French and Indian War, he totally underestimated the power of the town militias to control events in the countryside. Writing to Lord Dartmouth, three days after the Lexington and Concord fight, he noted, "The whole country was assembled in Arms with Surprizing Expedition, and Several Thousand are now Assembled about this Town threatening to attack and getting up artillery." Later, after Bunker Hill, he lamented, "In all their Wars against the French, they never Showed so much Conduct, Attention, and Perseverance as they do now."[52]

When William Brattle and Timothy Ruggles attempted to organize "parallel" loyalist militias, they could produce only a small force of about two hundred Boston Tories. They were simply too late and their patriot opponents too entrenched in the standing town militias for anything to change at this point. The town militias had won the first engagement of the war.

Notes

1. John Adams to James Warren, July 17, 1774, in *The Warren-Adams Letters* (Boston, 1917), 1:26; Pauline Maier, *From Resistance to Revolution: Colonial Radicals and the Development of American Opposition to Britain, 1765–1776* (New York: Alfred A. Knopf, 1972), p. 244.

2. David Hackett Fischer, *Paul Revere's Ride* (New York: Oxford University Press, 1994), pp. 44–45; Ray Raphael, *The First American Revolution: Before Lexington and Concord* (New York: New Press, 2002), pp. 113–14.

3. Fischer, *Paul Revere's Ride*, pp. 47–48.

4. Pension deposition of Jonathan Brigham, in John C. Dann, ed., *The Revolution Remembered* (Chicago: University of Chicago Press, 1986), pp. 1–3.

5. Quoted in Fischer, *Paul Revere's Ride*, p. 37.

6. Thomas Gage to William Brattle, quoted in Robert P. Richmond, *The Powder Alarm: 1774* (Princeton, N.J.: Auerbach Publishers, 1971), p. 5.

7. William Brattle to Thomas Gage, August 27, 1774, quoted in Richmond, *The Powder Alarm*, pp. 5–6. This letter was also printed in the *Boston Gazette* on September 5, 1774.

8. Quoted in Richmond, *The Powder Alarm*, p. 58.

9. Fischer, *Paul Revere's Ride*, pp. 48–51.

10. John R. Galvin, *The Minute Men* (Washington, D.C.: Brassey's Publishers, 1989), p. 92.

11. Gage to Lord Dartmouth, August 27, 1774, quoted in Galvin, *Minute Men*, p. 42.

12. Peter Force, *American Archives*, 4th ser., vol. 1 (Washington D.C.: M. St. Clair Clarke and Peter Force Publishers, 1837), p. 732.

13. *Gazetteer and New Daily Advertiser*, February 11, 1775; John C. Miller, *Origins of the American Revolution* (Stanford, Calif.: Stanford University Press, 1959), p. 371.

14. Richard Boucher, "The Colonial Militia as a Social Institution: Salem, Massachusetts 1764–1775," in *Military Analysis of the Revolutionary War: An Anthology*, by the editors of *Military Affairs* (Millwood, N.Y.: KTO Press, 1977), p. 39.

15. Howard K. Sanderson, *Lynn in the Revolution*, pt. 1 (Boston: W. B. Clarke Company, 1909), pp. 20, 22.

16. Action at the Worcester County Convention and the First Provincial Congress: *Journals of Each Provincial Congress*, quoted in Galvin, *Minute Men*, pp. 51–52.

17. Galvin, *Minute Men*, p. 52.

18. Boucher, "The Colonial Militia as a Social Institution," p. 40.

19. Fischer, *Paul Revere's Ride*, pp. 26–27.

20. Robert E. Brown, *Middle-Class Democracy and the Revolution in Massachusetts, 1691–1780* (Ithaca, N.Y.: Cornell University Press, 1955), p. 345.

21. Abigail Adams to John Adams, quoted in Richmond, *The Powder Alarm*, p. 31.

22. Paul Revere to John Lamb, September 4, 1774, in Elbridge H. Goss, ed., *The Life of Colonel Paul Revere* (Boston: Howard W. Spurr, 1902), 1:150–53.

23. John Andrews to William Barrell, September 9, 1774, quoted in Raphael, *The First American Revolution*, p. 146.

24. Quoted in Raphael, *The First American Revolution*, pp. 146–47.

25. Richard D. Brown, *Revolutionary Politics in Massachusetts: The Boston Committee of Correspondence and the Towns, 1772–1774* (Cambridge, Mass.: Harvard University Press, 1970), pp. 200, 202, 208.

26. Norman Castle, ed., *The Minute Men, 1775–1975* (Southborough, Mass.: Yankee Colour Corp., 1977), pp. 55–56, 207.

27. Castle, *Minute Men*, pp. 74, 260.

28. Castle, *Minute Men*, pp. 286–87; Force, *American Archives*, p. 1093.

29. Brown, *Middle-Class Democracy and the Revolution in Massachusetts*, p. 349.

30. Frank Moore, comp., *Diary of the American Revolution*, 2 vols. (New York: Arno Press, 1969), 1:12; *New York Gazette*, January 16, 1775.

31. Brown, *Revolutionary Politics in Massachusetts*, p. 231; Benjamin Church to Samuel Adams, September 29, 1774, Samuel Adams Papers.

32. Galvin, *Minute Men*, p. 58.

33. George Quintel, "Patriot Chronicles," unpublished manuscript on the "Lexington" army of 1775.

34. Maynard Historical Society, September 5, 2000 <http://web.Maynard.ma.us/history/society/minutemen2000>, accessed on June 6, 2005.

35. Alfred S. Hudson, *History of Sudbury, 1638–1889* (Boston: R. H. Blodgett, 1889), p. 370.

36. *The War Years in the Town of Sudbury, Massachusetts, 1765–1781*, Town Record Books, Book 6, 1755–1790 (Sudbury, Mass.: Sudbury Revolutionary War Bicentennial Committee, 1975), pp. 139–40.

37. Hudson, *History of Sudbury*, p. 363.

38. Hudson, *History of Sudbury*, pp. 370–72.

39. Hudson, *History of Sudbury*, pp. 375–82.

40. Robert A. Gross, *The Minutemen and Their World* (New York: Hill and Wang, 1976), p. 59.

41. Gross, *Minutemen*, p. 60.

42. Lemuel Shattuck, *The History of the Town of Concord* (Boston: Russell Odiorne & Company, 1835), pp. 93–94.

43. Shattuck, *History of the Town of Concord*, pp. 98–99.

44. Galvin, *Minute Men*, p. 131.

45. Gross, *Minutemen*, p. 131.

46. Fischer, *Paul Revere's Ride*, pp. 319–20.

47. George Quintel, "Patriot Chronicles," unpublished manuscript, 2004; Gross, *Minutemen*, p. 217.

48. William Pencak, *War, Politics, and Revolution in Provincial Massachusetts* (Boston: Northeastern University Press, 1981), pp. 201, 214.

49. Gordon Wood, *The Radicalism of the American Revolution* (New York: Vintage Books, 1991), p. 45; James W. Coburn, *The Battle of April 19, 1775*, 2nd ed. (Port Washington, N.Y.: Kennikat Press, 1970), pp. 170–71.

50. Gross, *Minutemen*, pp. 177, 189.

51. Lawrence Delbert Cress, *Citizens in Arms: The Army and the Militia in American Society to the War of 1812* (Chapel Hill: University of North Carolina Press, 1982), p. 49; John Adams, "Notes, September 6, 1774," in *Letters of the Members of the Continental Congress*, vol. 1: *1774–1776*, ed. Peter Smith (Washington D.C.: Carnegie Institution of Washington, 1921), p. 14.

52. Thomas Gage to Lord Dartmouth, April 22, 1775, in John Rhodehamel, ed., *The American Revolution: Writings from the War of Independence* (New York: Library Classics of the United States, 2001), p. 20; Gage, quoted in James Kirby Martin and Mark Lender, *A Respectable Army: The Military Origins of the Republic, 1763–1789* (Arlington Heights, Ill.: Harlan Davidson, 1982), p. 19.

2

THE MASSACHUSETTS
RANK AND FILE OF 1777

WALTER SARGENT

At the approach of the new year of 1777, Americans found themselves mired in a fierce struggle in their war for independence. At the end of November 1776, a twenty-two-year-old soldier stationed at Peekskill, New York, wrote home of his depressed morale:

> The present appearance is very Gloomy, the British troops making head wherever they attempt, our people instead of behaving like brave men, behave like Rascalls & to add to that, it seems that the British troops had gone into the Jersies only to receive the Submission of the whole Country, People join them almost in Captains Companies to take the oath of allegiance—beside those of the Militia Who have been sent for our Assistance leave us the minute their times are out & would not stay tho' their eternal Salvation was to be forfeited if they went home.[1]

In December, Commander-in-Chief George Washington wrote in a similar vein to Governor Trumbull of Connecticut, "The spirits of the people . . . are quite sunk by our recent misfortunes."[2] Washington's army was in difficult straits, receiving little local support in men or materials as they retreated just ahead of a relentless British advance toward Philadelphia.

In the final days of December, Washington managed to stem the tide of defeatism with bold assaults on British posts at Trenton and Princeton. The unexpected victories temporarily restored American control of most of New Jersey, dispelled for the moment the sense of gloom, and captured some 1,250 British troops in the process. The British setback prompted General William Howe to consolidate the winter quarters of the main British army in and around New York City. General Howe also deployed some six thousand troops to Newport, Rhode Island, under command of General Henry Clinton, there poised to strike into the heart of New England.[3] In the north,

British forces from Canada had successfully invaded the Champlain-Hudson corridor during the fall of 1776 in pursuit of the retreating American Northern Army, and only a burst of desperate resistance at Valcour's Bay on Lake Champlain had forced Sir Guy Carleton to withdraw his army into Canada for the winter. Thus, despite the American successes in capturing two British outposts in New Jersey, the main British armies were waiting for spring to move from their bases in New York City, Newport, and Canada against the rebel Americans.

Like the soldier at Peekskill, Americans who manned posts in the Champlain corridor were clearly discouraged at the start of 1777. Lieutenant Henry Sewall of York, Maine, vividly described the unraveling situation around Fort Ticonderoga. In a sequence of diary entries, he told of the army literally marching out of camp with the expiration of enlistments at year's end. His entries read as follows:

> Wednesday, January 1, 1777: The time of our Engagement being expir'd, the major part of the men left this Garrison.
> [Thursday] January 2, 1777: No Relief sent to this Garrison.
> [Monday] January 6, 1777: The remainder of the men having left the Garrison, the Officers followed after.[4]

Lieutenant Sewall's journal paints a comical vision of the troops marching off, leaving only a handful of officers with no one to command, and then, as the officers realized their predicament, they marched off as well. These letters and journal entries could be read as proof that Americans had lost their resolve as the war dragged into its third year.

There is wide agreement among Revolution scholars with the conclusion that people became "tired of serving, and . . . tired of contributing" after 1776, with the result that the Revolutionary armies grew dependent on the poorest stratum of colonial society to face the brunt of the fighting. American General "Mad Anthony" Wayne complained in 1777 that one-third of his troops were "Negroes, Indians, and Children." Robert Middlekauff writes, "As the war dragged on they [Continental soldiers] came increasingly from the poor and the propertyless . . . as substitutes for men who had rather pay than serve, or as the recipients of bounties and the promise of land." In his canonical *War of American Independence,* Don Higginbotham notes that "manpower requirements . . . inevitably led the Americans to scrape the bottom of the barrel of human resources." This study examines service records and social characteristics of Massachusetts troops to test the regional variability of Americans' response to mobilization and the extent to which the Revolution became "a poor man's fight."[5]

The first part of this essay outlines the campaigns and mobilization efforts of 1777 and demonstrates that Massachusetts state militia service in the Revolution was as essential to the war effort, though sometimes in different ways, as that of the national Continental Army. Second, attention turns to analysis of a compilation of comprehensive individual service records to reveal the patterns of enlistments and service in the field. Third, each individual's service data are linked to state tax lists and social characteristics to provide regional profiles of the Massachusetts Revolutionary soldiers of 1777. The findings of this study suggest that ordinary Massachusetts people, mostly of the middling sort, made complex calculations in reaching their own decisions on how, when, or whether to actively engage in the American war effort, and that the recruits and veterans of 1777 reflected the entire spectrum of the social structures of their regions.

The data collection for this study focuses on four regions proximate to Salem, Plymouth, Northampton, and York, Massachusetts, to provide a representative geographic and social cross section of the general population. Data collection begins with a compilation of soldiers' service records from all branches of the service, including local militias and state and Continental Army units. By including in the data-collection process all enlistments for an individual, it is possible to follow each individual's military service record throughout the war, a longitudinal component that has been underused in previous efforts to evaluate service patterns empirically. The second major set of variables in this data set is a group of measurements of the individual soldier's social and economic status. Correlating the service patterns and socioeconomic characteristics of a large sample of rank-and-file Massachusetts soldiers provides a window into the American mobilization, illuminating some of the intersections of individual decisions and community responses to the call to arms. The decisions about who served—and when and where they served—were shaped crucially by such personal concerns as family obligations, ambition, excitement, and opportunity, as well as by the larger political and ideological issues as seen through the lens of their local town meetings. Put another way, individual decisions reflected not only a personal calculation, but also the efficacy and solidarity of local town government, logistical and fiscal support from the state, and popular opinion in the individuals' own towns.[6]

Mobilization: 1777

About 30 percent of Massachusetts recruits signed on with Continental Army units, and the other 70 percent enrolled with state regiments and militia units in 1777. Most recruits reported to the army either at the critical posts along the Hudson highlands, to the Northern Department that defended the Lake Champlain region, or to garrisons surrounding the British army at Newport, Rhode Island.[7] Some recruits joined the Continental Army directly, others joined state regiments and militia companies, and every male from sixteen to fifty was a member of the local militia train band. The different branches often worked together on the same campaigns. Militias routinely rotated as reinforcements through camps anchored by state regiments under Continental command, especially at

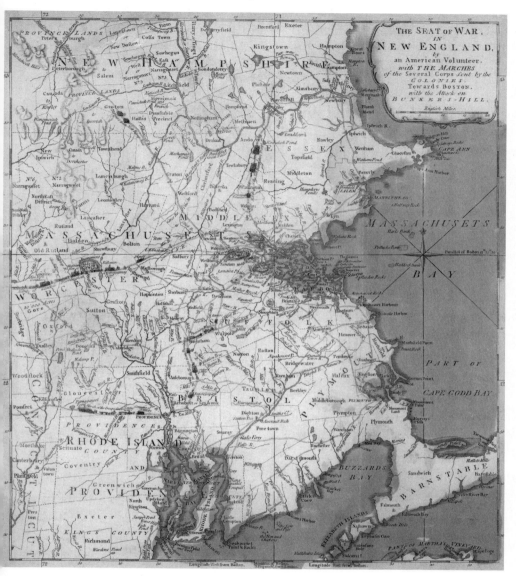

Map 2-1. Map of Massachusetts and Cape Anne. The map of the southern New England provinces provides the geographic context for the study of mobilization in the Cape Anne area of Massachusetts. The map is entitled the "Seat of War in New England" and was made by an American volunteer in 1775 to show the movement of militia from the New England provinces to Boston and the "Battle of Bunkers Hill." It was printed in London in September 1775. (Courtesy of the New Hampshire Historical Society.)

Peekskill and Ticonderoga, while others manned seacoast defenses and responded to British raids.

The first tour of duty of 1777 actually began just before Christmas 1776, when a call came into Massachusetts towns for reinforcements for Washington's Continental Army, soon to be wintering at Morristown, New Jersey. Altogether, Massachusetts sent about two thousand men to New Jersey that winter.[8] These soldiers went to the front as temporary reinforcements during a period of transition to a new long-term enlistment policy intended to expand and stabilize the Continental Army.

In the early spring of 1777, the American army sent many junior officers such as Lieutenant Sewall to their hometowns across the state to enroll recruits for the new three-year terms in the Continental Army.[9] In support of Congress, the Massachusetts General Court issued a resolve "demanding 1/7 part of the Militia to engage for 3 Years in the Continental Service."[10] This call—some call it a "draft"—for troops was read in meeting houses across the state and promulgated in town meetings.[11] In Hampshire County, the town of Northampton proposed incentives for recruits:

> To encourage and facilitate the raising of this town's proportion of men for the Continental Army. . . . That those persons that shall now engage in the service . . . shall have full compensation for all losses by them Sustained in Cloaths and other Articles where such losses were unavoidable and not through the negligence of those who sustained them. And as a further encouragement . . . any other able bodied men belonging to this Town who will engage in the Service, the Town Voted that they each of them shall receive from the Inhabitants of the Town of Northampton the sum of fifteen pounds which sum shall be paid to them at three several times viz five pounds before they shall march to Join the Army and five pounds more shall be paid to them or to their Order in the month of April 1778 And the other five pounds shall be paid in the month of April 1779.[12]

Accustomed to the colonial militia tradition of short-term engagements, the men were leery of the new call for multiyear tours of duty. To meet the quotas, towns employed the mechanism of "classing" to distribute the obligation for recruiting. The minutes of a town meeting in Northampton in April 1777 illustrate the process:

> The Town then voted that the Officers of the several Companies of the Militia within this Town should be directed to ascertain the number of men that are still wanting in their respective companies and [divide] them in so many classes as there are men wanting . . . and enjoin it upon each of those Classes to procure one good effective man to engage in the Continental Service.[13]

Despite reservations, more than 500 Massachusetts soldiers of the 4,071 in this data set enlisted for long-term Continental service during 1777.

Fearful of the threat posed by the major British garrison at Newport, New Englanders repeatedly called out the militias at each sign of enemy activity. The first alarm of the spring came on March 29, 1777, on intelligence that the British were planning a foray into the New England countryside, upon which news Captain James Harlow promptly led a company from Plymouth to Bristol, Rhode Island. That report, like many, proved to be a false alarm, and the men returned home in just two weeks. Nonetheless, throughout the spring, rotating contingents of soldiers from York and Plymouth remained stationed around Narragansett Bay. Enlistments were for sixty days on average, which effectively maintained a constant rotation of troops such that most recruits could still get their crops planted.

Maintaining vigilance at guard posts around British garrisons, while not high drama, was not unimportant either. The militia presence ensured that it would be difficult or impossible for the British army in Newport to supply themselves from the countryside, a fact that significantly raised the costs of the British presence.[14] Nonetheless, the presence of a powerful British force constituted a constant and a not-always-idle threat to the region, as British troops did occasionally execute extremely damaging raids like the costly raid on an American depot in Danbury at the end of May 1777. General Heath noted that "the loss to the Americans in stores, &c was considerable, and could but illy be spared at that time."[15] While local skirmishing continued intermittently, New England also braced for an expected British invasion from Canada.

Lieutenant General John Burgoyne arrived in Quebec on May 6, 1777, to take command of the British Canadian forces and energize the campaign against the American rebels. Upon his arrival in Canada, Burgoyne declared his determination to bring the Americans to heel by threatening to unleash his Indian allies to reignite bloody frontier warfare:

> I have but to give stretch to the Indian forces under my direction (and they amount to thousands) to overtake the hardened enemies of Great Britain and America. I consider them the same where ever they may lurk. If notwithstanding these endeavors, and sincere inclinations to effect them, the phrensy of hostility should remain, I trust I shall stand acquitted in the eyes of God and men in denouncing and executing the vengeance of the State against the willful outcasts.[16]

Burgoyne's threat "to give stretch to the Indian forces"—that is, to order Iroquois warriors to attack the northern New England frontier—touched a raw nerve among New Englanders, who had been involved in more than a century of bitter animosity and often bloody conflict with Native Americans. Burgoyne's threat was ill-advised in that it galvanized American resolve rather than undermined American resistance, much the way Virginia's royal governor, Lord Dunmore, ignited outrage in Virginia in 1775 with his proclamation to liberate runaway slaves.

Starting in May 1777, Captains Simeon Clap and Salmon White took companies of Northampton men on sixty-day enlistments to reinforce the Northern Army stationed at various camps around Lake Champlain. Despite the steady flow of reinforcements to Ticonderoga throughout the spring, in June 1777, American General Arthur St. Clair complained that he had as yet only about 1,900 poorly armed men at Fort Ticonderoga.[17] In response, Whig politicians brought out their most fiery orators to promote recruiting. Sylvester Judd recalled that, in Northampton, "When orders came for raising men, Major [Joseph] Hawley used to appear with a short sword and address the soldiers [the local militia] in the most animating manner. He used to tell them that they would be hewers of wood and drawers of water to British lords and bishops, if the great cause did not succeed."[18] Complementing Hawley's theatrics, the news of impending Indian attacks and the fact that the British invasion army fielded dreaded mercenary Hessians spurred Massachusetts men to action during the summer of 1777.[19]

At Fort Ticonderoga, the Americans were overwhelmed by British forces and were forced to pull back in disarray. Lieutenant Sewall's company withdrew with the rest: "The Enemey pursued us and had like to have taken some of our Rear." Amid great confusion, American commanders attempted to regroup the fleeing troops. Sewall wrote, "Our party consisting of about forty was composed of different regiments promiscuously collected under the command of Col Warner." Colonel Seth Warner, the thirty-four-year-old commander of the Green Mountain Regiment, rallied the Americans to mount a rear-guard stand against British General Simon Fraser at Hubbardton on July 7. Veteran Colonel Ebenezer Francis, of Beverly, who commanded the critical American center, was felled by a musket shot in his chest and died on the spot.[20] The following morning, Lieutenant Sewall wrote of his own close call, "British Regulars, Hessians, and Indians attacked us a little after sunrise . . . and I rec'd 2 balls thro' my Cloaths." Americans suffered about 125 killed or wounded and more than 200 captured, but enemy losses were estimated at 200 as well.[21] It was not a decisive action, but the skirmish at Hubberton began a trend in which American militias took an increasing toll on Burgoyne's invasion force, though not without a cost to Americans.

Word of the precipitous American retreat from Ticonderoga quickly reached the Connecticut River Valley, where the loss was considered a disaster of the first order. The symbolic importance of Ticonderoga as a bastion of defense for western Massachusetts was enormous. Brigadier General John Fellows and the Committee of Safety responded to a desperate plea from Major General Philip Schuyler for reinforcements by sounding the alarm. A loud urgent beating of a drum throughout town, accompanied by the ringing of the church bell or the firing of cannon, was the signal for the town's people to gather at the meeting house. Brookfield, Massachusetts, lacked a church bell or cannon, so the emergency call was issued by blowing on a conch shell. In Northampton, men who had served under John Fellows when he was a colonel at the Dorchester camp in 1775 responded quickly to his call. It was important to Massachusetts soldiers to know their commander, and men were particularly reluctant to entrust themselves to the orders of a stranger. Men preferred to serve with people they knew under a trusted local leader. The Northampton militia assisted General St. Clair's troops in executing critical delaying tactics that stymied Burgoyne's advance. The militia felled trees to block roads, removed crops, hid cattle, wrecked bridges, and built dams to flood low-lying portions of the trails, never knowing when fighting might engulf them. Meanwhile, eastern Massachusetts troops continued to rotate on short enlistments to the defensive positions around Newport. On the first of August, Captain Asa Prince led a company from Salem to Rhode Island, and a Plymouth company joined them on a five-month tour of duty at posts surrounding the British base at Newport. Their arrival was timely. On August 6, 1777, General Heath reported a probing foray into the countryside by British troops, which was quickly countered by Massachusetts militia.[22]

In mid-August, York men marched in two companies to reinforce the Northern Army on a four-month tour and were present at the eventual surrender of Burgoyne.[23] A few days after the York detachment marched toward the Northern Department, a messenger arrived in Northampton on August 17 with the disconcerting news that the British were on the move again and attacking the American post at Bennington. Northampton historian James Trumbull wrote that, on this occasion, "the news came in the night, and the alarm was sounded at once. It is reported that [Nathaniel Day] had 'a big drum, and in the stillness of the night it made a terrific noise.' The whole town was soon thoroughly aroused."[24] The alarm spread through the Connecticut River towns, and Northampton sent off a company of 104 men on the spot, including Dr. Hezekiah Porter, one of the town doctors, who signed on as a private with Captain Oliver Lyman for this crucial mission. Northampton men swarmed toward Bennington, expecting to join the battle, but it was already over by the time they arrived. They were assigned the mop-up duty of escorting the 700 Hessians taken prisoner by the Americans to Springfield, where they were to be held in custody. In August, Salem sent a sixth of its militia under Captain Zadok Buffington to Saratoga.[25] On August 25, Captain Samuel Flint led a troop of Danvers men to "the Northward" to reinforce the army. Typical of militia alarm enlistments, the Danvers Company served just over three months and returned home for winter after the fighting was over for the season.

In September, Burgoyne's British army struggled slowly southward, hoping to break through to Albany and rendezvous with reinforcements, while American troops were massing to block his escape. Massachusetts militias joined with Continental regiments to confront Burgoyne at Bemis

Heights. As the opposing forces drew near one another, Captain Silas Wilde recorded the growing tension in the standard order of the day: "Lay on Our Armes and Be Redey to Turnout at the Shortest Notis."[26] On September 19, the main forces clashed in a fierce battle, known as the First Battle of Freeman's Farm. One British soldier wrote of the intensity of the clash:

> Between 2 &3 [in the afternoon] the action became general . . . such an explosion of fire I never had any idea of before, and the heavy artillery joining in concert like great peals of thunder, assisted by the echoes of the woods, almost deafened us. This crash of cannon and musketry never ceased till darkness parted us . . . leaving us masters of the field; but it was a dear bought victory if I can give it that name, as we lost many brave men. The 62nd had scarce 10 men a company left, and other regiments suffered much, and no great advantage, honor excepted, was gained by the day.[27]

British casualties are estimated at 556, and on the American side, twenty-three-year-old William Preble of York and John Taylor of South Hadley were among the 80 Americans killed that day.

At nearby Stillwater, the expectation of renewed battle kept the American troops on edge. To counter the anxiety, the troops in Colonel Michael Jackson's regiment were especially rowdy, to the point that orders were issued to quiet the camp in the evenings:

> The Piquet and advance Guard complain that there is Such a Noise and Disturbance in Camp from 8 till 11 oclock at night that there is no possibility of alarming the Camp or hearing the approach of the Enemy. During that period the Sergeant Desires the Commanding officer of the lines and companys will be careful to see the men in their tents and camp silent as soon as the watch is set at 8 o'clock.[28]

One might speculate that the noise in camp was exuberant bravado in anticipation of the battle to come.

On October 7, Burgoyne attempted another assault on the American position on Bemis Heights and again suffered a major setback at the cost of many casualties on both sides. One of the Americans killed that day was Danvers militia Captain Samuel Flint, who had led a company to reinforce the Northern Army in late August. Ezra Tilden, a Massachusetts militiaman who was on the battle line, recorded that there was "Continual and incessant crackling of small arms and the roaring of cannon." Later he witnessed the carnage as the dead and wounded were brought in to General Gates's headquarters. "With regard to your Wounded Creatures: Some [shot] thro their Body & Crying to God, to Jesus, &c, to take away their lives. Poor Miserable Creatures Indeed!"[29] The battle exacted a steep price from militias and regulars alike.

Burgoyne retreated again to Saratoga, where he finally capitulated to conditional terms on October 17, 1777. The British surrendered six thousand men, some forty-two cannon, and quantities of valuable supplies. Ebenezer Wild described the occasion: "Gen'l Burgoyne and his Cheaf Off'rs Rode by us . . . at half after 3 O'clock Genl Burgoynes armey Began to Pass Us and thay Continued Passing Till Sunset."[30] This unprecedented victory and spectacle came at the hands of an American army, two-thirds of whom were militiamen.[31] As American guards marched the captured British and Hessian troops to Boston, patriot women heaped verbal and sometimes physical abuse on the prisoners to add to their misery.[32]

Back on the New England coast, soldiers from Plymouth and the Salem area continued to rotate on duty in Rhode Island throughout the fall. On September 25, Captain Nathaniel Goodwin marched a company from Plymouth on a "secret expedition" to Newport. There was a brief hope that American troops might combine with French naval power to capture another British army. In November, Plymouth sent another contingent of troops on a five-month enlistment to Rhode Island, while Essex sent new reinforcements to the New York highlands. Throughout the winter months, Massachusetts soldiers served as guards of Burgoyne's surrendered army in Cambridge and rotated on duty at posts in the highlands.

Recruiting for three-year Continental enlistments continued throughout the year as well. The demand for troops was seemingly incessant, with renewed calls every month throughout the year. Conditions were difficult for all American soldiers during the winter months, and they probably seemed worse for the soldiers who could not bask in the glow of a major victory. At winter camp at Valley Forge in December 1777, Doctor Albigence Waldo noted succinctly, "Provisions Scarce." He described an eerie chorus between the soldiers: "A general cry thro' the Camp this Evening among the Soldiers—'No Meat! No Meat!'—the Distant vales Echoed back the melancholly sound 'No Meat! No Meat!,' imitating the noise of crown of Owls." The refrains of this camp song told the story of hardship eloquently:

> What have you for Dinner Boys?
> Nothing but firecake and Water, Sir
> At night—'Gentlemen the supper is ready'
> What is your Supper Lads?
> Firecake and Water, Sir

The doctor echoed the rank and file as he penned his own warning to those in civilian comfort: "Ye who Eat Pumpkin Pie and Roast Turkies—and yet curse fortune for using you ill, curse her no more, least she reduce your Allowance of her favors to a bit of Firecake & a draught of Cold Water & in cold Weather too."[33]

Soldiers' families on the home front shared in the hardships, too. The toll of runaway inflation, combined with the meager pay of soldiers, drove many soldiers to resign, out of concern for their families as much as for themselves. Doctor Waldo wrote from Valley Forge,

> When the Officer has been fatiguing thru' wet and cold and returns to his tent where he finds a letter directed to him from his Wife filled with the most heartbreaking tender complaints a Woman is capable of writing— Acquainting him of the incredible difficulty with which she procures a little Bread for herself & Children—and finally concluding with expressions bordering on despair . . . that she begs of him to consider that Charity begins at home and not suffer his family to perish with want in the midst of plenty— When such is the tidings they constantly hear from their families—What Man is there whose soul would not shrink within him? Who would not be disheartened from preserving the Best of Causes—the cause of his Country when such discouragements as these lie in his way, which his country might remedy if they would?[34]

The hardships of the soldiers' lives were matched by the hardships imposed upon many soldiers' families, and it should not surprise us if the American people grew tired of the constant demands of the war. For the rank and file, the weather was often miserable and the travel exhausting. Soldiers walked everywhere they went, and they generally slept in barns or out of doors. Camp duties were tiresome, the food was bad, smallpox was a haunting specter in the camps, and there was never enough of anything.[35]

And the peril was real regardless of whether men served in local militias, state lines, or the Continental Army. Mashpee Indian and Plymouth resident Joshua Pockemet signed an enlistment for three years of Continental service during the last week of March 1777. He joined Captain Seth Drew's company in the Northern Department during the Burgoyne invasion. He was nineteen years old when he was reported dead on September 1, 1777. Among Massachusetts soldiers on active duty in 1777 the chance of death before the war was just more than 5 percent. In comparison, the death rate for all Massachusetts soldiers in the data set was only about half of that. The point is that however a Massachusetts soldier of 1777 served, he was liable to be killed, injured, or struck with disease regardless of his enlistment papers. On the other hand, most people lived to tell about it. Joshua Nasson of Berwick served several tours from Boston to the Hudson between 1775 and 1777, and, after returning home to Berwick, he went on to sire eleven children.

Service Data

The foregoing account of the military actions of Massachusetts soldiers illuminates the key roles they played in sustaining the war effort at a critical time in the northern theater. The energetic turnout of Massachusetts militias helped carry the day at the pivotal Battle of Saratoga, a turning point for America, and tenacious local defenses challenged any British movements anywhere in New England. To address the questions of whether Massachusetts soldiers continued to serve in greater or lesser numbers and whether they turned out for the burdensome service in the regular army after 1776, however, this essay turns now to the data on service records compiled by the author. The data offer the opportunity to analyze a representative cross section of Massachusetts soldiers in America's Revolutionary armies and also enable comparisons between cohorts of various years of the struggle.

The distribution of rank among the soldiers in the data set mirrors closely the actual organizational charts of America's Revolutionary armies. That means that ordinary rank-and-file soldiers comprise the vast majority; privates and corporals account for more than 84 percent of the total sample. Officers comprise just less than 6.5 percent of the total, and noncommissioned officers make up the balance. This distribution of military records provides an opportunity to assess carefully the service patterns of the Massachusetts rank and file during the Revolutionary years.

The importance of the campaigns of 1777 to New Englanders is underscored by the fact that almost 40 percent of all soldiers in this data set (4,071) who served at any time during the eight-year war performed some service during 1777. Forty-eight percent of the soldiers on active duty during 1777 (1,536) were first-time recruits, replacing or joining veterans from prior years. Complementing the green recruits, 34 percent were continuing in service from 1776, and 18 percent were returning veterans of 1775, signing on for a second tour after staying home in 1776. All told, 52 percent of soldiers in 1777 were veterans continuing in the service. The elevated level of participation and the proportion of new recruits reflect the immediate threat posed by British invasion that year. About a third of the 1777 soldiers came out only on one occasion of acute danger to New England, but more than two-thirds of the soldiers of 1777 served more than one enlistment during the war, some prior to and some after 1777. On average, among the cohort of soldiers with active duty in 1777, each enlisted 2.3 times during the course of the war, a rate notably higher than the average of 1.8 enlistments per soldier for all Massachusetts soldiers in the data set. The willingness to enlist for multiple tours of duty demonstrates a strong level of persistence in the face of often discouraging circumstances.

This apparent willingness translated into a greater absolute number of enlistments in 1777 than in either of the previous two years. The rate at which Massachusetts soldiers turned out during 1777 resulted in a total of 1,725 enlistments, exceeding the total for 1775 (1,418) or 1776 (1,053). The upsurge of enlistments in 1777 correlates closely to the imminence of a British invasion, which suggests that an immediate threat to the community and family was a powerful motivator for men to turn out.

GRAPH 2-1   Enlistments by Year and Region

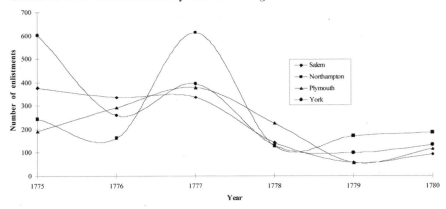

The enlistment patterns for the four regions of Massachusetts covered by this study varied in the response rates year by year, but the contours were consistent (see Graph 2-1). Most regions had a sharp increase in enlistments in 1777 from the prior year. The most dramatic increase, in the Northampton region in 1777, correlates directly to the timing and proximity of the Burgoyne-led British invasion through the Champlain-Hudson corridor that was bearing down on the western region of Massachusetts. The urgency of the situation acted as a powerful incentive for men to enlist to meet the crisis, if only for short terms. A second reason for the predominance of the Northampton surge was the logistics of American manpower resources. The manpower pool in the Northampton region was closest to the British invasion route through the Lake Champlain corridor and was the only viable American force of reinforcements able to make the required march in time to confront the British advance.

The drop-off in the number of enlistments in every region after 1777 reflects the transition from the rotation of short-term troops to increased reliance on soldiers with multiyear enlistments. The implementation of long-term duty in Continental regiments increased active-duty manpower and simultaneously reduced the number of men available for short-term militia enlistments. Although Congress originally hoped to recruit men for the duration of the war, an open-ended commitment did not sit well with the independent-minded Massachusetts people. Congress quickly amended the recruiting program to offer fixed three-year terms, a change that brought in enough recruits to restaff the Continental Army for 1777.[36] Continued popular reluctance to long-term service prompted Congress to compromise their wishes for a stable national army by offering shorter Continental enlistment terms. The most common alternatives were eight-month and nine-month tours of duty, which were still considerably longer than a typical militia tour of duty, but were more palatable to men who could not see their way to leaving their farms and families for years at a time.

TABLE 2-1 Comparable Unit of Service

Unit	Cohort of 1777	%	All Massachusetts Soldiers	%
Provincial/militia	766	49.9	2,506	61.5
≤1 year, Continental Army	173	11.3	638	15.7
≥3 years, Continental Army	597	38.8	927	22.8
Total	1,536	100	4,071	100

Despite reasonable reservations, 35 percent of all the soldiers who enlisted during 1777 agreed to the long-term three-year enlistments. The willingness to sign on for a three-year term in light of the known dangers and hardships demonstrates a profound commitment to the American war effort, but the jockeying for bounties and other incentives by recruits also shows that they expected to be fairly compensated. The cumulative impact of adopting a long-term enlistment policy in 1777 on the numbers of Massachusetts men in military service was to sustain the numbers of men in service even as enlistment rates gradually slowed. The number of individuals on active duty (1,536) in 1777 exceeded all other years. The number of soldiers on active duty in 1778 (1,157) and 1779 (989) continued to match the numbers from 1775 (1,181) and 1776 (983).

More Massachusetts soldiers were on active duty in 1777 than before, but a related question is the relative value or difficulty of service. The narrative of the campaign provides one view of the difficulty and importance of their service, but another measure is in the proportions of the soldiers of Massachusetts that served their active duty in the militias for short terms and those who accepted the dangers and hardships of long-term duty in the Continental Army. The service records of the soldiers on active duty in 1777 indicate that just more than 49 percent of enlistments were in Continental units, a rate just slightly higher than that for all Massachusetts soldiers in the data set. It should not be surprising in light of the push to multiyear terms that 1777 was the peak rate for three-year Continental enlistments, when nearly 40 percent of recruits signed on for three years or longer, nearly twice the overall rate for three-year Continental enlistments (see Table 2-1). All told, about half of the Massachusetts recruits in 1777 signed on with Continental units, while the other half turned out for brief militia terms during that year, including the many Northampton militiamen who marched to repel Burgoyne's invasion force, serving only a month or two before returning home.

The effect of the influx of many recruits coming in on the basis of longer enlistments in 1777 immediately began to contribute to a cumulative rise

TABLE 2-2 Total Man-Days Service

	Y E A R					
	1775	1776	1777	1778	1779	1780
Aggregate Days of Service	209,661[a]	160,000[b]	210,254	219,907	173,769	103,628

[a] Actual fighting began on April 19, 1775, so the 1775 campaign was eight months long, compared to twelve-month campaigns for subsequent years.

[b] The decline of man-days in 1776 is exaggerated by the loss of many returns from the army in Canada. Many records were lost or destroyed during the chaotic retreat from Quebec.

in active manpower levels in the American armies. The data show that, whereas enlistments and total service days may have dropped somewhat in 1776 from the enthusiastic levels of 1775, Congressional resolves in the fall of 1776 and other incentives prompted an upswing in both enlistments and in man-days of service for 1777 (see Table 2-2). The effect of long-term enlistments meant that aggregate man-days of service remained at relatively high levels among Massachusetts soldiers, even as the number of new enlistments tailed off in subsequent years, coincident with the major theaters of war moving southward. The man-days calculation includes service in all branches of the army.

Graph 2-2 depicts the number of enlistments per year and the simultaneous levels of Massachusetts manpower in the field during the first six years of the war. The boxed line tracks the number of enlistments over time, whereas the diamond line shows the actual cumulative man-days of service. Man-days of service in 1777 and 1778 were sustained at levels slightly higher than even 1775. Gradually the man-days of Massachusetts soldiers on active duty declined as the war moved into the Mid-Atlantic and South in 1779, but far more slowly than the drop in the rate of new enlistments.[37]

Understandably, Massachusetts men enlisted frantically when the threat of a British invasion from Canada loomed over New England in 1777. The drop-off in the rates of new enlistments after 1777 supports the perception that support for the war effort waned, but the data show that the cumulative effect of an increased proportion of long-term enlistments resulted in more men in the field despite the drop in recruiting rates. The introduction of three-year Continental enlistments and an intensified recruiting drive meant that more men stayed on longer in service than in previous years, and the momentum carried forward through the remaining years of the decade. Compared to the robust response from Massachusetts at the outbreak of the war, the response rates during the crises of 1777 demonstrate a strong level of continuity in commitment to the Revolution as measured by military service.

GRAPH 2-2 Enlistments and Days Served by Year

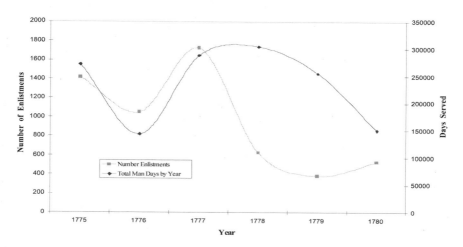

Social Characteristics

The social characteristics of America's Revolutionary soldiers are the third issue at stake in this discussion. The question is whether the social characteristics of Massachusetts soldiers continued to be representative of their communities as the war went into its third, fourth, and fifth years. The purpose of linking individual service records to socioeconomic characteristics is to see whether Massachusetts soldiers conform to the notion that the war became a "poor man's fight." Compilation and analysis of individual economic, social, and demographic characteristics of Massachusetts soldiers offers substantive evidence that Massachusetts soldiers were, in fact, largely representative of their communities, both in 1775–1776 and in the years thereafter. The following analysis of Massachusetts soldiers reports empirical evidence on variables of age in the ranks, social relationships, race, transience, and relative economic status.

The first issue is the notion that the army turned to boys and old men to fill the regiments. Of the 1,536 Massachusetts soldiers on active duty in 1777, military and church records document the ages of 576 individuals. Their median age was twenty-three years (see Table 2-3). A breakdown by percentiles shows that 20 percent of soldiers were thirty-three years of age or older and 20 percent were eighteen and younger, leaving 60 percent between the ages of eighteen and thirty-three. There were only three soldiers in their sixties: one was a colonel, one a surgeon, and one a sergeant. Officer ranks were coveted and prestigious, reserved to men admired within their respective communities. It is not surprising then that one-third of the soldiers more than forty years of age were officers. The prevalence of older soldiers among the upper ranks is evidence that recruiters were not necessarily scraping the social barrel. On the other end of the age spectrum,

TABLE 2-3   Ages of Soldiers on Active Duty, 1777—
Descriptive Statistics

	Percentile	Age (years)
	10	17
	20	18
	30	20
	40	21
Median	50	23
	60	26
	70	29
	80	33
	90	40

$n = 576$

of the 576 soldiers in the cohort of 1777 with known ages, there were just eight soldiers fifteen years of age, and six even younger. In some of those cases, boys accompanied their fathers, and the instances of boys younger than fifteen in service represent only 1 percent of the soldiers.[38] In the colonial context, the presence in camp of a few young men aged fourteen or fifteen was commonplace. Because traditional militia laws required service from all males from ages sixteen to fifty, it is anachronistic to read the frequency of seventeen-year-old recruits as a sign of desperation among recruiters. America was a young country, and a male sixteen years old was considered of a responsible age.[39] By way of comparison, the ages of the seventy-seven first-time recruits into Continental service whose dates of birth are known ranged from fifteen years (one case) to forty-seven years (one case). The median age of Continental recruits was twenty-one years, two years younger than the median for all soldiers.[40] Overall, the ages of rank-and-file Massachusetts soldiers of 1777 appear representative of the demographics of their society, the army not overly reliant on either "boys or old men."

Kinship relationships constitute a second social characteristic that links soldiers to their communities. Many of the younger soldiers enlisted with or alternated service obligations with fathers and brothers. A preliminary count of known kinship relations between soldiers shows that nearly 20 percent of recruits in 1777 had fathers, brothers, or sons who also served, consistent with the entire population of Massachusetts soldiers over the course of the war, of whom some 18 percent had close kin who also served as Massachusetts soldiers. In a test using surnames as a proxy for kinship, of the 350 Plymouth soldiers on duty in 1777, about one-fourth came from just seven family groups. Fifteen family groups account for 45 percent of the 485 soldiers from the Northampton region on duty in 1777. In contrast, only one Salem family group had more than 10 soldiers among the 315 on duty, a reflection of the higher mobility among the seaport residents.[41]

Marital status is another key indicator of a soldier's social standing and the strength of his ties to his community. The evidence for Massachusetts soldiers reveals that, of the recruits in 1777, at least 26 percent married within their own communities, almost exactly the same incidence as for the total data set. The marriage rates were a bit higher in 1775, 34 percent, which reflects the predominance of older heads of households who took active roles as respected community leaders in the opening hostilities. The statistics for reported marriage rates are conservative because of the incompleteness of surviving vital records—that is, the actual marriage rate was presumably higher than the rate that can be documented. The incidence of married men among the Massachusetts soldiers adds weight to the claim made here that most troops were fighting for and representative of the social structures of their communities.

As to General Wayne's charge that the American army filled their ranks with "Negroes" and "Indians" in 1777, there is no data to support that observation in the case of Massachusetts recruits. Among the 1,536 soldiers in the 1777 cohort, a mere twenty-six troops are identified explicitly as "black" or "negro" men in the service records. The twenty-six blacks represent less than 2 percent of the troops, a rate at the low end of the range of estimates of blacks in the general Massachusetts population.[42] Robert Wells lists the percentage of blacks in county populations as follows: Hampshire (Northampton), 1.1; Essex (Salem), 2.4; Plymouth, 2.1; and York, 2.1 percent.[43] Only two individual cases are specifically identified as "Indians" in the descriptive portions of service records. It is almost certain that the actual numbers of black and Indian recruits are underreported in the service records, but there is no evidence in the data of Massachusetts soldiers that there was a shift in recruiting those populations in 1777. Singling out data exclusively for Continental enlistments, one finds that nine of ten black recruits served in the Continental Army. Among the factors that contributed to the concentration of blacks' enlistments in Continental units during the later years of the war, two stand out: first, an official retreat from the exclusionist policies instituted in the early days of the war opened recruiting to blacks, and, second, the attraction of increasing bounties for Continental service in the later years of the war offered a unique opportunity for blacks to acquire a nest egg or a land grant. In some cases, owners of slaves could and did send their bondsmen as substitutes. There was also a traditional popular linkage between military service and citizenship rights, and at least some blacks saw military service as a vehicle to cement claims to freedom and full citizenship by way of fulfilling the military obligation expected of citizens.[44]

Only four Massachusetts soldiers of 1777 are explicitly identified as "transients." There are no standardized criteria for determining when individuals might be classified as transient, other than the occasions that town officials issued "warnings out" to unwelcome travelers. There is little guidance to explain how often recruiters made note of that qualification in their descriptive notes that appear in service records. The question of the recruitment of transients is further complicated by the fact that many young men did enlist for neighboring communities if they offered more favorable bounty incentives. An astute sense of the market does not make them mercenaries or strangers, just sharp Yankees seeking out the best terms in the best New England tradition. Massachusetts service records include innumerable entries in which a recruit credited to the enlistment quota for one town listed his residence in an adjacent community. Such young men were not identified as transients by contemporaries and should not be considered such when we search for social characteristics today. It was not commonplace to recruit strangers.[45] Continental Army recruiters were selected to recruit in their hometowns precisely because they personally knew everyone and were themselves known to the townspeople. In regard to recruiting immigrants, only five of the Massachusetts soldiers of 1777 are identified as foreign born: three British, one Scot, and one Guinean. It is interesting that one of the British-born was a John Barton from Duxbury, who went on to serve as one of George Washington's guards. Again, the reporting is doubtless incomplete, but the Massachusetts contingent does not appear to have significantly relied upon foreign-born recruits. One ready explanation is that New England towns were not among the prime destinations for immigrants in the decades preceding the Revolution, that honor falling to New York and especially Philadelphia.[46]

The economic status of Revolutionary soldiers is also difficult to assess concisely, because of incomplete records and the fact that the median age of the men in service in 1777 was twenty-three-years. At that age, young men generally had not achieved the status of property owners or heads of households and, as a result, do not appear in possession of real assets on state tax lists. It would be a mistake, however, to presume that these young men were all from the "lowest sort."[47] Through a process of linking soldiers with their families, it is possible to identify the young men whose families owned houses, commercial buildings, tillable land, pasturage, livestock, and so forth. By so doing, one can compare the median valuation of assets in several categories for soldiers from 1775 through 1777 with the median assets for all soldiers during the war and with all Massachusetts taxpayers (see Table 2-4).

A comparison of the asset category for the valuation of real estate, including dwellings and shops, shows Massachusetts soldiers on duty in

TABLE 2-4 Comparative Median Values of Asset Classes (£)

Category (n)	Real Estate[a]	Acreage[b]	Livestock[c]
Soldiers, 1775 (522)	2	1	4.2
Soldiers, 1776 (296)	3	0	3.4
Soldiers, 1777 (405)	3	4	7.1
All Soldiers (981)	3	2	4.4
All Massachusetts (37,938)	2.5	6	8.35

Note: The categories and asset values are based on *The Massachusetts Tax Valuation List of 1771*, ed. Bettye H. Pruitt (Boston: G. K. Hall, 1978).
[a] Annual worth (£) of the whole real estate.
[b] Acres of pasture, tillage, saltmarsh, upland hay, and meadowland.
[c] Value (£) of horses, oxen, cows, goats and sheep, and swine.

1777 possessed real estate assets in line with soldiers from the early war years and with soldiers overall, though exceeding the statewide level. Acreage refers to tillable land and pasturage. The median valuation of acreage for soldiers of 1777 is approximately two-thirds of the statewide median. Finally, the median valuation of livestock holdings indicates that the soldiers of 1777 were better off than their predecessors and only slightly lower than statewide levels. There are two main points to be gleaned from the comparison of median valuations. First, the similarity of the asset valuations of soldiers of 1777 with the statewide population suggests that the men in service were rather typical of Massachusetts society. Second, the median asset valuations among the soldiers on duty in 1777 compares favorably to the cohorts of 1775 and 1776, which suggests a fair degree of continuity in the economic profile of Massachusetts soldiers. The most important explanatory factor for the differential with statewide median valuations is the age factor: soldiers were predominantly young, single men not yet heads of households and thus not yet in possession of the land and livestock that they might expect to inherit in later years. Christopher Jedrey writes that, in eighteenth-century Massachusetts, few men received their inheritance of property or wealth before the age of thirty and that 67 percent of landless men on the tax rolls could expect an inheritance. John J. Waters adds that, in his research, he found that in the top quintile of wealth distribution, the norm was a married man almost fifty years of age, whereas the bottom quintile was typically single men younger than thirty.[48]

The proportion of soldiers with links to the tax valuation list remains steady from 1775 through 1777. Isolating the first-time recruits of 1777, one finds that there is no significant drop-off in median asset valuations (see Table 2-5). The median value of real estate holdings of new recruits is

TABLE 2-5—Comparative Median Values of Asset Classes (£)

Category (n)	Real Estate	Acreage	Livestock
All Active-Duty Soldiers, 1777 (405)	3	4	7.1
First-Time Recruits, 1777 (155)	3	3	7.8

Note: See Table 2-4 for explanation of categories and asset values.

TABLE 2-6—Comparative Median Values of Asset Classes (£)

Category (n)	Real Estate	Acreage	Livestock
Continental Recruits, 1777 (244)	2	0	4.2
Provincial/Militia Recruits (162)	3.9	6	10.6

Note: See Table 2-4 for explanation of categories and asset values.

the same as for all soldiers on active duty. The valuation of acreage is lower by one-fourth, but the valuation of livestock is slightly higher. That is largely a function of age, in that younger men may have had some stock but had not yet acquired title to land. The data do not point to significant decline in the economic status of the new recruits among Massachusetts soldiers in 1777.

A comparison of asset valuations of provincial militiamen and Continental recruits shows that Continental recruits in 1777 typically had about half of the assets of their militia counterparts (see Table 2-6). This strongly suggests that older men with more assets—that is, farms, businesses, and families—preferred service in the provincial militias, with the typically short-term commitments. In fact, the median age of provincial soldiers was twenty-six years, fully four years older than the median age of Continental enlistees. The differential in age correlates to the differential in asset valuations, as one would expect in colonial society where men typically did not become heads of households and property owners until their late twenties.[49] For young, single men, the Continental service offered the attractions of travel, new associations, excitement, possibly glory, and solid employment— not to be overlooked in a time of economic disruption.

Conclusions

Massachusetts mobilization in 1777 and the patterns of military service show that Americans were doubtless war weary, but continued to turn out in growing numbers. Burgoyne's 1777 invasion produced a surge of mobilization in Massachusetts, in Continental lines, state regiments, as well as militia companies. Throughout a steady barrage of calls for recruits and materials, the service records demonstrate that Massachusetts men continued to enlist and serve in increasing numbers in 1777 compared to prior years and that the cumulative effects of that surge carried forward into subsequent years. If we consult only General Washington's returns for January 1777 that show his army dwindling away, we lose sight of the cyclical trends and broader contours of service patterns, as well as the full range of options for military service.[50] The Continental Army was always an amalgamation of units. Militia troops served alongside the Continental regiments. Whenever soldiers served on campaigns under orders from Congress, they referred to such service as "continental." James Kirby Martin writes that "each time militiamen appeared in camp, they became part of an American Continental force."[51] Expanding our purview to include the full spectrum of military service through the course of the war, as the review of service records does here, offers a comprehensive picture of Massachusetts military service during the Revolutionary War and shows that Massachusetts sustained a high level of manpower in the field until 1779, when the theaters of the war moved away from New England. By examining soldiers' social and economic profiles in relation to their local communities, this study demonstrates that aggregately Massachusetts soldiers reflected colonial society—some rich, some poor, some young, some old, together a great body of yeomen. The application of this methodology to other states offers the promise of a more accurate appraisal of Revolutionary soldiers than we have previously had available, one sensitive to the variations of service during the various stages of the war in other regions.

The decentralized and voluntary organization of recruiting and mobilizing manpower meant that decisions to support the war were ultimately made locally. The continued service of Massachusetts soldiers in whichever branch they chose affirmed their belief in the cause, their sense of obligation to their communities, and their sense of their own best interests. Massachusetts soldiers were undoubtedly drawn to the most favorable bounties and land grants, but they were far from mercenaries. Henry Dearborn wrote, "We . . . had Something more at Stake than fighting for six Pence pr Day." Baroness Reese, who witnessed the fighting at Saratoga, attributed the Americans' bravery to the fact that they were fighting "for their country and for freedom."[52] Looking out for one's community, one's country, and oneself were not incompatible; self-interest and community interest were not mutually exclusive.

The data on Massachusetts soldiers of 1777 show strong social and economic ties to their communities, through marriage, kinship, and economic stakes in their towns. There is little empirical evidence in the service records to suggest that Massachusetts recruiters turned disproportionately to the youngest, the poorest, or the minorities of colonial society, despite complaints from commanders such as General Wayne. Complaints of this sort almost always came from officers who appear to have been anxious to pass any blame for failed operations onto their troops. To be sure, socially marginal men of no known property or no known ties to their towns were present in the Massachusetts military, but in similar proportions to their presence in colonial Massachusetts society.

This study of service and social profiles of Massachusetts soldiers illuminates the intersections of private lives and public obligations during the exigencies of the Revolutionary War. On a practical level, the multitiered military system of militias, provincial regiments, and Continental service was suitable for Americans. Massachusetts soldiers participated in different units at different times, depending on many circumstances, in both the ebb and flow of their own lives and the fortunes of the war. The service data show a clear preference for limited enlistments of the militia tradition and a clear popular preference for widely sharing the burden of military duty. There is a measurable economic differential between those who chose short- versus long-term enlistments, but that does not supplant or negate the social ties of Massachusetts soldiers to their families, towns, and regions or the cause of national independence.[53] The moments of manpower crises reflect to considerable degree the seasonal character of traditional colonial military service and are not necessarily strong indicators of the widespread commitment in Massachusetts to the success of the war. Take, for example, the incident with Lieutenant Sewall: his troops melted away in January of 1777, but new recruits swelled the ranks again in the spring. The coming and going of troops on active duty was certainly nerve-wracking, but it was also routine for American commanders during the Revolution.

The patterns of the service data show Massachusetts soldiers turned out with particular alacrity when threats were imminent but, on the other hand, were reluctant to take responsibility for fighting outside of their home region of New England. In fact, some enlistments stipulated that service was to be limited to the New England states. This was not unique to Massachusetts. New York law disallowed her militias from serving more than forty days outside the state, until 1779, when the limit was extended to ninety days, which, in light of travel times in the eighteenth century, precluded significant service beyond the state line.[54] Seen in the context of the times, soldiers' reluctance to serve abroad was reasonable based on their experience of militia tradition that centered obligation on defense of the community, while outward bound expeditions were voluntary. Men identified foremost with their local communities, and the sense of a national identity and national obligations was only in infancy. This study of Massachusetts soldiers' service records shows that people turned out when it counted most to them. In 1777, with Congress on the run and with Washington on the defensive, it must have seemed that the full brunt of the war bore down on New England. In the crisis of 1777, Massachusetts people turned out in record numbers. Many signed up for long-term commitments to the national army, and many more turned out to defend New England in its season of need.

In the course of their service, the soldiers of Massachusetts literally walked from the Maine coast to the Hudson River, from Salem to the Narragansett Bay, from Northampton to Morristown, and from Plymouth to Lake Champlain. Though it is true that Washington never assembled the professional army he wished for, one in parity with that of the British Empire, it is also the case that ordinary Americans never wanted a professional army on the scale of the British Empire. As Charles Royster succinctly notes, "Americans *were* farmers, tradesmen, mechanics, and planters—not soldiers—and they wanted to remain so."[55]

But perhaps the most significant point is that the willingness to turn out for alarms or enlist for long terms in a national army can be read as an ongoing popular referendum on the war itself. Individuals and families employed a complex calculus of what was at stake for them, their communities, and their states when determining whether to serve and when, where, and for how long to enlist. The driving forces behind enlistments ran the gamut from young men seeking excitement, to those with ambition who sensed an opportunity to advance themselves in society, to yet others who were attracted by the incentives and promise of army pay during a period of economic disruption. Certainly many were stirred by calls to defend their liberties—these were often expressed in earthy admonitions to potential recruits, like that of Joseph Hawley to fight or become "hewers of wood and drawers of water to British lords and bishops." Massachusetts Indians like Joshua Pockemet may well have fought to establish their right to an equal place in Massachusetts society. Black soldiers often engaged in military service in exchange for a promise of civil freedom or economic opportunity. Some rural debtors saw the war as a means to free themselves of an oppressive legal system that favored a distant privileged elite. But any of these individual motives could comfortably complement the sense of Massachusetts soldiers that they had "Something more at Stake."

In the final analysis, there was no centralized authority in Revolutionary America with coercive power to demand either manpower or material support. The decentralized patriot organization may have been less effective than the imperial machine, but the movement was "strong at the grass roots, in the local communities."[56] Congress could do no more than request the states for support, and the states could then order the towns to provide men and materials; moral suasion and uncollectible fines were the only enforcement mechanisms for quotas and drafts. In essence, the mobilization was ultimately voluntary, and, though the mosaic of motivations was as varied as the people themselves, the persistence of ordinary Massachusetts people in support of the war is clear during the course of

1777. Massachusetts soldiers represented the people and communities from which they came, and their service was critical to achieving the independence of the United States and did much to ensure their right to a place at the table in the new republic.

Notes

This essay draws from "Answering the Call to Arms: The Social Composition of the Revolutionary Soldiers of Massachusetts, 1775–1783," chapter 4, Ph.D. dissertation, University of Minnesota, 2004. I wish to thank John P. Resch, Richard Buel, and Wayne Bodle for their helpful comments in the preparation of this essay, and also John Howe, Russell Menard, and all participants at the Early American Workshop at the University of Minnesota. Thanks also to John Shy, Stanley Engerman, and Fred Anderson, who offered valuable comments at various stages of this project.

1. Ebenezer Huntington, *Letters Written by Ebenezer Huntington during the American Revolution* (New York: Charles F. Heartman, 1915), p. 53.

2. Washington to Governor Trumbull, December 14, 1776, in, John C. Fitzpatrick, ed., *The Writings of George Washington from the Original Manuscript Sources, 1745–1799*, 39 vols. (Washington, D.C.: Government Printing Office, 1931–1944), vol. 6.

3. Richard Buel, *Dear Liberty: Connecticut Mobilization for the Revolutionary War* (Middletown, Conn.: Wesleyan University Press, 1980), pp. 92–93; Robert W. Coakley and Stetson Conn, *The War of the American Revolution: Narrative, Chronology, and Bibliography* (Washington, D.C.: Center of Military History, 1975), p. 50; Christopher Ward, *The War of the Revolution* (New York: Macmillan, 1952), 1:281; Henry B. Carrington, *Battles of the American Revolution 1775–1781: A Military History* (New York: A. S. Barnes and Company, 1904).

4. Diary of Henry Sewall, Massachusetts Historical Society, Boston, Mass. (hereafter MHS).

5. John Shy, *A People Numerous and Armed: Reflections on the Military Struggle for American Independence*, rev. ed. (Ann Arbor: University of Michigan Press, 1990), p. 21; Robert Middlekauff, *The Glorious Cause: The American Revolution, 1763–1789* (New York: Oxford University Press, 1982), p. 506; Don Higginbotham, *The War of American Independence: Military Attitudes, Policy and Practice, 1763–1789* (Bloomington: Indiana University Press, 1977), pp. 393–94; Richard M. Ketchum cites Colonel Anthony Wayne in *Saratoga: Turning Point of America's Revolutionary War* (New York: Henry Holt and Company, 1997), p. 44; Robert A. Gross, *The Minutemen and Their World* (New York: Hill and Wang, 1976), p. 147. For a more comprehensive discussion of historiographic issues, see the historiographic essay that appears in the present volume.

6. The data set used here was compiled by the author as part of a dissertation at the University of Minnesota. Data collection focused on records of soldiers from the Massachusetts regions proximate to York, Plymouth, Salem, and Northampton. Taken together, these agricultural and maritime centers represent a cross section of late-eighteenth-century Massachusetts society, including old settled towns and expanding frontier communities, agricultural, mixed, and maritime economies, coastal and interior, urban and rural, and so on. For a full explanation of method, see Walter L. Sargent, "Answering the Call to Arms: The Social Composition of Massachusetts Revolutionary Soldiers, 1775–1783," Ph.D. diss., University of Minnesota, 2004 (UMI number 3154074), pp. 12–20, 259–68.

7. Gerald C. Stowe and Jac Weller state, "It [West Point] was by far the most important American fortification during the war." General Henry Knox also wrote that the Hudson highlands posts were "infinitely important." Stowe and Weller, "Revolutionary

West Point: 'The Key to the Continent,'" in *Military Analysis of the Revolutionary War: An Anthology,* by the editors of *Military Affairs* (Millwood, N.Y.: KTO Press, 1977), p. 154.

8. Judd Manuscripts, Revolutionary Matters, Forbes Library, Northampton, Massachusetts, p. 27.

9. For example, see William M. Dwyer, *The Day Is Ours! An Inside View of the Battles of Trenton and Princeton, November 1776–January 1777* (New Brunswick, N.J.: Rutgers University Press, 1998), pp. 49–50.

10. Diary of Henry Sewall, MHS.

11. Calls for recruits generally originated with commanders in the field and were forwarded to Congress. Congress, in turn, issued requests to the states. In Massachusetts, the General Court then sent out quotas to the county militia regiments or directly to the towns.

12. Town meeting, Northampton, March 3, 1777. Jay Mack Holbrook, *Massachusetts Vital Records: Northampton, 1654–1893* (Oxford, Mass.: Holbrook Research Institute, 1994), microfiche 138, #34, #65.

13. Town meeting, Northampton, April 15, 1777. Holbrook, *Massachusetts Vital Records,* microfiche 138, #34, #72.

14. For example, April 28, Plymouth company to Rhode Island under Colonel Titcomb; April 30, Captain Johnson's Salem company to Providence; May 1, Captain Silas Adams' Danvers company to Rhode Island; May 6, Captain Joseph Hiller's Salem company to Providence; May 7, Captain Samuel Grant's York company to Rhode Island; May 19, Captain Abel Moulton's York company to Rhode Island; June 29, Captain Silas Adams' Danvers company to Providence.

15. William Heath, *Heath's Memoirs of the American War: Reprinted from the Original Edition of 1798,* introduction and notes by Rufus Rockwell Wilson (New York: A. Wessels Company, 1904), p. 129.

16. William Digby, *The British Invasion from the North: Digby's Journal of the Campaigns of Generals Carleton and Burgoyne from Canada, 1776–1777,* Introduction by James Phinney Baxter (Albany, 1887; reprint, New York: Da Capo Press, 1970), p. 191.

17. Paul David Nelson, "Legacy of Controversy: Gates, Schuyler, and Arnold at Saratoga, 1777," in *Military Analysis of the Revolutionary War,* introduction by Don Higginbotham (Millwood, N.Y.: KTO Press, 1977), p. 184.

18. Judd Manuscripts, Revolutionary Matters, Forbes Library, Northampton, Mass., p. 167.

19. John Resch, *Suffering Soldiers: Revolutionary War Veterans, Moral Sentiment, and Political Culture in the Early Republic* (Amherst: University of Massachusetts Press, 1999), pp. 30–33.

20. Ketchum, *Saratoga,* p. 205; Digby, *Journal,* pp. 211–13.

21. Howard H. Peckham, ed., *The Toll of Independence: Engagements & Battle Casualties of the American Revolution* (Chicago: University of Chicago Press, 1974), p. 37.

22. Heath, *Heath's Memoirs of the American War,* p. 134.

23. Edwin Emery, *The History of Sanford, Maine, 1661–1900,* comp. and ed. William Morrell Emery. A Facsimilie of the 1901 edition with a new, comprehensive name index by Rachel Bean Perkins (Sanford, Maine: Harland H. Eastman, 1987), p. 61.

24. James Russell Trumbull, *History of Northampton, Massachusetts from Its Earliest Settlement in 1654* (Northampton, Mass.: Press of Gazette Printing Company, 1902), p. 402.

25. *Essex Institute Historical Collections* (Salem, Mass.: Essex Institute Press, 1869–1993), 42:315.

26. Manuscript journal, Ebenezer Wild, 1758–1794, entry of September 18, 1777, MHS.

27. Digby, *Journal,* p. 273.

28. Tuft's Orderly Book, 8th Massachusetts, kept by Francis Tufts, September 5–December 4, 1777, Part I: Michael Jackson's Regiment, Continental Army (Mass.) September 5–December 4, 1777. Revolutionary War Orderly Books, MHS, microfilm P-394.

29. Ezra Tilden (1751–1819), C. E. French Collection: "Extracts from Ezra Tilden's Journal," MHS.

30. Manuscript journal, Ebenezer Wild, 1758–1794, entry of October 18, 1777, MHS.

31. Robert K. Wright, Jr., *The Continental Army* (Washington, D.C.: Center of Military History, 1983), p. 117; James A. Huston, *The Sinews of War: Army Logistics, 1775–1953* (Washington, D.C.: Office of the Chief of Military History, 1966), p. 56.

32. Mary Beth Norton cites the diary of Baroness Frederica von Reese in *Liberty's Daughters: The Revolutionary Experience of American Women, 1750–1800* (Boston: Little, Brown, 1980), p. 172.

33. Doctor Albigence Waldo, Surgeon in Col. Prentices Regt. in the Continental Army, 1777–78: Diary Kept at Valley Forge. MHS, Ms.SBd-33. Entries dated December 21–22, 1777.

34. Waldo diary, MHS, Ms.SBd-33. Entry dated December 28, 1777.

35. Charles H. Lesser, *The Sinews of Independence: Monthly Strength Reports of the Continental Army* (Chicago: University of Chicago Press, 1976), pp. xxx–xxxi.

36. See Lesser, *Sinews of Independence*.

37. John Resch finds a similar pattern in New Hampshire. See *Suffering Soldiers*, p. 26.

38. See John Resch, "The Revolution as a People's War: Mobilization in New Hampshire," in the present volume.

39. Alice Hanson, *Wealth of a Nation to Be: The American Colonies on the Eve of the Revolution* (New York: Columbia University Press, 1980), p. 40; Robert Wells, *Revolutions in American Lives: A Demographic Perspective on the History of Americans, Their Families, and Their Society* (Westport, Conn.: Greenwood Press, 1982), p. 82.

40. Leroy Thompson, *The U.S. Army in Vietnam* (Devon, U.K.: David and Charles Publishers, 1990), p. 21.

41. On surnames, see Kenneth Lockridge, *A New England Town, The First Hundred Years: Dedham, Massachusetts, 1636–1736* (New York: W. W. Norton, 1970), pp. 63–65. On divided families, see Ronald Tagney, *The World Turned Upside Down: Essex County During America's Turbulent Years, 1763–1790* (West Newbury, Mass.: Essex County History, 1989); Thomas Hughes, *A Journal by Thomas Hughes: For His Amusement, & Designed Only for His Perusal by the Time He Attains the Age of 50 If He Lives So Long (1778–1789),* Introduction by E. A. Benians (Cambridge: Cambridge University Press, 1947), pp. 32, 42.

42. Jesse Chickering, *A Statistical View of the Population of Massachusetts, from 1765 to 1840* (Boston: Charles Little and James Brown, 1846); Robert V. Wells, "Population and the American Revolution," in William M. Fowler and Wallace Coyle, eds., *The American Revolution: Changing Perspectives* (Boston: Northeastern University Press, 1979), p. 108: Alice Hanson Jones, *Wealth of a Nation to Be: The American Colonies on the Eve of the Revolution* (New York: Columbia University Press, 1980), p. 40.

43. Robert V. Wells, *The Population of the British Colonies in America before 1776* (Princeton, N.J.: Princeton University Press, 1975), pp. 81.

44. Rhode Island, on the other hand, had a much larger percentage (8.5) of black residents than Massachusetts, and Rhode Island fielded considerable numbers of black soldiers, including one regiment composed almost entirely of black privates.

45. Resch, *Suffering Soldiers*, p. 26; Douglas L. Jones, "The Strolling Poor: Transiency in Eighteenth-Century Massachusetts," *Journal of Social History* 8 (1975): 28–54, and *Village and Seaport: Migration and Society in Eighteenth-Century Massachusetts* (Hanover, N.H.: University Press of New England, 1981).

46. See Jones, "The Strolling Poor."

47. Jones, *Wealth*, p. 384.

48. Christopher Jedrey, *The World of John Cleaveland: Family and Community in Eighteenth-Century New England* (New York: W. W. Norton, 1979), p. 63, table 2, p. 175;

John J. Waters, review of *Fathers of the Towns: Leadership and Community Structure in Eighteenth-Century New England,* by Edward M. Cook, Jr., *New England Quarterly* 50, no. 3 (September 1977): 543.

49. James A. Henretta, "Families and Farms: *Mentalité* in Pre-Industrial America," *William and Mary Quarterly,* 3rd ser., 35 (January 1978): 3–32.

50. Returns for the Continental forces are compiled in Lesser, *Sinews of Independence.*

51. Martin, in John Ferling, ed., *The World Turned Upside Down: The American Victory in the War of Independence.* Contributions in Military Studies, no. 79 (New York: Greenwood Press, 1988), pp. 33–34.

52. Dearborn and Reese, quoted in Ketchum, *Saratoga,* p. 369.

53. Charles Royster, *A Revolutionary People at War: The Continental Army and American Character, 1775–1783* (New York: W. W. Norton, 1979), p. 374.

54. Allen Bowman, *The Morale of the American Revolutionary Army* (Washington, D.C.: American Council on Public Affairs, 1943), p. 114.

55. Royster, *A Revolutionary People at War,* p. 11.

56. Coakley and Conn, *The War of the American Revolution,* p. 43.

3

THE REVOLUTION
AS A PEOPLE'S WAR

Mobilization in New Hampshire

J O H N   R E S C H

Beginning in 1973, John Shy, Edward Papenfuse, and Gregory Stiverson broadened the scope for studying the War for Independence by using military history to examine social structure, ideology, and political culture in Revolutionary America. Their work on the theme of war and society fostered more research on ordinary people, ethnic groups, women, Indians, blacks, urban and rural communities, and the composition of the army. Since their groundbreaking work, scholars have added richness, complexity, and controversy to the history of the Revolutionary society far beyond the benign view of the war as a struggle of a largely unified people for liberty.[1]

This essay adds a comparative study of mobilization in five New Hampshire towns, 1775–1782, to this body of literature. Peterborough, Exeter, Hollis, Canterbury, and Weare were chosen because they varied in their founding, population size, ethnic composition, and geographic location and because they preserved nearly complete lists of enlistments of town residents and tax records (three towns) or other data, such as genealogies and biographies, to link service and social standing. In addition, accounts of mobilization gleaned from scores of New Hampshire town histories and state records provide further insight into these communities' war efforts.[2]

In New Hampshire, mobilization, like politics, was a local matter. These case studies illustrate how different communities responded to the changing needs for manpower throughout the different stages and fortunes of war. In the first year of the war the towns were swept up by the *rage militaire* that brought out thousands of enthusiastic soldiers. Between 1776 and 1782 townsmen faced constraints on mobilization as a result of their democratic practices and market pressures and diminished enthusiasm to fight as the war became protracted and moved out of New England. What began as a people's uprising became a war of attrition conducted by a determined group of hard-core leaders who sustained war-weary townsmen and by young soldiers who were drawn from both the fringe of society and its establishment.

Peterborough, New Hampshire

Peterborough was settled in the 1750s in the southwestern part of the colony by Scots-Irish immigrants from northern Massachusetts and children of Scots-Irish in Londonderry, New Hampshire, some forty miles to the east. Between 1754 and 1763, Peterborough was deeply involved in the imperial struggle between Great Britain and France in North America. The French and Indian War (1754–1763) bloodied Peterborough, but it also seasoned men, such as Samuel Cunningham, Alexander Robbe, John Taggart, "Short Bill" Scott, and his cousin "Long Bill" Scott, who became military leaders and officers in the Revolution. In the 1760s, though still part of New England's frontier, Peterborough was linked increasingly to the region's economy. By 1775, the town had grown from a handful of settlers to 549 people, mostly young couples and their children. Many Peterborough families orbited around two large kin networks. One of these networks centered on the Cunningham, Robbe, Taggart, and Scott families, which had strong ties to communities in Massachusetts. The other centered on the Miller, Morison, Moore, and Smith families, which were linked to communities in the Merrimack Valley, in particular Londonderry. The town's social fabric was strengthened first by marriages within these two networks and, then, during the Revolution and following it, between them. On the eve of the Revolutionary War, Peterborough had grown from a precarious aggregation of Scots-Irish settlers carving out farms on the frontier under proprietor rule to a thriving, self-governing community of farmers and traders. The presence of one slave in Peterborough's first census of 1767, increasing to six slaves by 1773 and to eight by 1775, attested to the increasing wealth and rising social status of some residents.[3]

When word of the Battles of Lexington and Concord reached Peterborough on April 19, Short Bill Scott closed his store, mustered about a third of the townsmen of military age, including his cousin Long Bill Scott, into a company of troops, and marched them to Boston to join the war. Between 1775 and 1783, a total of 100 residents enlisted in the army. Of them, 94 men were drawn from the grand total of 150 males of military age, sixteen to fifty years of age, who were at risk of service during these eight years; six of the 100 soldiers were older than fifty. Enlistment patterns varied each year of the war. As shown in Table 3-1, the highest proportion of mobilization occurred in 1775, 1777, and 1778. After 1780, mobilization decreased substantially.

The Peterborough data permit a close examination of the enlistment cohort for each year of the war. As seen in Table 3-1, in 1775 Peterborough sent forty-two men to war. This enlistment cohort was the most representative of

Map 3-1. Detail from map of New Hampshire. This 1775 topographical map of the province of New Hampshire shows the five towns used in this study. Exeter is located in the eastern part of the province, near the capital of Portsmouth. From Exeter, Hollis is located about midway in the province, along the border separating New Hampshire and Massachusetts. Peterborough is located slightly north and west of Hollis. Weare can be found northeast of Peterborough and near the township of Concord. Canterbury is located north of Concord and touches that township. (Map surveyed by Samuel Holland and printed for William Faden, Geographer to the King in 1784. Courtesy of the New Hampshire Historical Society.)

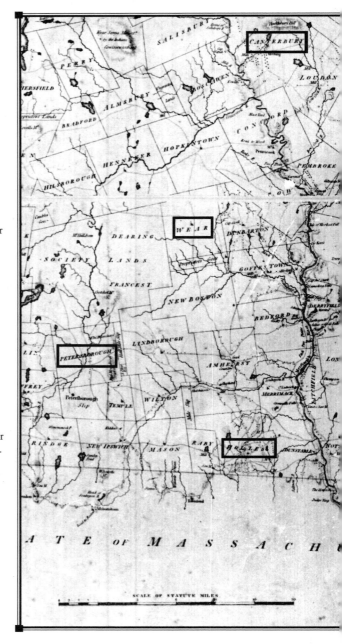

TABLE 3-1—Enlistment Patterns, Peterborough, 1775–1782—
New Enlistees Each Year

	YEAR							
Year	1775	1776	1777	1778	1779	1780	1781	1782
1775	42	18	23	19	12	10	7	4
1776		11	9	3	3	2	1	1
1777			34	16	5	5	2	2
1778				9	4	5	4	2
1779					2	0	0	0
1780						1	1	0
1781							1	0
1782								0
Total	42	29	66	47	26	23	16	9

the town's population for the eight years of war. These forty-two men represented a cross section of the town's population structure. They averaged thirty years of age, two years younger than average age of the 100 men at risk of military service in 1775. Nearly 40 percent of the soldiers were in their thirties or forties, about the same proportion of all Peterborough males. Many of the town's political leaders marched to war. Eleven of the forty-two soldiers (26 percent) had held or were holding a town office. Town leaders promoted community mobilization either by volunteering for duty or by seeing their sons off to war.

The soldiers represented the town's economic structure. Although some were propertyless, they were not part of a rural proletariat. They were young sons of Peterborough farmers, such as Samuel Moore, Jr., and William Smith, Jr., both aged nineteen. Nor were the older men who enlisted propertyless. Some were identified as "yeomen" who owned average-sized farms. These soldiers, part of the *rage militaire* of 1775, formed the core of troops provided by the town for the remainder of the war. Twenty-nine of the thirty-eight surviving soldiers (four had died either in combat or in camp) who first enlisted in 1775 either continued in service in 1776 or reenlisted at other times during the war (see Table 3-1). Soldiers who enlisted in 1775 contributed from a third to a half of the town's soldiers under arms each year of the war. Fourteen soldiers, nearly half of the thirty-one townsmen who served in the Continental Army from Peterborough, had first fought in 1775.

From 1776 to 1782, the number of men Peterborough sent to war varied with the fortunes and location of the conflict. Enlistments declined in 1776 but reached their highest point in 1777, when 66 of the 106 men at risk of service that year left town, some for just a few days, to repel Burgoyne's invasion of New York and Vermont. Service remained strong in 1778, with the call for men to reinforce troops laying siege to Newport, Rhode Island. Service declined steadily from 1779 through 1782, and new enlistments dropped dramatically in 1779 as the war moved to the Mid-Atlantic and Southern states. Between 1778 and 1780 only thirteen Peterborough residents became new recruits, bringing the town's total to 100 servicemen by war's end. Benjamin Alld was one of those soldiers. Alld's father had been a substantial landowner in Londonderry and Bedford, New Hampshire. Selling his property there, he moved with his family to Peterborough in 1778. In 1776, young Alld, age seventeen, had enlisted in Nahum Baldwin's state regiment, which was recruited to reinforce Washington's troops in New York. Alld fought in the Battle of White Plains. In July 1777, he reenlisted for three years in Long Bill Scott's Continental Company.

Kinship, friendship, birth order, and links to military units continued to shape enlistment patterns, as illustrated by recruits John Scott, David Scott, and Samuel Spear. In 1778 Captain Short Bill Scott recruited his son, John, age fourteen or fifteen, to serve as his company's fifer. That same year, Captain Long Bill Scott recruited his son, David, age fifteen, to be his company's drummer, and Samuel Spear, age sixteen, likely David's friend, to serve in the infantry. David was reunited with his brother, Honorable John, and his cousin, Thomas Scott, in Long Bill's company. The town relied upon such youths from established families to fill military ranks.

Community expectations that its leaders serve in the army produced recruits throughout the war. James Cunningham felt these pressures. In 1774, Cunningham was elected tithingman. In 1775, he advanced in Peterborough's political structure by being elected selectman. His lack of military service, however, diminished his status as a leader. He held no town office between 1776 and 1778, despite a general pattern of townsmen returning their leaders to office. In 1778, Cunningham, at thirty-four, enlisted under his brother Samuel, who commanded a company of New Hampshire troops sent to Rhode Island to reinforce Continental regiments near Newport. Samuel Cunningham, age forty, was a veteran of the French and Indian War and a prominent town leader. He had served as selectman in 1768 and in 1776. In 1775, Samuel was Peterborough's representative to the

Provincial Congress. Samuel had fought at Bennington and had been present at Burgoyne's surrender near Saratoga. In August 1778 Samuel and James returned from Rhode Island after three weeks of service. In 1779 James resumed his rise among town leaders when he was elected to the Peterborough Committee of Safety. He had to reestablish himself within the town by performing military service.

New recruits continued to come from established families that rotated service among their sons of prime military age and those who had yet to serve. For example, brothers Charles and Thomas Davison rotated service. In 1777, Thomas first enlisted at age nineteen to defend Fort Ticonderoga. In 1779 Charles, also nineteen, enlisted for the first time. He served for three weeks in Rhode Island. In 1780, Thomas, then twenty-two, returned to service for three months with the Continental Army at West Point while Charles stayed home. Other men, such as John White, Jr., thirty-one, took their turn under arms. White's brother and four cousins had marched with Samuel Cunningham in 1778. A fifth cousin had served in the Continental Army in 1776 and had enlisted in a state regiment that engaged Burgoyne the following year. In 1779, John White, Jr., enlisted for the first time for three weeks of service in Rhode Island. Households continued to serve as recruiting centers that rotated sons in and out of service.

By 1780, most men with military experience chose to stay home as the war moved to the Mid-Atlantic states and the South. Fighting far from home was left to the hard-core soldiers who first saw action in 1775, 1776, and 1777. Throughout the war, the town's selectmen or its Committee of Safety enlisted men into regiments formed by the state or filled the town's quota of troops for the Continental Army or mustered townsmen into mobilized militia units. Peterborough, like other towns, supplemented bounties paid by the state and Congress to entice enlistments in the Continental Army. Only rarely did the town hire strangers, as it did in 1779 when it recruited "transhant" Zaccheus Brooks to help fill its quota of Continental soldiers.

The contrast to Brooks was the Scott family. The Scotts were enterprising, ambitious, and active in Peterborough. Short Bill ran a store from his house and was a leader in the local militia. Long Bill was a farmer and shoemaker anxious to make his mark in the world. They were involved in running and building the town. Between 1762 and 1775, William Scott, one of the two "Bills," and John Scott held six minor town offices, including constable and hog reeve. In all, twelve of thirteen Scotts of military age, representing three generations and living in Peterborough and nearby towns, took up arms; seven Scotts served in the Continental Army. In 1775 Long Bill's son, Honorable John Scott, age ten, and Short Bill's son, John, age eleven, served their fathers as waiters. Later, both boys enlisted in the Continental Army. Other family members served in the army as well. In 1777 David Scott, age fifteen, enlisted in his father's (Short Bill) company as a drummer for the town of Attleborough, Massachusetts. In

1781, he reenlisted for a second three-year term for Townsend, Massachu-setts. David was described as a five-foot nine-inch "farmer," with "blue eyes," a "light complexion," and "dark hair." In both cases, Peterborough had filled its quota of troops and thus was not offering bounties. By enlist-ing first for Attleborough and then for Townsend, David would receive bounties from these towns and any other financial concessions he could negotiate that would be useful to this young man from an established family who was just beginning to build his own estate. His military service and gamble for gain, however, ended in tragedy. He died in 1782, possibly of camp fever.

Judging from their enlistments, the Scotts made no ideological distinc-tion between service in the Continental Army and other military units. Some family members, such as Alexander Scott, of Stoddard, New Hamp-shire, and his son James served only in local militia companies and state troops. In 1777, Peterborough's William Scott, age sixty-four, who had come to town in the 1750s as a homesteader, marched with Alexander Robbe's militia company to repel Burgoyne's invasion. In September 1777, William reenlisted into Colonel Daniel Moore's state troops, which reinforced the army opposing Burgoyne at Stillwater. His son David had served in 1775 under Short Bill and later served as a sergeant in the state troops raised in 1780 to repel a Tory raid on Royalton, Ver-mont. William's two other sons, Thomas and William Scott, Jr., served in the Continental Army.

By war's end twelve Scotts had collectively contributed about forty years of military service in Continental, state, and militia units. They were hard-core fighters from well-established and aspiring families who were mobilized into service through their kin network. For some, military ser-vice became one more avenue to improve their social status and stand-ing as community leaders. For most, the war was a family affair involv-ing fathers, sons, and cousins serving, often together, in militia, state, and Continental Army units. Furthermore, the Scotts belonged to an extensive kin network that included families like themselves—Robbes, Cunninghams, Nays, Taggarts, and Swans—which contributed troops. Three men from the Taggart family and two from the Swan family, both part of Peterborough's establishment, contributed soldiers to the Continental Army. And, as David Scott's case suggests, they were proba-bly careful to secure financial benefits either from their own town or by enlisting for other communities.

In this particular town, the general conclusion made by most modern historians that the Continental Army was unrepresentative of society failed to materialize when all of Peterborough's soldiers are examined within the context of their households and community. Peterborough's enlistees represented a cross section of the community whether serving in the Continental Army, state regiments, or the militia. Some men were on the margin of the town's society, a few were transients, possibly two were former slaves, but most recruits came from families such as Smith, Morison, Miller, Ferguson, Scott, Blair, and Alld. These soldiers were sons of well-to-do farmers, immigrant settlers, and homesteaders who, by the time of the Revolution, had established positions in the town's social, political, and economic structure. The army recruited young men, and Peterborough had a large pool of men between the ages of sixteen and twenty-five, the prime military ages. That the young soldiers would lack wealth or property was a function of their age or perhaps being lower in the birth order among males in their households.[4]

Many townsmen served alternately in militia companies, in state regiments, or in Continental units. Service was not stigmatized by class. Enlistments followed family lines. Once a family member left town under arms, others, including fathers, sons, brothers, cousins, and in-laws, could be expected to enlist. High social status influenced enlistment. Town leaders or their children and those aspiring to leadership were expected to serve in the military. Confidence in local commanders produced enlistments. Many Peterborough residents served with either Captain Short Bill Scott or his cousin Captain Long Bill Scott, who were company commanders in the First New Hampshire Regiment and Henry Jackson's Massachusetts regiment, respectively. Many mobilized under the town's militia captain, Alexander Robbe. All three captains were town founders, veterans of the French and Indian War, and seasoned officers. Thus, townsmen clustered around experienced and trusted officers whose units contained relatives, friends, and neighbors. Bounty payments did not cause Peterborough enlistments to shift to the lower sorts in the community. Rather, financial rewards were conventional, and thus expected, when responding to kin, peer, and community expectations to serve.

The war's changing character affected enlistment patterns. Conflict close to home aroused many men to arms, such that, during both the *rage militaire* in 1775 and the British invasion of New England in 1777, a large portion of the community's men bore arms. As the conflict became a long and dirty war from 1777 to 1782, recruits came from the manpower pool of newcomers, veteran soldiers, and young men from the town's established families. Only a handful of "hired" men were transients and, possibly, former slaves. The war appeared to politicize soldiers and stiffen their resolve, particularly those who fought in 1775 and 1776. Many of the men who saw action early in the war became hard-core troops. They frequently reenlisted when there was a call to arms. More than half (eighteen of thirty-one) of the town residents who served in the Continental Army first enlisted in either 1775 or 1776.

Viewed as a whole, Peterborough was a cohesive community whose town and military leaders were able to mobilize kinship networks to provide soldiers for the war. In Peterborough, the enlistments were not socially segregated. Enlistees, including Continental soldiers, came from various social ranks throughout the war. Enlistments resulted from a combination of factors such as kinship, community expectations, the war's proximity, trust in local military leaders, ambition for prestige, direct connections to the Continental Army through the two Scott captains, and politicization resulting from combat. In this town, family loyalties and self-awareness of community status and expectations for service, possibly fueled by revolutionary zeal, motivated men to fill military ranks.

Exeter

Exeter and Peterborough vary in their founding, composition, and involvement in the events leading to the War of Independence, but they were similar in having leaders seasoned by war. Exeter is located north of the mouth of Merrimack River and on the banks of Squamscot River that feeds into the Great Bay that is the site of Portsmouth, which became the colony's capital and major port city. The town was founded in 1637 by the Reverend John Wheelwright, who, along with Anne Hutchinson, was expelled from Massachusetts for his Antinomian beliefs.[5] Wheelwright moved to Wells, Maine, in 1643, when Exeter had grown to about 200 people and become part of the Massachusetts colony. Its inhabitants, many originally from Lincolnshire, engaged in farming, cattle raising, lumbering, fishing, and ship building. Although the town was little touched by King Philip's War, it was deeply involved in the eighteenth-century conflicts that embroiled New England. About fifty Exeter men participated in the siege of Louisburg in 1745. During the French and Indian War, the town mobilized its annual quota of troops and served as a "headquarters of one or more battalions." In 1755, Exeter sent eighty-four men as part of the expedition against Crown Point. Men from the town's leading families—such as Folsom, Gilman, Cass, Dolloff, Leavitt, Steel, and Thurston—appeared on 1745 and 1755 military rolls and later on Revolutionary rolls. More than half a century of colonial warfare appeared to have produced a civic tradition of community mobilization and the institutions to sustain its men under arms. On the eve of the Revolution, Exeter, like Peterborough, had experienced veterans and officers who would provide military and political leadership.[6]

Unlike Peterborough, Exeter had a long tradition of engagement in imperial politics. Townsmen actively opposed the Dominion of New England (1686–1689) that consolidated the New England colonies under a new government. They embraced the Glorious Revolution of 1688 that installed a Protestant monarch on England's throne. They defied the Crown and provincial authority to turn in the men who were responsible for the Mast Tree Riot of 1734, an incident where a few men dressed as Indians roughed up the king's officials who tried to enforce the law preventing the taking of trees marked for the Royal Navy. Beginning in 1765, the town actively opposed British policies that taxed the colonists or subverted their privileges.[7] After 1770, Exeter was at the center of New Hampshire's resistance to Britain's American policies. The Boston Massacre led to a town meeting that passed a nonimportation resolution and agreement to enforce nonconsumption of "unnecessary and superfluous foreign articles" and tea. The five-person committee charged with presenting this resolution to the assembly included future leaders of the state's Revolutionary assembly and army. Moreover, the town punished those who did not concur with its opposition to British policies. In 1771, Exeter did not return to office Peter Gilman, "the foremost citizen of the town," and speaker of the New Hampshire General Assembly, after he refused to allow the assembly to endorse Virginia's 1770 letter of protest over English duties. In 1774, Exeter protested the tax on tea and punitive treatment of Boston that followed the Tea Party. The town adopted the Philadelphia resolves that asserted that the tax on tea supported policies that "render assemblies useless" and "introduce arbitrary government and slavery." Adding intimidation to its assertions, the resolves branded anyone who consumed tea "an enemy to America."

More than paper protest, in July 1774 Exeter escalated protest from proclamation to action when it hosted the first Provincial Congress that established an extralegal government directly linked to the Continental Congress in Philadelphia. Exeter's Nathaniel Folsom was selected as one of this government's two delegates to Philadelphia. Through the fall of 1774 and spring of 1775, resistance to British authority became more intense and more intimidating for undecided and indifferent residents, to say nothing of Tories. The town formed a Committee of Safety to enforce nonimportation and to apply "Tar and Feathers" to violators. Exeter's enthusiasm, leadership, and strong organization secured the town's place as the center for the Revolutionary government. In December 1775, Exeter became the provincial capital of the state's Revolutionary government.[8]

Besides political resistance, Exeter had prepared for war. As of October 1775, Exeter reported 51 men "gone in the army" out of a male population of 324 men of military age, sixteen to fifty years of age. Over the course of the eight-year war, the town contributed at least 220 men to the Revolutionary Army. The figure is low because the muster rolls for 1775 are incomplete, and the one for 1778 is missing. Just over half, 112, served in the Continental Army by the town's count, which included men who enlisted for three, eight, or nine months, as well as those who enlisted for longer terms. An analysis of the military service of those 220 men provides more insight into the town's war effort. In 1775, even with some rolls missing for that year, the town's contribution to the war effort was substantial. Eighty-eight men, or more than a quarter of the men at risk of military service, left town that year under arms. As in Peterborough, the number of men under arms diminished in 1776, reached its peak in 1777 with Burgoyne's invasion, remained substantial for the next two years, and then dropped off dramatically from 1780 onward. At some time during the first five years of the war, one-fifth to one-third of the men of military age were out of town under arms, and most of those soldiers were between the ages of sixteen and thirty. Those entering the Continental Army were likely in their late teens and early twenties—the average age of enlistment based on 1818 pension applications.[9]

Burgoyne's invasion not only produced Exeter's largest mobilization of the war, but was also a catalyst for enlistments in the Continental Army. In 1777, forty-three of the fifty-four men who fought for the first time joined the Continental Army. As of 1780, most Exeter men had returned from the army, except for a few hard-core troops. Of the forty-one men in service in 1780, only thirteen of them were new recruits; and, in 1781 only eleven new men mustered. By the end of the war, 96 of the 112 men the town credited with Continental service came from the enlistments cohorts of 1775, 1776, or 1777. Like other New Hampshire towns, after 1780 Exeter relied upon veterans to fill ranks. Unlike nearly every other New Hampshire town, however, Exeter filled its Continental quota in 1781 and 1782.

Historians have claimed that Continental soldiers were lower class, that their motives for enlistment were driven by poverty and cash, and that ranks filled by dregs, blacks, and the poor are evidence of a political culture and social structure that were class ridden and exploitative.[10] Exeter's tax and town records along with genealogies, which pinpoint the social standing of most of its soldiers with greater precision than Peterborough's records, challenge that claim as it applied in this town. Tax information was gathered on 738 individuals who paid taxes in Exeter sometime between 1775 and 1783. Of these 738 people, taxes were recorded for 133 of the 220 men credited with service by the town. The tax rank of all 133 men who were credited with military service was somewhat lower than the town as a whole, but differences appeared when soldiers' tax status was analyzed by the type of service. The tax rankings of soldiers who did not serve in the Continental Army closely resembled the town as a whole. On the other hand, as a whole, those who ever served in the Continental Army occupied a lower tax ranking when compared to soldiers who served in the militia and state regiments as well as to taxpayers as whole.[11]

Although these general findings seem to conform to the view that Continental soldiers came from the lower classes, a closer examination of that cohort reveals that it was composed of men from across the economic ranks. In 1775, for example, 50 percent of the thirty-two men who would later serve in the Continental Army and who paid taxes that year ranked below the thirtieth percentile of taxpayers; a third fell between the thirtieth and sixtieth percentiles of town taxpayers. One-sixth, however, ranked between the sixtieth and ninetieth percentiles of taxpayers. In 1777 through 1780, the taxpayers who served, were serving, or would serve in the Continental Army were nearly evenly distributed among the town's taxpayers—just over a third below the thirtieth percentile, a third between the thirtieth and sixtieth percentiles, and 28 percent from the sixtieth through ninetieth percentiles. Though tending toward the lower rungs of the town's economic ranks as a group, as individuals those who served in the Continental Army did not come from the lower class. They included men above the median of taxpayers and even some from the upper tax ranks.

An even deeper examination of economic ranking of Continental soldiers was possible by comparing the tax rates of nine fathers whose ten sons went to war. These sons did not appear on the tax rolls. The profile of the fathers adds to our understanding of the connection between class, political culture, and mobilization because seven of ten sons served in the Continental Army for three years or until the end of the war. The three fathers whose sons only served in the militia or state troops were in the top tier of Exeter taxpayers, but so too were six fathers of the seven soldiers who enlisted in the Continental Army in 1777. These fathers ranged from the sixtieth through ninetieth percentiles of taxpayers in 1775, 1776, and 1777. The high economic status of these fathers further supports the conclusion that soldiers in the Continental Army from Exeter came from well-to-do households as well as those ranking lower economically. Living in the state's capital, home of leading Revolutionary figures, and being part of a civic tradition of mobilization led to a large turnout of men from all social ranks during the Revolutionary War. For Exeter, at least, the Revolution was not a *"Rich Man's War and a Poor Man's Fight."*

Hollis

The town of Hollis was incorporated in 1746, but its settlement occurred much earlier as part of the township of Dunstable, which was chartered in 1673 by the Massachusetts General Court. From 1673 to 1733 the settlement was on the frontier and for many years there was no town north or west of Dunstable in New Hampshire. During most of this period Exeter, fifty miles to the east, was the nearest New Hampshire town, while Chelmsford and Groton, Massachusetts, some fourteen miles to the south, were the closest communities. As the township became more populated, it divided into parishes, then in 1746 into four towns, including Hollis and its seventy-five taxpayers, who were mainly from towns in northern Massachusetts. Like Peterborough and Exeter, Hollis was heavily engaged in the French and Indian War. During that war, Hollis sent at least seventy-five men to the army, a conservative figure in light of the loss of the 1759 muster roll. After the war, Hollis's population increased substantially, from 809 in 1767 to 1,255 in 1775, a proportional increase that matched New Hampshire's overall population growth from 52,700 to 82,000 souls during the same time period. From its modest beginnings of nine families in 1736, Hollis had become the eleventh-largest town of New Hampshire's 152 communities in the 1775 census.[12]

Between 1773 and 1775, Hollis shifted its political allegiance from Royal Governor John Wentworth to leaders who resisted British imperial policies. On November 7, 1774, at a special town meeting, Hollis approved a resolution that its citizens "will at all times endeavor to maintain our liberties and privileges, both civil and sacred, even at the risque of our lives and fortunes." Hollis sent delegates to the Hillsborough County Congress to consider what actions the towns should take in response to British occupation of Boston. Hollis also chose delegates to the Provincial Congresses in Exeter that linked the towns to the Continental Congress. Thus, the town participated in extralegal assemblies that were called to respond to the growing division between the royal government and the towns. Besides protest, Hollis prepared for war. In 1774, it assessed residents to purchase ammunition and in January 1775 updated its militia roll. On April 19, 104 men from Hollis mustered to march to Boston. These men served eight days. Later that month, at an emergency town meeting, residents voted to raise a company of forty men to join the army at Cambridge. The town agreed to pay the men at the "same wages" as troops from Massachusetts. The town also voted to support the families of poor men in the army, "the amount to be deducted out of their wages." Thus, Hollis mobilized as it had in prior wars—providing men, paying their wages and expenses at the going rates, and caring for their families.

When the war began, Hollis relied on customary community practices that had served it well in mobilizing for the French and Indian War. Hollis, like other towns, took pains to find out who had "taken a turn" and kept careful records of wages paid troops and other expenses such as bounties, reimbursement for travel and billeting, compensation for the loss of personal property, and support for soldiers' families. In addition, Hollis, as did other towns where records exist, compensated residents who advanced money to pay town expenses. Hollis credited these expenses against taxes owed the state to support the war. Apart from any feelings of patriotism or fear of British tyranny, mobilization in Hollis included a bookkeeper's mentality.

Between 1775 and 1782 Hollis's pattern of mobilization resembled that described for Exeter and Peterborough.[13] Although the town census in the fall of 1775 reported 60 men under arms, a total of 154 residents marched from town sometime during that year. The average age of those who fought in 1775 was twenty-seven years; the median age was lower, twenty-three years. On the basis of age data from Peterborough and pension records, as the war continued, regiments looked for younger men, between the ages of sixteen and twenty-five. The 1775 Hollis census reported 306 youths and boys younger than sixteen. Many would become eligible for service during the next eight years. Hollis, like nearly all New Hampshire towns, had a huge pool of potential recruits.[14]

As in Peterborough and Exeter, service levels were highest in the first three years of the war, 1775–1777, when the conflict took place largely in New England and New York. Hollis soldiers who fought in those first three years composed 83 percent (255/305) of the residents who ever served during the war. A few of them either continued in service or reenlisted in the later years of the war, 1780–1782. Of the seventy-eight townsmen credited to the Continental Army, fifty, or nearly two-thirds, came from three enlistment cohorts, 1775, 1776, and 1777. Town effort lagged between 1778 and 1781 with relatively few men enlisting for the first time and only a few men taking a turn in the Continental Army. Enlistment cohorts of 1778, 1779, and 1780 contributed only 32 men to the total of 305 who served from the town, and of them 14 went into the Continental Army. As in Peterborough and Exeter, participation declined in the last five years of the war when the conflict in the New England was restricted to "alarms," raids, the siege of Newport, Rhode Island, reinforcing West Point, and repeated calls to fill the depleted ranks of the Continental Army.

Tax information was gathered on 547 individuals who paid taxes in Hollis for one or more years from 1775 through 1782 (see Tables 3-2, 3-3, and 3-4).[15] Of these 547 individuals, taxes were found for 223 of 305 resident-soldiers; 44 of those taxpaying soldiers served in the Continental Army. Measured by the mean and median, the tax rankings for Hollis's soldiers are similar to Exeter's soldiers. The tax rankings of non-Continental soldiers closely resembled the town as whole. The cohort of men who ever served in the Continental Army was in a lower tax bracket. From 1775 through 1782, between 76 percent and 86 percent of the Hollis men who ever served in the Continental Army fell below the median of town taxpayers. Although more men in the Hollis cohort of Continental soldiers were below the median than in the comparable Exeter cohort, Hollis's Continentals, like those from Exeter, were not exclusively from the lower tax ranks. In 1778, for example, whereas 61 percent of the men who ever served in the Continental Army fell within the tenth to thirtieth percentiles of town taxpayers, 22 percent fell between the fortieth and sixtieth percentiles and nearly 17 percent occupied the upper ranks of town taxpayers. Most of these soldiers appeared on the tax rolls at an age when men generally had little property and thus paid nominal taxes, mainly the poll tax. The average age of the thirty-six men at the time they first entered the Continental Army was twenty-three years. The median age was twenty-one years.

As in the study of Exeter, further insight into the status of these young men is gained by examining the tax status of twenty Hollis fathers who counted twenty-two of their sons in the Continental Army. The overall tax status of these fathers was substantially higher than Hollis tax payers as a whole. For example, in 1776 the mean and median tax ranking of the twenty fathers whose sons served in the Continental Army was 1,949 pence and 1,861 pence, respectively, compared to an average of 1,363 pence and median of 1,213 pence paid by taxpayers as a whole. This pattern

TABLE 3-2—Hollis Taxpayers, 1775–1782

	YEAR							
	1775	*1776*	*1777*	*1778*	*1779*	*1780*	*1781*	*1782*
No. Taxpayers	239	238	272	275	247	275	273	287
Mean Tax[a]	54	1,363	538	525	1,038	8,863	673	462
Median Tax[a]	44	1,213	420	432	927	7,084	546	361

[a]Calculated in pence.

TABLE 3-3—Hollis Non-Continental Soldiers on Tax Rolls, 1775–1782

	YEAR							
Year	*1775*	*1776*	*1777*	*1778*	*1779*	*1780*	*1781*	*1782*
No. Taxpayers	122	118	127	125	130	126	119	121
Mean Tax[a]	58	1,499	620	598	1,101	10,412	814	575
Median Tax[a]	50	1,315	523	540	1,030	9,669	768	520

n=169   [a]Calculated in pence.

TABLE 3-4—Hollis Continental Soldiers on Tax Rolls, 1775–1782

	YEAR							
	1775	*1776*	*1777*	*1778*	*1779*	*1780*	*1781*	*1782*
No. Taxpayers	17	13	18	18	15	16	28	26
Mean Tax[a]	45	946	344	353	710	6,230	456	301
Median Tax[a]	32	525	195	228	494	4,697	309	181

n=44   [a]Calculated in pence.

of soldiers coming from the town's well-to-do households continued after 1780, when enlistments declined dramatically. In 1781, as an illustration, the five fathers who had sons in the army during this period had a mean and median tax rankings of 1,383 pence and 1,302 pence, respectively, compared to 673 pence and 546 pence for all taxpayers.

These data suggest that the lower tax status of Hollis's Continental Army soldiers as whole represented the poverty of youth rather than poverty of class. Although not noted in the town's tax records, the lower ranking of soldiers may also reflect an abatement given to men in service. Hollis exempted Continental Army soldiers from paying the poll tax while still assessing their property. Moreover, the tax data found for fathers whose families provided more than a quarter of Hollis's Continental soldiers (22/78) revealed that the town's wealthiest families were a source of soldiers throughout the war, despite the hardships of military life and the effects of war weariness that dampened enlistments. Hollis enlisted men without property, some of whom were poor, others who were propertyless because of their young age, and others who were just building their estates. What is remarkable is not the presence of those with relatively little wealth, but that enlistments throughout the war continued to reflect the town's social structure. We see a pattern more clearly in Hollis than in Exeter: a core of town leaders and its wealthiest families sustained the war effort with material support as well as through the service of their sons in the Continental Army.

Canterbury

Unlike Peterborough, Exeter, and Hollis, which were founded by core groups revolving around kin networks or neighboring towns, Canterbury was composed of a scattering of young families from towns along New Hampshire's seacoast and from Massachusetts.[16] Though laid out by proprietors in 1727, lack of roads and frontier conflicts between 1744 and 1763 slowed settlement. Peace in 1763, following the conclusion of the French and Indian War, opened the area to rapid settlement. By the time the provincial census was taken in 1767, the town had grown from fewer than 200 to 503 people. Despite the division of the original tract into two additional towns, by 1775 Canterbury had grown to 723 residents, including four "Negroes and slaves for life." Canterbury, like Peterborough, Exeter, and Hollis, had a large manpower pool eligible for military service and, even more striking, a large number of youths and boys who would become eligible for service during the course of the eight-year war. Canterbury's 1775 census recorded 154 men of military age and 199 males younger than sixteen.

Like the other towns in this study, Canterbury turned out a large proportion of its men in 1775 and 1776. Despite support of the cause, in

1777 the town experienced difficulty—more so than Peterborough, Exeter, and Hollis—raising troops for the Continental Army. At its annual town meeting in March 1777, Canterbury counted only nine men enlisted from its quota of twenty. On March 31, the town voted to tax its polls to raise money for bounties of fifty dollars for those it had recruited and to encourage others to enlist. On April 23, the town had a special meeting to increase its bounty from fifty to a hundred dollars, the rate paid by other towns, to "stimulate enlistments."

Tensions caused by recruitment, bounties, and taxes divided the town. In late 1777 at another town meeting, opponents of the increased bounty tried unsuccessfully to rescind it. Even with the increase, Canterbury could fill its quota only by taking advantage of the waiver given by the State Committee of Safety that allowed delinquent towns like Canterbury to enlist men for eight-month terms rather than for three years to at least fill their quota for 1777 only. By contrast, Peterborough, Exeter, and Hollis were much more successful in enlisting men for the three-year duration. More than money played on the minds of Canterbury men as they considered service in the Continental Army. They appeared to lack the support and incentive provided by a cohesive community united in the war effort that favored enlistment of young men in Peterborough, Exeter, and Hollis.

A climate of persecution and intimidation dampened Canterbury's war effort. Possibly this oppressive atmosphere was a product of the town's diverse settlement and internal divisions that were accentuated by the war. In June 1777, the town took the extraordinary step to quell personal vendettas that exploited patriotic feelings by approving a warrant prohibiting anyone from calling his "neighbor a Tory, unless he has sufficient reason." Violators were to be censured by the town's Committee of Safety. The case of Captain Jeremiah Clough, Jr., son of a town leader who was a member of Canterbury's Committee of Safety, is particularly instructive in revealing community tensions that weakened mobilization. In May 1777, the State Committee of Safety, acting on information provided by the Committee of Safety of Boscawen, a town bordering Canterbury, ordered Colonel Thomas Stickney to round up the "set of most abandoned wretches" who were meeting in Canterbury to conspire "against the states and meditating how to assist our enemies." Among those arrested were Clough and Richard Ellison of Canterbury. Captain Clough had spent nearly two years in the army, first during the siege of Boston in 1775 and then one year's service in the Continental Army in 1776. While held in jail, Clough wrote to a friend that "since the commencement of this unnatural war . . . malicious persons are capable of construing common conversation to the disadvantage of any person." To his father Clough wrote that he "never did anything against my country deserving such treatment," except, as he wrote, "some unguarded words" uttered that past spring. Clough was vindicated and released, returning to Canterbury, but never again to fight for his country. His case reveals the malicious use of patriotism that turned men like Clough and maybe other townsmen against service.

Throughout the remainder of the war, Canterbury, like other towns, had to increase its bounties, make promises of support for soldiers' families, and make up for depreciated pay to get men to enlist. Despite the legal obligation of New Hampshire to pay its state troops and mobilized militias, and, despite the Continental Congress's obligation to pay the army, the financial responsibility for soldiers' pay and expenses fell directly on the towns in the form of "war taxes" voted by the towns. In the last years of the war, soldiers looked locally for compensation. As the cash economy collapsed, towns paid bounties and depreciated wages in kind and with promissory notes. In 1781, Canterbury paid its Continental soldiers Edmund Colby and William Rines one cow each, with the cost deducted from the balance of their depreciated wages and bounties owed them by the town. Canterbury's inability to get men to reenlist in large numbers or get new recruits after 1777 may be evidence of the town's incapacity or unwillingness to meet the financial demands of those who would serve.[17]

Despite the relative difficulties of Canterbury to sustain mobilization at levels comparable to Exeter and Hollis, the tax ranks of soldiers and their fathers resembled those two towns. The tax rank of men who did not serve in the Continental Army either mirrored Canterbury's tax structure or was somewhat higher than the town as a whole, and men who served in the Continental Army came largely from the lower tax ranks. In 1776, for example, 71 percent of those men who ever served in the Continental Army fell below the median of town taxpayers. A closer examination of rankings by individual tax ranks divided into deciles indicated a pattern similar to the other towns in this study. In 1777, 66.7 percent of the men who ever served in the Continental Army were in the lowest three percentiles of town taxpayers; 16.6 percent were in the fortieth through sixtieth percentiles; and the remaining 16.7 percent were in the top three percentiles—figures similar to Hollis, but lower than Exeter.[18]

The commitment of Canterbury town leaders, much the same as seen in Peterborough, Exeter, and Hollis, was crucial in sustaining the war effort, particularly near the end of the conflict, when the town wearied of war. Tax records showed that, as in Exeter and Hollis, fathers who ranked highest in wealth continued to see their sons enlist throughout the war. Tax information was found on thirteen men whose twenty-six sons went to war; ten of those sons did not appear on the tax list. Eight of the thirteen fathers had sons who served in the Continental Army. As a group, these thirteen fathers were in the top tier of the town's taxpayers. The median tax ranking for twelve of these fathers who paid taxes in 1777 was 2,379 pence, compared to a median of 1,487 pence for the town as whole. Eleven of twelve of those fathers ranked in the top 30 percent of taxpayers;

four of those eleven fell within the top 10 percent of taxpayers. Although the numbers are small, the eight fathers whose sons joined the Continental Army ranked nearly as high as those five fathers whose sons did not serve in the army. In these cases, service in the army was a matter of choice independent of class standing.

Benjamin Blanchard is illustrative of those well-to-do town leaders whose sons went to war. In 1777, two of his sons—Isaac, twenty-four, and Joel, eighteen—served in the state troops. In 1780, two more sons served. Abel, age nineteen, marched to West Point with his brother Reuben, age eighteen, who later enlisted in the Continental Army for six months in 1781. In 1780, at the time of these enlistments, their father's tax ranking had climbed to the eighty-seventh percentile. The elder Blanchard was a prominent leader against British policies in 1774 and 1775 and a central figure in the town's war effort as a member of its Committee of Safety. Archelaus Moore, Esq., on the other hand, had no sons, but still contributed a soldier, his slave. In 1781 Moore, who ranked in the top 2 percent of the town's taxpayers, sent his slave, Sampson Battis, for his second turn (his first being in 1777) into the militia and state troops for short terms. As in Peterborough, as well as in Exeter and Hollis, leaders such as Blanchard either felt compelled or moved by conviction to commit not only their treasure, but also to encourage or at least tolerate their children enlisting. In the case of Moore, he offered his slave, who returned to Canterbury to live the remainder of his 103 years a free man.[19]

Weare

The town was begun in 1750, but it was not until 1762, according to town historian William Little, that settlers "began to swarm into the woods" in the area about twenty miles west of Derryfield, now Manchester. Young men, many veterans of the French and Indian War, were attracted by the abundance of fish and game, especially beaver, and inexpensive land as they began the long process of turning wilderness into productive farms. Families settling in Weare came from various parts of New Hampshire and Massachusetts and may have been part of the migration from towns that had reached their capacity after several generations.[20] Like Canterbury, Weare was a collection of people rather than transplanted kin and community networks as occurred in Peterborough, Exeter, and Hollis. Weare's settlers shared only the experience of soldiering, the hardscrabble life of frontier living, and their Baptist church. Named after Meshech Weare, a political leader from Hampton Falls, favorite of Governor Benning Wentworth, and later president of New Hampshire's Committee of Safety, the town grew from seven families in 1754 to forty taxpayers in 1764.[21]

Although the prospect of joining fellow Baptists attracted an array of people to settle, ironically it was religion that fractured the town. In 1769, the town's Baptist church divided over whether the congregation should adopt the doctrine of exhorting sinners to repent or the doctrine of admonishing them to follow God's law. When the majority chose admonishment, the minority left the church. Alienation and hard feelings followed when the majority decided to both pronounce and enforce God's law as they saw it. Interrogated, admonished, and shunned, if not ostracized, one dissenter was reported to have said that sinners "would have an Easier Place in hell than in a Chh meeting in Weare." The schism dissolved the church. In 1773 townsmen brought elders and deacons from several New Hampshire towns to mediate the dispute and reconstitute the church. The differences were patched over and a new covenant signed that was "nearly identical" to the original, but it was understood to sanction both exhortation and admonition. In August 1773, the compromise failed when Elder Hovey gave a sermon declaring that the church's saints were followers of the devil's "counterfeit" gospel. "The church was now a ruin." Church meetings did not resume until the early 1780s.

At the beginning of the Revolution, Weare was a bitterly divided settlement, embroiled by religious doctrinal controversy and personal conflict. Although the 1775 census reported that Weare had grown to 987 inhabitants, including 150 Quakers, making it the nineteenth-largest of New Hampshire's 152 towns, it remained a rough, fragmented, and poor frontier settlement. In June 1775, the town closed its schools because it could not afford to finance both war and education. Weare entered the war largely unarmed, likely reflecting its poverty. The 1775 census recorded only sixteen muskets in the town and the need for the province to supply seventy-two weapons to arm the militia. Weare's principal military asset was a large population of males of military age and an even larger population of young men who would come of military age during the eight years of conflict. Not counting its Quakers, in 1775 the town recorded 159 men of military age and 248 youths and boys younger than sixteen.

War united the town at the beginning of the conflict. Even with some rolls missing, Weare's contribution of manpower to the conflict was substantial. A total of 199 townsmen left town under arms between 1775 and 1783 for various periods of service.[22] Like other New Hampshire towns, Weare's major contributions of manpower were made in the first three years of the war. In 1775, about 36 percent of the townsmen of military age served in New Hampshire and Massachusetts regiments for an average of 137 days. Fifteen Weare soldiers fought at Bunker Hill. Twenty-two men took part in the invasion of Canada. In light of Weare's exposure to the frontier, it is not surprising that its residents were particularly keen to secure the town from British and Indian attacks by taking the war to Canada.

Defending their town was tempered by the expectation of fair compensation. Those who went with Benedict Arnold to Canada received two pounds per month in wages, nine pence per day for billeting, and a bonus of one pound and six shillings for a coat and blanket. Weare's recruits also displayed the customary independence defined by contract that had appalled British officers in the French and Indian War. Ten of the seventeen soldiers from Weare in Arnold's camp left in December without being discharged, when their enlistment expired. Although they were labeled deserters, they viewed themselves as law-abiding citizen soldiers. Eight of them served in subsequent years.

In 1776, rather than being deterred by war's hardships, Weare put more men into the field than in any other year of the war. Their service, however, varied greatly. Some went to northern Vermont and Canada to reinforce the retreating American army and were later captured at the Cedars. Others joined the army at Boston until the siege was lifted in March. A few men volunteered for garrison duty in Portsmouth, New Hampshire. Twenty-five men enlisted for a year in the Continental Army. Overall, 105 men marched from town in 1776, a figure representing nearly three-quarters of the men of military age reported in the fall 1775 census. Twenty-seven of these men had served in 1775.

In 1777, the commerce of recruitment for three years or the duration in the Continental Army caused controversy in Weare and for a while stopped enlistments as it had in Canterbury. In view of the poverty of the state, the war created a financial strain upon the town to pay and equip its troops. Town records report individuals paying the wages of some soldiers who served for a few months in state regiments. Rather than substitutes, it appears as if the private payment of wages was a traditional form of subscription whereby townsmen with means used personal funds to pay a public expense. Weare compensated these individuals by reducing their taxes by the amount paid to soldiers.[23] In the spring of 1777, the town refused to vote a bounty that was needed to get men to volunteer to meet Weare's quota of sixteen three-year men in the Continental Army. The reason was equity, not ideology. Townsmen refused to do more to support the war until Weare compensated individuals who had paid wages, bounties, and expenses on behalf of the town and state and before it settled wages for past service. Moreover, this accounting contributed to recriminations as the town took stock of its residents' war effort. The town's historian later recorded that the differences between those who were making wartime sacrifices and those who did very little was "a matter of complaint among people in general." To resolve these differences and renew mobilization, townsmen created a committee to reimburse all private wartime expenses to date and to determine allowances for soldiers' past service.[24] So as not to prejudice enlistments, the committee was to report at the end of 1777.

The promise of payment and equity opened the way for recruitment. Weare provided men for state regiments and met its quota for the Continental Army. Through the spring and summer, the town hired ten men for three years and filled the rest of the quota with six men who served for eight months. Overall, seventy-two men marched from town sometime during 1777. Weare continued to use bounties paid by taxes and subscriptions to raise volunteers for state regiments and to get men, like Ebenezer Sinkler, to join the Continental Army. It is quite possible that Weare employed a variant of "classing" to get men like Sinkler to enlist. Described by Richard Buel in his study of Connecticut's mobilization, under this system militia units were divided into "classes" or small groups. Each was responsible for providing one recruit, or face a draft, which had gone into effect in New Hampshire in 1777. Men in a class would pool their funds to provide a bounty to induce one of their members or someone else to volunteer. The volunteer would receive not only the enlistment bounty from his class, but also wages, the bounties from the state and Continental governments, and any other concessions, such as guarantees of care for his family, that he could gain from the town.[25] If drafted, the soldier lost his bounty and concessions. The threat of draft, coupled with the loss of benefits, would likely persuade men like Sinkler to enlist.

Ebenezer Sinkler was a veteran. He was at the Battle of Bunker Hill and spent the remainder of the year in Cambridge. He did not march in 1776, but enlisted in 1777 for three years and was killed a few months later at Saratoga. One might imagine that Sinkler had been propertyless or impoverished, and thus attracted to service only by wages. The records of his estate, however, reveal a different portrait. Sinkler was a joiner who owned 150 acres of wild land in the town of Wentworth. It is likely that he saw the bonuses as an opportunity to help build his estate with cash bounties and wages. Sinkler received seven pounds and ten shillings from Jacob Tuxbury for one year of service and on the same day received three pounds and fourteen shillings from Caleb Atwood for an unspecified, but no doubt, shorter portion of this three-year enlistment. Although it may appear that Atwood was shirking his duty by hiring a substitute, town records suggest that Atwood was a subscriber rather than a shirker. Atwood had purchased land in Weare in 1760. In 1764, he ranked twelfth of forty-three taxpayers on Weare's first list. In 1775, he marched to Lexington, was among the "best citizens" who did a half-turn of two months and four days in the spring of 1776, and volunteered for thirteen weeks of duty at Fort Edward in 1777. Tuxbury, the other subscriber, was also a veteran who served in Cambridge in 1775 and then detached to join Arnold's march to Canada. In 1776 and early 1777, he served ten months of garrison duty in Portsmouth. Lieutenant Tuxbury, age twenty-six, ended his military service, which included some of the most arduous duty of the war, but not his support for the struggle. The commerce of war had united Atwood, Tuxbury, and Sinkler.

Despite the success of enlistments in 1777, the controversy over compensation festered. At a special meeting that December, the town rejected its committee's recommendation to settle wages and accounts. The committee's compensation was based on the length and difficulty of service. Men who enlisted for a year in 1776 were to receive three Spanish dollars for each month of their service; those who did garrison duty in Portsmouth or took part in the siege of Boston were to receive two dollars a month; men who reinforced Washington's army in late 1776 were awarded one dollar per month. Presumably, subscribers who had paid soldiers' wages would be compensated in a like manner. Rejecting the recommendation, the town dissolved the committee.

At its March 1778 annual town meeting, residents created a new committee to settle with its soldiers. The three men on the committee had served only briefly in the military during the prior three years. They were not town founders. Their names did not appear on the 1764 tax list, and they were not among the people prominent in doctrinal conflict that split the town and dissolved the church. Jonathan Martin, possibly the brother of early settler Nathaniel Martin, did not arrive in Weare until 1775, but he quickly rose to prominence as a member of the compensation committee and then as a selectman. Probably these committee members were viewed as untainted by the factional conflicts that had divided the town and dissolved its church. Possibly those conflicts were still percolating to the detriment of the war effort.

The new committee, like the one it replaced, was "to report in the fall [1778], thus keeping the matter in suspension so as not to chill and stop enlistments." That strategy appeared to work once again. Weare's enlistment pattern was similar to the more cohesive town of Hollis. It appears that the formation of the new committee on compensation reassured taxpayers that Weare would fulfill its obligations to its creditors and the town's veterans and would honor future financial commitments, despite the rapid rate of inflation and collapsing economy.

In December 1778, Weare accepted the report of the committee. Comparing that report to the first, the number of men who would receive additional compensation was reduced by nearly half, 141 to 79. Rather than scaling payment to various types of service, the town accepted the recommendation of the new report to pay all soldiers four dollars a month, except those who went to Canada who would receive six dollars a month for their services. Despite approval, compensation remained controversial. In March 1779, the town debated a resolution to rescind the settlement on the grounds that it was "illegal" and that some soldiers deserved higher compensation than had been awarded by the town. The town rejected the challenge, but no doubt the "complaint" over inequities and injustices in supporting the war continued to roil the town.[26]

The extent of the town's exhaustion with the war effort and internal divisions was recorded in its rejection of a call in 1779 for men to serve in Rhode Island for six months. The town expressed the view that Rhode Island should look after itself. Weare had done enough. Weare's participation in the war fell precipitously in 1779, when only seventeen men served, including the few who had enlisted for three years in the Continental Army. The committee charged with providing more troops for the

Continental Army found that potential recruits "drove sharp trades." Military service had become a buyers' market where those who were savvy and willing to enlist could make favorable terms for themselves. In 1779, New Hampshire improved the market conditions for towns like Weare to recruit men by exempting soldiers in the Continental Army from state taxes.[27] The next year marked the last substantial effort of the town to fill ranks of the Continental Army. To do so, it hired men for short terms, three months and six months. Despite short terms and new legislation in June that substantially increased individual fines to $500 for refusing to serve, the state failed to fill its quotas.[28] Inflation probably made punitive fines meaningless because worthless currency could be used to settled debts. Moreover, the collapsed economy made a shambles of payments. Recruits accepted promissory notes that had face values in cash, either in silver, pounds, or dollars but were in actuality proxies for payment in kind at the prewar levels set at four shillings for a bushel of Indian corn. When Daniel Clough enlisted for six months, he was paid with a note with the face value of twelve pounds silver, for which he received sixty bushels of corn in two installments. Citizens were taxed in kind for corn—later beef and rum—to pay and provision the army.

Though lacking tax records, the brief sketches of town founders and early settlers found in the town history provide a view of the men who enlisted in the Continental Army. Jotham Tuttle, who enlisted in 1777 for eight months of service in the Continental Army, was probably the same Tuttle who settled in Weare in 1759, a propertyless young man who acquired land as a gift from his father-in-law, Thomas Worthley of Weare. Joshua Atwood, who enlisted in 1780 for eight months, appears to be the son of Caleb Atwood, a founder of Weare. Caleb was "a prominent man," active in town matters, who, late in life, retired to his son Joshua's home in nearby Antrim. Stephen Dustin, who served four years in the Continental Army, 1776–1780, may have been the son of either Paul Dustin or William Dustin, who were related. Both Paul and William came to Weare from Chester, New Hampshire. Both men arrived in town poor, purchased lots, and began their farms. In 1764, William purchased ninety acres to add to his earlier parcel acquired in 1762. A veteran of the French and Indian War, he was considered a "thrifty farmer," who acquired "considerable property," including a female slave. Paul marched to Canada in 1776 to reinforce the American army, and, in 1777, both Paul and William marched to repulse Burgoyne's invasion, William's only service during the war. Two of Samuel Caldwell's sons fought in the war. The soldiers' father had arrived in Weare in 1770 from Merrimack, New Hampshire. He was an enterprising man who built a saw- and gristmill, ran a tavern and store, held town offices, owned a slave, and was considered "one of the first citizens of the town." James Caldwell spent twenty-one days in Rhode Island. His brother Samuel, Jr., fought at Bunker Hill, participated in the siege of Boston, and continued his service in 1776 in the Continental Army. A

Samuel Caldwell—possibly the same person as Samuel, Jr.—enlisted for three years in 1777. Samuel Page was the son of Colonel Samuel Page, who moved to Weare in 1772 with his four sons and settled on a plot that became known as Page Hill. Samuel, Jr., served a year in 1776, an eight-month enlistment in 1777, and a final enlistment of eight months in 1778. John Flanders appears to be the poorest of the soldiers who enlisted in the Continental Army. He was reported to be squatter or tenant on Thomas Packer's farm. Flanders's service began at Cambridge in 1775, followed by a year's enlistment in the Continental Army, then three years more beginning in 1777, and finally eight months in 1780. He was paid wages and bounties, and his family was supported by the town, causing controversy. These biographies indicate that, except for Flanders, the Continentals identified with town families were either young men who had recently settled or the sons of household heads who had established themselves in town. Most finished serving by 1781.[29]

Town records show that, at the beginning of the war, enlistment was grounded in custom and the market. Weare's soldiers expected to be paid wages comparable to those of other towns in New Hampshire and Massachusetts and for their wages to increase as inflation eroded the value of their pay. Individuals who acted on behalf of the town to pay soldiers through subscription or loans awaited compensation by the town for their expenses. Weare recorded carefully the bounties and tax abatements that were given to induce enlistments, with the belief that its military expenses would be reimbursed by the state either directly or through reduced taxes. As the war dragged on, Weare, like other towns, had to become sharp in its dealings with soldiers and would-be recruits because the state and Continental Congress lacked funds. Townsmen hired men as cheaply as possible, paid only the going rates for wages and bounties, ensured compliance by making payments in installments, and saved money by deducting the cost of family support from the soldiers' wages. On the other hand, the need for soldiers increased the leverage of recruits who negotiated with the town to make up for depreciated wages, receive payments in kind rather than in worthless currency, and bargain for concessions such as the kind of support the town would provide for their families. Although some historians have interpreted these deals as exploitation, they appear in Weare's records to be calculations by town and soldiers to gain their best advantage in the market for soldiers. Market and military service, and financial gain and patriotism, were not mutually exclusive.

Conclusion

Overall, seven general features emerge in this comparative study. First, the turnout of men from these five towns is similar. A large portion of residents enlisted in the first three years of the war, 1775–1777. Beginning in 1777, however, the failure to fill Continental ranks with three-year enlistments led to short-term enlistments of from three to nine months. The 1777 draft law that imposed a fine on those who refused to serve in the militia or Continental Army appears to have been unenforceable in these towns. Beginning in 1780, enlistments declined dramatically as the conflict became more remote. The June 1780 law that increased fines and threatened court martial seems to have been ineffective in producing recruits. The use of "classing," accompanied by stiff fines, also appears to have had little effect on recruitment. Groups or "classes" of men in towns were responsible for hiring recruits and were subject to a penalty, approved in 1781, of "double the sum it shall cost to hire" a recruit should they fail. To force compliance, the state passed a law in January 1781 fining towns sixty pounds lawful money for each man deficient as of May and rewarding towns that met the quota with a promissory note valued at twenty pounds for each man. Despite these efforts, in 1782 the New Hampshire Committee of Safety reported that 149 towns were deficient in filling their quotas for the Continental Army; only half the men—674 of 1,345 called for in 1781—were in the army. Neither the stick nor the carrot proved effective to fill ranks, especially in the last years of the war. Ultimately, mobilization depended upon voluntary enlistments made fair by compliance with the market value for service paid in bounties, wages, and concessions.[30]

Second, enlistments in these five towns were neither socially nor economically segregated into marching militias, state regiments, and the Continental Army. Whereas men in the Continental Army tended to come from the lower tax ranks when compared to the militias, their status was more a product of age than of class. More important perhaps, many of the men not found on the tax rolls—thus giving the impression of poverty—came from families that ranked high among town taxpayers. The tax rankings of fathers of Continental soldiers were, for the most part, among the highest in the three towns where records exist. Furthermore, these wealthy households by town standards continued to be sources of soldiers when enlistments in the army lagged after 1780. What is remarkable is not that young and relatively propertyless men filled ranks, but that the Continental soldiers from these towns continued to represent the social structures of their communities. Mobilization in these towns appeared to place a special burden on town leaders to support the war with wealth and manpower from their own families and kin networks.

Third, regardless of the type of unit or stage of the war, men "hired" for service. Military service, apart from any ideological motivations or community pressure, was a form of employment. Beginning with the *rage militaire* in 1775, soldiers expected to be paid at the going rate, reimbursed for expenses, and compensated for the loss of personal property. Private Ezekiel Larned received two pounds and fourteen shillings from his town of Rindge for the loss of his coat, two shirts, one gun, an iron strike sword, and a pair of hose at the Battle of Bunker Hill. Service and employment were one.[31]

Fourth, financing and fighting the war were two sides of the same coin. Towns retained control over the state's purse strings. The burden in New Hampshire for paying for the war fell on town selectmen and constables, who were responsible for rating polls and estates and collecting taxes. Towns used creative financing to encourage men to volunteer as well as to pay them. In July 1776, the town of Windham voted to pay a forty-dollar bounty to men who enlisted to reinforce the Northern Army under General Sullivan. Later that year, the town collected taxes to pay this expense but, in a move to compensate past service, exempted the tax for soldiers who had spent eight months at Boston in 1775. In 1776, instead of offering a bounty to enlist, Weare voted to abate the tax for any man who served in the Continental Army for a year. Besides soldiers' pay, individuals who advanced money to meet town expenses, or who pooled their funds to hire a soldier or pay his bounty, expected to be reimbursed by the town. Advancing private funds to pay a public wartime expense was one way to support the cause. In 1777, the town of Weare voted to accept such bills for compensation, though it took two years and two committees to reach a settlement. Extra payments and tax breaks were intended to encourage men to volunteer and those with means to finance the war. Paying for the war was a constant issue at the annual town meetings and special meetings called during the year to vote for the collection of funds to pay town, state, and Continental assessments. In 1778, for example, Rindge collected taxes on polls and estates six times to meet wartime expenses. The carefully kept records of Weare and fragments from other towns suggest that selectmen kept close accounts of public and private expenses, including compensation to soldiers for depreciated pay, and contributions made by residents to the war effort in the form of "turns" served, taxes paid, and private funds advanced. After the war, towns sought compensation from the state for these expenses. In 1791, the town of Amherst submitted a bill to the state for £3,511 for "Bounties, etc., paid by the town that were not paid by the State or the United States."[32]

Fifth, despite quotas for men imposed by the state and Continental Congress, towns interpreted these demands to suit themselves, as illustrated in Colonel Enoch Hale's report to the state's Committee of Safety in February 1777. Hale had been ordered to raise 119 men for New Hampshire's Continental Line from his regimental district. The number of recruits from each town was apportioned by population. The towns returned a total of 118 men but not in the manner expected. Peterborough, for example, had a quota of fourteen men and returned a list of twenty-two, but only twelve were in New Hampshire regiments. The remainder were with Long Bill Scott's company in Colonel Hendley's Massachusetts regiment. The town refused to send more men. The town of Fitzwilliam reported that its men were in Massachusetts regiments and would send no more. Hale reported, "They plead nothing extraordinary only that every town has a right to their own men." The town of Dublin defiantly replied that it would not send three-year men, as ordered, but would send men for nine months. In May 1777, when the state informed towns that short-term men were not eligible to receive Continental and state enlistment bounties, objections led the state Committee of Safety that August to authorize payment of a proportion of those bounties to men who enlisted for a few months. The state and Continental governments could pass laws, but towns would enforce them only if they met local approval; local democracy governed community war efforts.[33]

Sixth, as the economy collapsed after 1777 under the weight of depreciation and inflation, made worse by counterfeit currency, the strain on towns to pay soldiers whether in cash or in kind adversely affected enlistments and led to hard bargaining between towns and potential recruits. By 1781, the state was virtually bankrupt. In February, the New Hampshire Committee of Safety informed the Continental government "that we can by no means fully satisfy the Demands upon us. Our funds have already been exhausted." Towns were forced to raise the amounts of their bounties to match the market because of the expectation of equity. In the latter years of the war, when towns sought men to fill quotas, recruits enjoyed a market where they could strike the best deal for themselves and families. When Samuel Fugard agreed in 1780 to enlist in the Continental Army for Bedford, he negotiated for a $2,000 bounty and for the town to pay a $10 debt valued in "1774" currency he owed fellow townsman, James Martin, for the town to purchase twenty-five acres for him in Bedford or, failing that, deliver a bushel of corn to his wife for each month he was in the army. Fugard also got the town to agree to recover his goods seized for debt by Robert Merrill.[34]

Finally, although town leaders did their best to meet requests for troops and supplies, they were limited by the degree the community wished to or was able to support the war effort. Worthless currency made fines for refusal to serve ineffectual. In January 1781, the state began to fine towns rather than individuals for failing to meet enlistment quotas. These fines were ineffective because the state could not enforce them. Moreover, towns contested fines by deducting all of the expenses they claimed were owed them by the state, including bounties, wages, and provisions and would withhold those amounts from state taxes. Towns kept track of expenses and contested state claims. In 1783, the town of Rye refused to pay the state's penalty of $800 for failing to provide four men to the Continental Army. The town used a curious logic to turn the state's claim of a debt owed it into a counter-claim that the state owed the town money. The selectmen stated that, early in the war, Rye had sent more men than had been requested and, thus, when the town's oversubscription early in the war was deducted from its shortfall of enlistments later in the war, "we have had more than our full proportion of Men in the Service during the War comparing one time with Another." Contention and negotiation marked relations between towns and the state as they responded to the changing demands of war over an eight-year period. In the last few years of the war, towns evaded their quotas by claiming men returned by other towns. Between 1781 and 1782, the Committee of Safety had to resolve 102 cases where several towns lay claim to the same soldier in the army. Towns suspended recruitment until these cases were resolved. They used this delaying tactic to avoid confronting townsmen with yet another call for men and taxes.[35]

Overall, as historians look deeper into the war through microhistories of towns, regions, military units, and racial and ethnic groups, the Revolution becomes an even richer era. These histories remove the romanticized patina that obscures the human dramas of resistance, war, and revolution. Mobilization in these five towns was local, personal, and familial, rather than imperial, national, or even provincial. Community, peer, and kin pressures, more than central Revolutionary authority, lay behind decisions to fight and support the war. In 1775, there was a general uprising of resistance and unity of purpose in these towns. Anticipating a short conflict, townsmen drew upon the ready resources and generosity of well-to-do townsmen for their wages, expenses, and losses of property. After 1775, the towns had to adapt to a unique conflict that was transformed from an uprising to a protracted and international war of attrition.

Central to war making was the role of the town leadership, whether in the form of committees of safety, officers capable of rallying men to arms, or, as in the case of Weare, individuals who could restrain vengeful patriotism or resolve complaints over inequitable soldiers' wages and unpaid bills incurred to support the war. Those towns like Peterborough, Exeter, and Hollis that had strong community foundations were able to do more to support the war than those like Canterbury and Weare, which were more fragmented and contentious. As early as 1777, wartime unity was challenged by the practical demands of sustaining the conflict. In Weare, paying for the war produced new divisions in a town already split by religious and personal conflicts. After 1777, the burden for fighting the war fell increasingly on a smaller portion of the population, especially after 1780, when the number of new enlistments fell precipitously despite unfilled ranks, continued pleas for soldiers, and increased numbers of young men of military age. Towns such as Peterborough, Exeter, and Hollis were able to fill ranks by drawing on kin networks, especially where townsmen, such as Peterborough's Scotts, were officers on active duty. In Canterbury and Weare, on the other hand, town leaders had difficulty filling ranks except with men willing to serve only a few months. Weare even refused to muster men when called upon by the state in 1779.

By 1781, state laws increasing individual fines for failing to serve and penalizing towns if they failed to meet quotas revealed both the desperation for more troops and the unwillingness of towns to comply fully with orders. Regardless of their own views, town leaders were constrained by a combination of democracy and market. Community action depended on consensus, rather than coercion. Several times each year, town residents had to vote to tax themselves for bounties to entice enlistments and hire, provision, and pay the travel expenses of troops, as well as compensate them for depreciated wages. Despite orders from afar, town leaders could only do as much as local residents allowed at frequent town meetings. By 1777, the face of war for the few thousand people in this study belonged to those they elected—the taxman, militia officers, selectmen, and committees of safety.

In general, the Revolution began in these towns as a people's war, a unifying general uprising that cut across social and economic lines. After 1777, the towns exhibited various degrees of war weariness and at times even grudging support for the war. By 1778 and certainly 1780, the conduct of the war shifted from the population as whole to the shoulders of a few town leaders, those men already in service, a small number of veterans willing to march again, and a tiny fraction of young men who could be persuaded or enticed to enlist for the first time. Towns failed to fill their quotas despite pleas and penalties. The Revolution, nevertheless, had not become a poor man's war in these towns, because local leaders continued to set an example through their own children going off to war. In New Hampshire, mobilization was at times both a people's war and a war by a few on behalf of the people. A small cadre of town leaders and veteran soldiers sustained the struggle for independence among war-weary and at times grudging townsmen who continued to vote for taxes and to send men into the army, tasks made easier in those towns that had begun the war as cohesive communities.

Notes

I wish to thank John Shy, who inspired me to pursue the study of soldiers, veterans, and pensions during his National Endowment for the Humanities Summer Seminar. I also thank the Humanities Center at the University of New Hampshire—Durham for its Gustafson Senior Faculty Research Fellowship, which made it possible for me finish the research and draft this essay, and the Institute of United States Studies at the University of London, for its Visiting Research Fellowship. I appreciate the help of the staffs of the New Hampshire Historical Society, the New Hampshire State Library, the University of New Hampshire—Manchester, and the historical societies and town offices of Canterbury, Exeter, Hollis, Peterborough, and Weare. My thanks go to Professor John Cerullo, chair of the Humanities Division at the University of New Hampshire—Manchester, for his support of a sabbatical leave to revise this essay and work as the coeditor on this book. Special thanks go to Professor Walter Sargent, my coeditor, for his significant contributions to this project and for his helpful comments on my essay. I also wish to thank the anonymous readers of my manuscript for their insightful criticisms. Not all of the tables created for this study could be included because of publishing restrictions. Readers wishing to see those tables should request them from the author. Finally, I wish to thank the scholars who have contributed to this volume. They have been thoughtful, timely, responsive to criticisms, and good natured in accommodating their coeditors and publishing requirements.

1. John Shy, *A People Numerous & Armed* (Oxford: Oxford University Press, 1976); Edward C. Papenfuse and Gregory A. Stiverson, "General Smallwood's Recruits: The Peacetime Career of the Revolutionary War Private," *William and Mary Quarterly*, 3rd ser., 30 (January 1973): 117–32; Benjamin Quarles, *The Negro in the American Revolution* (Chapel Hill: University of North Carolina Press, 1961); Robert Gross, *The Minutemen and Their World* (New York: Hill and Wang, 1976); Charles Royster, *A Revolutionary People at War* (New York: W. W. Norton, 1979); Richard Buel, *Dear Liberty: Connecticut Mobilization for the Revolutionary War* (Middletown, Conn.: Wesleyan University Press, 1980); Linda K. Kerber, *Women of the Republic: Intellect and Ideology in Revolutionary America* (Chapel Hill: University of North Carolina Press for the Institute of Early American History and Culture, 1980); Alfred F. Young, "George Robert Twelves Hewes (1742–1840): A Boston Shoemaker and the Memory of the American Revolution," *William and Mary Quarterly*, 3rd ser., 38 (October 1981): 561–623; James Kirby Martin and Mark Edward Lender, *A Respectable Army: The Military Origins of the Republic, 1763–1789* (Arlington Heights, Ill.: Harland Davidson, 1982); Steven Rosswurm, *Arms, Country, and Class: The Philadelphia Militia and the "Lower Sort" during the American Revolution, 1775–1783* (New Brunswick, N.J.: Rutgers University Press, 1987); Don Higginbotham, *War and Society in Revolutionary America: The Wider Dimensions of Conflict* (Columbia: University of South Carolina Press, 1988); Joan R. Gundersen, *"To Be Useful to the World": Women in Revolutionary America, 1740–1790* (New York: Twayne, 1996); Holly A. Mayer, *Belonging to the Army: Camp Followers and Community during the American Revolution* (Columbia: University of South Carolina Press, 1996); Charles Patrick Neimeyer, *America Goes to War: A Social History of the Continental Army* (New York: New York University Press, 1996); Woody Holton, *Forced Founders: Indians, Debtors, Slaves, and the Making of the American Revolution in Virginia* (Chapel Hill: University of North Carolina Press for the Omohundro Institute of Early American History and Culture, 1999); Wayne E. Lee, *Crowds and Soldiers in Revolutionary North Carolina: The Culture of Violence in Riot and War* (Gainesville: University Press of Florida, 2001); Wayne Bodle, *The Valley Forge Winter: Civilians and Soldiers in War* (University Park: Pennsylvania State University Press, 2002); Judith Van Buskirk, *Generous Enemies: Patriots and Loyalists in Revolutionary New York* (Philadelphia: University of Pennsylvania Press, 2002); Gregory T. Knouff, *The Soldiers' Revolution: Pennsylvanians in Arms and the Forging of Early American Identity* (University Park: Pennsylvania State University Press, 2004); Michael McDonnell, *The Politics of War: Race, Class, and Social Conflict in Revolutionary Virginia* (Chapel Hill: University of North Carolina Press for the Omohundro Institute of Early American History and Culture, 2007).

2. Richard D. Brown, "Microhistory and the Post-Modern Challenge," *Journal of the Early Republic* 23 (Spring 2003): 1–20.

3. John P. Resch, *Suffering Soldiers: Revolutionary War Veterans, Moral Sentiment, and Political Culture in the Early Republic* (Amherst: University of Massachusetts Press, 1999), pp. 13–46.

4. Gloria L. Main, *Peoples of a Spacious Land: Families and Cultures in Colonial New England* (Cambridge, Mass.: Harvard University Press, 2001), pp. 156–67.

5. Charles H. Bell, *History of the Town of Exeter* (Boston: J. E. Farwell, 1888), pp. 3–41.

6. Bell, *History of the Town of Exeter*, pp. 78, 215–39.

7. Bell, *History of the Town of Exeter*, pp. 72–79.

8. Bell, *History of the Town of Exeter*, pp. 80–87.

9. Bell, *History of the Town of Exeter*, pp. 84–88, 240–57, and Genealogy; Resch, *Suffering Soldiers*, p. 219.

10. Neimeyer, *America Goes to War*, pp. xiii–26; Martin and Lender, *A Respectable Army*, pp. 90–91; Buel, *Dear Liberty*, p. 179.

11. Exeter Tax Records, 1763–1792. N.H. Town Records, reel 097. New Hampshire State Library. For purposes of statistical analysis, all tax figures used in this study are

sums created by converting pounds, shillings, and pence to a grand total of pence for each individual. The tax figures were analyzed using the Statistical Package for the Social Sciences, better known as SPSS. The tax numbers recorded from 1777 through 1780 reflect the devaluation of currency.

12. Samuel T. Worcester, *History of the Town of Hollis, New Hampshire*, (Nashua, N.H.: O. C. Moore, 1879), pp. 19–145. John Avery Butters, "New Hampshire History and the Public Career of Meshech Weare, 1713 to 1786," Ph.D., diss., Fordham University, 1961, pp. 80, 206–7.

13. Worcester, *History of the Town of Hollis*, pp. 139–207.

14. Nathaniel Bouton, ed., *Documents and Records Relating to New Hampshire*. 40 vols. (Concord and Manchester: State of New Hampshire, 1867–1954), 7:724–81; 10:624–35, 638–89.

15. Hollis Town Records, vol. 1: 1739–1871, N.H. Town Records, reel 146. New Hampshire State Library.

16. James Otis Lyford, *History of the Town of Canterbury, New Hampshire, 1727–1912*, 2 vols. (Concord, N.H.: Rumford, 1912), 1:2–50, 54–6, 75–88, 93–98, 107–67.

17. Lyford, *History of the Town of Canterbury*, 1:129–67.

18. Canterbury Town Records, vol. 2: 1727–1864. N.H. Town Records, reel 039, New Hampshire State Library.

19. Lyford, *History of the Town of Canterbury*, 2:21–22.

20. Philip Greven, Jr., *Four Generations: Population, Land, and Family in Colonial Andover, Massachusetts* (Ithaca, N.Y.: Cornell University Press, 1970), pp. 175–221.

21. William Little, *The History of Weare, New Hampshire* (Lowell, Mass.: S. W. Huse & Co., 1888), pp. 93–179, 185–246.

22. Little, *History of Weare*, pp. 192–246.

23. Richard Upton, *Revolutionary New Hampshire* (Hanover, N.H.: Dartmouth College Publications, 1936), p. 95.

24. *Records of Weare*, vol 1: 1749–1816, pp. 180–82. Reel 346. New Hampshire State Library.

25. Buel, *Dear Liberty*, p. 111.

26. Little, *History of Weare*, p. 225.

27. Upton, *Revolutionary New Hampshire*, p. 195; Little, *History of Weare*, p. 230.

28. Upton, *Revolutionary New Hampshire*, p. 95.

29. Little, *History of Weare*, pp. 93–120.

30. Henry Harrison Metcalf, ed., *Laws of New Hampshire: The Revolutionary Period, 1776–1784*, 10 vols. (Bristol, N.H.: Musgrove Printing House, 1916), 4:77–78, 294–95, 305–7, 345–50, 394–95, 407–8, 443–46, 654–70, 707.

31. Ezra S. Stearns, *History of the Town of Rindge, New Hampshire* (Boston: George H. Ellis, 1875), p. 113.

32. Little, *History of Weare*, p. 210. Leonard A. Morrison, *History of Windham in New Hampshire* (Canaan, N.H.: Phoenix Publishing, 1975), pp. 76–77 (reprint of 1883 history by Morrison). Little, *History of Weare*, p. 125. Stearns, *History of the Town of Rindge*, p. 164. David F. Secomb, *History of the Town of Amherst* (Concord, N.H.: Evans, Sleeper and Woodbury, 1883), p. 402.

33. Stearns, *History of the Town of Rindge*, pp. 133–34. Metcalf, *Laws of New Hampshire*, 4:654, 670.

34. Metcalf, *Laws of New Hampshire*, 4:796–97. *History of Bedford, New Hampshire, from 1737* (Concord, N.H.: Rumford, 1903), p. 486.

35. Metcalf, *Laws of New Hampshire* 4:849–52. Langdon B. Parsons, *History of the Town of Rye, New Hampshire* (Concord, N.H.: Rumford, 1905), p. 271.

4

"FIT FOR COMMON SERVICE?"

Class, Race, and Recruitment in Revolutionary Virginia

MICHAEL A. McDONNELL

When we think of Virginia in 1781, we usually remember Washington's famous victory over Cornwallis at Yorktown. But only a few months before that battle, Virginians were at war with themselves—over who should fight against the British. Even as the British launched a ferocious invasion of the state in the spring of 1781, hundreds of ordinary Virginians from all around the state rose up in armed protest against attempts to draft them into the Continental Army. Some of these men believed that, by paying high taxes throughout the war, they had the right to force lower-class Virginians into the army. At the same time, many ordinary Virginians refused to turn out as militiamen against the British because they believed "the Rich wanted the Poor to fight for them, to defend [their] property, whilst they refused to fight for themselves." Still others complained that slaveholders ought to contribute more to the war effort, because nonslaveholders found it "burthensome" to serve in the armed forces when they had "not a slave to labour for them" in their absence. Whatever the complaints, it meant that army recruiters were desperate for men. So desperate, that some of them proposed the seemingly unthinkable. Major Alexander Dick, for example, suggested that Virginia formalize an already informal practice of allowing enslaved Virginians to enlist in the army. Believing that there was "no probability" of filling his regiment with white Virginians, Dick argued that they should consider accepting "likely young negro fellow's" from planters who would then be given compensation for their loss of property. In turn, the enslaved recruit would "be declared free upon inlisting for the War at the end of which, they shall be intitled to all the benefits of Conl. Soldiers." Dick believed that the plan would succeed because enslaved soldiers would make for good recruits and, apparently without a trace of irony, felt that "the men will be equal to any."[1]

The situation in the Old Dominion in the spring of 1781 seems to clash with what we thought we knew about the Continental Army, and about Virginia. Not only were white Virginians reluctant to serve even in the very midst of a massive British invasion that threatened to overrun the slaveholding state, but they also seemed to divide along class rather than racial lines. More generally, such images certainly seem to fly in the face of the pervasive but romantic images we have of the American Revolution as a contest between embattled but willing and unified American farmers and the disciplined lower-class veterans who made up the ranks of the mighty British Army. As the editors of this volume point out, scholars have worked hard to challenge the images and myths that have commonly shrouded our perspectives on the Revolutionary War. But one area that has been left relatively unstudied is Virginia—the largest, most populous, and arguably the most important British colony, and one of the states initially at the forefront of the independence movement.

What greater attention to mobilization in Virginia reveals is that both class and racial tensions shaped—and were, in turn, exacerbated by—efforts to raise soldiers for the Continental Army. From the very start of the war, patriot leaders in Virginia created a clear division and hierarchy in the military services. While celebrating the virtues of the militia, patriot leaders at the same time created a regular army and tried to recruit those they believed to be "fit for common service," in the words of one gentleman. Part of the reason why Virginia's patriot leadership believed that only the "lower Class of People"—as George Washington put it— should join the regular army was because in Virginia's racially divided society, service in the Continental Army was clearly analogous to another important institution in the province: slavery. Service in the regular army required white recruits to give up their independence and accept the rigors of discipline, subordination, and obeisant service to superior officers. The parallels were all too obvious in slave-rich Virginia—particularly after many enslaved Virginians themselves sought freedom in the ranks of the army. As a result, most middling independent farmers resisted any and all attempts to persuade, entice, or coerce them into service in the Continental Army. Most preferred to retain their independence and remain at home doing occasional but short tours of duty in the militia.[2]

But slavery affected mobilization in other ways. Many middling farmers, for example, were reluctant to serve for long periods of time because they worried about their families in their absence. Some feared domestic slave insurrections, whereas others, especially nonslaveowning farmers, worried about their economic independence if they served in the army or even militia for long durations. Middling farmers without slaves lashed out at planters with slaves, but they also joined their wealthier neighbors in making it clear that property holders should not have to serve in the army. Throughout the war, but certainly by the end of it, most middling farmers resisted service in the Continental Army as did Virginia's patriot leaders.

In turn, some lower-class Virginians willingly gave up their own independence to serve in the army, but they demanded a high price for their services. They forced legislators to offer high bounties, and they forced their more well-to-do neighbors to offer increasingly larger payments for serving as substitutes during the war. Many simply refused to serve. And, as recruits became increasingly scarce, and the price of bounties too high to sustain, lower-class Virginians resisted any and all attempts to draft or coerce them into the army, curtailing and at times paralyzing Virginia's mobilization efforts. As a result, patriot leaders in the state were forced to debate some revolutionary proposals of their own to solve their mobilization problems.[3]

From the start of the war, patriot leaders in Virginia were influenced by concerns about both race and class, which shaped their military response to the resistance movement. In the first place, patriot leaders drew on past experience in shaping their military policy. And in previous conflicts, and like many other colonies, Virginia's leaders drew on a limited martial tradition that placed the poor and marginal in society front and center of most efforts to raise soldiers. During the War of Jenkins' Ear (1739–1741), for example, the Burgesses conscripted, or drafted, only "able-bodied persons, fit to serve his majesty, who follow no lawful calling or employment." In the Seven Years' War (1754–1763), Governor Dinwiddie and the Burgesses fell upon the same expedient, making their intentions clearer when they exempted all those who could vote from the draft. This meant that only the propertyless would be conscripted, and the middling classes, who could vote, would be left alone. In previous colonial wars, then, provincial elites raised soldiers by coercing and exploiting the lowest classes of whites—the poor, the needy, and the vulnerable.[4]

When mobilizing for war, Virginian elites were also concerned about the lowest class of all in the colony—enslaved Virginians. Enslaved Virginians had panicked white Virginians on numerous occasions during previous wars. Black Virginians knew that war among whites presented opportunities for freedom; the new imperial dispute gave black Virginians further hope. As early as November 1774, some enslaved Virginians had already met and selected a leader "to conduct them when the English troops should arrive." They believed that by "revolting to them they should be rewarded with their freedom."[5]

Under the circumstances, most patriot leaders in Virginia wanted to send a clear and forceful message to enslaved Virginians contemplating insurrection in the midst of the imperial dispute. They thus followed colonial practice and ordered the creation of two regiments of regular troops that would act as a permanent home guard both to deter black Virginians from planning a coordinated revolt and to warn Governor Dunmore that Virginians were ready for a fight. Patriot leaders also resurrected a largely defunct militia, gave commanding officers new powers to appoint and lead slave patrols, and exempted from service altogether all overseers of at least four enslaved Virginians. Leaders also called for the recruitment of sixteen battalions of elite militia called the "minutemen" who would serve as a first line of defense for the colony against the British. Patriot leaders hoped that a permanent regular force, combined with a reinvigorated militia and an elite group of minutemen, would provide both a sufficient internal, as well as external, line of defense.[6]

But if these initial proposals reflected a concern about race and slavery within Virginia, they also reflected patriot leaders' class-based perspectives on mobilization, for it was clear from the outset that most patriot leaders believed that the two regiments of Continental soldiers should and would be composed of men similar in social standing as those drafted to serve in regular units in the French and Indian War. For example, patriot leader George Mason, the chief architect of the military plan, made it clear that his own son should not even think about serving in the regular army. Instead, young men of standing ought to join the minuteman service because it was, the elder Mason asserted, "the true natural, and safest Defence of this, or any other free Country." Another prominent patriot, George Gilmer, hoped the new minuteman plan would be "on such footing as inevitably to draw in Gent'n of the first property in the Colony" and immediately signed up. On the other hand, Francis Willis of Fredericksburg told his son he would be happy to see his son serve in the regular forces, but only "as an Officer." Willis was "absolutely in the strongest Terms against his enlisting as a common Soldier." Thus, while the minuteman service would be filled with virtuous yeomen defending hearth and home, most patriot leaders believed that the ranks of the regular service would be filled with poorer men who would help the propertied classes secure their rights and privileges.[7]

Unfortunately for patriot leaders in Virginia, too few virtuous yeomen stepped forward to make the minuteman service a viable defense force, despite the fact that Governor Dunmore had upped the ante in Virginia by declaring the slaves of rebel masters free if they could reach his lines and join him against the patriot forces. In late 1775, even the renewed threat of racial war failed to mobilize middling white Virginians in sufficient numbers, and not for the last time in the conflict. Consequently, by December 1775, patriot leaders had all but scrapped the minuteman service and, in desperation, instead called for a vastly enlarged regular service that they hoped would serve as a permanent wartime professional army for the protection of the state. At the same time, they also pleaded with Congress to include this contingent as part of Virginia's contribution to the Continental Army. In doing so, patriot leaders signaled that they would not rely on middling citizens in the militia for the colony's defense. Rather, they would award generous enlistment bounties and regular pay to anyone who would give up their independence and submit to the more onerous regulations governing the Continental Army. To put it another way, as early as the end of 1775, Virginia's leaders had concluded that it was better to pay the poor to fight on behalf of taxpaying citizens and the ruling class than to send the sons of the elite and middling classes to war.[8]

Subsequently, patriot leaders neither encouraged nor expected middling Virginians to join the Continental Army. Drawing upon their experience of mobilization in prior wars, most patriot elites assumed that only the marginal should or would need to join the regular forces. The laws they passed encouraged this general impression. At the end of 1776, for example, the new state government made it clear what kind of men they expected to serve in the Continental Army and what other purpose the armed forces might serve. Noting the "great increase" of "idle and disorderly persons" in the state, the Virginia Assembly decided to do something about the "rogues and vagabonds" plaguing their towns and lanes. Struggling to raise men for the new Continental regiments, the legislature decided to take more draconian measures to deal with both problems. If vagabonds could not give security for their good behavior or future job prospects, the General Assembly gave justices of the peace and the governor wide powers to imprison and ultimately impress such people into the armed services. Significantly, the representatives defined vagabonds quite broadly as any able-bodied men who neglected or refused to pay their public county and parish levies and who had no visible estate.[9]

But if patriot leaders were keen to push lower-class Virginians into the army, lower-class Virginians had their own agenda. Many looked warily at the lengthening terms of required service, particularly when Washington made it clear that he wanted a more disciplined army. From early on, officers around Virginia encountered problems recruiting men for the Continental Army. Reports from all across the new state brought bad news to the capital throughout most of 1776. There was a brief flurry of successful recruiting activity near the end of December, as news reached Virginia of Washington's successes at Princeton and Trenton. As it became apparent that Washington's victories were only temporary successes, however, recruiting fell off once again. John Page wrote from Williamsburg at the end of February that "Inlistments . . . I fear will never be compleated—several Counties have not raised a Man."[10]

There were, of course, some who did decide to take advantage of the seemingly liberal bounties and promises of land held out to potential recruits. Although few studies have been done on the social composition of the earliest cohort of regular soldiers because of the lack of detailed extant sources, it seems that most recruits fit the profile of earlier wars. In one of the only studies of Virginia's Revolutionary soldiery in these early years, Richard Bush has concluded that the majority of recruits for the Continental Army were "young, single, and had relatively little wealth." Those recruited just one year later, in early 1777, were even poorer, and slightly younger. Certainly, few gentlemen, or sons of gentlemen, joined the army, except as officers. Many gentlemen, like William Allason, revealed that he believed he had a right to claim an exemption on the basis of his status or rank in life. He protested that a "Soldiers duty would also go exceedingly hard with me never having been accustomed to that way of Life that renders a man fit for common service."[11]

With so many white Virginians reluctant to serve, it was left to the very lowest classes to fill the ranks of the Army. Many men, for example, were willing to exchange one kind of bondage for another. In 1775, the Third Virginia Convention had forbidden recruiters to enlist any servants at all, unless they were apprentices who had the written consent of their masters. Yet desperation drove recruiters to enlist anyone that seemed willing to serve. Indentured and convict servants took full advantage. Several owners of escaped indentured servants believed that their servants were headed straight for recruiting officers. Samuel Love of Loudoun County lost two convict servants in the early summer of 1777. Love thought that twenty-year-old, London-born George Dorman (alias Holderness) and David Hinds, a thirty-five-year-old Irish ropemaker and sailor, would try to enlist "at the first opportunity." By mid-1777, George Washington believed that the Virginia line of the Continental Army was full of convict servants especially. "Convict Servants," he explained to Congress, "compose no small proportion of the Men from the Upper and more interior Part of that State." Some servants may have been coerced into service by masters wishing to make a profit on their sale, but no doubt many welcomed the bargain as a swift way to end their servitude. Even if they stayed in the army for the length of service contracted, it was likely shorter than the time they had remaining on their indentures. It was also easier, however, to escape the army than ever-watchful masters. Both Washington and other observers believed that most servants would "desert the first opportunity."[12]

Enslaved Virginians also took advantage of the desperate need for soldiers by offering themselves to recruiters under the guise of being freemen. The 1775 prohibition against enlisting servants presumably applied to enslaved Virginians, for on that front the Convention was completely silent. At some point between 1775 and early 1777, however, desperate recruiters began allowing free blacks into the Virginia line. This, of course, led to many enslaved Virginians presenting themselves to recruiters as free men. Certainly, enslaved Virginians seemed to believe that they could find refuge in the army. Early in 1777, for example, Joe escaped from his master, Charles Jones, in Alexandria. Joe was about twenty-one years of age and could "read and wright," according to his more illiterate owner, who understood that Joe wanted to "enlist as a freeman."[13]

Enslaved Virginians knew that, in the face of a shortage of white enlistments, recruiters were more likely to enlist blacks, enslaved or free. Indeed, whereas for most of Virginia's history, whites had been collecting rewards for catching and returning escaped blacks to their masters, the new recruiting law meant that some whites at least could make money by helping enslaved Virginians find freedom through enlistment in the army.

The new law stipulated that recruiting officers would get ten dollars for each recruit they could bring into the army. With such an incentive, blacks knew that recruiters were happy to accept their claims to freedom. By May 1777, enough enslaved Virginians had run away and enlisted in the army to alarm the General Assembly. Legislators complained about the number of "negro slaves" who had deserted their masters and enlisted with the army and tried to close the loophole by declaring the practice of enrolling black or mulatto Virginians unlawful unless they produced a cer-tificate affirming their free status from a local justice of the peace. In doing so, of course, they gave official sanction to the practice of enrolling free blacks into the army, a practice not adopted in Maryland until 1780 and not adopted at all south of Virginia. They also opened the door for enslaved Vir-ginians to gain their freedom from their masters by offering to serve as substi-tutes for them if they were drafted. Thus, by the middle years of the war, blacks constituted a significant minority in Virginia's line in the Continental Army. Because middling and upper-class whites refused to fight for them-selves, and because even lower-class whites only reluctantly joined the army, necessity forced white Virginians to rely on blacks for their defense.[14]

The total number of the increasingly motley crew of men who did step forward, however, was small. Washington reported in early April 1777 that, as far as he could ascertain, Virginia's nine old regiments did not ex-ceed 1,800 effective men when there should have been approximately 4,500 men in service, and Governor Patrick Henry told him that he did not think more than four of the six new regiments ordered raised would actually be filled. As late as May 1777, only twelve Virginia battalions had joined Washington to the north. Of them, the largest battalion consisted of only 326 men who were present and fit for duty. Full battalion strength was 738 officers and men. In the twelve battalions serving with Washing-ton in May, there were only a total of 2,512 Virginia troops present and fit for duty in total, or about a *quarter* of the total number of troops Virginia had been asked to provide. Nor was there much chance of recruiting any more men. By the end of March, Governor Henry concluded that "enlist-ments go on badly. Indeed they are almost stopped."[15]

With Washington and Congress pressuring them to do something about the understrength regiments in 1777, Virginia's leaders devised new plans to enlist marginal men. Richard Henry Lee, a Virginia congressional delegate, told Jeffer-son that there were too many "lazy, worthless young Men" in the state who ought to be forced into service. Washington was more explicit—he believed that the army could only be filled with "the lower Class of People." Although he had hoped they could hold out sufficient inducements for "the lower Class of People" to enlist voluntarily, Washington believed that they could not now avoid the "necessity of compelling them to inlist." Virginia's leaders, then, wanted to fight for liberty by curbing the liberty of others.[16]

Some of Washington's officers had already taken matters into their own hands. Much like the hated British Navy, Nicholas Cresswell reported in

March 1777 that recruiting officers in Loudoun County, perhaps hoping that the new vagrancy law had established a precedent already, had begun "pressing the young men into the Army."[17] The first Virginia Assembly to advocate a draft for the Continental Army followed a similar model. Contrary to congressional recommendations that they draft men indiscriminately, Virginia legislators decided that draftees would not be picked by open lottery, but by the opinion of the field officers and "four first magistrates" of the county. From among the ranks of the militia, these officials would "fix upon and draught" one man, who, in their opinion, could "be best spared, and will be most serviceable." The new recruits, or picked draftees, were to serve for a full three years and receive the same bounty and pay as voluntary recruits.[18]

Virginia's Revolutionary leaders, then, fell back on a colonial strategy of targeting the more vulnerable in society. Although this new draft affected respectable middling farmers who would, by virtue of their enrollment in the militia, be responsible for procuring recruits, propertied farmers were unlikely to be targeted in the draft. There seemed little doubt among legislators about who would ultimately serve. Recruiters were to target apprentices, servants, free blacks, and debtors. Draft officials were to pick out only those men who they felt were expendable, or, in the words of one recruiting officer, all "Lazy fellows who lurk about and are pests to Society." Most of these men would have no political rights. The fact that draftees would be picked not by lottery, but by field officers and county officials, only ensured that the troublesome or powerless would be chosen. Indeed, in this respect, the draft would also allow legislators to deal with the vagrancy problem that worried them the previous summer and fall.[19]

Initially, it looked as if legislators' plans might work. More liberal bounties—in the form of land, money, and clothing—seemed to attract more enlistees on to the parade ground. At the same time, though, the threat of a draft created opportunities for poorer Virginians to get something more in return for their now badly needed service. All members of the militia were divided into groups, or divisions. Each division was then responsible for producing one recruit; if no one was forthcoming, someone would be drafted. Without being certain who would be picked, many divisions began offering large sums of money—legal "private gratuities" in addition to the Continental bounty—to potential recruits to exempt themselves from the draft. One man in Caroline County forced a division there to pay eighty pounds for his services. As a result, the other divisions in the county could not afford to hire anyone. Edmund Pendleton reported that the field officers and justices in Caroline, who were ordered by the law to pay fifty shillings each to hire a man to exempt themselves from the draft, paid in the full twenty pounds and "offered it for a man, but in vain." Instead, potential recruits hired themselves out to the highest bidders. Landon Carter, one of the four first magistrates of Richmond County, grumbled that he and his colleagues could hire a man only for twice the stipulated rate.[20]

But lower-class Virginians at risk of being drafted and who could not afford to pay such sums for substitutes resorted to other means to try to avoid service. Even before the draft, some men tried to disrupt the recruiting service, perhaps to sabotage the act altogether. As the day of the draft approached, and fewer and fewer potential recruits stepped forward, militia who felt themselves under threat of being picked out stepped up their general resistance to the act. In Richmond County, Carter reported that he had attended court only because a "worthy member begged I would come to give weight and order to the Proceedings." Then, just after the actual draft took place, two men—John Jones Griffin and William Sutton—were summoned to answer a charge of "Contempt offered by them to the Officers of this State." In Loudoun County, eight men were brought before the court just after the draft law went into effect, charged under the new law with having resisted the government and raised "Tumults and Disorders in this State." Under the same law, and immediately following the draft, at least two men were also brought before the Mecklenburg County Court.[21]

Those who could not stop the draft from taking place could and often did evade it if they were actually picked for service. Many of those targeted for the draft were footloose, so they took the opportunity to seek new fortunes in other counties, or even other states. Robert Honyman later wrote that he thought not half of the conscripts ever joined the army. Most deserted and ran off to the Carolinas, Georgia, or the Ohio backcountry. From Hanover County alone, twenty of twenty-seven drafted men had deserted. Nor was this unusual. In the aftermath of the draft, the newspapers were full of advertisements for deserters.[22]

Ironically, advertisements for deserters may also have contributed to faltering voluntary enlistments in the army. Though patriot leaders had made it clear among themselves who they wanted to target for service in the army, and had made it more explicit in the provisions for drafting men in 1777, the advertisements for deserters painted a more graphic picture of the kinds of men who were compelled and coerced into the army. Advertisements for deserters from the army are a particularly rich source of information about soldiers in Virginia. They tell us much. Not just about the kinds of men that joined—or were picked out to join—the army, but also about officers' perceptions of them. Patriot officers were often scathing about the quality of the recruits that had joined the army.

Newspaper advertisements for deserters from the army gave readers a colorful impression of the motley crew that came to compose the army. Like advertisements for runaway slaves, officers gave names, a short description, and any distinguishing characteristics of the deserters, usually accompanied by a measure of verbal abuse for their transgression. In early September, for example, Alexander Spotswood, colonel of the 2nd Virginia Regiment, put a notice in the *Virginia Gazette* advertising thirteen deserters from his regiment who were then in service in New Jersey. They included thirty-five-year-old Francis Dryskil, an Irishman who chewed tobacco and was "very fond of Liquor," and Joseph Bryant, who was also "fond of Liquor" but who had a "remarkable scar on one of his lips." William Denny had also deserted. Denny was another Irishman, about thirty years of age, who was "much pitted with the Smallpox" as well as being "fond of Liquor." His younger countryman, John Saunders, was only about eighteen, and "smooth faced." Thomas Trap was a thirty-year-old sergeant in the army who was also "pitted with Smallpox" and who, according to Spotswood, "talks in a whining Manner." Trap had left the army with his wife—"who was heavy with Child"—who had been with him during the campaign. Finally, the deserters included brothers Philip and Brice Ragan, who were twenty-two and twenty years old, respectively. Philip, a corporal, "speaks fierce" and had a "dark Complexion" whereas his brother Brice was of a "fair Complexion" and a more "agreeable look."[23]

These advertised descriptions in the public papers helped shape public opinion about just who was in the army. Indeed, if, like Nicholas Cresswell, more middling Virginians did not already think of the army as a "ragged crew," they could have only recoiled at the thought of joining the dregs described by Spotswood and other officers. Most deserters were described as being "fond of liquor" and/or ravaged by smallpox. Of the thirteen, four were described as Irish, one as English, and only one was specifically listed as a "Virginian." Five (three of whom were foreigners) were listed as being between the ages of thirty and thirty-five, and the ages of the four others were given as between eighteen and twenty-two. None seemed to have a home to speak of. Colonel Spotswood thought Benjamin James would flee to Baltimore, where his parents lived, and Joseph Bryant might try to go to King George County, where his parents lived. Richard Lewis, the twenty-five-year-old Englishman, "formerly" lived in Loudoun, and of course Trap and his wife presumably had made a "home" anywhere on the road.[24] Although patriot leaders had made it clear among themselves who they wanted to target for service in the army, the advertisements for deserters painted a more graphic public picture of lower-class men and immigrants who were enticed and coerced into the army.

In the end, the combined effects of evasion, resistance, protest, and desertion rendered the first draft for the Continental Army a failure. At best, perhaps fewer than a thousand men enlisted or were drafted into the army. In May 1777, there was a total of 3,561 men listed in the ranks of the Virginia line, including those sick and on furlough. By December, there were at most just over 4,000 Virginia troops with Washington at Valley Forge. This included hundreds of men who were listed as sick, who were on furlough, or who were listed as "wanting shoes, etc." The 7th Virginia Regiment, for example, headed by Colonel Alexander McClanachan, listed a total of 427 men in the battalion. Eighty of these men, however, were missing shoes and thus out of action, 139 were on furlough in Virginia, 104 were sick and not present, and another 10 were sick at camp. This left only forty-six men present and fit for duty, as well as another forty-eight men who were on duty elsewhere. Altogether, the number of men from Virginia who were present and fit for duty by the end of 1777 was at best about 1,500, or almost 1,000 fewer than in May.[25]

With Washington's army falling apart in early 1778, the Virginia Assembly again turned to the vexed question of the army. Virginia needed at least 8,000 new recruits or reenlistees to fill its quota. Delegates to the Virginia Assembly still believed that enticements were the best way to recruit the majority of the men needed. They also hoped they could again lean on the same men that had already joined up. Thus, they held out good inducements for men to reenlist in the army. Invariably, however, most delegates believed that enticements would only help, but not solve, the recruiting crisis. Although the last draft had engendered so much opposition, most legislators seemed to believe that another draft was the only way to complete their quota. There was much less agreement, however, on what kind of draft there ought to be. Lower-class Virginians' resistance had divided the legislators.[26]

Delegates discussed three different alternatives; significantly, none of these alternatives replicated the experiment of "picked men" tried by the previous assembly. One group of legislators was of the mind that they ought to target "Vagabonds" more specifically. If vagabonds could not be had, "those who approach nearest to them" should be picked. The second alternative was to draft men from the whole militia "indiscriminately," or regardless of economic status. This, of course, was the most equitable manner by which to choose drafts. But some leaders, such as Pendleton, objected to it on the grounds of the damage it would do to established families. He thought it would be "cruel to force men from their Families to a distant Countrey for two or three years." The assembly then considered and finally adopted a third proposal—a "middle way"—between the two other measures proposed. This was to draft only "the Single men" by a fair lottery. Pendleton believed that most would agree that "the young men are properest to go, and then it follows that all of them should take a fair and equal Chance." Eventually, the assembly decided to draft only single men, whether officers or privates, older than eighteen who had no children. Pendleton thought this was the best possible choice in the circumstances. "It is every way disagreeable," he acknowledged, "but being of absolute necessity, we must take a mode the least exceptionable." Lower-class Virginians, then, had forced Virginia legislators to widen the net for potential recruits.[27]

The new draft would only deepen divisions between white Virginians, but this time between elites and middling Virginians. Having watched the army fill up with an increasingly motley crew, few middling Virginians, even if single and young, were keen to serve in it. About a week after the draft was scheduled to take place, Robert Honyman noted that "It was very generally disagreable to the people, & in some counties occasioned considerable disturbance." Honyman's own county of Hanover was spared any violent "disturbance." They paid an expensive price, however; the inhabitants of Hanover and elsewhere had to raise "large sums" of money by subscription and offer it to those who would enlist voluntarily. Recruits in Hanover were thus paid almost sixty pounds each. Taken together with the bounty allowed by law, new enlistees were paid a joining bonus of sixty-nine pounds.[28]

In other counties, however, the draft produced swift and bloody resistance. In the lower Northern Neck, reaction to the draft law was dramatic. At least four men tried to disrupt the draft or lead a protest against it in Westmoreland County. In neighboring Northumberland County, at least five men led a protest against the draft that brought proceedings to a halt. The county court there charged them for "behaving in a riotous manner on the day of the Draught." Several of these men were confined and put under guard by local militia officers following the incident, but others organized a rescue mission. Problems were not confined to the Northern Neck. Thomas Jefferson reported problems in Fluvanna County in the Piedmont as well. Even in counties that had previously produced many willing recruits and full support for the patriot cause, there was vocal opposition to the draft. Two men from Culpeper County, for example, complained publicly about the draft and found themselves in prison. They had, they claimed, voiced their concern "against unjust discriminating draughts."[29]

Other men made similar complaints, backing up their concerns with force of arms. In Loudoun County, "the People" prevented the draft from taking place with "violent & riotous behaviour" according to one report. Lund Washington, who was minding Mount Vernon, told his cousin General George Washington that people were in arms over the draft. On the first attempt to conscript men, the militia mutinied and successfully prevented the draft from taking place. In the confusion, however, "one of the Mutinous got shot," though not fatally, probably by one of the field officers of the militia. Already angry, the militia then threatened to kill the county lieutenant, Colonel Francis Peyton, in reprisal. Shaken, but undeterred, Peyton ordered another draft for March 11. He was pessimistic, however, over whether he would fare any better. He believed that they needed to be more forceful but that, without state help, they could never overawe the draft resisters. "Without some exertions of Government," he complained to the council, "there was little reason to expect a more successful Issue than before." The county was in a state of civil disorder for at least two months. In the end, officials in Loudoun brought a total of fourteen men to court in April and tried them in May, but they were only the ringleaders. The court charged the men with "Riotous and disorderly behaviour in withstanding the draught."[30]

In places where the draft was not stopped by collective and active opposition, draftees themselves either opted out or banded together to bid defiance to local officials. Forty-seven men were drafted in Fauquier County, for example, but only just more than half reached the army. Twenty-six men were actually delivered to the army, two men moved to other counties, and nineteen others stood their ground. They "alledged the Law was partial & would never join." Similarly, Lund Washington noted that, even if there had not been a riot in Loudoun because of the draft, they would have to do it over again anyway, because "the men who were draughted cannot be found." Other men waited for a better opportunity to escape. Many deserted on route to the army. Until the middle of May 1778, only 799 men marched from Virginia. Of them, forty-one had been left on the road for various reasons and another forty-two deserted. Officials reported that men were leaving in numbers daily. Draftees were particularly prone to deserting. Of twenty-eight drafts one Lieutenant Campbell escorted northward, twenty-two deserted.[31]

In the end, opposition to the draft again short-circuited recruiting plans. Unable to afford substitutes and unhappy with the discriminatory application of the law, many ordinary Virginians fought back against what they perceived to be an unjust law. Their strategy worked. By late May 1778, only 716 men of the 8,000 men asked for had been raised through the draft or through substitutions. George Washington wrote at the time that even of the 1,500 recruits requested from the previous draft, together with the 2,000 men the assembly ordered drafted in February 1778, they had only received 1,242 men. Washington lamented that this was "so horrible a deficiency." Of all the drafts and volunteers ordered raised, Patrick Henry thought that "not one half of the Number voted by the Assembly have got to Camp." "Virginia," wrote one army chaplain definitively, "makes the poorest figure of any State in the Recruiting way."[32]

Yet, despite the continued poor performance of Virginia in fielding new recruits for the Continental Army, protests against the indiscriminate draft of single men in 1778 shocked Virginia legislators into abandoning altogether the idea of raising men by force. They turned instead to high bounties and short terms of service—much to the frustration of officers like Washington, who wanted a long-term, more permanent army. Moreover, when the assembly made economic enticements the sole inducement to join the army in 1778 and 1779, the inflation of bounty rewards grew—fueling the already rampant inflation that had begun to cripple the economy. By early 1779, Robert Honyman reported that recruiting officers were paying up to $450 more than the prescribed bounty of $300 to procure recruits. By the fall of 1779, the sums needed to recruit for the army had become prohibitively expensive. Pendleton thought that almost each man enlisted had cost, on average, about £5,000.[33]

Even when account is taken of the rapid devaluation of currency in these years, wealthy Virginians were angry because they had to pay out so much for so little. David Jameson complained that, though such exorbitant sums had been paid out to hire recruits, only a temporary army had been raised. Pendleton also despaired that by the time the new recruits became proficient soldiers their terms of service would run out. Virginians would again have to incur the "ruinous expence of recruiting." The bounties paid out during the summer of 1780, he claimed, were far too expensive. "At any rate of depreciation," he concluded, the sums paid out "must exceed the ability of any Countrey frequently to repeat."[34]

Many gentlemen were furious that lower-class Virginians could and would protect their own interests. Edmund Pendleton could not believe that potential recruits could act so selfishly. By holding out for more money for their services, potential recruits were, according to Pendleton, being self-interestedly greedy. In a letter to George Washington, he revealed his prejudice toward the kinds of recruits he felt ought to join the army. The "demon of avarice, and spirit of extortion," he exclaimed, "seem to have expelled the pure patriotism from the breasts of those who usually compose armies." But, having been treated with years of contempt by Virginia's leaders, lower-class Virginians were having none of it. Raleigh Colston, the captain of the sloop *Liberty,* learned the limits of patriotism as a call to arms when he tried to invoke the principle as a good reason for his crew to take lower wages. The spokesman for the crew declared, "Country here or Country there, damn my Eyes and limbs but I'll serve them that give the best wages."[35]

In the face of such resistance, the war effort simply ground to a halt. The returns of the 1st Virginia Regiment, probably the strongest regiment from the state at any given time during the war, showed the shortcomings of Virginia military policy in the midyears of the war. In September 1776, there were 590 men enrolled in the regiment, though only 406 were present and fit for duty. By the end of 1779, even after being reinforced with remnants of the 9th and 10th Virginia Regiments, the First consisted of only 295 men, most of whose terms of service were expiring. Finally, just before its capture at Charleston, South Carolina, in May 1780, the strength of the regiment was listed at just 195 effective men. Governor Jefferson wearily summed up the situation in a letter to Washington in November 1779, assuring the general that the government was doing all it could, "but we find it very difficult to procure men."[36]

In late 1778, the British began to bring the war to the South and open up a new front. Believing themselves at a stalemate in the North, the Southern colonies began to look more inviting to the British by 1778–1779. More thinly settled than the Northern colonies, more vulnerable by sea, more dependent on foreign markets for imports and their exports, and arguably much more valuable to Britain, the Southern colonies loomed large in British thinking in late 1778 and early 1779. Moreover, intelligence reports of loyalist support encouraged the British to think that they might make more progress in the South than they had hitherto made in the North. These reports, combined with the knowledge that enslaved Americans might help make up a fifth column, or at least keep a vulnerable people at home, encouraged the British to think that they could still save the Southern colonies.[37]

Beginning in May 1779, the British began a series of devastating raids in Virginia, which would eventually culminate in the rendezvous of Arnold and Cornwallis, the near-capture of Governor Jefferson, and the complete breakdown of mobilization in Virginia by 1781. The Virginia Assembly, squeezed by lower-class resistance from below and mounting pressure from Congress and Washington to pull its own weight, was forced to put even more pressure on the middling sort in Virginia—both by requiring them for more frequent and longer militia service and, finally, by reinstituting and expanding the draft for the Continental Army to include all men.

In the first place, calls on the militia for more frequent service in Virginia and in neighboring states escalated after 1778. But the more the assembly and the governor called on the militia, the more middling white Virginians protested. Ordinary farmers and planters first demanded that calls on the militia be limited, for short terms of service, and only for service close to home. Most were adamant that they would not serve outside the state and particularly in the hotter climates of the states to the south of them. But middling men in the militia were equally insistent that their taxpaying status should exempt them from fighting altogether and that the state ought to spend their tax money on raising a proper army and filling it with their lower-class neighbors. Petitioners from Berkeley County, for example, complained that, for the money they had spent raising recruits, they could have enlisted troops for the duration of the war. These complaints also revealed a class-based vision of society. Distinguishing themselves from the kind of people most likely to join the army, the petitioners from Berkeley claimed that volunteers for the army were driven by profit, not patriotism. They contrasted their situation with "that Class of men" who had come to "depend upon the field for his living." The present laws gave such men the "power" and encouragement to "Fleece from the virtuous and good part of our Citizens Whatever their avaricious inclinations may prompt Them to exact." The Berkeley militia pointed to a deepening divide between themselves and those whom they expected to do their fighting for them, and they claimed that full citizens of the new republic had the right not to serve but to pay others to do that for them. Only by pushing these men into a permanent army, they warned, could the government quell the "great uneasiness and disquiet in the Country" caused by militia call-ups and high taxes.[38]

But the middling class was equally concerned about serving in the military because of the shadow of slavery. Slavery and the presence of a large number of enslaved Virginians in the state affected mobilization in several significant ways. In the first place, many slaveholders were worried about losing their valuable property amid the British raids and invasion. After all, the British had come to Virginia with an eye on the rich resources of the state, which included the thousands of enslaved Virginians who could either be turned into extra plunder or help bring the state to its knees. But many white Virginians harbored a deep-seated fear that Virginia's enslaved population might do more than just take the opportunity to escape to the British. With firsthand accounts raising alarms, they feared that enslaved Virginians would revolt and kill their masters.[39]

Such worries, perhaps predictably, kept many militia at home when the British invaded the state. By 1781, most state officials were resigned to the fact that militia in the immediate vicinity of British forces would not turn out. When the British came calling at Hampton, in Elizabeth City County, in the fall of 1780, for example, militia officers told their men that "every man who had a Family" could retire and "do the best for them they could." The officers later told the assembly that they had been forced to put the "Personal welfare of their wives Children and themselves with their property" above the cause and make terms with the British.[40] Edmund Randolph later recalled that the poor militia turnout in the face of the British raids in 1780 and 1781 was due to enslaved Virginians. He wrote that the "helpless wives and children were at the mercy not only of the males among the slaves but of the very women, who could handle deadly weapons; and these could not have been left in safety in the absence of all authority of the masters and of union among neighbors."[41]

Significantly, slavery also had a less obvious impact on mobilization in Virginia. Although many historians have assumed that slavery helped unify white communities in times of trouble, the ownership of enslaved Virginians actually aggravated deep divisions among whites. Nonslaveholders, for example, were quick to claim that military service for slaveholders was much less of a burden than for those without slaves. Slaveowners still had someone to labor for them in their absence. Nonslaveholders, Chesterfield petitioners claimed, found militia service particularly "burthensome" for the "poorer sort who have not a slave to labour for them." Such complaints grew more commonplace as the demands of war put a greater strain on farmers' abilities to maintain their livelihoods in the face of numerous and intrusive militia call-ups.[42]

Slaveholding, then, particularly toward the end of the war, increasingly became the touchstone for class divisions among white Virginians. Time and again, on different issues surrounding mobilization, militia from across the state, not just slave-poor regions, made claims based on slaveholding inequality. Sometimes their claims implicitly contrasted slaveholders with nonslaveholders. At other times, however, militia were explicit about perceived inequalities in Virginia. In the spring of 1780, for example, the Charlotte County militia, in a petition to the legislature, rendered an explicit analysis of the problem of wartime mobilization by laying bare what they saw as the class-based injustice of military service. The petitioners were angry that the "great & oppulent who contribute very little personal labour in support of their families, often find means to screen themselves altogether from those military services which the poor and indigent are on all occasions taken from their homes to perform in person." What was worse, they claimed, was that slaveholders benefited twice over; while nonslaveholding whites risked their lives, their families, and their estates through their personal service in the militia, slaveholding planters exempted themselves from service and grew personally rich on the backs of their slaves' labor.[43]

Thus, mobilization efforts in Virginia showed the depth of class divisions and their relationship to slavery in the state. By 1780, class antagonisms weakened Virginia's ability to resist British forces at a critical point in the war when leaders were struggling to maintain order on the home front by suppressing potential slave rebellions and trying to mobilize forces against British invasion. When Virginia was forced to confront again the problem of raising recruits for the Continental Army under the pressure of the British invasions of 1780–1781, legislators had to take into account the draft resistance of earlier years, the reluctance of lower-class Virginians to volunteer readily, the class-based complaints of the middling sort that they had paid enough toward the war, *and* complaints from diverse sectors of society that wealthy slaveholders in Virginia had not borne their fair share of the costs of the war. But these class-based complaints were also intricately linked with slavery in the state. Indeed, slavery helped bring the British to Virginia in the first place—and the threat from enslaved Virginians kept many militia at home. But slavery was also at the center of many of the divisions among whites over who ought to serve in the army. In light of these seemingly intractable considerations, patriot leaders were forced into thinking about some revolutionary proposals to overcome these problems.

In the fall of 1780, Joseph Jones revealed the outlines of a radical new plan to raise a more permanent army. A committee, of which Jones was a member, had drafted a bill to raise Continental troops for the duration of the war, by offering volunteers—in addition to the Continental bounty, which still included a parcel of land—an enslaved Virginian between ten and forty years of age. As striking as this new policy was, the committee went further. It suggested that enslaved Virginians used for bounties should be taken from wealthy slaveholders only. All masters who owned more than twenty bondsmen would be forced to contribute every twentieth slave.[44]

Jones believed that, if they could make the plan work, it would be the best solution possible to their mobilization problems. He thought that the "Negro bounty cannot fail to procure Men for the War" because it would be an attractive enticement for those with little property. A slave bounty taken from the wealthy, however, would also placate middling Virginians' complaints about the burden of war falling disproportionately on their shoulders. Indeed, one representative from the near-western county of Botetourt, Thomas Madison, believed that the legislature introduced this scheme precisely because they wanted to make the wealthy pay their share of the war. Madison told William Preston of Montgomery County that "the principle on which this Bill was founded was . . . that Negroes were a desireable Property, and it would be obliging to the Wealthy, who perform little personal duty, to contribute largely."[45]

Slaveholders, and those sympathetic to slaveholders, however, fought back and managed to defeat the plan. Nevertheless, legislators retained the idea of giving enslaved Virginians to potential recruits as a bounty coupled with increased financial incentives. Representatives proposed to

entice as many of the 3,000 new recruits they had decided to raise to enlist voluntarily, offering very generous bounties, before they resorted to a
draft, which would, according to Jones, be "the dernier resort." Soldiers
who enlisted for the duration of the war would receive $12,000. Those
who enlisted for three years would earn $8,000. On top of that healthy
bounty money, those enlisting for the duration of the war would also receive a "healthy sound negro" between the ages of ten and thirty or sixty
pounds in gold or silver, at the option of the soldier. The soldier would receive his slave or the money at the end of his service. Finally, recruits for
the duration of the war would also get 300 acres of land. After years of resistance and holding out for the best leverage for their services, lower-class Virginians were finally able to extract a huge windfall in return for their services
to the state. They would not only get enough land to vote, but also receive
money enough to establish themselves and even an enslaved Virginian to
make that land more productive. In doing so, legislators may have hoped
that, in addition to raising a more permanent army, they were also making a
judicious move to shore up what was clearly a tenuous alliance between
poor whites and wealthy slaveowners to resist the British invasion.[46]

Significantly, patriot leaders stopped short of making the most obvious
move of enlisting slaves rather than using them as part of the bounty to
enlist poor whites. James Madison, sitting as an observer in Congress,
thought the idea of giving enslaved Virginians away as bounties was "inhuman and cruel." Like Major Alexander Dick, with whom this essay began, Madison thought it would be much better if patriot leaders in Virginia took the more obvious step and allow enslaved Virginians to serve
themselves. "Would it not be as well to liberate and make soldiers at once
of the blacks themselves as to make them instruments for enlisting white
Soldiers?" he asked Joseph Jones. Madison thought that such a move
would "certainly be more consonant to the principles of liberty which
ought never to be lost sight of in a contest for liberty."[47]

Most of Madison's elite colleagues in the General Assembly, however,
were not prepared to move so far. The war had already chipped away at
the institution of slavery on a number of different fronts. Arming enslaved
Virginians and offering them their freedom would amount to a virtual
emancipation call across the state, Joseph Jones asserted. The offer would
also draw away "too many laborers from farms, so as to ruin many individuals." As it was, what they helped produce, Jones asserted, was "but
barely sufficient to keep us joging along with the great expence of the
war." Although the freedom of enslaved Americans in a contest for American freedom was an important object, Jones protested, it should be done
gradually so that they could find laborers to replace them, "or we shall
suffer exceedingly under the sudden revolution which perhaps arming
them wod. produce." Arming and freeing enslaved Virginians, then,
would deprive slaveholders of valuable property, drastically reduce the
number of laborers available, and create a new class of freemen who could

later claim a level of patriotism that would exceed that of their masters.[48] They would also be living examples of the principles that made slavery theoretically incompatible with the Revolution. Patriot leaders were not going to go that far, regardless of the costs.

As it turned out, the new recruiting law was undermined by a fresh British offensive in the state that began in January 1781. Increased militia call-ups and general protests against the new law ensured that it was ineffective. Few recruits actually stepped forward, and many counties refused to implement the recruiting law in sympathy with their militia, or in fear of what might happen if they did. Worse, though, when local officials forcibly tried to draft men, it caused widespread unease, discontent, and in some cases collective and violent resistance. As the British made further inroads into the state, Virginians fought among themselves. In the critical year of 1781, leaders in Virginia would reap what they had sown over the past years of war.[49]

Where local officials could or would carry out the draft, it followed predictable patterns. A sole surviving return of recruits and draftees from Loudoun County following the 1781 draft provides perhaps the fullest picture of how a wartime community dealt with a difficult and potentially divisive call for men. The Virginia Assembly had mandated that Loudoun, one of the largest counties in the colony, had to provide a substantial contingent of 119 recruits for the Continental Army. Despite the increased incentives offered for doing so, a mere fourteen men enlisted voluntarily. These men were all landless laborers in their mid-twenties and included one sailor and one "waggoner." Volunteer laborers included Frederick Sexton, an eighteen-year-old from Loudoun, Robert Bryan, a thirty-six-year-old also from Loudoun, and James Smith, a twenty-five-year-old from Montgomery County, Maryland, who subsequently deserted. Most volunteers who did step forward enlisted for the duration of the war, preferring to take advantage of the better bounty that included cash, an enslaved Virginian, and the promise of land. Although these men ranged in age from eighteen to forty-seven, none of them appeared on the 1784 personal property tax lists for Loudoun and were probably propertyless, transient, or both. All, it can be presumed, enlisted for the financial rewards.[50]

The vast majority of recruits on the Loudoun County list were draftees or substitutes for draftees. Forty-four drafted men hired substitutes after they were picked to serve. All of the substitutes waited until the draft took place to see whether they could secure even more bounty money from individuals desperate to avoid being dragged off for eighteen months of service. Seven men signed on as substitutes on the day of the draft. Thirty-nine men held out longer and, because of the temporary suspension of the draft in the county, were procured between March 26 and April 30. Again, these were generally men in need of cash to obtain a stake in society. Nineteen of these substitutes were from outside of the county—mainly from neighboring counties, but also from across the river in Maryland, including a "sailor" from Baltimore, and from as far away as

Pennsylvania, North Carolina, and Kentucky. Nineteen, or 43 percent of these substitutes were listed as laborers. The rest were mostly low-skilled tradesmen, including four tailors, three weavers, three shoemakers, a sailor, a wagonner, a butcher, and a "distiller." From the more highly skilled trades, there was a single blacksmith, a cabinetmaker, two coopers, and two fullers. Significantly, only four of these substitutes listed themselves as farmers—two from Loudoun and two others from outside the county. The average age of the substitutes from Loudoun was twenty-four, while the outsiders were of an average age of twenty-seven.[51]

Most middling farmers sought ways to avoid the draft. Some did all they could, for example, to find substitutes. However desperate they were, farmers in Loudoun did not turn to their sons or other kin to avoid the draft. Indeed, although farmers often sent relatives as substitutes for militia duty within the state, military duty in the Continental Army appeared too risky to send close relatives. None of the substitutes listed in the "Return" from Loudoun had the same names as those they replaced. Instead, middling farmers generally turned to men less well off than themselves. Thirteen of the men who hired substitutes can be identified on the tax lists of 1784, and, of them, five were slaveholders. One of the men, James Cleveland, a militia captain and Commissary of the Specific Tax in Loudoun, owned twelve slaves, fifteen horses, and forty-nine head of cattle in 1784. He hired one John Bevers (or Beavers), a twenty-one-year-old laborer from Cleveland's own neighborhood, who by 1784 owned no slaves, three horses, and three head of cattle. Similarly, Nathaniel Skinner hired Nicholas France from a nearby district. Although neither man owned any slaves by 1784, Skinner owned seven horses and twenty-six head of cattle, while France, listed as a shoemaker and about twenty-six years old in 1784, owned only two horses and three head of cattle.[52]

Far less information is available for the forty-eight men who were drafted but did not find substitutes. Most of these men were probably absent for the draft or failed to show up for the rendezvous. Only six draftees provided information about themselves, presumably the only draftees who actually made it to the rendezvous. Of these six, three were listed as laborers, one a weaver, and two farmers, and they ranged in age from nineteen to thirty-one.

The kind of recruits Loudoun officers managed to scrape together with offers of large bounties, with the coercion of the draft looming overhead, were not unlike those from other places in the state. In Culpeper, for example, another large county—and, like Loudoun, situated far from the vulnerable coasts—only seven men stepped forward voluntarily to fill the quota of 106 men. These included Enoch Cox, a nineteen-year-old shoemaker, and William Wedgroof, a nineteen-year-old free mulatto who lived in Culpeper town and engaged for the war. John Tim, also a Culpeper town resident, was a carpenter. None of these men owned land or appeared in the property tax records. Because of the lack of volunteers, ninety-nine divisions were subject to a draft. Of them, forty-six of the men drafted managed to find substitutes. The substitutes were generally needy men. Nine of the fourteen who actually appeared in the property tax records owned no slaves, and none of them owned more than two horses. Although they earned less from the state for stepping in as substitutes, they earned rich and more immediate rewards from their neighbors. Moreover, by stepping in as substitutes rather than volunteers, they also only had to serve eighteen months—the length of the tour of duty prescribed for conscripts.[53]

It was one thing to raise recruits, but it was something else altogether to get them into the army. The new levies from Culpeper County, the tax commissioner reported, would not budge until they had received their full bounty money. They became mutinous and refused to march to their rendezvous. In the end, of the fifty-three draftees who did not find substitutes, twenty-one never made it into the army. Eleven of the volunteers or substitutes also did not make it into the army, which meant that, of 106 men required from Culpeper, only seventy-four made it into the army, or 70 percent of the quota.

It is significant to note that Culpeper probably provided the highest proportion of its quota of Virginia's counties.[54] Likewise, Loudoun actually did quite well when compared to other counties. At first, some counties, divisions, and individuals evaded the draft in ways similar to previous acts of resistance. This time many did so with the aid of company or even field-grade officers who either agreed or felt compelled to help undermine the draft. Some divisions in Fairfax County, for example, sent men who included, according to the county lieutenant, Peter Wagener, "Invalids and altogether unfit to do the duty of Soldiers." Baron von Steuben complained that too many counties had drafted and recruited "little dwarfs and children," knowing full well that they would be returned.[55]

By late April, however, the intensity of resistance to the draft had risen dramatically. Henry Lee, an ex-Continental Army officer and commander of the Prince William militia, was determined to carry out the draft in his county. He proceeded to recruit, draft, and round up the forty-eight new soldiers needed from his county. Much to his frustration, however, many had taken drastic measures to avoid being sent to the army. Lee complained that of those recruited, "2 of whom cut off their fingers after the draft, 1 was discharged as being a Lunatick, 9 deserted & 1 remains in the County armed." In James City County, which lay between the York and James rivers, the county lieutenant, Nathaniel Burwell, stated that the draft had been held on Tuesday, April 17, but three days later the British occupied Williamsburg and Yorktown. Most of the recruits took the opportunity to flee. Some of them were captured by the British, while others "through choice" joined the British.[56]

The lengths to which eligible draftees in Prince William and James City counties went to avoid serving in the Continental Army presaged confrontation elsewhere in the state. Trouble began in the western part of the state when the county lieutenant of Augusta reported that he was forced to stop the draft because of threats from his militia. The contagion of violence against the draft laws spread through the western counties. After hearing about the success of the Augusta protest, militiamen from Rockbridge also put a violent end to local officials' attempts to draft them. As many as a hundred men invaded the county courthouse and stopped officials from carrying out the paperwork for the impending draft. Further north, in Hampshire County, more than 700 people reportedly launched a "dangerous insurrection" when local officers tried to draft soldiers for the Continental Army, while in the southern Piedmont county of Bedford, recalcitrant militia also banded together with draftees to defy local officials. Meanwhile, on the state's eastern frontier, riots broke out in Northampton and Accomack counties. In Accomack, local officials reported that upwards of 200 men "armed with Clubs" gathered to oppose the draft.[57]

In the end, collective violence or the threat of it helped undermine the draft in counties other than those that actually reported their problems to the state government. Major Thomas Posey later reflected that it was "obvious to everybody" that many local officials had either been "prevented" from drafting men or refused to draft men because of "an opposition of men in arms." William Davies wearily pointed to the inaction of many county officials when he told the Virginia General Assembly in November that "in many counties nothing has been done in this business."[58]

Thus, resistance, evasion, and collective violence crippled the search for soldiers in Virginia in the spring and summer of 1781. Even before the extent of recruiting problems had become clear, General Steuben complained that "the opposition made to the law in some counties, the entire neglect of it in others, and an unhappy disposition to evade the fair execution of it in all afford a very melancholy prospect." He was correct. Later in the year, when asked to fill out returns of soldiers raised under the recruiting act, only fourteen of seventy-three counties bothered to do so.[59]

As for the permanent army Washington wanted, in 1781 Virginia managed to find just 248 men who actually volunteered for three years or for the duration of the war. Even of these men, three remained in their counties, twenty-two absconded at some point after enlisting, and ten were refused by the Continental receiving officers, probably because they were unfit for duty. Officials reported that a total of 775 men were actually drafted into the service. Of these, at least 49 remained in their counties, 118 had absconded, and 48 had been refused for service. Thus, 39 volunteers and 560 draftees made it to their rendezvous points within Virginia. The state's recruiting act had called for raising 3,250 men. If all of the men who reached their rendezvous points stayed with the army, Virginia contributed a total of just 773 men, or a mere 24 percent of what the state was required to contribute to their Continental quota. Pressure from below thoroughly disabled mobilization for the regular army in 1781. Although repeated British invasions helped undermine the draft in Virginia, the militia's sometimes intense, sometimes passive, but persistent local resistance to state laws had brought recruiting to a standstill.[60]

Nor did white Virginians do much better in rallying themselves to the battlefield as militia. Resistance to militia call-ups actually intensified during the British invasion. Under the strain, some class resentments became glaring divides. In the midst of one British raid up the Potomac in the early summer of 1781, for example, the militia of the Northern Neck was called out to defend the vulnerable rivers. Instead, several militia members organized a barbecue in Richmond County to rally support among those who were fed up and unwilling to serve any longer. The leaders made class-based appeals to their friends and neighbors. One man told authorities that the ringleaders of the conspiracy declared "the Rich wanted the Poor to fight for them, to defend there property, whilst they refused to fight for themselves."[61]

The Richmond barbecue was in fact the tip of the iceberg. Significantly, perhaps the most intriguing aspect of Virginia's mobilization throughout the war, but especially in 1780–1781, is that, despite the immediate threat posed by both the British and enslaved Virginians, white Virginians failed to act in concert. As the British roamed freely across the state in May and June, many militia throughout Virginia actually rioted in protest against the draft for Continental soldiers *and* against militia call-ups. While Washington and Lafayette hurried to Virginia with the remains of the Continental Army in the hopes of trapping Cornwallis at Yorktown, white Virginians squabbled among themselves and protested against military service in the very face of the threat.

The end of the war did come at Yorktown, but only with an indifferent contribution from Virginians. Robert Honyman, who raced to Yorktown to see the showdown between Washington and Cornwallis, was disappointed with the small number of Virginia troops he found there. He believed that there were "but few" in the camp before York, and thought that no more than about 1,500 of the 15,000 troops he estimated he saw there were Virginia militia. Most, he reckoned, were French troops. Even the best estimates of the number of militia at Yorktown show that perhaps no more than 3,000 Virginia militia out of a potential 50,000 participated in some way, while 7,800 French troops, and more than 5,000 Continental troops—mainly from states north of Virginia—played the greatest role.[62]

Slavery and class, then, profoundly shaped mobilization for the Revolutionary War in Virginia, the most populous state in the Confederation and a critical theatre for the conflict in the latter stage of the conflict. In the first place, most middling and upper-class Virginians expected that only lower-class Virginians should serve in the Continental Army, and their recruiting drives and enticements were aimed at these groups. In turn, lower-class Virginians refused to be coerced into serving for the state, and almost all fought to secure the best deal they could in return for doing the bidding of others. The lowest classes of Virginians—indentured and convict servants and enslaved Virginians—were sometimes able to earn the ultimate reward for serving in the army, their freedom. Others hoped for a steady wage, held out for ever-increasing joining bonuses, or joined on a promise of land and independence after the war.

Slavery also caused or exacerbated other, often class-based, divisions among white Virginians and helped undermine mobilization in more profound ways. While a restive enslaved population kept many potential soldiers or militia at home, the ownership of slaves also proved a divisive issue during the war. Nonslaveholders, for example, resented the fact that more wealthy slaveholders either exempted themselves from service, could buy themselves out of service more easily, or would suffer less even if they had to serve in the militia because they had slaves to labor for them in their absence. Slavery exposed class divisions in Virginia, then, even while it contributed to creating them, and these divisions were exacerbated by the strains of wartime mobilization.

Although slavery played a significant role in the mobilization process, white racial solidarity was no protection against class divisions during Virginia's Revolutionary War. Indeed, white Virginians more often fought among themselves even in the face of the combined threat of British invasion and black insurgency. Late, and largely unsuccessful, efforts to offer enslaved Virginians as bounties to entice poor whites to enlist only highlight the desperation of patriot leaders to paper over class divisions to fill Virginia's militia and Continental regiments.[63]

Notes

I wish to thank Walter Sargent, John P. Resch, Richard Buel, and Wayne Bodle for their helpful comments at all stages in the preparation of this essay, and also Terry Bouton, Seth Cotlar, Matthew Dennis, Ron Hoffman, Woody Holton, Marjoleine Kars, Alan Taylor, Fredrika Teute, Peter Thompson, Peter Way, and the many participants at an Organization of American Historians panel in Memphis, April 2003, and at the Class & Class Struggles in North America and the Atlantic World, 1500–1820, Conference at the 320 Ranch in Montana, September 2003, for their insightful comments and informed discussion on a different version of this chapter. Parts of this chapter have also been used in a different guise in Michael A. McDonnell, "Class War? Class Struggles during the American Revolution," *William and Mary Quarterly*, 3rd ser., 63, no. 2 (April 2006): 305–440. My thanks to the Omohundro Institute of Early American History and Culture for allowing me to use this material here. I also wish to acknowledge my intellectual debt to and appreciation of the pioneering work of John Shy, which inspired my work in this field from the start.

1. Testimony of Vincent Redman, "Proceedings of a General Court Martial," June 18, 1781, Executive Papers, Library of Virginia (hereafter LiVi); Proceedings of the Fifth Virginia Convention, May 7, 1776, in William Van Schreeven, Robert Scribner, and Brent Tarter, eds., *Revolutionary Virginia: The Road to Independence*, 7 vols. (Charlottesville: University Press of Virginia, 1973–1983), 7:47; Pittsylvania County Petition, [June 19, 1781], Virginia Legislative Petitions, LiVi; Alexander Dick to the Speaker of the House, May 11, 1781, box 2, Executive Communications, LiVi.

2. See Michael A. McDonnell, "Popular Mobilization and Political Culture in Revolutionary Virginia: The Failure of the Minutemen and the Revolution from Below,"

Journal of American History 85, no. 3 (December 1998): 946–81.

3. For a full explication of my use of "class" and "class conflict" in this context, and an elaboration of many of the themes and issues raised in this essay, see Michael A. McDonnell, "Class War? Class Struggles during the American Revolution," *William and Mary Quarterly*, 3rd ser., 63, no. 2 (April 2006): 305–440.

4. James Titus, *The Old Dominion at War: Society, Politics, and Warfare in Late Colonial Virginia* (Columbia: University of South Carolina Press, 1991), pp. 4, 59, 80, 98–99; Edmund S. Morgan, *American Slavery, American Freedom: The Ordeal of Colonial Virginia* (New York: W. W. Norton, 1975), p. 340. This was standard colonial practice. See Don Higginbotham, "The Military Institutions of Colonial America: The Rhetoric and the Reality," in Don Higginbotham, ed., *War and Society in Revolutionary America: The Wider Dimensions of Conflict* (Columbia: University of South Carolina Press, 1988), p. 19; E. Wayne Carp, "Early American Military History: A Review of Recent Work," *Virginia Magazine of History and Biography* (hereafter *VMHB*) 94 (1986): 272.

5. Madison to William Bradford, November 26, 1774, in William T. Hutchinson and William M. E. Rachal, eds., *The Papers of James Madison*, 17 vols. (Chicago: University of Chicago Press, 1962–1991), 1:129–30; Peter H. Wood, "'Liberty is Sweet': African-American Freedom Struggles in the Years before White Independence," in Alfred F. Young, ed., *Beyond the American Revolution: Explorations in the History of American Radicalism* (DeKalb: Northern Illinois University Press, 1993), pp. 154, 160; Titus, *Old Dominion at War*, pp. 75–76.

6. Van Schreeven, *Revolutionary Virginia*, 3:406, 463, 466, 471, 476; William Walter Hening, ed., *The Statutes at Large: Being a Collection of all the Laws of Virginia, from the First Session of the Legislature, in the Year 1619*, 13 vols. (1809–1823; Charlottesville: University Press of Virginia, 1969), 9:27–35.

7. Mason to Martin Cockburn, August 5, 1775, Mason to George Washington, October 14, 1775, in Robert A. Rutland, ed., *The Papers of George Mason, 1725–1792*, 3 vols. (Chapel Hill: University of North Carolina Press, 1970), 3:245–46, 255–56; Gilmer to Charles Carter, July 15, 1775, Gilmer, Commonplace Book entry, [summer 1775], in R. A. Brock, ed., "Papers, Military and Political, 1775–1778, of George Gilmer, M.D., of 'Pen Park,' Albermarle County, Virginia," Virginia Historical Society, *Collections*, new ser., 6 (Richmond, Va., 1887), pp. 90, 91; Francis Willis to Robert Carter, July 19, 1775, Carter Family Papers, Virginia Historical Society (hereafter VHS).

8. For full details of the rise and fall of the minutemen in Virginia, see Michael A. McDonnell, "Popular Mobilization and Political Culture in Revolutionary Virginia," *Journal of American History* 85, no. 3 (December 1998): 946–81, and *The Politics of War: Race, Class, and Social Conflict in Revolutionary Virginia* (Chapel Hill: University of North Carolina Press for the Omohundro Institute of Early American History and Culture, 2007).

9. Hening, *Statutes at Large*, 9:216–17.

10. John Page to R. H. Lee, February 27, 1777, in Paul P. Hoffman, ed., Lee Family Papers, 1742–1795 (Microfilm Publication, Charlottesville, Va., 1966). For reports of recruiting problems, see John Smith, on behalf of the Frederick County Volunteers, to the House of Delegates, December 12, 1776, in "Virginia Legislative Papers," *VMHB* 18:29–31; December 31, 1776, January 2, 1776–March 11, 1782, Diary of Robert Honyman, Alderman Library, University of Virginia (microfilm) (cf. entries of April 10 and April 30, 1777); Pendleton to R. H. Lee, December 28, 1776, in David John Mays, ed., *The Letters and Papers of Edmund Pendleton, 1734–1803*, 2 vols. (Charlottesville: University Press of Virginia, 1967), 1:204; Patrick Henry to R. H. Lee, January 9, 1777, in H. R. McIlwaine, ed., *Official Letters of the Governors of the State of Virginia*, 3 vols. (Richmond: Virginia State Library, 1926–1929), 1:90; January 7, 1776, Nicholas Cresswell, *The Journal of Nicholas Cresswell* (London: Dial Press, 1925), p. 180.

11. Richard C. Bush, "'Awake, Rouse Your Courage, Americans Brave': Companies Raised in Northumberland County for the Virginia Continental Line, 1776 and 1777," *Bulletin of the Northumberland County Historical Society* 29 (1992): 7–10; Allason to Col.

Humphrey Brooke, September 9, 1777, "Letters of William Allason," *Richmond College Historical Papers* 2, no. 1 (June 1917): 168–69.

12. Hening, *Statutes at Large*, 9:12; *Virginia Gazette* (Purdie), August 8, 1777, supplement; *Virginia Gazette* (Purdie), September 5, 1777; March 3, 1777, Cresswell, *Journal*, p. 186; Washington to the President of Congress, May 13, 1777, in John C. Fitzpatrick, ed., *The Writings of George Washington from the Original Manuscript Sources, 1745–1799*, 39 vols. (Washington, D.C.: Government Printing Office, 1931–1944), 8:57; December 14, 1776, January 7, 1777, March 3, 1777, March 10, 1777, Cresswell, *Journal*, pp. 176, 180, 186, 187. The Assembly formalized the practice in May 1777, when its members allowed recruiting officers to enlist servants and apprentices, apparently without their masters' consent (see Hening, *Statutes at Large*, 9:275–76.)

13. *Virginia Gazette* (Purdie), September 12 and October 31, 1777.

14. Hening, *Statutes at Large*, 9:280, 454–55; Gerald W. Mullin, *Flight and Rebellion: Slave Resistance in Eighteenth Century Virginia* (New York: Oxford University Press, 1972), p. 133; Benjamin Quarles, *The Negro in the American Revolution* (Chapel Hill: University of North Carolina Press, 1961), pp. 56–57; Don Higginbotham, *The War of American Independence: Military Attitudes, Policies, and Practice, 1763–1789* (Boston: Northeastern University Press, 1983), pp. 395–97.

15. Washington to the President of Congress, April 12, 1777, in Fitzpatrick, *Writings of Washington*, 8:397; Patrick Henry to Richard Henry Lee, March 28, 1777, in McIlwaine, *Official Letters*, 1:129; "General Return," Executive Papers, LiVi; Returns of the 8th and 10th Regiments, dated April 10 and 12, 1777, Miscellaneous Revolutionary Collection, W. H. Cabell Papers, LiVi; Henry to Washington, March 29, 1777, in McIlwaine, *Official Letters*, 1:130; Henry to Charles Lewis, February 21 and March 15, 1777, Governor Patrick Henry Papers, LiVi; Charles H. Lesser, ed., *The Sinews of Independence: Monthly Strength Reports of the Continental Army* (Chicago: University of Chicago Press, 1976), 46); March 25, 1777, in H. R. McIlwaine, ed., *Journals of the Council of the State of Virginia*, 4 vols. (Richmond, Va., 1931–1967), 1:375–76, and, generally, March–April 1777, *passim*.

16. R. H. Lee to Jefferson, April 29, 1777, in Julian P. Boyd, ed., *The Papers of Thomas Jefferson*, 32 vols. (Princeton, N.J.: Princeton University Press, 1950–2005), 2:13–14; Washington to Patrick Henry, May 17, 1777, in Fitzpatrick, *Writings of Washington*, 8:77–78.

17. March 22 and March 29, 1777, Cresswell, *Journal*, pp. 189–90, 191; Jesse Lemisch, "Jack Tar in the Streets: Merchant Seamen in the Politics of Revolutionary America," *William and Mary Quarterly*, 3rd ser., 25 (July 1968): 371–407; Peter Linebaugh and Marcus Rediker, *The Many-Headed Hydra: Sailors, Slaves, Commoners, and the Hidden History of the Revolutionary Atlantic* (Boston: Beacon Press, 2001), esp. pp. 228–29, 235–36.

18. Hening, *Statutes at Large*, 9:275–80; August 29, 1777, Honyman Diary; Pendleton to William Woodford, June 28, 1777, in Mays, *Pendleton Papers*, 1:215; John Chilton to his brother [Charles Chilton?], August 11, 1777, in Keith Family of Woodburn, Fauquier Co., Papers, VHS.

19. John Chilton to his brother [Charles Chilton?], August 11, 1777, in Keith Family of Woodburn, Fauquier Co., Papers, VHS.

20. Pendleton to William Woodford, September 13, 1777, in Mays, *Pendleton Papers*, 1:224; September 2, 1777, in Jack P. Greene, ed., *The Diary of Landon Carter of Sabine Hall, 1752–1778*, 2 vols. (Charlottesville: University Press of Virginia, 1965), 2:1128.

21. September 1, 1777, Richmond County Order Book, no. 18, LiVi; July 7 and August 8, 1777, Carter, *Diary*, 2:1107, 1121; August 12 and September 9, 1777, Loudoun County Court Records, 1776–1783, LiVi; September 8, 1777, Mecklenburg County, Order Book 4, 1773–1779, LiVi.

22. January 6, 1778, Honyman Diary; *Virginia Gazette* (Purdie), November 1 (supplement) and November 28, 1777; *Virginia Gazette* (Dixon & Hunter), September 26, 1777; *Virginia Gazette* (Purdie), October 3 and October 31, 1777; *Virginia Gazette* (Purdie), October 3, 1777; Rutland, *Mason Papers*, 1:373n., cf. *Virginia Gazette* (Dixon &

Hunter), October 3, 1777; *Virginia Gazette* [Purdie], November 14, 1777. The *Virginia Gazette* (Purdie), of November 28, 1777, contained an advertisement for twenty men from Hanover, "draughts from the *Hanover* militia" for the 14th Regiment, who had failed to appear at the appointed time.

23. *Virginia Gazette* (Dixon & Hunter), September 5, 1777.

24. *Virginia Gazette* (Dixon & Hunter), September 5, 1777; December 14, 1776, January 7, 1777, March 3, 1777, March 10, 1777, Cresswell, *Journal*, pp. 176, 180, 186, 187.

25. Lesser, *The Sinews of Independence*, pp. 46–47, 54–55.

26. Pendleton to Woodford, November 29, 1777, January 2, 1778, in Mays, *Pendleton Papers*, 1:238–39, 240; November 26, 1777, in Worthington C. Ford et al., eds., *Journals of the Continental Congress, 1774–1789*, 34 vols. (New York: Johnson Reprint Corp., 1968), 9:967; Hening, *Statutes at Large*, 9:337–38, 342.

27. Hening, *Statutes at Large*, 9:339–40; Pendleton to Woodford, November 29, 1777, in Mays, *Pendleton Papers*, 1:238–39; Rutland, *Mason Papers*, 1:365, 369–72.

28. February 2, 1778, February 22, 1778, Honyman Diary.

29. February 24, 1778, Westmoreland County Court Orders, 1776–1786, LiVi; March 9, 1778, Northumberland County Order Book, 1773–1783, LiVi; Jefferson to Isaac Zane, February 26, 1778, in Boyd, *Jefferson Papers*, 2:175; *Journal of the House of Delegates*, November 18, 1778, f.70.

30. February 27, 1778, in McIlwaine, *Council Journal*, 2:93–94; Lund Washington to George Washington, March 11, 1778, Lund Washington Letters to George Washington, LiVi; April 14 and May 12, 1778, Loudoun County Court Records, 1776–1783, LiVi.

31. "Abstract of Men Raised under the Former Laws Passed for Raising Soldiers for the Continental Service—November 1782," *Virginia Military Records: From the Virginia Magazine of History and Biography, the William & Mary Quarterly, and Tyler's Quarterly* (Baltimore: Genealogical Publication Co., 1983), pp. 661–62; Lund Washington to George Washington, March 8, 1778, Lund Washington Letters to George Washington, LiVi; John Robert Sellers, "The Virginia Continental Line, 1775–1780" (Ph.D. diss., Tulane University, 1968), p. 291.

32. Washington to R. H. Lee, May 25, 1778, in Fitzpatrick, *Writings of Washington*, 11:452; cf. ibid., 438n.; Patrick Henry to Henry Laurens, June 18, 1778, in Hutchinson and Rachal, *Madison Papers*, 1:245; David Griffith to Leven Powell, June 3, 1778, in Robert C. Powell, ed., *A Biographical Sketch of Col. Leven Powell, including his Correspondence during the Revolutionary War* (Alexandria: G. H. Ramey & Son, 1877), p. 79; R. H. Lee to Jefferson, May 2 and May 3, 1778, in Boyd, *Jefferson Papers*, 2:176, 176–77. Cf. Baylor Hill to Theodorick Bland, May 5, 1778, Bland Family Papers, VHS. For a full discussion of lower-class resistance to draft laws in Virginia in the middle years of the war, see McDonnell, *Politics of War*, esp. chaps. 8–10.

33. March 12, 1779, Honyman Diary; Arthur Campbell to Patrick Henry, March 15, 1779, in W. P. Palmer et al., eds., *Calendar of Virginia State Papers and Other Manuscripts, 1652–1781, Preserved in the Capitol at Richmond*, 11 vols. (New York: Kraus Reprint Corp., 1968), 1:317; Pendleton to James Madison, September 25, 1779, in Mays, *Pendleton Papers*, 1:308–9.

34. David Jameson to Madison, September 20, 1780, in Hutchinson and Rachal, *Madison Papers*, 2:94; Pendleton to James Madison, September 25, 1780, in Mays, *Pendleton Papers*, 1:309.

35. Pendleton to Washington, May 21, 1778, quoted in Sellers, "The Virginia Continental Line," p. 289; Pendleton to George Washington, December 22, 1778, in Mays, *Pendleton Papers*, 1:276–77; Raleigh Colston to William Aylett, October 24, 1777, "Correspondence of Aylett," pp. 152–53.

36. Lesser, *The Sinews of Independence*, p. 33; Lists of Officers of the First Va. Regt., June 1, 1777, December 9, 1779, and May 1, 1780, Miscellaneous Revolutionary Papers, Box 3, LiVi; Jefferson to Washington, November 28, 1779, in Boyd, *Jefferson Papers*, 3:204–5; Robert K. Wright, Jr., *The Continental Army* (Washington, D.C.: Center of Military History, 1983), p. 147.

37. Higginbotham, *War of American Independence*, pp. 352–54.

38. Berkeley County Petition, [November 18, 1780], Virginia Legislative Petitions, LiVi.

39. For losses of enslaved Virginians in the midst of this invasion, see May 11 and May 27, 1781, Honyman Diary; Ira Berlin, *Many Thousands Gone: The First Two Centuries of Slavery in North America* (Cambridge, Mass.: Harvard University Press, 1998), p. 259; Richard Henry Lee to William Lee, July 15, 1781, Richard Henry Lee to George Washington, September 17, 1781, in James Curtis Ballagh, ed., *The Letters of Richard Henry Lee*, 2 vols. (New York, 1911), 2:242, 256; John Banister to Bland, May 16, 1781, in Charles Campbell, ed., *The Bland Papers: Being a Selection from the Manuscripts of Colonel Theodorick Bland, Jr.*, 2 vols. (Petersburg, Va.: E. & J. C. Ruffin, 1840, 1843), 2:68–70; John E. Selby, *The Revolution in Virginia, 1775–1783* (Williamsburg, Va.: Colonial Williamsburg Foundation, 1988), p. 275; Sylvia R. Frey, *Water from a Rock* (Princeton, N.J.: Princeton University Press, 1993), pp. 159, 167. For reports of slave revolts, see Palmer, *Calendar of Virginia State Papers*, 1:477–78; Patrick Lockhart to Governor Nelson, November 16, 1781, ibid., 2:604–5.

40. Elizabeth City County Petition, [March 8, 1781], Virginia Legislative Petitions, LiVi. Cf. James Innes to Jefferson, October [21?], 1780, in Boyd, *Jefferson Papers*, 4:55; General Assembly of North Carolina to Jefferson, February 14, 1781, ibid., 4:610–11.

41. Edmund Randolph, *History of Virginia*, ed. Arthur H. Shaffer (Charlottesville: University Press of Virginia, 1970), p. 285.

42. Proceedings of the Fifth Virginia Convention, May 7, 1776, in Van Schreeven, *Revolutionary Virginia*, 7:47; Pittsylvania County Petition, [June 19, 1781], Virginia Legislative Petitions, LiVi. Cf. Amherst County Petitions, [May 29, 1781], Virginia Legislative Petitions, LiVi.

43. Robert Lawson to Jefferson, May 1, 1781, George Skillern to Jefferson, April 14, 1781, in Boyd, *Jefferson Papers*, 5:583–84, 449–50; Charlotte County Petition, [May 26, 1780], Virginia Legislative Petitions, LiVi.

44. Joseph Jones to Madison, November 18, 1780, in Hutchinson and Rachal, *Madison Papers*, 2:182–83; Undated Bill, Legislative Department, Rough Bills, LiVi (brought to my attention—to my thanks—by Brent Tarter at the LiVi).

45. Joseph Jones to Madison, November 18, 1780, in Hutchinson and Rachal, *Madison Papers*, 2:183; Thomas Madison to William Preston, November 30, 1780, Preston Papers, VHS.

46. JHD, November 27, November 28, November 29, and November 30, 1780, pp. 47, 49–50, 51–52; Jones to Madison, November 18 and November 24, 1780, in Hutchinson and Rachal, *Madison Papers*, 2:183, 198; Pendleton to James Madison, November 27 and December 4, 1780, in Mays, *Pendleton Papers*, 1:324, 325; Thomas Madison to William Preston, November 30, 1780, Preston Papers, VHS; Hening, *Statutes at Large*, 10:326–37.

47. Madison to Jones, November 28, 1780, in Hutchinson and Rachal, *Madison Papers*, 2:209, 210. Maryland, in fact, did authorize the enlistments of enslaved men into the army in their legislative session in the fall of 1780. The following year, however, they stopped short of raising an entire regiment of enslaved Marylanders (see Hutchinson and Rachal, *Madison Papers*, 2:210n.; Quarles, *Negro in the American Revolution*, pp. 56–57).

48. Edmund Pendleton to Madison, January 1, 1781, Joseph Jones to Madison, December 8, 1780, in Hutchinson and Rachal, *Madison Papers*, 2:268, 232–33.

49. McDonnell, *Politics of War*, chap. 12.

50. Return of the Recruits raised for the County of Loudoun under the Act of Assembly for October 1780 . . . , [May 1, 1781], Auditor of Public Accounts Inventory, Militia Lists, 1779–1782, LiVi. Few documents like this list this still survive. The average age of the volunteers was twenty-six, whereas the average age of the substitutes residing in Loudoun was twenty-four and those living outside of Loudoun twenty-seven.

51. Return of the Recruits of Loudoun, LiVi. For an analysis of one group of recruits in neighboring Maryland in 1782, see Edward C. Papenfuse and Gregory A. Stiverson, "General Smallwood's Recruits: The Peacetime Career of the Revolutionary War Private," *William and Mary Quarterly*, 3rd ser., 30 (January 1973): 117–32.

52. Return of the Recruits of Loudoun, LiVi.

53. John R. Van Atta, "Conscription in Revolutionary Virginia: The Case of Culpeper County, 1780–1781," *VMHB* 92 (July 1984): 279.

54. Tax Commissioners of Culpeper County to Jefferson, Mar. 29, 1781, in Boyd, *Jefferson Papers,* 5:278; Van Atta, "Conscription in Revolutionary Virginia," *VMHB* 92 (July 1984): 279; William Preston to the Governor, March 15, 1782, in Palmer, *Calendar of Virginia State Papers,* 3:100; Robert Jones to William Davies, August 7, 1782, ibid., 3:252.

55. William Davies to Steuben, March 10, 1781, Peter Wagener to Jefferson, April 3, 1781, in Boyd, *Jefferson Papers,* 5:178, 335–36; Major Thomas Posey to William Davies, October 2, 1781, in Palmer, *Calendar of State Papers,* 2:521. Cf. William Davies to the General Assembly, November 26, 1781, War Office Records, LiVi.

56. "Abstract of Men Raised—November 1782," *Virginia Military Records,* p. 669; Nathaniel Burwell to William Davies, February 1, 1782, in Palmer, *Calendar of State Papers,* 3:50.

57. George Moffett to Jefferson, May 5, 1781, in Boyd, *Jefferson Papers,* 5:603–4; Jefferson to Samuel McDowell, April 23, 1781, Samuel McDowell to Jefferson, May 9, 1781, in Boyd, *Jefferson Papers,* 5:541–42, 621–22; Garret van Meter to Jefferson, April 11, 14, and 20, 1781, in Boyd, *Jefferson Papers,* 5:409–10, 455, 513–14; Lafayette to Nathanael Greene, June 3, 1781, in Stanley J. Idzerda, ed., *Lafayette in the Age of the American Revolution: Selected Letters and Papers, 1776–1790* (Ithaca, N.Y.: Cornell University Press, 1977), 5:162–65; Lafayette to Wood, June 4, 1781, James Wood Papers, Alderman Library, University of Virginia (photocopies); James Callaway to Jefferson, June 4, 1781, David Ross to William Davies, May 27, 1781, Recommendation of the Justices of the Peace for Bedford County, May 1781, in Boyd, *Jefferson Papers,* 6:77, 23–24n., 55; Commissioners for Collecting Taxes in Accomack County to Thomas Jefferson, May 15, 1781, George Corbin to Jefferson, May 31 and June 17, 1781, in Boyd, *Jefferson Papers,* 5:651–54, 6:44–47, 47n. For Northampton, see "Abstract of Men Raised—November 1782," *Virginia Military Records,* p. 666.

58. Major Thomas Posey to William Davies, October 2, 1781, in Palmer, *Calendar of State Papers,* 2:521; William Davies to the General Assembly, November 26, 1781, War Office Records, LiVi.

59. "Representation of the State of the Virginia Line" [May 28, 1781], enclosure in Steuben to Jefferson, May 28, 1781, in Boyd, *Jefferson Papers,* 6:31; General Return of Recruits, November 26, 1781, War Office Records, LiVi; "Abstract of Men Raised—November 1782," *Virginia Military Records;* A Return of the recruits raised for the County of Henry under the Act of Assembly of October 1780 . . . , September 30, 1782, LiVi.

60. "Representation of the State of the Virginia Line" [May 28, 1781], enclosure in Steuben to Jefferson, May 28, 1781, in Boyd, *Jefferson Papers,* 6:31; General Return of Recruits, November 26, 1781, War Office Records, LiVi; "Abstract of Men Raised—November 1782," *Virginia Military Records.*

61. Testimony of Vincent Redman, "Proceedings of a General Court Martial," June 18, 1781, Executive Papers, LiVi.

62. September 3, September 5, September 15, October 7, and October 15, 1781, Honyman Diary; Emory G. Evans, *Thomas Nelson* (Williamsburg, Va.: Colonial Williamsburg Foundation, 1975), pp. 117–18; William Davies to David Jameson, July 14, 1781, in Palmer, *Calendar of State Papers,* 2:219; Evans, *Thomas Nelson,* p. 118; William Davies to Thomas Nelson, September 15 and October 10, 1781, War Office Orders [Letters], August 15–November 1, 1781, LiVi; Thomas Nelson to William Davies, September 19, 1781, in McIlwaine, *Official Letters,* 3:59; James Clay to Thomas Nelson, September 13, 1781, Executive Papers, LiVi.

63. For an extended treatment of the impact of such class conflict on the course of the Revolution in Virginia, see McDonnell, *Politics of War,* esp. conclusion.

5

CLAIMING THEIR DUE

African Americans in the Revolutionary War and Its Aftermath

JUDITH L. VAN BUSKIRK

On May 18, 1821, John Harris stood in the Petersburg, Virginia, Superior Court to make a claim on the United States government. Whether his palms were moist or his heart beat faster, Harris was there to apply for a pension for his services during the Revolutionary War, some forty years before. The sight of court clerks, witness box, and judge might have inspired little confidence in Mr. Harris, an African American man seeking justice in a Southern court. Courthouses everywhere, but especially in the South at this time, were hardly associated with blind justice and fair outcomes for black men. Although Harris stood in the Petersburg courthouse thanks to federal legislation that rewarded veterans of the Revolution, he and thousands of other black men were accustomed to laws and promises that, by dint of their race, did not apply to them. One had only to harken back to the founding documents of the land for proof of this. So John Harris confronted an unpredictable situation as he waited for the proceedings to begin.

Despite intimidating circumstances, this sixty-nine-year-old "free man of color" dutifully recited what the federal government wanted to know. He joined the military struggle in 1778 and was immediately marched to Valley Forge, Pennsylvania, some 250 miles away. After surviving the rigors of that encampment, he went with Washington's army into New Jersey on a grueling march through stifling heat to cut off the British army retreat from Philadelphia to New York. He must have impressed his superiors because, at some part in this march, he was pulled out of the ranks and made to serve a young Virginia major by the name of James Monroe. Together, the two soldiers survived heat exhaustion and the British army at the Battle of Monmouth. If Harris provided details of the battle or further adventures of his service, the court clerk did not record them. Harris's narrative closes with his activities in 1780 when he was building barracks at Chesterfield Courthouse back in Virginia. Once Harris finished his story, Judge Richard Parker pronounced himself satisfied as to Harris's veracity and his financial need for a pension. This was enough for the soldier-turned-barrel-maker to collect eight dollars a month, the sum mandated by law for all privates in the Continental line during the Revolution.[1]

The federal government, during the presidency of John Harris's commanding officer, James Monroe, passed Revolutionary War pension legislation in 1818 that gave support to veterans of the Continental line who served at least nine consecutive months and could prove financial distress. In 1832, Congress extended the benefit to all officers and enlisted men in the state militias as well, regardless of their financial situation, who served a sum of at least six months during the war. In both cases, a national scandal erupted after each bill's passage, necessitating regulations to stem fraud and deception on the part of some applicants. Despite such start-up problems, some 60,000 veterans received pensions for their service in the Revolutionary forces. Among the thousands are hundreds of African American men like John Harris who left testimonies of their participation in the American Revolution as well as paperwork relating to their applications. These sources provide a moving picture (in both an emotional and cinematic sense) of the veterans' lives from the hopes associated with their enlistment to the challenges of their old age in a republic that was keen to acknowledge the services of the old vets of '76. The 1818 pension records reveal a fair, dispassionate process on the federal level, where race is seemingly preempted by service performance and legislative stipulations that applied to every applicant. This operation is all the more remarkable because it carried out its mandate in a society that increasingly vilified people of color. By the 1832 legislation, however, African American veterans confronted a much less accommodating pension office whose regulations and unwritten rules made it harder for black men to obtain their due. However daunting the system turned out to be, these veterans were the men who brought down Burgoyne and Cornwallis. In approaching the U.S. government years later, these old soldiers surveyed the terrain, secured allies, and persevered when confronted with defeats. Three hundred African American pensioners, largely forgotten, will tell us the story. They began with high hopes.[2]

Why African Americans Fought

In a country that denied basic civil liberties to free and enslaved African Americans alike, individuals joined the Continental Army, state troops, or local militia for a variety of reasons. But fifty years later, as old men, the veterans often narrowed their motives to one cause—liberation. Samuel Bell, an eighty-three-year-old free black man from North Carolina, spoke of liberation in a social rather than a personal sense. He summarized his complex emotions when he told the Robeson County court that "he enlisted in the service of the United States because he believed it was his duty to support his countrymen in arms in achievement of their independence," which was generally understood to mean liberation from British tyranny. Bell's use of pronouns is instructive. By saying "his" countrymen in arms, Bell claimed membership in his integrated unit and the arduous endeavor that culminated in independence. The state government of North Carolina certainly supported a black man's sanguine expectation of full citizenship by stipulating that *all* men between the ages of sixteen and fifty had to serve in the militia. Unlike its neighbors to the north and south, North Carolina did not distinguish between white and black men when it came to militia service. But whatever civic expectations he harbored at enlistment, Bell found them dashed by the ensuing years. In 1833, he speaks of "their" independence, a realization that full life-and-limb engagement in the struggle did not result in full civil rights for people like him in the war's aftermath.[3]

Enslaved men were motivated by a more personal definition of liberation than the broader civic definition of Bell's pension application. Slaves were one crucial step behind Bell: liberation from slavery had to precede full citizenship. Their concept of liberation was tied directly to servitude. Richard Rhodes, an enslaved Rhode Islander, enlisted "in the black regiment so called to obtain his freedom." Ichabod Northup signed up with the same regiment as Rhodes, thus acquiring "his freedom by his service in the army." Northup was born into slavery, and when his chance for liberation came at age thirty-five, he did not hesitate. Approximately 200–250 other African American men joined Rhodes and Northup in this unique Rhode Island regiment, for a time largely peopled by Rhode Island's black men. These enslaved men grabbed the opportunity of freedom provided by the Rhode Island assembly in February 1778, when, hard-pressed to fill its army quotas, the legislators passed a law that stipulated that "every able bodied Negro, mulatto, or Indian man slave" who enlisted for the war's duration and passed muster, would be freed. Masters who released their slaves would be paid as much as $400 with funds provided by the Continental Congress. Worry over the state's ability to fill quotas was not the only reason for such an extraordinary offer. Since December 1776, the British had occupied Newport, Rhode Island's major seaport, and put out the word that any slave owned by a rebel need only enter the British lines to be a freeman. Or, to put it another way, as one Rhode Islander did in 1821, Rhode Island was the "seat of war" for several years and had to find a way "to assure the fidelity of the slaves to the country." Aside from state-guaranteed freedom after the war, these recruits had the opportunity of serving in a unit overwhelmingly composed of black men. Although officered by whites, these new soldiers were free and working in an African American environment instead of being one of the isolated few in a white regiment.[4]

New York, Connecticut, and Maryland emulated Rhode Island and offered similar inducements to enslaved men, though the recruits did not enter exclusively black regiments. Other states, like Massachusetts and Virginia, considered fielding all African American regiments, but the idea went nowhere. Although regiments of armed black men induced fear, smaller units (companies) of men of color were deemed acceptable and effective entities, particularly in New England. Edward Sands enlisted in a company of blacks in Colonel Joseph Vose's First Massachusetts Regiment. Caesar Shelton, born in Africa but residing in Bridgeport, Connecticut, at time of enlistment, joined an all-black company in the Fourth Connecticut. Peter Jennings, of Providence, Rhode Island, recalled that in 1776 he signed up with "the fifth Regiment of Artillery of Blacks in the Continental Line." These men enlisted in all-black companies, a fact that they need not have mentioned in their pensions a half-century later. That they specifically indicated their units as such is an indication that they were proud of their units and that all-black companies might have been an inducement to enlist.[5]

Legislatures paved the way, but black men were the ones to negotiate with masters and neighbors on the subject of substituting for drafted white men. As early as the spring of 1777, state legislatures condoned what their white citizens were inclined to do anyway—namely, find another man to take their place in the ranks. Freemen like Jacob Francis could earn some money (he received seventy dollars on one occasion) by fulfilling white men's obligations. Other substitutes won their freedom by relieving masters of their patriotic responsibilities. William Hinton, a slaveholder, signed up for a five-year hitch in the Virginia Navy only to fall ill after one year. Hinton's slave, Lewis, took his master's place and saw action against a British schooner and, later, the British fleet. As a result of his efforts, Lewis was freed by his master at the end of the war. In another part of Virginia, Rolling Jones, a white farmer, signed his name to enlistment papers during a "drunken frolic." As the fog lifted from Jones' brain the next morning, the sickening feeling in the pit of his stomach expanded as he realized what he had done. His slave, Tim, bailed him out and became a witness to such historic battles as Camden and Yorktown. At the end of the war, Tim Jones had gained his freedom but lost a leg. In Rhode Island, London Hazard, an enslaved man, made a career out of substituting on short militia duty for various members of his master's family and neighbors as well. Black substitutes permitted white masters to continue making a living. The freedom of one slave was a small price to pay for uninterrupted earning potential through the eight years of war.[6]

Along with the prospect of freedom and bounty money, some men entered the service because personal commitments induced them to go. In Massachusetts, Samuel Dunbar was one of six brothers who fought on the American side. Other African American men followed their masters into the war, though whether by free choice or by coercion is not always evident in the pension. Joseph Johnson simply stated that he enlisted in Captain James Rosekrans's company, fought in Sullivan's Campaign, and was discharged at the end of the war. The government rejected his pension application because muster rolls indicated that he deserted in 1780. The soldier later explained to the government that his captain was his master's son. When Captain Rosekrans lost his sanity and was discharged in 1780, Joseph Johnson left the company to take his master's son home. Perhaps he was ordered to do so and never returned or perhaps he made a decision to decamp with the man who had shared his childhood, an indication that he felt some affection for the white man.[7]

Whether moved by money, Revolutionary rhetoric, or future hopes, some black men might have been coerced into enlisting or substituting. African Americans in the loyalist claims often talk of being "compelled" or "obliged" to take up arms for the Americans. Of course, it behooved a loyalist applying for aid from the British government to characterize the military service with the Americans as being forced. It likewise made sense for a Continental Army veteran to emphasize free choice in applying for an American government pension.[8]

Black and white men shared many of the same motivations for enlistment in that they saw their best opportunity in the military. Poor white immigrants joined the Pennsylvania line in significant numbers. One soldier in five joined the New Jersey line as a substitute for more-affluent townsmen.[9] Adventure, camaraderie, passion for the Revolution's ideals, hope for a better future, poverty—all these inducements played on black and white men alike. But, with the exception of a poor apprentice who wanted to part from his master, white veterans could not begin to appreciate the high stakes experienced by men enslaved for life. Laws opened the way for black participation in the war, but the men themselves had to make the decision. They had to calculate the odds that state laws would be honored after the war, that masters would live up to their word, that they would survive to reap the benefits. None of these eventualities was a foregone conclusion when African American men made their marks on enlistment papers.

Military Experiences

Evidence of racism aside, the pension records reveal strikingly similar war experiences for white and black soldiers. The pension system itself accounted for much of this similarity in that it asked for specific information: unit, time enlisted, and time and manner of leaving the service. As the War Department gained experience with fraudulent applications, it asked for more information: officers, battles, property schedules, and supporting testimonies from fellow veterans, clergymen, and neighbors. The government was not interested in stories, however riveting, but in processing an overwhelming number of applications. John Roe's application is representative. A veteran of the Second Virginia, he served under Captain William Taylor and participated in the Battles of Monmouth, Stony Point, and Yorktown. Roe begins and ends with the place-names. He does not elaborate on what he saw, what he did, or how he felt. Yet he participated in two major battles (the battles most frequently cited by African American veterans) as well as a famous surprise attack at Stony Point in which a small number of soldiers, singled out for that service, shocked the British out of occupying the Hudson Highlands.[10]

Black and white pensioners tell remarkably similar stories. All veterans tended to label the great patriot victories with the names of the defeated British general. Before the history books assigned place-names to identify these battles, the veterans had personalized them with "the taking of Burgoyne" (Saratoga) or "the capture of Cornwallis" (Yorktown). Humble soldiers were, of course, an integral part of the fall of these great men. One notable exception to the similarities of white and black pension depositions is the number of Washington sightings. African Americans rarely mention him.[11]

While all soldiers, both black and white, marched long distances, participated in battles, and shared gnawing hunger, the African Americans' skin color made for experiences that were unique to these men. One might expect that black soldiers suffered from racist treatment within the army or militia, but such evidence in the pension records is subtle at best. The path to a life-transforming pension subsidy ran through a white-dominated local court and white civil servants in Washington. It would not behoove a black veteran to relate instances of racial prejudice on the part of whites. Caesar Shelton, a Connecticut man, went about as far as a black veteran could go in describing the racist behavior on the part of his white comrades. Although he adopted the family name of his master, Caesar Shelton explained that, in the army, he was called "Caesar Negro or Caesar Nig."[12]

Most African American veterans were not this explicit in pointing out the problems within their regiments. Rather, many related that they served as waiters to white officers without noting that their skin color had anything to do with this kind of service. In none of these cases did the veterans serve their fathers or brothers as some young white boys did in the military. Some veterans did, however, note their color as a reason they were treated differently from whites. William Wanton, from Rhode Island, explained that as a "coloured man," he could not be enrolled in the militia, but he could serve as a substitute. Pomp Magus, of Massachusetts, related that "being a man of colour, myself and some others were left on fatigue." Other veterans felt the need to explain why they did not immediately assume combat positions in their companies. James Hawkins from Virginia explained that, "being a coloured man, he was taken as a waiter to Major Crughan." Joel Taburn, a North Carolinian, noted that "being very young and a person of colour, he was first taken and employed as a servant to the officers," but a short time later was put in the ranks.

Southern states, with most of the African American population, were particularly loath to put guns into black men's hands. When the Virginia legislature admitted free blacks into the state's companies in 1777, it stipulated that these "free mulattoes . . . shall be employed as drummers, fifers, or pioneers." Officially, the black men of Virginia could either play an instrument or dig a ditch. South Carolina eventually instituted a similar law. Although North Carolina's 1777 militia act demanded that all men had to serve, the state passed laws early in the war disarming persons of color.

Despite these restrictive laws, the pension applications indicate that black men found their way into battle. Whether as line soldiers or as drummers and fifers providing crucial communication links during battle, black men served in the line of fire. Seventy-five percent of the Southerners in this sample noted specific battles in their pensions compared to a little less than half of the New England and Mid-Atlantic veterans. (Many veterans did not mention battles although their units figured prominently in certain actions of the war.) While being present at a battle does not necessarily mean a combat position, evidence of a wound indicates that the veteran was likely in the thick of battle. More Southerners noted being wounded than soldiers from north of the Mason Dixon line.[13]

Northern states, too, had a tendency to place black recruits in support positions. In fact, the overall percentage of black soldiers in this sample who admit servant status at some point in their service is the same for Northerners as for Southerners (10 percent). Despite the surprising lack of regional variation on the servant issue, the possibility of waiting on an officer, driving a wagon, or digging a trench was higher for African American recruits than for their white counterparts.

At the end of the Revolutionary War, most African American veterans could probably say that, to use Tom Paine's words, they "deserved the love and thanks of man and woman." Of the men in this sample who noted enlistment and discharge dates, the average black veteran served a little over four years in the fighting forces of the Revolution, a longer term than the average white soldier. Certainly, every black man who served in the Revolution had a reasonable expectation that his life would be better after the war. The pension records show, however, that the Revolution's black veterans did not enjoy the same fruits of victory as whites. These differences reflect not only the lower status held by most blacks at the time of the Revolution, but also the effects of increased racism following the war, especially in the nineteenth century, when opportunities for black veterans to improve their lives dwindled.[14]

Measures of opportunity, such as literacy, mobility, and property, all indicate that white veterans had a distinct advantage over their African American counterparts. Only 16 percent of the black veterans of this study could sign their name, and those signatures reveal a shaky, tentative hand.

New England produced most of the literate veterans. Twenty-one percent of black Yankees could sign their names compared to only 11 percent each for the Southern and Mid-Atlantic states. Illiterate African Americans were prey to tireless shysters who took advantage of these vulnerable people in making off with their pension benefits.[15]

The difference between the geographic mobility of black veterans and that of white veterans is striking. Three-quarters of the black men in this study remained in the state where they enlisted as compared to approximately half of whites. If they did move out of state, it was usually to other seaboard states. Only 12 of 300 veterans moved to a frontier area such as Ohio, Indiana, Kentucky, or Tennessee. Although the Northwest Ordinance of 1787 declared that all territory north of the Ohio River would be free of slavery, states in that area concocted laws to keep African Americans away from their borders. In addition to concern over racial hostility toward them as strangers, African Americans may also have preferred to stay where they could find other people of color in familiar neighborhoods. Only 12 of 300 pensioners ended up in a major city. Even in New England, the most liberal area of the country for blacks, poor African Americans recently emancipated would often be warned out of towns they moved to for fear that they would eventually live at public expense. As a result, most African American Revolutionary War veterans stayed in familiar surroundings.[16]

Another reason for the lack of African American mobility was their poverty. John Harris, who served with James Monroe during the war, lived on the outskirts of Dinwiddie, Virginia, with two small broken pots, one old basket, one old table, two old chests, and some coopering tools. Of the black veterans whose property was valuated in their applications, Harris was one of the poorest. Most inventories were so paltry that no dollar figure was affixed to them, and the belongings of the majority of African American pensioners whose property merited such a figure were valued at less than fifty dollars. Only a handful of pensioners in this study owned a house, most of whom were in New England, and they were described as "shabby . . . old . . . small . . . one story." White veterans, on the other hand, averaged property holdings of $129 and showed much more debt than African Americans, an indication that they could get credit more readily. Examining the inventory lists of white veterans, one finds items that never appear in black households: teacups, saucers, and looking glasses. Blacks had knives and forks, but no spoons; they had buckets, but no washtubs. Whites had more of everything—more animals, more tools, more furniture. The 1818 pension law required that all recipients be "in reduced circumstances," but, even in indigence, men of color were poorer than their white counterparts.[17]

The poverty of African American veterans is highlighted in a December 1818 letter written by David Howell, a district judge in Rhode Island. In the wake of the 1818 pension law, there were many abuses of the system, particularly with respect to applicants hiding their property to qualify. In response, the federal government stipulated that the local courts would have to verify a list of property to be submitted to the pension office. All past cases had to be revisited. Judge Howell was irritated. It was through his court that the veterans of Rhode Island's black regiment were processed. Howell had already stated that these veterans were sufficiently poor and for this reason saw no need to call on these men to prove what was already apparent. "It has been a very unpleasant circumstance to me," complained Howell, "that I have been called on for proof of the poverty of so many Negroes whose almost universal poverty is notorious among us here." Identifying them as a group apart, Howell still exhibited some sympathy for these veterans, who, according to his lights, deserved to be left in peace. So even among Revolutionary War veterans, the most cherished characters in the nation's memory, skin color denoted the poorest of the poor.[18]

Experiences with the Pension Office

In proving their service, black and white veterans shared common problems. At forty to fifty years' remove from the events in their declarations, the old men could not, at times, recall dates or could only remember a happening in relation to some other event—for example, "It was the spring after the taking of Burgoyne" or "We arrived there when they were gathering oats." Veterans jumbled the order of events and sometimes had to receive help from their fellow comrades in summoning up memories. They lost discharges, had difficulty finding witnesses, and received the dispiriting news that certain work performed during the war was not deemed sufficiently military in nature to merit a pension.

As with their services in the war, African American veterans also labored under their own unique set of problems with the pension process. Name issues, slave status, and the vulnerability brought by local prejudice were additional hurdles to negotiate. In each of these challenges, however, the African American veterans demonstrated their determination to claim a greater civic role assisted by a white cast of characters who either served with them in the war or lived with them in a neighborly capacity over several years.

In applying for a pension, many African Americans had to cope with complications concerning the basic signifier of identity—their name. Once set free from enslavement, African Americans often shed as much of their old status as possible, including their masters' names. Consequently, the name found on the muster rolls was not necessarily the current identity of the veteran. Some men adopted the names of their fathers at the end of the war. Cuff Cousins enlisted under the name of his master, but, once "freed by the laws of the state" of Massachusetts, he recovered his father's surname and became Cuff Tindy.[19]

Some African American men were encouraged by their officers to change their names. When Ben Roberts applied for a pension in 1818, he had to explain that he enlisted as Benjamin Black, "a name by which he was then called." His captain, Elijah Humphrey, suggested that he change his name, and so dropped "Black" in favor of "Simmons." After the war, Ben learned that his father's name was "Roberts," a name the veteran owned for the rest of his life.[20]

Joseph Johnson's identity issues were even more labyrinthine than the others. While never identifying himself as a slave, Johnson had lived since childhood in Henry Rosecrans's household. Although his father's name was Thomas Peters, Joseph was called only by his first name. Rosekrans's son asked Joseph to enlist in his company as a substitute for one Thomas Johnson. "I recollect that an officer took hold of my hand," said Joseph, "and made me write my name that I would serve during the war and that I would be true to my country." Despite the fact that he was "made" to write down his name, he was known in the company as Joseph Johnson "on account (as I suppose) of my having taken Johnson's place." After the war, Joseph moved around and eventually encountered "a man from Litchfield" who took to calling him "Tom." When word got out that "Tom" had served with Major James Rosekrans during the war, Joseph Johnson became "Thomas Rosekrans," ending his life with both his master's and his officer's name.[21]

In adopting surnames, the African American community claimed their right to identify themselves, thereby chipping away at the obstacles to full civic participation in their communities. And whether taking a father's name or an officer's name, these veterans, along with newly freed African Americans in general, did more than reject slavery or claim civic rights when they adopted surnames. They proclaimed that they were members of a family, that they belonged to one another and not to some outsider, and that there was a moral violation in splitting up parents and children.

Although black veterans chose their own surnames to identify themselves, local courts often fixed them with another identifier when they came to claim a pension—their race. This worked in only one direction, as whites were never labeled as such, their names sufficing to designate them. When "John Harris, a free man of colour," entered the Prince George County Courthouse in Virginia, it is highly unlikely that he himself stated the obvious about his appearance. The court clerk, however, found it necessary to label him as such.[22] The African American pension applicants could not have but realized that race was always pertinent to their condition, and so when they cast about to find fellow veterans to testify on their behalf, they overwhelmingly chose white men. At times, these white supporters demonstrated ingrained racism when talking about their black neighbors. One of the white men who supported Caesar Shelton's pension application characterized this veteran as "an industrious and good Citizen for a Black Man." A white supporter of Isaac Perkins, a North

Carolina veteran, claimed that Perkins would never have falsified his financial situation, for, "though a man of *Colour,* we do believe him to be too honest in principal to practice anything like a fraud." These white supporters were all the more notable because they had to skirt their unapologetically racist views to identify black veterans as members of the community who deserved respect and a pension. The camaraderie of the war prevailed over the entrenched views of black men's inferiority and untrustworthiness.[23]

More representative, however, of the support depositions were white veterans who praised their old comrades with no racist qualifiers. The black men were "industrious," "good soldiers," "faithful." Aside from complimentary qualities, white veterans could enhance a black comrade's deposition. Pomp Magus, an African American veteran from Massachusetts, recited the bare bones of this three-year stint in the Revolutionary War. Perhaps his eleven-month ordeal as a prisoner-of-war in British-occupied New York City was too painful or too shameful to resurrect, because he makes no mention of it in his first deposition. It is his white comrade, Asa Hart, who not only tells of their joint confinement, but also relates how Magus afforded him "much assistance" while imprisoned. Another New Englander, Prince Crosley, experienced resistance from white residents when he moved his house to a new location. It was a Revolutionary War captain who told the protesting whites "that Prince had been one of the Revolutionaries, an old warrior, and deserved to live among folks." His service in the Revolution seems to have trumped racial prejudice, because it appears that Crosley succeeded in moving.[24]

With declarations of their service duly notarized by a local court and depositions from neighbors, local notables, and old veterans, the African American applicants waited for word from Washington. Despite the fact that race directly followed an African American's name in most court documents and racism was rife in the land, a man's race seemed to have had little effect on the pension administrators of the 1818 act. The rejection rate for white veterans is higher than that of African Americans (8 percent versus 3 percent). This surprising finding could be due to the cases of fraud resulting from the 1818 act. It was a national scandal that so many veterans lied about their wealth. Black men did not have to lie about their poverty. It could also be that black men were less likely to hoodwink the system because the consequences of such action would be doubly hard for a black man. In a society riddled with racial prejudice and double standards, this seemingly fair treatment stands as a beacon in an otherwise unfair and racist world. Perhaps fellowship in the war trumped skin color. At least during the first general pension legislation in 1818, there were still many veterans in society and government who saw firsthand the significant contributions of black soldiers. Just as the Revolutionary War captain defended Crosley's right to live where he wanted, thousands more veterans could remind their intransigent neighbors of the undeniable service contributed by veterans during the war. While a good number of veterans still lived, the general culture might have been more tolerant with respect to these old, black men whose age made them less threatening to the white community.

A less sanguine explanation of the rejection rates in the 1818 cohort is found in the legislation itself. The pension act required a veteran to tell his story to the local court "and on its appearing to the satisfaction of the said judge that the applicant served in the Revolutionary War, he [the judge] shall certify and transmit the testimony in the case . . . to the Secretary of the Department of War." The process, then, included a threshing operation at the local level that may well have turned away more blacks than whites. We do not know how many black and white men were told to go home. The only evidence we have is from one African American veteran who explained how it happened to him. James Weeks served more than three years in New York units during the war. When he approached his local county court, the judge told him he could not assist the veteran, having no copy of the legislation on his person. The judge palmed off the sixty-six-year-old veteran to another judge, who declined to assist him because Weeks did not have the money to pay for the processing of his application. Beyond that technicality, the judge discouraged him from making any further application. Five years later, Weeks tried again, and this time his paperwork reached "the seat of government," which deemed him worthy to join the pension roll.[25]

However discouraging the local climate, once an application reached Washington, D.C., the pension clerks under the 1818 act behaved like true bureaucrats, authorizing pensions according to the evidence presented. Presence on a muster roll or the possession of a discharge from the war period were both considered golden evidence. If such "direct proof" were not available, "two disinterested witnesses" were needed to testify to the veteran's service. There was, then, some room for a judgment call on the part of the pension office bureaucrats. It appears that these government clerks exercised this flexibility with astounding color-blind impartiality, at least for the 1818 cohort. By 1832, the world had changed such that African American veterans had to clear new obstacles to obtain a pension.[26]

The 1832 Experience

The new 1832 pension legislation broadened the field of potential applicants by admitting those who served in the militia and state lines, provided they served a total of at least six months during eight years of war. The poverty requirement was dropped. (The 1818 law considered only Continental army veterans who served at least nine consecutive months and could prove indigence.) The amount of the pension varied according to rank and length of service. A veteran who served two years or more received full pay for life according to his rank. All who served between six months and two years received their annuities in proportion to their lengths of service.[27]

Under the new legislation, former African American militiamen, as well as the small number of economically solid black men who were barred by the 1818 poverty requirement, could apply for a benefit. While Congress widened the field, the pension office created regulations that made it more difficult for African American veterans to receive a pension. The 1818 and 1832 regulations stipulated that those who worked for the army through any kind of civil contract were ineligible. Examples were provided: "clerks to commissaries and to shopkeepers etc., teamsters, boatmen, etc." The rule affected black veterans more than it did whites because black men were far more likely to be ordered into support jobs like commissary duty or service to officers. If muster lists could not be found— a more likely occurrence in 1832 because militia lists were generally not preserved—the assumption was that the applicant fell under the "civil contract" stipulation and so was ineligible, no matter how many support depositions he had that said otherwise.[28]

Whereas the "civil contract" stipulation was printed in the act's official regulations, other practices of the pension office were not. Absent in the 1832 act or regulations was the new unwritten rule affecting men who were servants during their military service. These men did not fall under the civil contract. The 1818 bureaucrats rejected both white and black men who worked as servants to officers usually on the basis of age. An eleven-year-old, argued the office, would never be mustered into a unit. But once these youth had attained manhood, the practice in the army varied according to one's skin color. White boys of military age usually became regular soldiers, but black men of comparable years often remained as servants or served some part of their enlistment as servants. What did the pension office do with such applicants? In 1818, it gave these black men pensions; the office did not penalize adult males who enlisted in the services and were then ordered into servant duty. In 1832, with militia muster records largely nonexistent, the office rejected veterans with such a record. All those black veterans who were rejected because of servant status fell under the 1832 legislation. As in the case of "civil contracts," the system did not set out to purposely discriminate against African Americans, but the net result was a higher hurdle for black veterans.

While the servant issue could work against white veterans as well, the last of the pension office policies addressed only black men. In 1832, the pension office refused pensions to any black man who enlisted while still enslaved. This proviso appears in neither the 1832 legislation nor the act's regulations. In 1818, veterans who enlisted while enslaved received pensions. In 1832, enslaved status served as grounds to disqualify black men.

Perhaps these stipulations help explain why the rejection rate for African American applicants is significantly higher than that of white men in 1832. That the rate went up is no surprise. A half-century after the war, memory further failed, the pool of veterans who could support an application dwindled, and militia rolls were harder to obtain than the Continental Army records. In 1818, whites experienced more rejection, but in 1832 the rejection rate for African American applicants was more than double that of white applicants (31 percent versus 13 percent).[29]

By 1832, the pension office often used both slave status and job type to reject black men. Peter Nash suffered just such a double-stroke against his pension. Nash joined his master in 1778 to guard the Connecticut coast. He initially served as a waiter but was so well respected that he also acted as a private, manning the field piece on the boat whenever the need arose. The pension office rejected Nash's application at first because he "was a slave at the time the duty was performed." The office turned a blind eye to a Connecticut law that exempted any two men who could provide a substitute of any color. Elsewhere in a letter from the pension office, Nash's service was disqualified because the office found one of the support depositions to have claimed that Nash was a waiter. As the letter stated, that "description of service was not contemplated in any act." Nash's advocate fired back that the pension office's version was a "mistake." He reminded the pension office that there was more than one support affidavit and that one of the veterans pointed out that Nash was "usually attached to the field piece," putting him in the center of the action during any military engagement. Such clarification was in vain. Peter Nash, an active participant in the defense of his state, was denied a pension. The office had adhered to its rules and procedures.[30]

Although there are other cases of this sort in the pension records, one case in particular highlights a clear chronology in the shifting reasons for denying a black man a pension. In the case of Primus Hall, however, J. L. Edwards, the commissioner of pensions, met formidable opponents in the persons of Hall and his attorney, Reuben Baldwin. The story begins with Hall's deposition in 1835. He enlisted in 1776 in the Fifth Massachusetts under Thomas Nixon and fought in the battles for New York City as well as at Trenton and Princeton. Having fulfilled his service requirement after Trenton, he stayed on for six more weeks at the "earnest request" of General Washington. Honorably discharged in early 1777, he enlisted later in that year on a three-month tour of duty that saw him at "the surrender of Burgoyne." At that battle, he caught his captain, Samuel Flint, when the officer was shot and "set him down against a tree" when it was obvious that the wound was mortal. Another three-month hitch took Hall to Rhode Island, where, "with another coloured man," he was detached to a French corps of sappers and miners. Finally, in 1781 and 1782, he served as a steward to Colonel Timothy Pickering and assisted him in accounting for the contents of British military chests after the Battle of Yorktown. While in Virginia, his pocketbook containing his freedom papers and his earlier discharges was stolen. Like most veterans, he had lost his final discharge. The local court in Massachusetts expressed its belief that Hall was indeed a veteran. He signed his deposition and waited for the bureaucratic process to take its course.[31]

Instead of a pension certificate, Hall received a letter from Edwards, who rejected his application on three counts. First, Edwards required supporting affidavits from fellow veterans, or, as Edwards put it, "from the numerous survivors of the revolution still residing in Massachusetts." Second, Hall's service as a steward to the Commissary General in 1781–1782 was "not embraced in the provisions" of the pension act. A suspicious Edwards also wondered why Hall had taken so long to apply.

Reuben Baldwin, Hall's attorney, wrote back that Hall had thought to apply for the first pension act but had too much property to make an application. Hall learned of the 1832 act only when informed of such by another pensioner in the fall of 1835. In addition to the two already submitted, Baldwin enclosed more affidavits from fellow veterans who were eyewitnesses of Hall's service. Within a week, Edwards replied, but this time, departing from the points he had before made. Edwards's new complaint was that Hall did "not disclose whether he was free-born or emancipated, and if the latter, at what time?" The gatekeeper at the pension office demanded another deposition.

Baldwin showed Edwards's correspondence to his client, who "expressed much disappointment . . . perticularly of that clause requiring 'evidence whether he was free born or emancipate.'" Hall also mentioned his father's name, Prince Hall, which may have raised a flag at the pension office as a man of that name was a prominent abolitionist in Boston. Primus Hall was not brought up by his father, but rather by Ezra Trask, a white man who never considered Primus Hall a slave. To protect Hall from future challenges, Trask signed a paper that proclaimed Hall free at age twenty-one. But Hall's attorney did not see how any of this was pertinent. He was "at a loss to conceive how that question can have any influence or bearing on the case under consideration." Baldwin knew of "many coloured persons" who were slaves at enlistment and received pensions. And so, Hall and Baldwin appealed.

In a week's time, Edwards fired back that he needed paperwork pertaining to Hall's emancipation. Baldwin responded that it would be "impracticable" to produce evidence from sixty years before. Still, the attorney related that in Dumfries, Virginia, in 1782, Hall found himself in a crowded tavern laying on animal skins with many other men. Someone had stolen his pocketbook that night with freedom papers and discharges therein. In addition to Baldwin's letter explaining the lack of paperwork, Hall once again deposed in court, adding more details about his life.[32]

The new packet of evidence and argument was still not satisfactory. It would have been "more satisfactory," claimed Edwards, if Hall had provided the "instrument which he avers he received from his former master." Edwards further stated that, while he had no doubt that Hall "was with the army," he wondered if Hall had been no more than a waiter in his first three tours of service. Edwards's groundless speculation—Hall had three support affidavits that said otherwise—must have struck Hall as racist rationalization. Just as his lawyer knew of enslaved men at enlistment who had received pensions, Primus Hall personally knew at least one black veteran who served with him in Pickering's quartermaster department and qualified for a pension back in 1818. Hall had testified at that time in support of Asabel Wood's successful application. By 1835, times had changed and called for more energetic measures to successfully secure a pension.[33]

In extreme exasperation, Hall and Baldwin decided to cease their appeals because it seemed the pension office was determined to believe that Hall was a "waiter" despite three affidavits (two from veterans and one from the son of Captain Flint, the officer who had died in Hall's arms) that said otherwise. Furthermore, Baldwin explained that his client was "not well pleased at the reiterated and often repeated inquiries as to the manner, how, and in what manner he became free since he has been so over 64 years." Before ending his correspondence with Edwards, the attorney felt impelled to point out that when Ezra Trask became too old and poor to support himself, Hall rented a farm for the white man who raised him. Hall and Baldwin would circumvent the pension office to appeal to the "national Legislature," where they hoped for justice "without distinction of colour."

On January 4, 1838, a congressional oversight committee on Revolutionary pensions found in favor of Hall. The committee noted that the commissioner of pensions had refused "from time to time to allow a pension to this free colored man on different grounds." While perhaps merited at the time, the committee said, the objections were "obviated" by the testimony produced. The committee's findings, passed by congressional act in June 1838, would seem the end of the story, but it was not. On August 16, 1838, Baldwin objected to new requirements demanded by the pension office. Edwards wanted another formal declaration by Hall that included proof that Hall was who he said he was! Baldwin had had enough. He was not going to submit a fifth declaration that would be *"line for line, word for word, comma for comma"* the same as the first four depositions. He informed Edwards that Richard Fletcher, a member of Congress, would carry on this appeal. Fletcher would "be able to substantiate" Hall's identity. In September 1838, Hall's new advocate sent a copy of the congressional act to Edwards, instructing the pension office to forward Hall's certificate to the congressman.

The Hall case highlights both promising and discouraging developments in early nineteenth-century America. By 1832, African American veterans confronted a much more daunting process in their pursuit of a pension. Hall, as a man who fought the British Empire and examined British officer-gentlemen's chests after the decisive Battle of Yorktown, was not about to acquiesce to government authorities. Despite the repeated blockages of 1832, he persisted and won. Military service and a man's determination could trump even the rising racist tendencies in American life.

The sense of confidence imparted by military service in the nation's founding military struggle is highlighted in the cases of two veterans for whom more copious documentation exists. Samuel Sutphin and Jeffrey Brace fought battles before, during, and after the Revolution. Both slaves at enlistment, Sutphin and Brace gambled on the probability that fighting for the cause would lead to freedom. Both encountered sobering experiences after the war that did not prevent them from applying for Revolutionary War pensions. In the process of claiming their right to the nation's gratitude, they both encountered setbacks, enlisted the help of white veterans, and eventually succeeded in securing official recognition for their sacrifice in the war.[34]

Samuel Sutphin

Samuel Sutphin was born enslaved on January 1, 1747 in Hunterdon County, New Jersey, as noted in his master's Bible. Sometime in 1775, he was sold to a neighbor, Casper Berger, who told Sutphin that if he substituted for Berger in the militia service throughout the war, he would be freed. "I believed the white man's word," Sutphin later recalled.

Between 1776 and 1778, the aspiring freeman signed up on eight separate occasions and participated in some of the most significant military actions of the early war. Two hours after his unit arrived on Long Island in 1776, the British and Hessians poured off their ships to start the battle for New York City. Sutphin reported that he fought for six hours as the American army retreated and then enlisted the aid of another black man to ferry Sutphin and some of his comrades to the New Jersey shore. Sutphin was also present at the Battle of Princeton, where he related that a group of British soldiers, cornered in Nassau Hall, were flushed out by American cannon fire. On his fourth tour of duty, Sutphin captured a soldier and received a gun from General Dickinson as acknowledgment for his services. Telling of his service in Sullivan's campaign, Sutphin remembered the names of the two Indian scouts, Shawnee John and Indian Ben, who helped them defeat the Iroquois warriors who had attacked Cherry Valley, a white settlement on the frontier. On returning from that action. Sutphin related that he had killed a Hessian, whom he "watched fall." Shortly thereafter, in late 1778, he was wounded in the leg, which sidelined him for a few months.

Because his last tour was deemed to be so considerable, Sutphin's master was never called up again and so ended Sutphin's military career. The master, however, reneged on his promise to free him and instead made more profit on the veteran by selling him. Three masters later, Samuel purchased his freedom from Peter Sutphin's widow by selling rabbit, raccoon, and muskrat skins.[35]

In June 1832, at the age of eighty-five, Samuel Sutphin applied for a pension from the federal government. In this first attempt, he mentioned neither his race nor his enslavement, limiting his statement to the information relevant to the pension. He substituted for a man called Casper Berger, listed seven short militia hitches and one nine-month service replete with officers' names in every case. He did not, however, provide any support depositions from fellow veterans. Perhaps it is for this reason that in August 1832, Sutphin was back in court to flesh out the details of his service. Here, his race was placed by his name and the substitution deal with his master explained. The court made an extraordinary addendum to this deposition in which the judge explained that Sutphin was a respected church member in his community and no longer lived in the county in which he enlisted, thus making it difficult to obtain support from other veterans. Sutphin's "arduous duties in the revolution ably and nobly performed," claimed the court, made him "highly meritorious of a pension." In accordance with the pension act, which stipulated that if no support depositions could be had two "respectable persons" (a clergyman was preferable) should testify, the Reverend John C. Van Dermont swore to his belief that Sutphin was indeed a veteran.

Lacking muster rolls for the New Jersey militia and an eyewitness account of Sutphin's service, the pension office wanted more details and further proof. In 1833, Sutphin made two court appearances, the first of which was to explain that extreme age and bodily infirmity made it difficult to recall dates with any precision. Indeed, Sutphin often dated events along the agricultural cycle, at "hay and harvest season" or "about the season of early corn planting." In his second court appearance, Sutphin answered the seven interrogatories required of militia applicants. Here Sutphin mentioned that a former governor of New Jersey, a justice of the peace, and a postmaster could attest to his character. His frustration with the process was evident as the word "again" was underlined when he swore to certain particulars.[36]

The pension office remained unmoved, claiming that "being a slave originally, Sutphin was not bound to serve in the militia and the circumstances of each tour of actual service not having been stated as was required, the claim is rejected." In May of 1834, Samuel Sutphin was once again in the courthouse to explain himself. Concerning the first argument, Sutphin reiterated the deal with his master. He was not drafted; he was a substitute. He admitted that his memory of his commanding officers was often limited to men of Dutch descent as he "could talk but little English" at the time of the war. He was more specific about his wounds. A musket ball hit the button of his gaiters, lodging button and ball into his flesh. He cited many other veterans' names in the Long Island and Sullivan campaigns. After dealing with the particulars of his military service, Sutphin turned his attention to the flawed process at his county courthouse. He fingered the court clerk or, as he put it, "the writer of my story" who was "much hurried" in the first depositions and so provided a sketchy outline of his service. He reminded the pension office that he served in the militia "fighting for the white man's freedom." And at the bottom of the fifth page of miniscule writing, Sutphin closed his deposition by saying that he had told the same story in all his depositions but whether court clerks "were willing to hear it," he doubted, as "they omitted all the particulars, asked me but few questions and hurried over it as soon as possible."

When this latest deposition was sent to Washington, it was accompanied by the testimony of a doctor (who happened to be a former member of Congress), validating Sutphin's war injuries. A local justice of the peace attested to Sutphin's scars and the gun he was awarded and still treasured from the war. And finally, a veteran pensioner swore to Sutphin's presence "under arms" at Princeton and around Monmouth. Sutphin had done his best to date his stints by the year and season of their occurrence, specify officers' names for each of his hitches, obtain the testimony of an eyewitness to his service, and enlist the support of two character witnesses, "one of whom should be a clergyman."

The pension office found the new testimony unpersuasive, but not for the reasons previously stated. They shifted their objections from the issue of slaves and the draft to a problem with discrepancies in Sutphin's declarations (without specifying what they were) and skepticism about Sutphin's hitch under Sullivan. A nine-month militia stint, claimed the pension office, was "an improbable length."

Nine months later, Lewis Condict, a former member of Congress, requested a final appeal, highlighting an issue that should have been addressed at the beginning—Sutphin's name. The reason it could not be found on the muster rolls was that, as a slave, "his second name always changed as he changed masters." Sutphin's advocate advised the pension office to look for "Sam Berger or Bergher" or "Sam, a coloured Man" on the rolls. In a last emotional appeal, the writer pleaded that the government keep its promise to this "sober, industrious, meek, humble, and devout" man. Perhaps this list of adjectives was another strategy meant to appeal to white elites in Washington, who wished that all poor people could behave accordingly. It might have struck a chord with J. L. Edwards, the commissioner of pensions, who was himself a Southerner, had black servants in his home, and whose office denied black men who were slaves at enlistment, a policy with no authorization from the pension act or its regulations. But finally, Sutphin's advocate noted what was perhaps the real problem at the pension office. "Without your aid," he wrote, "his unfortunate color will stand between him and his country's justice."

The pension office stood its ground, resuscitating one of its previous objections for the final response. Sutphin was a slave "and was not, of course, bound to serve in the militia." The black man's repeated declarations that he was not drafted but substituted for another man were in vain. Such an acknowledgment would land the pension office squarely against the existence of the May 1777 New Jersey law that rewarded masters economically when they enlisted servants—no race disqualified. The government also claimed that, without proof of Sutphin's participation in Sullivan's campaign, he would not meet the six-month requirement under the law. The pension office did not believe the lengthy militia hitch, part of which took place during General Sullivan's campaign against the Indians. Finally, Edwards's office wanted more officers' names. The names that Sutphin had supplied were not adequate.[37]

Three years and many depositions later, Samuel Sutphin gave up, at least at the level of the federal government. In 1836, his supporters asked the return of his papers from the pension office so they could prepare a case for the New Jersey legislature. On March 10, 1836, Samuel Sutphin, at age eighty-nine, finally received his pension.

Many a man in his eighties would have given up on the first rejection letter, but there is a sense in these sources that Samuel Sutphin would not be denied his right to a pension and the official acknowledgment that accompanied it. On this point, he was adamant—and not, I believe, because of the money. He was, after all, nearly ninety years old when the state of New Jersey approved his pension. Rather, he had children, grandchildren, and neighbors whom he had been regaling with war stories for decades. Nobody was going to tell this wounded veteran that he had not served in the Revolution. Despite a duplicitous master, indifferent court clerks, and, from his perspective, an intransigent pension office, Samuel Sutphin persevered, buoyed by a fellow veteran, a clergyman, neighbors, a postmaster, judges, and even a member of Congress. Samuel the Meek was also Samuel the Persistent.

Jeffrey Brace

Unlike Samuel Sutphin's long and detailed narratives, Jeffrey Brace confined himself to the bare essentials at his court appearance in April of 1818. He enlisted in the Connecticut line and fought at the Battles of White Plains, Stamford, Westchester, and Fort Mifflin, where he was wounded. Brace thought he had signed up for a three-year commitment but found that he was expected to serve for the duration. He "cheerfully served" for five years and nine months and received a discharge and badge of merit, which he had lost.[38] Brace was an exceptional pensioner in that he provided posterity with his memoirs that flesh out these bare details, turning Brace from an abstraction associated with a few battles to a flesh-and-blood man, who, according to his own narrative "passed through so many varying scenes of life."[39]

Eight years before Brace applied for a pension, he had related his life story to an abolitionist, who published the result in 1810. Like the pension applications, this narrative was filtered through the mind of a white man. Unlike hurried court clerks who transcribed pension applications, however, B. F. Prentiss, an abolitionist, was truly interested in the pageant of Jeffrey Brace's life from which he culled colorful details and moral lessons, and no doubt added a stroke or two of his own to drive home his point. Although Brace's memoir was fashioned to convince a broad audience of a certain point of view, the narrative provides unique glimpses into one veteran's life before the war and his experiences afterward.

Born and raised in Africa, Brace was sixteen years old when kidnapped and forced aboard a slave ship bound for the Caribbean. He sailed with the British fleet during the French and Indian War, earned the name Jeffrey for a reckless courage that reminded his superiors of Sir Jeffrey Amherst, and continued to sail the Atlantic until he was sold to a religiously strict Puritan with sadistic tendencies. Several masters later, he ended up with a kindly widow in Woodbury, Connecticut, who taught him to read by studying scriptures. When the old woman died, Jeffrey "descended like real estate in fee simple" to her son, Benjamin Stiles, Esquire.

In 1777, at the advanced age of thirty-seven, he entered the Connecticut line with his master and his master's brother. It is unclear whether he entered the service as a servant to his master or whether he took advantage of a 1777 Connecticut law allowing blacks to be hired as substitutes for white men. The latter possibility seems more likely, because shortly after his enlistment he was drafted into a company of light infantry that wanted men above six feet tall. (Brace was six feet three inches). Whether his editor's sentiments or Jeffrey Stiles's—as he was now known—own sense of irony, he wrote, "Alas! Poor African Slave to liberate freemen, my tyrants." In the ensuing years, Stiles marched all over the northern theater of war, participating in major battles like Monmouth and minor skirmishes like the one at Horseneck, Connecticut. Unfortunately, he provided no details of the battles because he felt (or perhaps his editor felt) that history books could do a better job of enlightening his readers. Stiles did, however, relate with great relish some stories that feature his ingenuity and daring.

One "soldier-like frolic" entailed stealing a pig from a loyalist in the neighborhood and bringing the animal back to camp. In short order, the "frothing Tory" stormed into their encampment and complained to Stiles's commanding officer, Colonel Return Meigs. When called on the carpet by the angry Meigs, Stiles "answered immediately" that the owner had brought the animal to camp for sale and that he and his comrades "unanimously suspected" the farmer as a spy and so held the pig until the officers could interrogate him. A mollified Meigs turned on the Tory farmer and "severely reprimanded the man for his insult on him and his soldiers." The frightened Tory hastily decamped with his dead pig. The black men had bested both the Tory and their commanding officer. Stiles's glee was apparent thirty-five years later.

On another occasion, Stiles served as a lookout for a small band of soldiers in search of stolen cattle. Suddenly a man rode up to him with pistol in hand and ordered Stiles to lay down his arms. Fearing that this might be a prank concocted by fellow soldiers who had pulled this kind of thing before on "the soldiers belonging to our line"—he was in an all-black company—Stiles questioned the man, ascertaining at some point that he was a British light horseman in disguise. Stiles managed to kill the enemy soldier and tore off down the road on the dead man's horse, pursued by more men with swords in hand. As the enemy gained on the spurless Stiles, he saw his captain and comrades up ahead on the road who whistled at seeing the "long shanked negro soldier with a leather cap, mounted on an elegant gelding light horse." Within twenty or thirty rods, Stiles heard his captain order the men not to fire as they might hit Jeffrey. But the men fired anyway, killing four British soldiers and striking Stiles's coat and bayonet belt. While only "two or three jumps of me," the British "being so handsomely saluted," made the best retreat possible.[40]

Once back in camp, Stiles realized he was wounded, thus effectively sidelining him for three months from service in Meigs's regiment, famous for its leather caps. Stiles's recuperation gave him plenty of time to reflect on the close shave he had with death. Why did his pursuers hold their fire as they thundered down the path and came within "two or three jumps" of him? Stiles surmised that his pursuers thought they could question this sentry about the state of the lines. Or perhaps they saw the opportunity to "enrich their coffers" by selling this black man in British-occupied New York. The only person to enrich himself from Stiles's adventure was, ironically, an American officer who agreed to pay Stiles $250 for the horse, saddle, and bridle and then "thought proper never to pay the same."

At war's end, the newly freed Jeffrey Stiles changed his name to that of his father—anglicized to Brace—and moved to Vermont, a sparsely settled area at that time. He hired himself out and was often cheated out of his pay to the point that he wondered whether there was any difference between freedom and slavery. Yet, he managed to buy twenty-five acres of uncleared land, though he still had to work for wages to afford the cost of setting up his own farm and to support his African-born wife with two children of her own. These children became a source of great concern to Brace and his wife, for as soon as they were old enough to work, white neighbors made the claim that they were not properly raised and so had to be hired out on a long-term contract. Although Brace said that "the majesty of Guinea rose indignant in my breast," the authorities prevailed and the two children were bound away. As he explained it, "The corruption and superstition, mingled with the old Connecticut bigotry and puritanism, made certain people think a Negro had no right to raise their own children."[41]

Years later, when Brace's own children came of a likely age to be hired out, a white neighbor who coveted the black man's land tried the same trick. By this time, Brace was a viable farmer and landholder in the community and had sufficient pull to resist the attempt. The incessant feuding with his white neighbor induced him to consider a move to Kentucky. A Revolutionary War colonel was leading a group of settlers there, but Brace thought the better of it, opting not to live so near slavery. "They might haul me in," he said, or prosecute him for sedition if he said something out of line. His children did not understand why he tolerated so much abuse. They wanted to avenge his wrongs, while their father counseled that the best chance for redress was to turn the other cheek. "This to them seemed like false doctrine," he said.

Finally, he found a reasonably good situation in 1804, when he moved to Georgia, Vermont, a town on Lake Champlain. It was here in 1818 that Brace called on the government to acknowledge his services during the Revolutionary War by awarding him a pension. His first attempt failed. Even though supported by the testimony of another soldier, who maintained that "there was no better soldier in the army," the pension office did not believe the truth of Brace's deposition and could not find his name on the muster rolls. Brace's supporters managed to interest a member of Congress, Samuel Crafts, into lodging a protest with J. L. Edwards. The tone of Edwards's reply suggests that Congressman Crafts had applied some pressure. No, said a defensive Edwards, his doubt concerning Brace's service did not imply that the judge handling Brace's case was a fraud. (Fraud cases in Vermont were particularly numerous in 1818). Edwards admitted that none of Brace's deposition clashed with the known facts about the regiment to which he belonged. All that was needed, claimed Edwards, was an explanation of the name change and two veterans who would vouch for him. Jeffrey Brace did better than that. He provided three more veteran testimonies, one who mentioned that Brace was part of an all-black company and another who complicated matters further by relating that Jeff Brace, alias Jeff Stiles, was also nicknamed Pomp London! But this last glitch did not stop the eventual issuance of a pension certificate in July 1821.

By that time, eighty-one-year-old Jeffrey Brace, in his own words, had "passed through so many varying scenes of life." This old, frail man who stood in the Franklin County courthouse had swum the Niger River, survived the Middle Passage and several sadistic masters, sailed around the Atlantic world, fought in the American Revolution, and published his life story to further the abolition movement. He pursued the American dream, moving to a frontier area and purchasing land. Despite rapacious selectmen and neighbors, he continued to soldier on, picking up stakes for greater opportunity. He was helped along the way by men with military titles. Colonel Lyon provided the opportunity to move to Kentucky, and Majors Clark and Sheldon helped him in northern Vermont. Perhaps they felt moved to aid a fellow veteran. Despite a strict pension office, which at that time was doubly vigilant about fraud in Vermont applications, Brace reapplied when rejected, enlisting the help of four white veterans and a member of Congress. Although no fuss was made when this extraordinary man passed away in 1827, his children, who did not accept humiliation and injustice so placidly, passed on his stories to their children, providing a strong, historical claim to their quest for liberation.

As Jeffrey Brace's memoir attests, court clerks bled out the personality from veterans' pension narratives. And so when one might expect to find differences, for example, between white and black depositions, there is little to be detected. The same applies when trying to find regional differences among the applicants. The narratives of freemen of Connecticut are strikingly similar to those of enslaved Virginians. Between the two pension acts of 1818 and 1832, the first national debate on slavery took place around the entry of Missouri into the union. By 1832, slavery was more an issue, abolitionist voices were stronger, and more numerous black voices in the movement more apparent. Yet there is no discernable change in the tone or content of the latter group of applicants compared to those who applied in 1818.

The bureaucracy of the pension system itself no doubt accounts for some of this uniformity. But perhaps the veterans' service in the war that forged the nation also left a positive memory that transcended regions, national debates, and mounting racism in American life. With few exceptions, the veterans in their old age looked back to their Revolutionary War service as the adventure of their lives. These young recruits burst forth from the confines of their neighborhoods and masters' oversight to experience new locales. Although ordered about in the army, African Americans were used to taking orders, and they could see that white men were subject to the same officer's bark. These men wore uniforms and were part of an organization that had to be respected. Black men were part of units that requisitioned white farmers' corn and shot at men who in civilian life would have lorded over them. Jeff Stiles and his comrades even got away with personally requisitioning a Tory farmer's pig. On many levels, then, military service proved a liberating time in itself. It also often resulted in individual emancipation and sparked a movement to gradually emancipate all slaves in the North. Military service freed the slave and servant from the narrow optic of everyday survival to a broader vision of active participation in a larger cause. And that cause was not only the white man's freedom, but also their own. Such was the pride and emotional connection to the Revolutionary days that some veterans put up a fight about handing over their discharges to get their pension. Agrippa Hull's attorney requested the prompt return of the discharge signed by George Washington, because his client "had rather forego the pension than lose the discharge." Another Massachusetts veteran, Artillo Freeman, showed his patriotic sensibility in another way. While putting a dollar value on the few pieces of crockery and clothing he possessed to prove his poverty under the 1818 act, he also included a line for "revolutionary uniform," which he estimated as "invaluable."[42]

Although some black men found it harder to obtain a pension, those who succeeded reaped a reward that made an enormous difference in their lives, particularly for penurious veterans under the 1818 legislation. Caesar Wallace, a veteran of Bunker Hill, Monmouth, and Newtown, had no belongings to speak of when he obtained his eight-dollar monthly pension. Two years later, when the government demanded a list of property for every veteran who had received a pension, Wallace noted the presence of one cow as the sum total of his assets, purchased with some of the pension money he had thus far received. Another veteran, in slightly better financial shape, Prince Bailey, obtained a pension in 1818, only to have it taken away in 1820 when he, like many other white veterans, did not pass the government means test. He owned thirty-five acres and a small house. When this bad news had gotten out, Bailey's creditors swooped down upon him, necessitating the sale of his house and land. In 1825, Bailey came back to court to apply for another pension because the actions of the federal government had just made him destitute. He was restored to the rolls.[43]

When Bailey reapplied for his pension, his white creditors and the town selectmen verified the sale of his land and praised Bailey's good morals. As in Bailey's case, the pension records show extensive support for black veterans by the white community surrounding them. White veterans and neighbors, former masters' children, clergymen, judges, and, in some cases, high government officials supplied supporting depositions for black veterans. Even if imbued with racist beliefs, white associates could enthusiastically support an individual black man who had regaled them for years with war stories. Their belief in his upstanding character may also have been aided by the fact that a government pension would put the black veteran in a position to pay his remaining debts or, at the very least, take the burden of his upkeep off the local authorities. The African American veterans understood the value of a white man's word over that of a black man's, and so tapped their white acquaintances for support. (There are very few support depositions from African Americans, and what few there were, typically appear in rejected applications.)

At times, their war service elevated them into heady company. Peter Jennings, a veteran of the First Rhode Island and one of the few black veterans to move to the western frontier, was acknowledged by General Lafayette when the famous general passed through Tennessee during his 1826–1827 tour. Up in New England, Nancy Daley, daughter of veteran Cato Fisk, testified twice to help her mother obtain a widow's pension.

Nancy was not sure of the exact date of her father's death, but she remembered that he died in the same week as a prominent local general—which would put her father's death in March 1824. She distinctly remembered this connection because the following Sunday "the minister preached a sermon on their deaths and mentioned my father before he mentioned the General, and some people in the Parish were offended at it." The minister, whose own father was a Revolutionary War veteran, had paired Nancy's father with a general, resulting in a miffed congregation. As was often the case for African American veterans, even the little victories were tinged with resentment and resistance.[44]

The old, undaunted warriors continued to fight well after the cannons were silenced on the battlefield. Although participants in the making of the country, most African American veterans were still far away from the world they had dreamed of for their children. The applicants were still largely limited to jobs that paid a pittance. Jack Gardner, a three-year veteran in the 4th Massachusetts regiment, was described in 1818 as "a regular perambulator of our streets with wheel barrow and swill tub in search of daily food for himself and swine." But while poor and limited by skin color in the new republic, he and other veterans became celebrities in their own communities, particularly when they aged. Countless neighbors in supporting affidavits testified that they had been listening to the veterans' stories for decades. The veterans talked to their children, too, and could take satisfaction from the strides made by the next generation. The pension files reveal that more than half of the male children of these veterans could write their names. Jeff Brace's sons exhibited less patience than their father over injustices committed by white neighbors. These children joined others who gathered around the old veterans and took inspiration from their actions. Jeremiah Asher, a grandson of an African-born veteran, wrote his memoirs in 1850 as a way to trumpet the evils of slavery and raise money for his church in Philadelphia. The younger Asher characterized the Revolution as an "eventful period [that] will never be forgotten by us whose fathers fought for liberty, not from the yoke of Britain but from the yoke of American slavery." William Cooper Nell, the son of a Massachusetts veteran, became an abolitionist, journalist, and historian, writing three books in the 1850s chronicling the history of "colored Patriots" in the American Revolution.[45]

By the first half of the nineteenth century, the Revolution was generally considered to be the epochal event in our nation's past. In 1818 and again in 1832, the government looked back and rewarded past-due recognition to the old Revolutionaries. But, unlike the power structure, African American veterans were involved in a forward momentum because the struggle of '76 was an ongoing one that they passed along to the next generation, bequeathing the example of their lives to inspire bolder action and greater risk.

Notes

I wish to dedicate this article to the memory of my mother's brother, William Raymond Hendricks, who at the age of seventeen enlisted in the Marine Corps during World War II and fought in the Pacific theater. It was in the last major battle at Okinawa that a sniper ended his life at age twenty. His service records appear to have burned in a fire at a government depository. He had no children. He will leave even less of a trace than the men of this study. The niece he never saw salutes his memory. I wish to thank the David Library of the American Revolution and the American Philosophical Society for funding this project. Special thanks go to David Library archivists Kathie Ludwig and Greg Johnson, who were my partners in finding these veterans. Many thanks go to John Resch, Patricia Bonomi, Jacquelyn Miller, and the anonymous readers for their helpful comments.

1. John Harris, Revolutionary War Pension Files, S37997. Having had enough of military service in 1780, Harris allegedly hired a substitute. See Luther P. Jackson, *Virginia Negro Soldiers and Sailors in the Revolutionary War* (Norfolk, Va.: Guide Quality Press, 1944), p. 36

2. For an estimate on the number of soldier pensions, see William Henry Glasson, *History of Military Pension Legislation in the United States* (New York: Columbia University Press, 1900), p. 51. This study is based on only those soldiers who provided pension depositions. Bounty Land Warrant recipients did not leave their stories and so do not figure in this sample. If bounty land warrants, half-pay Virginians, and widow-only applications were added, the total number of applications would rise to 80,000. See National Genealogical Society, Special Publication no. 40, *The Index of Revolutionary War Pension Applications in the National Archives* (Arlington, Va.: National Genealogical Society, 1976). The sample for this study was drawn from the following sources: Virgil White, ed. *Genealogical Abstracts of Revolutionary War Pension Files*, 3 vols. (Waynesboro, Tenn.: National Historical Publishing Company, 1992); Richard S. Walling, *Men of Color at the Battle of Monmouth, June 28, 1778* (Hightstown, N.J.: Longstreet House, 1994); Robert Ewell Greene, *Black Courage, 1775–1783: Documentation of Black Participation in the American Revolution* (Washington, D.C.: National Society of the Daughters of the American Revolution, 1984); David Oliver White, *Connecticut's Black Soldiers, 1775–1783* (Chester, Conn.: Pequot Press, 1973); George Quintal, Jr., *Patriots of Color, "A Peculiar Beauty and Merit": African Americans at Battle Road and Bunker Hill* (Washington, D.C.: U.S. Department of the Interior, 2000). On occasion, names on these lists contained pensions with no indication of race therein. These names were then checked in the census records to substantiate race. Muster lists also occasionally provided descriptions of soldiers. In addition to working off already existing lists, the 1790 census records were examined for all African American heads of household and their names were then checked against Virgil White's abstracts. Through this process, several new African American veterans have come to light. The sample includes 118 Southerners; 24 middle states; and 158 New Englanders. Seventy percent of the sample applied under the 1818 legislation, and 30 percent under the 1832 law.

3. Samuel Bell, S6598; "An Act to Establish a Militia in this State: April 8, 1777," in Walter Clark, ed., *The State Records of North Carolina,* 26 vols. (Goldsboro, N.C.: Nash Brothers, 1886–1907), 24:1–5; Benjamin Quarles, *The Negro in the American Revolution* (New York: W. W. Norton, 1961), p. 124.

4. Richard Rhodes, W22060 & Ichabod Northup, W20279; Lorenzo Greene, "Some Observations on the Black Regiment of Rhode Island in the American Revolution," *Journal of Negro History* (April 1952): 142–72; for text of 1778 law, see John Russell Bartlett, ed., *Records of the Colony of Rhode Island and Providence Plantations in New England,* 10 vols. (Providence, R.I.: A. C. Greene, 1856–1865), 8:358–60.

5. Edward Sands, W16148; Caesar Shelton, S19764; Peter Jennings, S4436.

6. Jacob Francis, W459; Lewis Hinton, S10831; Tim Jones, S18063; London Hazard, S17463. For legislation pertaining to masters who broke their word, see "An Act Directing the Emancipation of Certain Slaves Who Have Served as Soldiers in This State," October 1783, in William Walter Hening, ed., *The Statutes at Large; Being a Collection of all the Laws of Virginia, from the First Session of the Legislature in the Year 1619,* 13 vols. (1809–1823; Charlottesville: University Press of Virginia, 1969), 11:308.

7. Samuel Dunbar, S15106; Joseph Johnson, R5636.

8. Alexander Mourice (A012–10074), Black London (AO12–99–86, John Ashfield (AO12–99–135), Henry Howe (AO12–101–107). Thanks to Cassandra Pybus for sharing these sources.

9. Charles Patrick Neimeyer, *American Goes to War: A Social History of the Continental Army* (New York: New York University Press, 1996), pp. 21–26.

10. John Roe, S39045

11. Gregory T. Knouff, *The Soldiers' Revolution: Pennsylvanians in Arms and the Forging of Early American Identity* (University Park: Pennsylvania State University Press, 2004), p. 247.

12. Caesar Shelton, S19764

13. William Wanton, S22035; Pomp Magus, S33059; James Hawkins, S37991; Joel Taburn, S42037; for 1777 law, see Hening, *Statutes at Large.*

14. Thomas Paine, *The American Crisis #1,* December 23, 1776, in *Common Sense and the Crisis* (Garden City, N.Y.: Anchor Books, 1973), p. 69; John Resch, *Suffering Soldiers: Revolutionary War Veterans, Moral Sentiment, and Political Culture in the Early Republic* (Amherst: University of Massachusetts Press, 1999), p. 178.

15. The white literacy rate has been calculated at 91 percent in 1840. See Lawrence A. Cremin, *American Education: The National Experience, 1783–1876* (New York: Harper & Row, 1980), p. 491; for examples of veterans and their widows who were duped, see Job Primus, W10256 and Scipio Watson, W18240.

16. Leon Litwack, *North of Slavery: The Negro in the Free States, 1790–1860* (Chicago: University of Chicago Press, 1961), pp. 70–71; Theodore J. Crackel, "Revolutionary War Pension Records and Patterns of American Mobility, 1780–1830," *Prologue* 16 (Fall 1984): 155. See also Resch, *Suffering Soldiers,* p. 218.

17. Resch, *Suffering Soldiers,* p. 179. Resch's estimate includes white veterans with no dollar value. My black estimate does not include this cohort.

18. Levi Caesar, S39269.

19. Cuff Tindy, S33804.

20. Ben Simmons, W24974.

21. Joseph Johnson, R5636.

22. When race is mentioned, the most frequently used terms are "man of colour" and "coloured." Two-thirds of my sample are identified as "man of colour"; one-fourth as "coloured man" (particularly popular in the middle states); 8 percent use the term "black"; and 2 percent designate "Negro."

23. Caesar Shelton, S19764; Isaac Perkins, S41953.

24. Pomp Magus, S33059; Prince Crosely, W24833

25. James Weeks S33269

26. "An Act to provide for certain persons engaged in the land and naval service of the United States, in the Revolutionary War," March 18, 1818, in "Public Acts of Congress," pp. 2518–19; *American State Papers,* Claims, 682–84.

27. "An Act Supplementary to the Act for the Relief of Certain Surviving Officers and Soldiers of the Revolution," June 4, 1832, *Statutes at Large,* 22nd Congress, sess. 1, chap. 127, pp. 529–30.

28. "Execution of the Act Providing for Persons engaged in the Land and Naval Service of the Revolution," January 4, 1820 in *American State Papers,* Claims, 682–84. For 1832 regulations, see "Pension Act of 1832 with the Instructions of the War Department for carrying it into Effect," June 7, 1832 in Hdoc 298 (22-1), pp. 221–40.

29. The rejection rates for African American veterans are based on the 300 men of this study. The white veterans are based on a random sample of 600 white veterans.

30. Peter Nash, R7558; Quarles, *The Negro in the American Revolution,* p. 54.

31. Primus Hall, S43677.

32. Gary B. Nash, *Race and Revolution* (Madison, Wis.: Madison House, 1990), pp. 65–67; William Cooper Nell, *Colored Patriots of the American Revolution* (Boston: R. F. Wallcut, 1855), pp. 29–30.

33. Asabel Wood, S22947.

34. Samuel Sutphin, R10321; Jeffrey Brace, S41461.

35. Mark F. Lender, *The New Jersey Soldier* (Trenton: New Jersey Historical Commission, 1975), p. 10.

36. Resch, *Suffering Soldiers,* pp. 167–68.

37. Quarles, *The Negro in the American Revolution,* p. 70; by 1777, "New Jersey even gave up asking for freemen in its appeals. Any able-bodied and effective volunteers would do." Lender, *The New Jersey Soldier,* p. 17.

38. Jeffrey Brace, S41461.

39. Benjamin F. Prentiss, ed., *The Blind African Slave, Or, Memoirs of Boyrereau Brinch, Nick-named Jeffrey Brace* (1810; Chapel Hill: Academic Affairs Library, University of North Carolina, 2001), found at the following Web site: <http://docsouth.unc.edu/neh/brinch/menu.html> (accessed July 2003).

40. Brinch, *Memoirs,* pp. 164–65.

41. Gary B. Nash and Jean R. Soderlund, *Freedom by Degrees: Emancipation in Pennsylvania and Its Aftermath* (New York: Oxford University Press, 1991), pp. 175–86.

42. Agrippa Hull, W760; Artillo Freeman, S44853; see also Oliver Cromwell, S34613; Colin Powell and Joseph E. Persico, *My American Journey: Colin Powell* (New York: Random House, 1995), p. 114.

43. Caesar Wallace, S43250; Prince Bailey, W17230.

44. Peter Jennings, S4436; Cato Fisk, W14719.

45. Jack Gardner, W1593; Jeremiah Asher, *Incidents in the Life of Rev. J. Asher* (London: C. Gilpin, 1850), p. 18; William C. Nell, *Services of Colored Americans in the Wars of 1776 and 1812* (Boston: Prentiss & Sawyer, 1850); *The Colored Patriots of the American Revolution* (Boston: R. F. Wallcut, 1855); and *Property Qualification or No Property Qualification: A Few Facts from the Record of Patriotic Services of the Colored Men of New York, during the Wars of 1776 and 1812* (New York: Thomas Hamilton & William H. Leonard, 1860).

Part II

COMMUNITIES

Retribution, Allies, and Women at War

6

RESTRAINT AND RETALIATION

The North Carolina Militias and the

Backcountry War of 1780–1782

WAYNE E. LEE

The worst of the American Revolutionary War came late to North Carolina. North Carolina's rebels had quickly gained control of the colony at the outset of the war, defeated the most dramatic loyalist counterstroke at Moore's Creek Bridge in 1776, devastated the Cherokees' country for their attempt to join the British war effort, and then more or less contained any serious intrastate resistance for the next three years. The Tories never entirely ceased their efforts to organize and resist, but by and large a kind of seething calm held the countryside until 1780 and the British capture of Charleston.

The fall of Charleston brought war back to North Carolina with a fury unallayed by the delay. The fratricidal nature of that war has become something of a truism, and many stories attest to its ugliness. In 1781, a volunteer militia company commanded by Colonel John Moffitt captured the "grayheaded" father of a known Tory clan and questioned him severely as to the whereabouts of his sons, repeatedly threatening him with death. At one point, a fellow soldier handed an improvised spear to our witness for this story, one James Collins, and suggested that he run the old man through.[1] On the loyalist side, the notorious David Fanning recounted how in May of 1781 he and a small party of his men were surprised and surrounded in a friend's house. They rushed out to overwhelm the ambushers and successfully reached the woods.

Two of his men were taken, however, "one of which the Rebels shot in cold Blood, and the other they hanged on the spot where we had Killed the man a few Days before." "Exasperated," Fanning retaliated on a party of rebels plundering a house. In a half-hour skirmish Fanning and his men killed two, wounded three, and captured two more. Following up on his success, over the next few days he attacked several other rebel parties, killing seven, wounding ten, and capturing eight.[2] In a yet more brutal example of the internecine

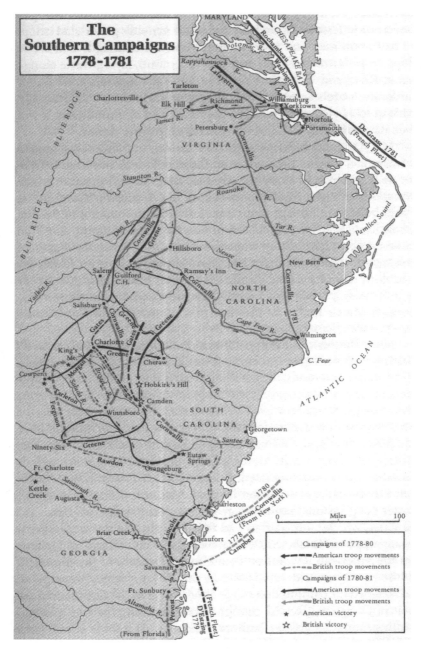

Map 6-1. The southern campaigns saw British and American units ranging widely across the countryside, in addition to widespread localized militia activity. (From *A Leap in the Dark: The Struggle to Create the American Republic* by John Ferling, copyright 2003 by John Ferling. Used by permission of Oxford University Press, Inc.)

struggle during those years, in February 1781, a combined force of Continental cavalry and North Carolina militia used confusion over uniforms to surprise and decimate a loyalist column. The next day, prodded by his comrades, militiaman Moses Hall wandered over to see some of the prisoners. "We went to where six were standing together. Some discussion taking place, I heard some of our men cry out, 'Remember Buford,' and the prisoners were immediately hewed to pieces with broadswords."[3]

These and similar tales of murder, mistreatment, and plunder litter the records of the Southern war in its later years. But in examining such stories, we must be careful to consider contemporary values and understandings of violence. Careful analysis will show that these are stories of both restraint and of escalation. Values and hopes for a virtuous way of war did not always hold together, but often they did. A careful look at the nature of the war in North Carolina from 1780 to 1782 reveals a complex story of a society struggling with the strains of war, hoping for restraint, fearing escalation, all while trying to bring their cause to a successful conclusion.

Values and Restraint

Violence is always judged. Observers and participants evaluate its legitimacy or criminality, but they do so from within their own cultural framework. The battlefield and nonbattlefield quasi-military violence of the War of Independence can only be understood within that era's cultural understanding of what war was and how it should be conducted. Those values and understandings in turn shaped individual reactions to the war they saw, and their reactions then formed part of the landscape of the war. Precedents and preconceptions shape decisions about wielding violence, in part by creating communal standards that individuals hesitate to violate for fear of social censure. Preconceptions also shape reactions to violence, whether outrage at violations of precedent or grudging acceptance of certain inevitabilities. The social and political environment in turn sets other conditions: the speed and reliability of reports of violence, the level of sensitivity to certain types of violence (for example, racial dynamics in response to reports of violence by Indians or slaves); and, the probability of censure. To precedent and environment, one must add contingency. Individuals pursue their own purposes, ignore social convention, or might, to use one historian's phrase, have a "sadistic predisposition to violence."[4] Such individually contingent acts then feed back into the wider social expectations and environment of war, shaping more collective responses. The norms of war alone, therefore, did not determine behavior, but they did condition it. Individual decisions about violence were pressured by concern for what others would think, and thus a substantial part of explaining the war's escalation lies in examining the ways in which individual and small-group decisions made under the stresses of war had become separated from prewar communal values and pressures.

To see the peculiar nature of the backcountry war, we must first understand the general conventions and prevailing values that governed the conduct of war during the American Revolution. We must then analyze the incarnation of those values in the militia. The values and expectations can be reduced to four groups. The first group includes the traditional limits on military violence rooted in popular morality, European military formalism (the "rules" of war), and the cult of honor. These conventions limited gratuitous violence. They prescribed treatment of enemy troops and civilians that was considered to be lawful and fair. Revolutionary Americans had developed a second group of values revolving around republican notions of virtuous war waged by citizens. Historians have long noted how republican ideology incorporated a belief in the military efficiency and political safety of an armed citizenry.[5] But also imbedded in the idea of a virtuous republican army was the expectation that its use of violence would be restrained, avoiding the wanton destruction of innocent life and property. This belief generated frequent comparisons of restrained American behavior to the excessive violence of the British.[6] A third set of beliefs recognized that war brought sacrifices. A certain amount of loss brought about by the need for armies to eat, and the normal killing and dying in battle, were only to be expected. Finally, although military convention and the republican notion of virtue acted as restraints on warfare, their effect on violence in North Carolina was diminished by the cultural legitimacy of retaliation or retribution. Behavior that exceeded normative limits on violence merited retaliation in kind. Just what those limits were and what kind of retaliation was meted out resulted from individual decisions and from the norms established by communities and institutions. Thus, the type and level of violence would be varied and dynamic, but not necessarily chaotic. Between 1780 and 1782, military conventions and republican ideals that restrained violence weakened as boundaries on retribution and retaliation expanded. Furthermore, embedded in that process of weakening restraints and expanding retaliation was another process whereby both individuals and the Revolutionary government justified the legitimacy of new levels of violence. They knew they were rewriting the rules, and in rewriting them they sought not only to "cover" their actions, but also to find ways to impose a modicum of order even on this more violent vision of war.

The extent to which the limits on military violence continued to function, even within these worst years of the war, is illustrated in Collins's experience of interrogating the "grayheaded" old Tory. While Colonel Moffitt questioned the old man and he pleaded ignorance of his sons' whereabouts and begged for his life, another member of the militia company pulled Collins aside, handed him a spear, and asked him to quickly run the old man through. Collins's horrified refusal and his reasons reveal not only the values in play, but also the structures reinforcing them. Collins said, "He is too old; besides the colonel would never forgive me;

he is a prisoner and he don't intend to kill him." Both traditional morality and European military formalism suggested that the old were not proper targets of war, and the colonel's adherence to that formal code put a protective shield around the prisoner. Furthermore, Collins's respect for Colonel Moffitt, which his memoir makes clear, prevented him from going against Moffitt's presumed wishes. Note also how his statement implies Moffitt's past history of restrained treatment of prisoners. Collins continued his account, recalling that the other militiaman then offered him money to kill the old man. Collins persisted in his refusal, scorning the instigator who "would bribe me to do a deed that he himself would be ashamed of." Here we see the judgment of the community of soldiery, particularly that of a respected officer, restraining each other from "shameful" acts. Collins ceased to respect the other man, avoided that soldier thereafter, and believed him "rotten at the core." Collins even suspected that the man later "ran distracted and died so" from a "remorse [which] had overtaken him." As for the old man, he was set free.

This is merely one anecdote, but other evidence reveals both the nature of restraints on war and their continued, though weakening, function in North Carolina from 1780 to 1782.[7] One way to see how those values continued to function was in the judgments the combatants made of each other on the basis of their conscious gradation of violent acts. The basic distinction appeared simple enough: in an oft-repeated phrase, there were Tories who were proper soldiers or were noncombatants, and then there were Tories "who have been guilty of murder, robbery, house-burning and offences out of the military line."[8] Murder and house burning were in a clear-cut category of their own, and men guilty of such acts repeatedly were excluded from late-war truces or pardons, or became the specific targets of retribution.[9] Collins, for example, noted that "those we called the 'pet Tories,' or neutrals, we never disturbed," but with the war in the rebels' hands in 1782, his company "commenced ferreting out the Tories . . . such as had been in the habit of plundering, burning, and murdering."[10] A similarly clear-cut category was desertion and fighting for the other side. Elijah Alexander, a militiaman in company with Continental Army troops in 1781, recalled taking a group of prisoners, five of whom proved to be deserters. They were "all hung on one gallows." It is important to point out, however, that Alexander continued on to record how the other Tories were guarded, some court-martialed and whipped, and others "sent to jail or headquarters."[11]

If murder, house burning, and desertion were clearly unacceptable, the question of robbery was somewhat thornier. After all, violence in the "military line" was to be excused, but the exact moment when provisioning became plundering was a fine line. The Reverend Samuel McCorkle laid out the ideological basis in a sermon against plundering, noting that it had "degrees of aggravation." Where "taking . . . victualls from their foes" was one thing, "the taking of money to a considerable amount. . . . The taking of horses and cattle, and slaves, and furniture" aggravated the offense to a felony.[12] Whig soldiers and politicians made similar distinctions. William Davie, a partisan leader sometimes accused of excesses, turned some of his prisoners over to Continental control and, when asked about them, said they were guilty "of no particular crime, but the general one of their being Kings Militia."[13] Witnesses in the 1782 treason trial of Samuel Bryant, a leading Tory officer, acknowledged that he had not "committed any violences more than any other Army would have done in similar circumstances, in supplying themselves with Arms, ammunitions, provisions, horses, &c., there being no proof of [him] having been guilty of any murders, house-burning or plundering except as above mentioned for the support of their Army." In light of this testimony, the governor reprieved Bryant, changing his status from a criminal punishable by death to an exchangeable prisoner.[14]

In short, some kinds of plundering were worse than others. Official impressment of needed provisions was more or less accepted, provided it was done with the appropriate formality (by officers, preferably with advance notice), and some attempt was made to pay or at least provide receipts.[15] Soldiers "carving for themselves" for subsistence was considered an offense, but not so much as soldiers taking nonmilitary necessities.[16] Finally, and most egregious, were the situations in which officers were seen to direct soldiers in the taking of nonmilitary necessities.[17] This sense of gradation, often ignored by historians, was of great concern to the populace and to the soldiers themselves, who can be found avoiding stepping over certain lines within this "hierarchy" of plunder. A number of examples from the Moravian communities are particularly vivid in this respect. Members of one militia company tried to take blankets but, when asked, were unable to show their "press warrant" authorizing such impressment and so left with nothing. Another group accosted a rider named Graeter on the road, threatening to shoot him if he did not give up his horse. "He risked that and they let him alone." Some militiamen expressed remorse at their previous behavior in the Moravian towns and were more restrained in later visits, whereas some stepped in to prevent the depredations of other militiamen. One militia company even took the time to repay the Moravians with provisions when their own official supplies caught up with them.[18] These distinctions of plunder and the consequent judgments of plunderers, however fine, continued to be made, and were even applied in the courts-martial of Tory prisoners.

The treatment of prisoners provided the clearest view of the Whig government's struggle to restrain itself and its military arm under traditional norms of war. In the main they succeeded, but with notable lapses. Most prisoners faced three decisions about their fate. The first came as they tried to surrender. Soldiers or militiamen in the heat of battle were known to refuse requests for quarter, and, though such "hot-blooded" killings were condemned by eighteenth-century military ethics, it was considered less of a crime than killing them in cold blood later. Being a captive was the second decision point. What would the leaders and men of the capturing unit decide to do with their prisoners? Most tales of mistreatment and murder occur at this point in a prisoner's transition from freedom to captivity, perhaps because such treatment at this stage was the most illegitimate—and therefore remembered and recorded. The leaders and men of militia units might seek vengeance, and sometimes exact it from their prisoners, but when doing so they sought to clothe their behavior in as much judicial legitimacy as possible, perhaps to assuage their consciences and perhaps to provide a legal shield. Whigs used courts-martial (formal and informal) to decide the fate of many loyalist prisoners. When William Gipson's company captured two Tories in 1779 they took the trouble to escort them a full fifteen miles to the Guilford County courthouse and there held a court-martial. The Whig company condemned Hugh McPherson, a "notorious" Tory, and shot him. They sentenced the other to "be spicketed," that is, suspended over a sharp pin, with his bare foot tenuously perched on the point. This was nominally a traditional disciplinary punishment for cavalrymen, but in this instance they went beyond the norm and actually slowly drove the pin through his foot.[19] There are many similar reports of Whig militias bringing in Tories and sentencing them to be whipped, and even occasionally to be hanged or shot, after a quick court-martial.[20] In one extended example, around a hundred Tory prisoners trickled into the Moravian towns in August and September of 1780. The militia held a series of trials, whipped some of the prisoners—a few more severely than others—hanged one on his own confession, enlisted many in the rebel forces, and released others on "certain conditions."[21]

The most famous incident was that of the prisoners from British Colonel Patrick Ferguson's loyalist corps taken at King's Mountain. In the week following the battle, several loyalists were tried and hanged, but the process also tells a tale of restraint and a desire for legitimacy. The Whig field officers convened a court-martial, supposedly motivated by reports of hangings of rebels by loyalists in South Carolina, and convicted thirty-six Tories (out of hundreds of prisoners) of "breaking open houses, killing the men, turning the women and children out of doors, and burning the houses." Determined to inject an air of legality into the proceedings, someone retrieved a copy of the North Carolina law that authorized two magistrates to summon a jury, and, because several militia officers present were in fact also magistrates, it was cited as the basis for the trial. Three men at a time were hanged until nine were dead, and then the officers ended it.[22] Even the manner of execution is significant. In the case of the King's Mountain prisoners, and in many of the more "informal" and illegal executions, the method of choice was hanging.[23] Hanging as a method of execution not only lent a judicial aspect to the killing, but also emphasized the supposed criminality of the victim.

A loyalist prisoner who survived his initial period of capture, as the evidence suggests the vast majority did, then faced the judgment of the North Carolina state government. They were even more likely to survive this judgment, though the Whigs continued until the end of the war to debate how to define the status of prisoners and thus how to treat them. For the most part, however, they fell back on the standard eighteenth-century utilitarian solution of treating them as exchangeable prisoners of war.[24] The process of exchange was never perfectly formalized between the American and British militaries during the war (especially for loyalist prisoners), but it achieved a kind of regularity that made preserving the lives of loyalist prisoners worthwhile.[25] There were exceptions. Public pressure operated to exact vengeance, and the government's consequent wavering over whether to treat a loyalist as a civil prisoner or as an exchangeable prisoner of war resulted in what were probably somewhat random decisions. Typically, however, the government tried to distinguish between "types" of Tories by relying on definitions of violent acts to decide the issue. Those Tories who could be shown to have "been guilty of murder, robbery, house-burning, and offences out of the Military Line" were likely to be treated as civil criminals under the treason law.[26] Persons who had not committed such crimes could be exchanged. There was also a temptation among some Whig leaders to forcibly enlist captured loyalists into the Continental Army or active militia service. For example, several hundred of the nearly 600 prisoners taken at King's Mountain were paroled on the condition that they enlist for a three-month tour in the militia.[27] Such service would not only earn the loyalist a pardon, but would also help the Whigs fill the ranks.[28]

In the end, it is critical to emphasize that dramatic stories notwithstanding, the vast majority of prisoners taken on both sides were either paroled or held until exchanged, with a significant percentage of loyalist prisoners being forcibly enrolled into Continental service.[29] Perhaps the clearest evidence for this effort to restrain the spiral of wartime violence can be found in the fate of the leading men of Colonel David Fanning's loyalist militia. David Fanning was easily the most notorious, and probably the most successful, of the North Carolina loyalist leaders. His success and his violence made him and his men the most feared and hated partisans in North Carolina. Despite that fact, when Fanning sat down in New Brunswick in 1790 to write his memoir of the war, he was able to report that a startling number of his officers were alive and living in North Carolina. Of fifty-six officers whose fates he knew (seven were either unknown or in Charleston at the time of the British evacuation), he reported that twenty-two were living in North or South Carolina (plus one more in Pennsylvania). Six had been "killed," apparently in battle, five had been executed more or less judicially, and only five had been, in his words, "murdered." The remainder had either died, fled to other British possessions, or joined the rebels (three men).[30] That a full 41 percent of the *offi-*

cers of the *most notorious* loyalist unit in North Carolina would still be living in the American states—the majority still in North Carolina—speaks volumes for the survival rate, if not the pleasantries, of being a prisoner.

The Breakdown of Restraint

One historian has characterized the war in the South as creating a "society altogether lacking a sense of civic polity."[31] In fact, the story is more complex than that. This was a society struggling to contain the savagery of war, sometimes succeeding and sometimes failing. Between 1780 and 1782 the failure of restraint became more marked, but never disappeared. So how and why did restraint break down?

Fundamentally the war outside Continental or British lines was a "people's war," waged by transient and institutionally weak militias, using operational techniques that undermined traditional restraints on military violence.[32] Furthermore, the militias' failures of restraint played out in an environment that by 1780 was charged by the Whig government's demands for men and material to support the war effort, and especially by the government's confiscations of loyalist property.[33] The Whig control of the countryside since 1776 had not kept tensions from escalating, and when the British army arrived in the area after the capture of Charleston, it catalyzed loyalist resistance. Throughout the war, wherever the British army could project its power, loyalists surfaced.[34] Added to this environment were the true "Banditti," small groups of individuals determined to take advantage of the war for purely personal gain.[35] Finally, and perhaps most often cited as the cause of the Southern war's violence, the British army struggled internally over whether to treat the Americans as rebels deserving only fire and the sword or to try and win back their allegiance with an eye to postwar reconciliation. The British never fully committed to either path, and individual officers followed the course of their personal preference. Those who chose the fire and sword policy quickly became notorious, and their activities rapidly led to retaliation in kind.[36] Pointing to the British army's presence or their atrocities, however, does not suffice to explain the escalation of violence by the militias, largely because the Continental Army also operated in the same area and, in general, did not respond with greater violence.[37] For similar reasons, it is not enough merely to say that war naturally engenders such violence. It is also inaccurate to call this a "backcountry" war and then explain it on the basis of the particularities of the backcountry—its less-developed political institutions or its rougher breed of men.[38] Among other factors, the "backcountry" war was not confined to the backcountry, at least not in North Carolina. The militias scourged each other right up to the edge of Wilmington and New Bern.[39] A better explanation lies in the weakness of the new state, the cultural value placed on retaliation, and the nature and history of the militia.

With the reigniting of war in the South, one finds not only a continued struggle to maintain traditional restraints on violence, but also a process of rewriting the rules of warfare to effectively legitimize a greater latitude of violence. At the outset of the war, North Carolina's Whigs struggled to fight the virtuous war demanded by republicanism and as defined by the traditional mores supporting restraint in war—morality, military formalism, and honor. As the war progressed, however, three factors combined to undermine their efforts. First, the new state lacked the political coherence to regularly supply its troops or to make consistent judgments about prisoners. In essence, war making was decentralized, and it was left to local communities and militiamen to set the standards of permissible violence. The second factor was the basic cultural legitimacy of retaliation. One violation of norms led to another. The third factor was inability of the militias to contain the plaguelike spread of the desire for revenge. This inability was rooted in the militia structure itself. Its basic organization undermined preexisting community restraints because, when mobilized, the militias came to resemble mercenaries seeking plunder and revenge in contrast to the more disciplined and professional Continental Army. Furthermore, its enforcement missions and operational techniques were ill suited to restraint. Rather than containing the plague of revenge, the militia structure often spread it.

The Infant State

The weak administrative power of the new state meant that the local militias acted with a minimum of centralized oversight. Militia units were largely local and on their own. They mobilized and demobilized in rapid succession, and, because they lacked a reliable source of supplies from a financially prostrate state, militiamen often ravaged the countryside for their needs. By contrast, even though it too was desperate for supplies, the Continental Army attempted to maintain at least the pretense of reimbursement (providing receipts or certificates) and was committed to restraining the troops.[40] The Moravian Frederick Marshall admitted that one "must say for the regular troops . . . that their officers kept good order among them." He blamed the excesses on "camp followers, single soldiers, and especially by the militia."[41] The Continental officers also helped prevent abuses by their more consistent practice in sending quartering officers ahead of troops to systematize the collection of supplies.[42]

The militias lacked this sort of institutional regularity and were even less likely to come equipped with a method of payment. State officials recognized the problem and created a Board of War in an effort to streamline the provisioning system. Among other emergency measures, they shifted to a tax "in kind" in response to the extraordinary depreciation of the currency which had dramatically accelerated in 1779.[43] Their fears were clear.

The board wrote to Thomas Polk in 1780 that "if we do not feed the soldiers they must take care of themselves, and will do it at the point of the Bayonet," or, employing the more common phrase, they "will carve for themselves."[44] Residents too recognized that many of the unpleasant confrontations with soldiers arose from their unexpected arrival and peremptory demands for supply.[45] Militia soldiers put to the necessity of supplying themselves found it all too easy to take more than necessities. As one militia officer summed up, the militia was "without regular supplies of provisions or forage," and so each man, when out of food, would supply himself from local homes, "which all considered they had a right to do at the house of friend or foe." The officer grimly concluded that this system provided "men of dishonest propensities an opportunity of taking many things which necessity did not require."[46]

The second problem created by the lack of state oversight was the absence of a consistent policy for defining who was a prisoner of war and the conventions for treating prisoners. As discussed previously, militia units often were free to contrive their own definitions and methods of treatment. The temptation of both rebel and loyalist militias was to treat prisoners as traitors. The proximity of regular troops, however, could restrain militias from executing captives. In the case of loyalist David Fanning, for example, as long as the British army maintained its base in Wilmington, he regularly turned over prisoners to the British commander who would either hold or parole them. When the British evacuated Wilmington in November 1781, we find Fanning more regularly killing prisoners, though he continued to parole some on his own authority until the very end.[47]

Legitimizing Retaliation

More important than weak state authority, the cultural legitimacy of retaliation that had existed prior to the war took on a new and frightful dimension for both rebels and loyalists. Both expanded retaliation to include retribution against groups of people who were, or were believed to be, sympathetic to opponents. The customary right of retaliation had been explicitly codified in European notions of war. The legal theorist Emmerich Vattel wrote in 1758 that retaliation should be avoided, but a sovereign who "is dealing with an inhuman enemy who frequently commits atrocities such as . . . [hanging prisoners without cause] may refuse to spare the lives of certain prisoners whom he captures."[48] Vattel thus acknowledged a "Law of Retaliation," a phrase frequently used by combatants in North Carolina. In their minds, retaliation was not only a human urge but a quasi-legal right. Even colonial religious leaders admitted the right to retaliate, emphasizing only that it should be a carried out by the state, not indulged in privately.[49] This legalistic view of retaliation blended with the more generalized popular ideology of an individual's right of self-redress—the right "to make themselves whole" in response to injury or affront.[50] This expansive and quasi-legal vision of retaliation played the crucial role of making previously immoral acts into legitimate acts of war, thereby clearing consciences.[51]

Consider the issue of conscience in militiaman Moses Hall's tale of the killing of six prisoners. We have already seen how the men who "hewed to pieces" the prisoners did so after some discussion among themselves, followed by their shouts referring to the treatment of Buford's command at the Waxhaws—their justification for retaliating. Hall, not privy to the discussion, was initially horrified. The next day, however, Hall "discovered lying upon the ground . . . [what] proved to be a youth of about sixteen who, having come out to view the British troops through curiosity, for fear he might give information to our troops, they had run him through with a bayonet. . . . The sight of this unoffending boy, butchered . . . relieved me of my distressful feelings for the slaughter of the Tories, and I desired nothing so much as the opportunity of participating in their destruction."[52] Hall's conscience, through *eight* previous tours of duty as a militiaman, had survived intact. This incident cleared it.

Hall was not alone in his reaction to atrocity. Numerous militiamen from both sides explained how atrocities motivated them to retaliate. Such accounts repeat phrases like "excusable and justifiable retaliation," or "just retaliation."[53] Furthermore, certain aspects of the British war effort were seen to violate expectations of war, stimulating rebel responses. Most notable in this category was the use of Indians as allies— a people seen as adhering to no limits and whose use in and of itself therefore constituted an atrocity. North Carolina militia general Griffith Rutherford described Tories who worked in concert with the Indians as "inhuman hostile wretches" and "unchristian foes in strong alliance with [a] savage enemy."[54]

Rumor and propaganda of atrocities reduced restraints on violence by justifying retaliation against men whose crimes were merely alleged. The formulaic nature of atrocity accusations heightened real tensions over violence, which were further aggravated in the Southern backcountry by rumor spread through a diffusely settled countryside. News arrived by word of mouth, which usually told only one side of the story. Militiamen fed on these kinds of stories. They entered the fray prepared to believe the very worst of their opponents and, even if they were not retaliating for personal injury, could do so for atrocities that had no basis other than rumor.

In North Carolina and elsewhere, Continental Army officers and Whig leadership recognized the political benefits of withholding retaliation and thereby winning the hearts and minds of the countryside. Washington himself admitted to being tempted "to retaliation," but both "humanity and policy forbid the measure." He believed that "their wanton cruelty injures rather than benefits their cause; that with our forbearance, justly secured to us the attachment of all good men."[55]

Unfortunately, the militias frequently proved incapable of such restraint. The cultural and quasi-legal legitimacy of retaliation not only "cleared consciences." Collective agreement within a militia unit to commit acts of retribution could neutralize both individual reservations and opposing communal social norms. If at least some collective agreement existed that retaliation was justified, neither the individual's conscience nor the community would object. Lacking communal support for retaliation, an individual who feared social or judicial censure might withhold violence. The crucial, unstated issue here is the definition of "community." In republican theory, a militia was a group of armed citizens who carried the community's republican values with them into military service. The "military community" and civilian society were supposed to be congruent. In fact, North Carolina developed two different kinds of militia units—the regular enrolled militia and the volunteer militia—neither of which proved to be congruent to civilian society. For both types, their wartime structure and mission weakened powers of judicial censure. The structure of the regular militia undermined community-based social censure, whereas the volunteer militia tended to create a new community altogether, obeying a different set of values. In whatever form, the militias failed their revolutionary purpose to demonstrate the power of virtue in a righteous cause. Instead of functioning as the arm of controlled state justice and defense, the militias all too often became instruments of private retaliation.

Militia Organization and the Breakdown of Community Restraint

Within a military, or even a paramilitary organization, there are two sets of outside pressures on individual behavior: the formal threat of punishment by a military hierarchy and the informal, internal threat of communal disapproval by one's peers.[56] As seen above, the state had little or no control over its militias. Moreover, regular troops were a source of restraint only if they were nearby or acting in concert with the militias. The structures and practices of North Carolina's regular enrolled militia tended to weaken both formal and informal censure that could restrain wanton violence. Militia officers were ill equipped to punish their soldiers, and the units themselves were usually all-too-temporary fraternities, lacking either a wide cross section of their home communities or sufficient permanence to develop their own sense of community.

One way for a military organization to maintain a sense of community and the consequent power to exert peer pressure is to recruit units from an existing community and from a relatively wide cross section of that community's social structure. The other is to take a diverse assortment of recruits and inculcate a sense of community first through training and then through sustained service together. The wartime militia laws in North Carolina undercut both possibilities. Before the war, the peacetime militia law required nearly universal male service. Some exemptions existed for various professions, but North Carolina's militia system included the vast majority of white men within its umbrella, including even servants after 1746.[57] Although most settlers in the North Carolina Piedmont had not settled in towns, and each farm could be quite distant from the next, they were nevertheless perceived as neighborhoods, usually ethnically cohesive, and often defined by the creek lines upon which all their homes lay.[58] Companies were formed from such neighborhoods, and regiments from counties. "Private" musters for companies were supposed to be held three to five times per year, whereas "general" musters for the full regiment were held annually. All officers were nominally appointed by the governor, but the governor usually appointed captains and below on the basis of recommendations by the counties' senior officers. In essence, a peacetime militia company was very likely to closely reflect the inhabitants of a given district, up and down the social scale, without including slaves. James Bartholomees has reconstructed the membership and homestead locations of a representative peacetime militia company, demonstrating its neighborhood coherence.[59] With the outbreak of war, however, the new North Carolina government divided each company into five divisions: four for active service and the fifth as a reserve composed of the old and infirm. The idea was that each company when called up for service would send one-quarter of its strength (one division) for a three-month tour. That division would join with other company "quarters" to form a composite company.[60]

This divisional structure had a variety of negative effects on the enrolled militia's ability to contain violence. First, actively serving companies were composites of a variety of neighborhoods, breaking down the sense of community that might have existed in a neighborhood company. This reduced the concern members had for condemnation by their peers: these were men with whom they had had no dealings in the past and might not again in the future. Their judgments of each other did not have a lasting impact. At the same time, the system's standard three-month tour not only prevented the building of a strong military community, but also tended to shift officers around frequently or even randomly.[61] The Wilkes County militia was drafted twice in 1778: once for men and once for officers.[62] This shifting of officers and soldiers undercut the mutual personal respect between the leaders and the led that formed the theoretical keystone of a militia system. Robert Kincaid, recounting his tour of militia service in 1781, had difficulty remembering all of the different officers under whom he had served in just a three-month stint.[63] Jesse Ausley, a resident of Wake County, recalled being commanded by officers from Orange County and for one tour simply noted that "there was very little Regularity as to officers."[64] Nathan Grantham's experience might be extreme, but he recalled serving five successive three- to four-month tours, under different captains, and usually in a different regiment.[65] Consider again James Collins's story. In this case, his is the exception that proves the rule. Collins's company was a cohesive and stable volunteer company that had already served together around eight months, under the command of Colonel Moffitt, who had been elected to the position. Collins served in a military community where his respect for Moffitt and the unnamed instigator's fear of condemnation by his military peers helped save a prisoner's life.

Collins's story brings up the distinction between regularly called-up militia and "volunteer" militia units. Moffitt's volunteer unit appears to have been fairly restrained, in this case relying on a sense of community and a respected leader's observance of the formalities of war. Being volunteer units, however, did not guarantee adherence to conventional rules of war because the men who joined them were often those motivated to fight either for personal revenge or for personal profit.[66] Once in service with other such men, and serving for longer periods of time, they developed divergent community standards of behavior that condoned plunder as their own just reward or revenge. It comes as no surprise that volunteer units were the ones most often blamed for plundering.[67] William Gipson, the militiaman who recalled "spicketing" a Tory prisoner, had joined that volunteer unit in 1779 after his mother had been "tied up and whipped by the Tories" and his own home "almost entirely destroyed."[68] British outrages could also precipitate rebel volunteer retaliation on the more vulnerable Tories. The British expeditionary force from Wilmington to New Bern in August 1781 stopped to burn the homes of General Bryan, William Herritage, William Coxe, and Longfield Coxe. Almost immediately thereafter, Bryan, Herritage, and the Coxes "raised a party & burnt up all the Houses of the Tories near them."[69] The North Carolina Board of War feared the uncontrolled behavior of these units and sought to place them under regular command.[70]

In addition to the separate structural problems inherent to the "regular" militia and the volunteer militia, the substitute system also may have weakened the military sense of community. When a call went out to raise the militia for a given period, the usual procedure was first to prescribe a quota for a specific locale and then call for volunteers (individual volunteers to such a call-up were distinctly different from "volunteer units"). Usually there were insufficient volunteers to meet the quota, so a draft was needed.[71] Persons drafted could hire a substitute. Many veterans recalled serving as substitutes, but they rarely made clear in their pension claims whether they did so within their communities—substituting for family members or friends—or were doing so on a more "professional" traveling basis.[72] In the one case—substituting one neighborhood man for another—the substitute system would have had little effect on the cohesion of neighborhood units about to be split up anyway. In the case of the "professional" substitute, they might be thought to have contributed to a new military community, but the militia tours in which they served were too brief. In short, the substitute system may not have further hurt the system's ability to sponsor community and restrain violence, but it certainly did not help.

In summary, the divisional system, the short tours, the frequent change of officers, and possibly the substitute system all interfered with the capacity of soldiers in the regular enrolled rebel militia to influence and restrain each other's violent behavior in the field. The normal mechanisms of worrying about one's reputation in the eyes of one's community did not function in this environment. Volunteer units, in contrast, developed a peer community based on longer service, but—with the exception of units such as Moffitt's—their initial motivations to serve actually encouraged a more violent standard of behavior.

Both volunteer and regular militia units were unable to rely on the authority of officers alone to control violence. To borrow an eighteenth-century term, the militia in North Carolina had long been "democratical."[73] General Nathanael Greene's comment on the subject remains the most famous: "With the militia everybody is a general, and the powers of government are so feeble, that it is with the utmost difficulty you can restrain them from plundering one another."[74] In practice, many of the junior officers were elected, and, when the officers were not of their choosing, the militia might refuse to serve. Sixty men from Cumberland County voluntarily turned out and found themselves put under the command of Captain John Matthews. Because they had not been consulted on Matthews' appointment, the soldiers at muster refused to act under him, citing his previous cowardice, and they demanded the "liberty to choose their officer."[75] A man's reputation was critical to his suitability to serve as a militia officer, and part of that reputation was that he not be too strict and "disgust the militia."[76] Thus, militiamen tended to select officers who reflected their values and wishes.[77] This became a serious problem for military order when men volunteered intent on revenge or plunder. In their minds, officers were to aid them, not deter their lust for violence.

Many soldiers, particularly in volunteer units, entered service with the expectation of plunder, either from purely profit-seeking motives, as a substitute for pay, or to "make themselves whole" in retaliation for having been plundered themselves.[78] The Whig leadership did not always help matters in this regard. In their desperation to find ways to encourage the enlistment of soldiers whom they could neither supply nor adequately pay, they often resorted to the promise of plunder instead. Most notoriously, South Carolina militia general Thomas Sumter promised enlistees a captured slave.[79] Further south, the Georgia Council offered commissions and the right to keep plunder to any man who would raise fifteen other men to raid British Florida.[80] North Carolina Whig Whitmel Hill regretted using plunder as an incentive: "Our distrest Militia . . . will claim to themselves some compensation for their services. . . . This plundering I should not generally encourage, but in the present instance I think it justifiable."[81]

This hope to profit from soldiering within a "democratical" officer-soldier relationship meant that even officers who wanted to prevent plundering often had to give in to their soldiers' preferences. The Moravians recorded one officer's internal struggle to find "pluck enough" to order the restoration of plundered property, but only after he had been confronted by the victims of his soldiers' greed.[82] British Major Patrick Ferguson acknowledged the problems of controlling loyalist troops, advising that "some latitude" should be allowed for the lesser acts of plundering, so as to contribute to greater overall discipline.[83] Similarly, rebel militias in southwest Virginia plundered, divided, and sold loyalist property, "to which the officers have submitted, otherwise it would be impossible to get men on these pressing occasions."[84]

Besides the hopes for plunder, militia units often set their own standards for the treatment of prisoners. In some instances, soldiers demanded harsher treatment than that preferred by officers; in others, they were the restraining influence on more bloody-minded officers. Such incidents rarely appear in the official records of the war but are common in the early oral history and folklore compilations and occasionally surface in the usually laconic pension records. Two examples will suffice here. In late 1781, some of loyalist Colonel David Fanning's men captured rebel militia colonel Thomas Dugan and brought him to Fanning. Fanning determined to execute him, "but some of Fanning's men being his intimate acquaintances, and personal friends, wished to save him. . . . One man particularly, . . . interested himself so warmly that he got a decided majority opposed to his execution, and Fanning was compelled, much against his will to revoke the sentence." Instead, leaning on the continued presence of the British army in Wilmington, Fanning turned Dugan over to British control.[85] The British commander in Wilmington sentenced Dugan to be executed, and on the day he was to be hanged Major John Elrod spared his life. Ironically, a few months later a released Dugan found himself leading a band of militia that captured Elrod in a nighttime retaliatory raid. According to the oral history of the area, Dugan, obliged to Elrod for saving his life, was nevertheless unable to deflect his soldiers' desire to execute Elrod for Elrod's earlier killing of another Whig. After a "kind of court martial or consultation" he was tied to a tree and shot.[86]

Neither the officers themselves, nor even the more distant authorities of the state, seemed to possess the willingness or the capacity to punish militiamen for their misdeeds. There are virtually no records of courts-martial being held to discipline militiamen for civilian or military offenses.[87] Furthermore, the North Carolina militia law was quite lenient, specifying only a ten-pound fine for desertion, mutiny, or quitting one's post. The old colonial corporal punishments that had been retained under the 1774 militia law were absent from the 1777 version.[88] Fines seem to have been preferred, though militia officers were allowed discretion to administer punishments other than death. The initial militia law of 1776 specified that "each and every Company make such regulations as to them shall seem best, for non-attendance, disobedience, and misbehavior, at Musters by Companies."[89] Flaws within the militia law made it difficult to hold punitive courts at all. Governor Burke pointed out that the law required all of the officers making up the court be from the same regiment as the offender, but too often the officers themselves were the offenders.[90] Near the end of the war, Burke complained that the militia law contained "no adequate provisions . . . for restraining or governing either men or officers when in actual service."[91] There are reports of unofficial punishment being meted out in cases of disorder; one such convict received seventeen lashes. But there are as many examples of plunderers being slapped on the wrist; several such men were merely made to return the stolen items and promise not to steal again.[92] Lieutenant Colonel Thomas Taylor of Orange County, accused of permitting "the men under his command to plunder and maraud in a most offensive and disgraceful manner," was suspended, but only after a special act of the North Carolina Senate.[93]

In contrast to the weakness of state law and the tenuous authority of militia officers, the Continental Army followed strikingly different rules. It adopted fairly stringent articles of war from the outset, and they became more severe over the course of the war, especially in the punishment of plunderers.[94] Continental Army order books are filled with warnings to soldiers not to plunder, with dire threats of punishment and even death. Those same order books often record infliction of such punishment, to include flogging and execution. One historian has argued that, although George Washington often commuted sentences for various offenses, he very rarely showed mercy to plunderers.[95] Unlike the militias, courts-martial were exceedingly common and punishment for plundering was severe.[96]

The state's and the militia officers' weaknesses undermined both types of militias' efforts to live up to societal expectations of restrained virtuous war. The regularly raised, "official" militia lacked the communal coherence necessary for internal systems of censure. The volunteer militia took the field fired by motives that legitimated more extreme visions of acceptable violence—they had "communal coherence," but of a different quality than the wider society. Even when not simply self-interested bandits, they felt their violence legitimated by the law of retaliation. Finally, both the regular and the volunteer militias lacked the social distance between officers and men necessary for authoritarian control of excessive violence. All of these weaknesses were exposed and accentuated by the missions required of militias and by the tactics they adopted to fulfill them.

From the very beginning of the war, one of the most important of the rebel militias' roles was the maintenance of loyalty to the Whig cause. Militias became the investigative arm, the police force, and the enforcers of a partisan government.[97] This mission grew naturally out of the extralegal activities of the committees of safety as the state moved from resistance to rebellion in 1775. In November 1775, militia units were found tarring and feathering loyalist Cullen Pollock in Chowan County, whereas in New Hanover County the militia went from door to door confiscating loyalists' weapons, leaving one per white man in each house.[98]

As the war progressed, the Whig government continued to use militias as political enforcers, to make arrests, administer loyalty oaths, confiscate arms, and eventually confiscate loyalist property. Such practices put the militiamen in the very awkward position of making individuals and individuals' homes the focus for their activity. Eighteenth-century Euro-American notions of war did not include warring against specific individuals. Military activity was supposed to be conducted between armies, the formally constituted bodies representing opposing states. Although individual houses could be the targets of foraging or even quartering, the individuals within those houses were not supposed to be harmed or carried away. The reality of European warfare often belied this expectation—particularly if an army was ordered to devastate the countryside for military reasons. Nevertheless, the expectation of restraint remained.

Unfortunately, the service experiences of many militiamen broke down this restraint against war on individuals, and, because most militiamen served a number of tours, they brought that experience with them in each succeeding tour.[99] As the war dragged on, there was a logical devolution of the militias from enforcement of provincial law to the more violent late-war "scour." The rebel militias took it upon themselves to "scour" the countryside for Tories. Restraint on militia enforcement diminished when the North Carolina Senate officially authorized such scouring in August 1778. The law empowered the county court or any three justices of the peace to call out the militia to "compel tories or other disorderly people of their county to a due observance of the law."[100]

Where scourings may have begun as missions to enforce the law, they quickly deteriorated into punitive expeditions. William Lenoir's account highlights this deterioration. In 1778 he went on three expeditions, ostensibly to enforce the loyalty oath. In the first, he and his companions found no Tories in three days of searching. In the spring, however, while pursuing some Tories into the Blue Ridge Mountains, they captured some who "were mostly permitted to go at large, after an examination, in which they generally made recantation, and [illegible] promises of loyalty to the cause of independence and in some instances . . . [took] the oath." Immediately after returning home, however, Lenoir and his company set out again in pursuit of yet more Tories. On capturing one, they tried to get information from the prisoner about other Tories. When the man refused, "Colonel [Benjamin] Cleveland adopted the expedient of Hanging him for a while to the limb of a tree or a bent down sapling, but which did not produce the desired effect until the dose was repeated a second time with more severity then the first."[101] Later in the war, Frederick Smith crossed the path of a party of Whig militia, who questioned him as to his loyalties. Unsure who was asking, he guessed wrong, and they proceeded to hang him briefly from a tree, cutting him down before he died. Not to be outdone, a loyalist militia unit that later crossed paths with Smith asked him the same question. Again Smith guessed wrong as to the identity of those asking and again was "half-hanged" for his trouble.[102]

The deterioration was even more marked as militiamen on a scouring expedition deliberately sought out those they "knew" were Tories. Scouring became a means to intimidate suspected Tories. The experience of John Evans is instructive.[103] Sometime in 1780, the light horse militia company of Nash County arrived at his house, arrested him, carried him to the courthouse, and "threatened [him] . . . with hanging, a Gallows being erected on the spot." Terrified, he agreed to enlist for eighteen months. When he asked the reasons for his arrest, the militia told him that they had heard that he wanted to take up arms and join a Tory band in Edgecombe County and that he had asked someone else's advice on the matter. Although the determination of Evans's loyalties may have been a little cavalier, others' loyalties were often accurately known, leading to nighttime expeditions to surprise partisans of the other side in their homes. The victims of many such raids did not survive.[104] Many did, however, and James Collins's account of his units' methods of scouring testifies to the continued functioning of some restraints. He claimed that they would surprise a Tory house, force the doors, extinguish the lights, back the man of the house into a corner, and swing away with swords, "but taking care to strike the wall or some object that was in the way." They would then pull down the house to the roof joists, and spare the Tory himself, provided he left. Collins further claimed that the only property disturbed was the house itself.[105]

The militiamen's experience with Indian warfare also weakened restraints on the use of force. The history of Indian wars in the colonies had led the militia to develop tactics that included a preference for night or dawn attacks, ambushes, and harassing parties.[106] Gregory Knouff has argued that this preference was reinforced by the backcountry men's investment of their masculine identity in a frontier style of war. They wanted to be seen as tough, independent, even violent men who fought Indians while using an Indian style of war.[107]

There were consequences to this style of warfare. Ambushes and night attacks were notoriously difficult to control once begun.[108] In situations like these, quarter was often refused.[109] In his pension statement, Thomas Cummings simply noted of one of his militia tours that, although no engagement was entered into, "a number of Tories were shot and cut to pieces" in the swamps.[110] For many militiamen, their only knowledge of war had been of the particularly unrestrained kind practiced against Indians. The most-common technique of waging war against elusive Indians was to burn their fields and towns, depriving them of sustenance; this was known in the seventeenth century as the "feed fight."[111] Frustrated militiamen could easily turn such a strategy against a white enemy. Stephen Cobb complained to the governor in July 1779 that he had been repeatedly threatened by a Tory band led by "the Basses." He pointed out that he had tried everything in his power "to take them without killing them." He had failed, and, if he did not get state help soon, he wanted a warrant to "take them dead or alive, and to destroy what they have if they will not surrender themselves."[112] This combination of using an Indian style of war that was difficult to control with an experience of scorched earth war *against* Indians helped pave the descent into retaliatory war.

Militia violence in the latter years of the war in North Carolina was neither unadulterated carnage nor the virtuous war that many had hoped for. The violence of the war was shaped more by collective values *about* war and the past and present experience *of* war. Honor and morality restrained violence, while the right of self-redress unleashed it. Past experience of war both demanded restraint according to the "customs and usages of war" and bore witness to unlimited destruction previously waged against Indians. Historians' explanations for the devolution of the war's violence into savagery have emphasized either preexisting social tensions or simple lashing back at British misbehavior. Those explanations account for neither North Carolinians' values about war nor the nature of the militia as an institution. Communal values about violence in war not only attempted to moderate behavior, but also set the conditions under which retaliation became "necessary." People lashed out with violence because they were angry about violence. They soon discovered that, when they did lash out, censure from within or from without the military community did not exist. In part censure did not exist because the culture authorized retaliation and because the infant state lacked the bureaucratic mechanisms necessary to enforce military conventions. And finally, censure did not exist because some militia units had redefined their values to include actions formerly beyond the pale, such as plundering and vengeance.

Two final anecdotes can best capture the complexity of violence. Both incidents are found in the pension claims of militiamen, whose memories were sometimes dimmed by time, but also sometimes freed from constraint by their age. In November 1781, Bryan McCullen avoided a draft by volunteering to serve a three-month tour under Captain John Grantham. His company went scouring for Tories in Dobbs County, found some, and a skirmish ensued. Then, in McCullen's extraordinarily blasé phrasing, "one of the Tories viz. Absalom Davis was taken prisoner and afterwards killed."[113]

In contrast, Robert Knox's group, during a tour at about the same time, went in pursuit of the notorious Tory Colonel John Moore. Unable to find him, they instead went to the home of his father, Moses Moore. There the soldiers took a rather simple revenge: "destroy[ing] his oats by throwing them over to the horses." This "the officers prevent[ed] when they came up."[114] These two simple stories actually tell a complex tale. In them we find short militia tours, Tory "scourings," the use of local knowledge to target the homes of "known" individuals, the "feed fight" tactic, and the casual killing of a prisoner contrasted with the intervention of officers at a more trifling offense. Many other such complex tales could be told, and in each of them we would find a struggle between the desire for a virtuous war and the urge for personal retribution.

184 WAYNE E. LEE

Notes

I am indebted to many people for their help with this essay. In particular I would like to thank the members of the Kentucky Early Americanist seminar, Glenn Crothers, Brad Wood, Debra Meyers, and Ken Williams. I also appreciate the close readings provided by John Resch and Rhonda Lee and the research assistance of George Stevenson at the North Carolina Archives. Although there is new evidence and argumentation here, portions of this essay appeared in Wayne E. Lee, *Crowds and Soldiers in Revolutionary North Carolina: The Culture of Violence in Riot and War* (Gainesville: University Press of Florida, 2001), chaps. 5–7, and are reprinted here by permission of that press.

1. James Collins, *Autobiography of a Revolutionary Soldier*, ed. John M. Roberts (Clinton, La.: Feliciana Democrat, 1859; repr., New York: Arno Press, 1979), pp. 55–56. Bobby Gilmer Moss, *The Patriots at King's Mountain* (Blacksburg, S.C.: Scotia-Hibernia Press, 1990), pp. 51–52, 186; Lyman C. Draper, *King's Mountain and Its Heroes* (Cincinnati: Peter G. Thomson, 1881; repr., Baltimore: Genealogical Publishing Co., 1997), p. 465.

2. David Fanning, *The Narrative of Col. David Fanning*, ed. Lindley S. Butler (Davidson, N.C.: Briarpatch Press, 1981), pp. 35–36 (hereafter *DFN*).

3. John C. Dann, ed., *The Revolution Remembered: Eyewitness Accounts of the War for Independence* (Chicago: University of Chicago Press, 1980), p. 202. "Remember Buford" was a reference to the massacre of surrendering Continentals under Abraham Buford's command at Waxhaws, S.C., by Colonel Banastre Tarleton in 1780.

4. David J. Fowler, "Egregious Villains, Wood Rangers, and London Traders: The Pine Robber Phenomenon in New Jersey during the Revolutionary War" (Ph.D. diss., Rutgers University, 1987), p. 21.

5. Charles Royster, *A Revolutionary People at War: The Continental Army and American Character, 1775–1783* (New York: W. W. Norton, 1979), pp. 25–53; James Kirby Martin and Mark Edward Lender, *A Respectable Army: The Military Origins of the Republic, 1763–1789* (Arlington Heights, Ill.: Harlan Davidson, 1982), pp. 30–34; John Morgan Dederer, *War in America to 1775: Before Yankee Doodle* (New York: New York University Press, 1990), pp. 196–97, 208–9; Lawrence Delbert Cress, *Citizens in Arms: The Army and Militia in American Society to the War of 1812* (Chapel Hill: University of North Carolina Press, 1982), p. 26.

6. James Kirby Martin, ed., *Ordinary Courage: The Revolutionary War Adventures of Joseph Plumb Martin*, 2nd ed. (New York: Brandywine Press, 1999), p. 120; James Thacher, *Military Journal of the American Revolution, 1775–1783* (Gansevoort, N.Y.: Corner House Publications, 1998), pp. 107–12. The same ideology of virtuous restraint can be found in John Adams's prewar tract, "On Private Revenge, no. 1," in C. Bradley Thompson, ed., *The Revolutionary Writings of John Adams* (Indianapolis, Ind.: Liberty Fund, 2000), pp. 6–7; and the sermon of the Reverend William Emerson, cited in Robert A. Gross, *The Minutemen and Their World* (New York: Hill and Wang, 1976), p. 73.

7. Wayne E. Lee, *Crowds and Soldiers in Revolutionary North Carolina: The Culture of Violence in Riot and War* (Gainesville: University Press of Florida, 2001), pp. 179–94.

8. Walter Clark, ed., *The State Records of North Carolina*, 26 vols. (Winston and Goldsboro, N.C.: various publishers, 1895–1907), 16:416–18 (hereafter *NCSR*).

9. *NCSR*, 17:1049, 16:566.

10. Collins, *Autobiography*, p. 66.

11. Elijah Alexander (W5201), Revolutionary War Pension and Bounty-Land-Warrant Application Files, National Archives, Washington (hereafter PenRec with claim number).

12. "Sermon against Plundering," Samuel E. McCorkle Papers, Duke University Special Collections, Durham, N.C.

13. Davie to Sumner, October 7, 1780, Horatio Gates Papers, Microfilm edition prepared by the New York Historical Society and the National Historical Records and Publications Commission (hereafter HGP).

14. *NCSR,* 16:268–69, 22:610–11.

15. Petition of Sundry Inhabitants of Salisbury and Parts Adjacent, April–May, 1782, Joint Standing Committees, Propositions & Grievances—Report and papers, General Assembly Session Records, North Carolina Department of Archives and History, Raleigh, N.C. (hereafter NCA); *NCSR,* 15:503–4; Martin, *Ordinary Courage,* p. 69; Samuel McCorkle, "Sermon against Plundering"; Adelaide L. Fries, ed., *Records of the Moravians in North Carolina,* 11 vols. (Raleigh, N.C.: North Carolina Historical Commission, 1922–1969), 3:1409 (hereafter *MR*); William Henry Foote, *Sketches of North Carolina: Historical and Biographical* (New York: Robert Carter, 1846), p. 417; Nathanael Greene, *The Papers of General Nathanael Greene,* 13 vols., ed. Richard K. Showman, et al. (Chapel Hill: University of North Carolina Press, 1976–2005), 6:589–90 (hereafter *NGP*).

16. *NCSR,* 14:392. The "carving" phrase was a common one.

17. *New Jersey Gazette,* August 5, 1778; *MR,* 4:1622, 1910; *NCSR,* 16:527–28; Thacher, *Military Journal,* p. 77.

18. *MR,* 3:1253–54; 4:1549; 3:1277–78; 4:1644, 1666, 1678–80, 1701–1702; 4:1759. All of these examples are taken from situations where officer intervention is either absent or not directly mentioned in the source. There are many more examples of restraint imposed or attempted by officers.

19. Dann, *Revolution Remembered,* pp. 188–89. For the traditional use of spicketing, or picqueting, see R. E. Scouller, *The Armies of Queen Anne* (Oxford: Clarendon Press, 1966), pp. 268, 390; Scott Claver, *Under the Lash: A History of Corporal Punishment in the British Armed Forces* (London: Torchstream Books, 1954), pp. 12–13. "Picqueting" was still listed as a punishment in the North Carolina militia law in 1774. *NCSR,* 23:943. Such a punishment was also described as appropriate for slaves in Hunter Dickinson Farish, ed., *The Journal and Letters of Philip Vickers Fithian: A Plantation Tutor of the Old Dominion, 1773–1774* (Charlottesville: University Press of Virginia, 1968), pp. 38–39.

20. Elijah Alexander Papers, NCA. Other incidents in E. W. Caruthers, *The Old North State* (originally published as *Revolutionary Incidents and Sketches of Character Chiefly in the "Old North State"* [Philadelphia: Hayes & Zell, 1854–1856; repr., Greensboro, N.C.: Guilford County Genealogical Society, 1994], pp. 87–88); Pension Record of Robert Love, transcribed in The David Schenk Papers, NCA; Pension Record of Peter Banks in Betty J. Camin, ed., *North Carolina Revolutionary War Pension Applications,* 3 vols. (Raleigh, N.C.: privately published, 1983) (Camin's volume is a typescript of pension documents found in county courthouses, which may or may not also be in the National Archives), 1:18.

21. *MR,* 4:1625–28.

22. *NCSR,* 15:109. Draper, *King's Mountain,* 332.

23. John H. Wheeler, *Historical Sketches of North Carolina, from 1584 to 1851,* 2 vols. (Philadelphia: Lippincott, Grambo and Co., 1851), 2:444; fn.35.

24. *NCSR,* 14:462–64; 17:668; 16:269, 318, 565–69, 685–86.

25. British prisoners, once taken, were usually treated according to the customs of war. Charles H. Metzger, *The Prisoner in the American Revolution* (Chicago: Loyola University Press, 1971), pp. 1–2; Betsy Knight, "Prisoner Exchange and Parole in the American Revolution," *William and Mary Quarterly,* 3rd ser., 48 (April 1991): 202, 210ff.

26. *NCSR,* 16:416–18. See also *NCSR,* 16:684.

27. Exact numbers are elusive; Greene repeatedly struggled and failed to get returns of prisoners taken, paroled, or held. *NGP,* 6:544, 7:48, 67; *NCSR,* 14:727, 15:xiv, 17:668; *MR,* 4:1574, 1576, 1633; Draper, *King's Mountain,* pp. 357–60. Emory G. Evans, "Trouble in the Backcountry: Disaffection in Southwest Virginia during the American Revolution," in Ronald Hoffman, Thad W. Tate, and Peter J. Albert, eds., *An Uncivil War: The Southern Backcountry during the American Revolution* (Charlottesville: University of Virginia Press, 1985), pp. 199–200, 205; *MR,* 4:1626–28; Harry M. Ward, *Between the Lines: Banditti of the American Revolution* (Westport, Conn.: Praeger, 2002), p. 88.

28. General Gates to the Board of War, November 15, 1780; Colonel Thomas Wade

186 W A Y N E E . L E E

to General Gates, November, 23, 1780, both HGP; *NCSR,* 17:668, 1049; 16:229–31, 511, 522, 689–90. *NCSR,* 15:151–52. South Carolina instituted a similar system in the summer of 1781. Jerome J. Nadelhaft, *The Disorders of War: The Revolution in South Carolina* (Orono: University of Maine at Orono Press, 1981), p. 71.

29. To attempt to quantify the survival rate of prisoners is impossible, because the records simply do not exist. Examining the pension records of North Carolina militiamen, however, one finds the experience of taking, delivering, and/or guarding prisoners to be extraordinarily common, far more common than accounts of killing them, even of killing them after a court-martial. Of 110 randomly selected pension records of North Carolina militiamen, ten (9 percent) specifically recalled an entire tour spent guarding or escorting prisoners. In Camin's collection of the pension statements of sixty-two militiamen, twelve (19 percent) recalled such tours. Although these numbers may seem small, when one considers how laconic most pension records are, the survival of this detail in 9 percent and 19 percent of them is significant.

30. *DFN,* pp. 39–43.

31. Richard R. Beeman, "The Political Response to Social Conflict in the Southern Backcountry: A Comparative View of Virginia and the Carolinas during the Revolution," in Hoffman, Tate, and Albert, *An Uncivil War,* p. 232; Ward, *Between the Lines,* pp. 221–27.

32. For the "people's war" characterization, see Stephen Conway, *The War of American Independence, 1775–1783* (London: Edward Arnold, 1995), pp. 245–47; John Resch, *Suffering Soldiers: Revolutionary War Veterans, Moral Sentiment, and Political Culture in the Early Republic* (Amherst: University of Massachusetts Press, 1999), pp. 1–46.

33. Lee, *Crowds and Soldiers,* pp. 164–75; Robert O. DeMond, *The Loyalists in North Carolina during the Revolution* (Durham, N.C.: Duke University Press, 1940), pp. 153–80.

34. John Shy, "Hearts and Minds in the American Revolution: The Case of 'Long Bill' Scott and Peterborough, New Hampshire," in *A People Numerous and Armed,* rev. ed. (Ann Arbor: University of Michigan Press, 1990), p. 178; Fowler, "Egregious Villains," p. 38ff; Wallace Brown, *The King's Friends: The Composition and Motives of the American Loyalist Claimants* (Providence, R.I.: Brown University Press, 1965), pp. 58–61.

35. Martha Condray Searcy, *The Georgia-Florida Contest in the American Revolution, 1776–1778* (Tuscaloosa: University of Alabama Press, 1985), p. 128; Ward, *Between the Lines.*

36. Armstrong Starkey, "War and Culture, A Case Study: The Enlightenment and the Conduct of the British Army in America, 1755–1781," *War and Society* 8 (1990): 1–28; Stephen Conway, "To Subdue America: British Army Officers and the Conduct of the Revolutionary War," *William and Mary Quarterly,* 3rd ser., 43 (July 1986): 381–407, and "'The Great Mischief Complain'd of:' Reflections on the Misconduct of British Soldiers in the Revolutionary War," *William and Mary Quarterly,* 3rd ser., 47 (July 1990): 370–90; Paul H. Smith, *Loyalists and Redcoats: A Study in British Revolutionary Policy* (New York: W. W. Norton, 1972); Shy, "Hearts and Minds," pp. 163–80; Nadelhaft, *Disorders,* pp. 55–58; Louis D. F. Frasche, "Problems of Command: Cornwallis, Partisans and Militia, 1780," *Military Review* 57 (1977): 62; Jac Weller, "The Irregular War in the South," *Military Affairs* 24 (1960): 133; Russell F. Weigley, *The Partisan War: The South Carolina Campaigns of 1780–82* (Columbia: University of South Carolina Press, 1970), pp. 12–13.

37. Don Higginbotham, "The American Militia: A Traditional Institution with Revolutionary Responsibilities," in Don Higginbotham, ed., *Reconsiderations on the Revolutionary War* (Westport, Conn.: Greenwood Press, 1978), p. 100.

38. Jack Greene, "Independence, Improvement and Authority," in Hoffman, Tate, and Albert, *An Uncivil War,* pp. 3–36.

39. Ward, *Between the Lines,* pp. 153–68, 222; Nadelhaft, *Disorders,* pp. 64–66; Weigley, *Partisan War,* pp. 22–23; Searcy, *Georgia-Florida.*

40. Lee, *Crowds and Soldiers,* pp. 212–19.

41. *MR,* 4:1910.

42. *MR,* 4:1573.

43. *NCSR,* 24:344–47, 390–94. *MR,* 4:1623, 1629–30.

44. *NCSR,* 14:392, 405. See also *NCSR,* 15:329; William A. Graham, *General Joseph Graham and His Papers on North Carolina Revolutionary History* (Raleigh, N.C.: Edwards & Broughton, 1904), p. 312.

45. The Moravians made this problem explicit, complaining that the real blame for the impromptu demands made on them for provisions was that the "Commissary does not look after the soldiers and does not provide for them." *MR,* 4:1758. Two weeks after that comment, another militia company repaid the Moravians in food once their own supplies came up with them. *MR,* 4:1759.

46. Graham, *Graham's Papers,* p. 348.

47. *DFN,* pp. 35, 36, 45, 48, 51, 53, 55–56, 60, 68, 72, 76. The details of Fanning's admittedly self-serving account are usually confirmed by pro-Whig sources.

48. Emmerich de Vattel, *The Law of Nations,* trans. Charles G. Fenwick. The Classics of International Law (New York: Oceana Publications, 1964), pp. 280–81.

49. Reginald C. Stuart, "'For the Lord is a Man of Warr': The Colonial New England View of War and the American Revolution," *Journal of Church & State* 23 (1981): 523; McCorkle, "Sermon against Plunderers."

50. Bertram Wyatt-Brown, *Southern Honor: Ethics and Behavior in the Old South* (New York: Oxford University Press, 1982), pp. xv, 34; Richard Maxwell Brown, *No Duty to Retreat: Violence and Values in American History and Society* (Oxford: Oxford University Press, 1991), and *Strain of Violence: Historical Studies of American Violence and Vigilantism* (New York: Oxford University Press, 1975); David H. Fischer, *Albion's Seed* (Oxford: Oxford University Press, 1989), pp. 765–68. Quote is from McCorkle, "Sermon against Plunderers."

51. Ward, *Between the Lines,* pp. 78, 126; *DFN,* p. 106; Metzger, *The Prisoner,* pp. 154–58; Knight, "Prisoner Exchange."

52. Dann, *Revolution Remembered,* pp. 202–3.

53. Quotations are from Petition of William Linton to General Assembly, October 3, 1783, April 20–May 18, Reports and Papers, Joint Select Committees, General Assembly Session Records, NCA; Petition of Henry Reed and others, [January 3, 1787] Gen. Assy. Sess. Recs., Nov. 1786–Jan. 1787, Senate Joint Resolutions, Jan. 1–7, NCA.

54. *NCSR,* 13:283.

55. George Washington, *The Papers of George Washington,* 14 vols. Revolutionary War Series, Philander D. Chase, ed. (Charlottesville: University Press of Virginia, 1985–2004), 9:223.

56. A third force would be individual conscience, but it is less visible in the records and is frankly almost inseparably tied to the second; however, it can occasionally be observed in the sources. For example, Frederick Smith, a would-be neutral in the war, was left hanging by a group of militiamen (of which side is unclear). One individual from the group doubled back and cut him down before he strangled. Caruthers, *Old North State,* p. 171. In a more striking example, militia captain James Devane refused orders to round up Tory women and children and carry them into Wilmington, describing it as "repulsive to his feelings." Camin, *Pension Applications,* 1:87.

57. *NCSR,* 23:29; 244–47; 25:334–37; 13:518–22; James W. Titus, *The Old Dominion at War: Society, Politics, and Warfare in Late Colonial Virginia* (Columbia, S.C.: University of South Carolina Press, 1991), p. 2.

58. Robert W. Ramsey, *Carolina Cradle: Settlement of the Northwest Carolina Frontier, 1747–1776* (Chapel Hill: University of North Carolina Press, 1964); S. Scott Rohrer, "Searching for Land and God: The Pietist Migration to North Carolina in the Late Colonial Period," *North Carolina Historical Review* 79 (2002): 432–35; Rachel N. Klein, "Frontier Planters and the American Revolution," in Hoffman, Tate, and Albert, *An Uncivil War,* p. 46.

59. James Boone Bartholomees, Jr., "Fight or Flee: The Combat Performance of the North Carolina Militia in the Cowpens-Guilford Courthouse Campaign, January to March 1781" (Ph.D. diss., Duke University, 1978), pp. 214–34. These peacetime structures during the colonial era were rarely mobilized intact. The militia served as a pool of manpower from which volunteers were preferred, but drafts would be made when necessary.

60. NCCR, 10:196–201.

61. This was not only true in law, but is borne out by virtually every pension application that refers to militia service.

62. Pension Record of Richard Allen, Sr., in Camin, *Pension Applications*, p. 98.

63. Robert Kincaid, PenRec (W26186).

64. Jesse Ausley, PenRec (W27520); Sterling Cooper, PenRec (S6776).

65. Nathan Grantham, PenRec (S31716).

66. *NGP*, 6:546 n.9; Foote, *Sketches*, pp. 315, 326; NCSR, 15:105.

67. Smallwood to Gates, October 31, 1780, HGP.

68. Dann, *Revolution Remembered*, pp. 186–87.

69. *NCSR*, 15:626–27.

70. *NCSR*, 14:451.

71. *NCSR*, 24:154–55; MR, 3:1113, 1250; NCSR, 12:iii–iv.

72. Of ninety-nine randomly sampled pensioners who served in the North Carolina militia, twenty-four (24 percent) had either served as or hired substitutes. If one counts the number of tours as a substitute versus the total number of tours served by those same men (340 total tours versus 30 tours as substitutes), it is only 8 percent. These numbers cannot be precise. Most pensioners tried to be clear on what basis they served, whether as volunteer, draftee, or substitute, but their petitions clearly do not reflect perfectly their service. The ninety-nine men sampled here are only those whose pension records were sufficiently clear to distinguish tours, but that only excluded a very few.

73. Lee, *Crowds and Soldiers*, pp. 130–31; Fred Anderson, *A People's Army: Massachusetts Soldiers and Society in the Seven Years' War* (Chapel Hill: University of North Carolina Press, 1984), pp. 48, 167–95; Harold E. Selesky, *War and Society in Colonial Connecticut* (New Haven, Conn.: Yale University Press, 1990), p. 187; Titus, *Old Dominion at War*, pp. 33–41.

74. *NGP*, 6:547.

75. *NCSR*, 11:628, 658; 13:4; James Shipman, PenRec (W17810); William Lenoir, PenRec (S7137); Wheeler, *Historical Sketches*, 2:385.

76. *NCSR*, 17:679.

77. William R. Davie, *The Revolutionary War Sketches of William R. Davie* (Raleigh, N.C.: Division of Archives and History, 1976), p. 16.

78. Graham, *Graham's Papers*, p. 312. Graham had interrupted a group of plunderers in the Moravian towns, who claimed that the Moravians were loyalists and "remonstrated that they had been plundered by Tories and had a right to make themselves whole."

79. Hugh F. Rankin, *The North Carolina Continentals* (Chapel Hill: University of North Carolina Press, 1971), p. 353.

80. Searcy, *Georgia-Florida*, p. 128

81. *NCSR*, 15:56.

82. *MR*, 4:1565.

83. Hugh F. Rankin, "Ferguson's 'Proposed Plan for Bringing the Army under strict discipline,'" in Howard H. Peckham, ed., *Sources of American Independence: Selected Manuscripts From the Collections of the William L. Clements Library* (Chicago: University of Chicago Press, 1978), 2:337.

84. Preston to Jefferson, August 8, 1780, Preston Papers, Draper Manuscript Collection, State Historical Society of Wisconsin, 5QQ50, cited in Evans, "Trouble in the Backcountry," p. 200.

85. Caruthers, *Old North State*, p. 86; DFN, p. 73.

86. Caruthers, *Old North State*, pp. 87–88.

87. Court-Martial of Captain Aaron Hill, Miscellaneous Papers, Military Collection, NCA; *NCSR,* 14:468–69; Charles McDowell Papers, NCA (the entire collection is a record of his court-martial for "countenancing Tories"); *NCSR,* 22:956. See also *NCSR,* 12:712–13; 14:17; 15:431–32; NCCR, 10:560–63. The long-established system for militia courts-martial, primarily used to regulate absences from muster or inadequate equipment, does not seem to have been used as a disciplinary tool. There are few surviving examples of these regular muster courts-martial from the Revolutionary period. That they continued to occur, however, is clear. There are, for example, numerous references to them in petitions referring to irregularities in the draft process. See, for example, Petition of the Freeholders and Freemen of the District of Salisbury, December 1781, April–May 1782, Joint Standing Committees, Propositions & Grievances, General Assembly Session Records, NCA.

88. *NCSR,* 23:943; *NCSR,* 24:1–5.

89. NCCR, 10:199.

90. *NCSR,* 22:1039–40.

91. *NCSR,* 16:10. In South Carolina, it was not until 1782 that a law mandating severe punishment for plundering by militia men and officers was passed. S.C. Senate Journal, February 10, 1782, cited in Klein, "Frontier Planters," p. 65.

92. *MR,* 4:1681, 1683, 1776.

93. *NCSR,* 17:689.

94. Robert H. Berlin, "The Administration of Military Justice in the Continental Army during the American Revolution, 1775–1783" (Ph.D. diss., University of California at Santa Barbara, 1976).

95. Holly A. Mayer, *Belonging to the Army: Camp Followers and Community during the American Revolution* (Columbia: University of South Carolina Press, 1996), p. 41.

96. James Neagles's extensive survey of courts-martial recorded in order books found 194 examples of soldiers charged with plunder or theft from civilians (7.3 percent of the total number of courts-martial). There were undoubtedly more, but the order books often did not include enough details to determine whether certain offenses such as stealing were committed against civilians or other soldiers. James Neagles, *Summer Soldiers: A Survey & Index of Revolutionary War Courts-Martial* (Salt Lake City: Ancestry Incorporated, 1986), p. 34.

97. The Journal of the Committee of Safety for Rowan County, July 18, 1775, Wheeler, *Historical Sketches,* 2:365, 368–69; NCCR, 10:48, 125–29, 363.

98. NCCR, 10:1027–33; Samuel Johnston to Joseph Hewes, November 26, 1775, enclosed in the letter of Vice Admiral Graves, January 29, 1776, PRO CO 5/123 transcript in English Records 13-2, NCA; *North Carolina Gazette,* December 22, 1775.

99. There was a very strong trend of individuals having multiple tours of duty in the North Carolina rebel militias. Thus, the "experience of the institution" was the multiple repeat service of individuals within it. Ninety-nine randomly selected militia pensioners served an average of 3.4 tours in the North Carolina rebel militias. The fifty-one pensioners with militia service (and distinguishable tours) transcribed in Camin averaged 2.7 tours each. In reality, both averages should be higher, because many of those pensioners lost count of their tours, and others combined one or two short militia tours with a long enlistment in the Continentals. (Continental tours are not figured into the average and militia tours are not weighted for length of service.)

100. *NCSR,* 12:775, 811.

101. William Lenoir, PenRec (S7137).

102. Caruthers, *Old North State,* pp. 171–72.

103. Petition of John Evans, *NCSR,* 15:236. See also *MR,* 4:1561, 1613.

104. Caruthers in *Old North State* and in *DFN.*

105. Collins, *Autobiography,* p. 66.

106. Higginbotham, "The American Militia," p. 99; Weigley, *Partisan War,* p. 15 and passim. Although it is true that North Carolina had escaped relatively lightly

from the Indian attacks of the mid-eighteenth century, many North Carolinians had arrived there from more northerly colonies. Of 114 North Carolina pensioners (militia and Continental), 32 percent had been born in Virginia, Pennsylvania, or Maryland (25 percent in North Carolina and 36 percent unknown). And, in view of the age of pensioners, these figures are weighted toward those born in North Carolina, perhaps after their parents had migrated there from the north.

107. Gregory T. Knouff, *The Soldiers' Revolution: Pennsylvania in Arms and the Forging of Early American Identity* (University Park: Pennsylvania State University Press, 2004), pp. 155–93.

108. Armstrong Starkey, "Paoli to Stony Point: Military Ethics and Weaponry during the American Revolution," *Journal of Military History* 58 (1994): 7–27

109. Davie, *Revolutionary War Sketches*, p. 12.

110. Thomas Cummings, PenRec (S6780).

111. William L. Shea, *The Virginia Militia in the Seventeenth Century* (Baton Rouge: Louisiana State University Press, 1983), pp. 20, 33.

112. *NCSR*, 14:176–77, 185–86, 15:212; Caruthers, *Old North State*, p. 64.

113. Bryan McCullen, PenRec (S9018).

114. Robert Knox, PenRec (S8803).

7

INCOMPATIBLE ALLIES

Loyalists, Slaves, and Indians in Revolutionary South Carolina

JIM PIECUCH

From the outset of the American Revolution, British officials recognized that their prospects of regaining control of the colonies were more promising in the South than in any other region. Southern governors informed the king's ministers that large numbers of loyalists waited only for arms and the assistance of regular troops to join in overthrowing the rebel state governments. Superintendent of Indian Affairs for the Southern District, John Stuart, held tremendous influence over the powerful Cherokee, Choctaw, and Creek Indian nations, all of which wished to halt the colonists' expansion into their territories. Finally, the large number of African American slaves in South Carolina and Georgia represented an internal threat to the rebels that British leaders hoped to exploit when they directed their military operations southward.

Although their assumption that they could count on support from loyalists, Indians, and slaves was accurate, officials in London failed to recognize that serious divisions existed both within and between the three groups; to make full use of their aggregate assistance would require careful planning and skillful management. The ministry in London, unwilling to grapple with such a difficult problem, however, preferred to sidestep the complex issue. The Secretary of State for the American Department, Lord Dartmouth, held principal responsibility for devising Britain's strategy, and he chose the easiest course, relying primarily on loyalists for assistance in the effort to regain the Southern colonies, with the expectation that Indians and slaves could be employed as needed in support of British operations. Lord George Germain, who succeeded Dartmouth in late 1775 because his advocacy in parliament of a firm stance against the colonists won him the favor of King George III, followed Dartmouth's path in placing his main reliance on the loyalists for aid in the South. The ministers' unstated assumptions were that loyalists were a cohesive group committed to the royal cause and that both slaves and Native Americans would assume an essentially passive role until such time as British officials might desire their assistance. Such decisions could be left to local officials and military commanders on the spot. As a result of this lack of policy, the British were never able to employ their diverse supporters in a unified manner that might have made the most of their combined strength. British activities in South Carolina, and the actions of loyalists, Indians, and slaves there, provide a case study in the problem of attempting to mobilize these internally divided groups and incompatible allies to act in the service of the king.

When the dispute between Britain and the American colonies erupted into open warfare in the spring of 1775, Britons and loyal Americans flooded Dartmouth's desk with proposals for retaking the Southern colonies. When Germain replaced Dartmouth in November, he continued to receive plans for a Southern campaign, and, although it was Dartmouth who approved the plan for Southern operations that was carried out in 1776, it was Germain who ultimately faced the task of determining how such a campaign should be conducted.

All of the writers who offered suggestions agreed on one point: loyalist sentiment was strong in the South Carolina backcountry. One loyalist leader, Moses Kirkland, told Dartmouth that in his travels through the backcountry he had gotten "near four Thousand Men" to sign a resolution affirming their allegiance to the king. Thomas Fletchall, who commanded a backcountry militia regiment, likewise informed Governor Lord William Campbell that he believed that "four thousand Men would Appear in Arms for the King here if necessary." Campbell forwarded Fletchall's letter to Dartmouth, but added a note of caution. "The friends of Government here have been so sunk, so abandon'd to despair, for some time, that it is hardly possible to make them beleive" that British assistance was forthcoming. Although Dartmouth initially expressed some doubt regarding loyalist strength in the Southern colonies, he soon became convinced that if organized and supported by British troops, the loyalists could hold both North and South Carolina.[1]

If Dartmouth and other ministers agreed that the loyalists would play a key role in the effort to regain South Carolina, they were less certain about employing Native Americans. When John Stuart informed Dartmouth that the rebels in the Northern colonies were attempting to turn the Indians there against the British, Dartmouth instructed all the Indian agents to be "upon their guard against any Attempt of the like nature to debauch the Indians in their respective Districts." The agents should do all they could "to keep all the Indians firm in their love and Attachment to the King and in a temper to be always ready to Act in His Service."[2]

Although Dartmouth hesitated to call upon the Indians, several military officers urged the ministry to employ Native Americans to assist in crushing the rebellion. The commander in chief in America, General

Thomas Gage, wrote Dartmouth in June 1775, suggesting that "we must not be tender of calling upon the Savages," because the rebels were using New England Indians to aid in the siege of Boston. From Nova Scotia, General James Grant wrote that same month that "a few scalps taken by Indians and Canadians would operate more upon the minds of these deluded distracted People than any other Loss they can sustain." General John Burgoyne similarly advised King George III to employ Indians to support the army's operations. Both the King and Lord North, however, shared Dartmouth's reluctance to take such a step, fearing it would reduce the chance for peaceful reconciliation.[3]

Loyalists were more cautious than British officers when it came to the use of Indians. Chief Justice Egerton Leigh of South Carolina believed that a tight naval blockade, along with the mere threat of Indian attacks and slave uprisings, would be sufficient to cause his province to submit to British authority. Leigh asserted that the colonists were nearly as "impotent & Dependent" as an infant in the South, where they were trapped "between Hawk & Buzzard, Indians Keep them in Awe on one Hand, & their slaves (a circumstance of humiliating Disgrace to these bawling Sons of Liberty) on the other." Leigh was one of the few loyalists to consider Indians a potential asset to the royal cause, and even then he envisioned them as playing only a passive role as a potential threat that would keep the rebels from devoting their full attention to resisting the British.[4]

Three key factors affecting the Indians' role did not arise directly in discussions of British policy. The first was the question of how loyalists might react to an Indian war, even if Indians and loyalists shared the goal of preserving royal authority in South Carolina. Second, in determining how to employ Native Americans, British officials paid scant attention to differences between tribes, or even to divisions within the tribes themselves. Third, the ministers assumed that the Indians would cooperate with British forces only if and when the government determined that they should do so, thus overlooking the fact that Native Americans had their own concerns and goals and might choose to pursue these regardless of the instructions of Stuart and his agents.

Most South Carolina loyalists lived in the backcountry, on land wrested from the Cherokees during the Seven Years' War. Having belatedly entered that conflict in 1759, the Cherokees suffered defeat two years later at the hands of a combined British-colonial army and were forced to surrender some of their territory. Tensions between the tribe and white settlers on the frontier remained high in the years after the war. In 1768, for example, the Reverend Charles Woodmason, an Anglican missionary, had preached a sermon to the settlers at the Waxhaws, in which he noted the presence of "an External Enemy near at Hand . . . to be guarded against. These are our *Indian* Neighbours." Woodmason urged his listeners to unite for "our Common Security." Thus, any British effort to employ Cherokees or other Indians against the rebels in South Carolina risked alienating many loyalists. Rebel leader Pierce Butler recognized that, if the British instigated an Indian war, loyalists and rebels would put aside their political differences in the common interest of safety. Butler expressed confidence that, "if the Indians are prevail'd on to attack us," all of the militiamen from the frontier districts would unite to protect their homes.[5]

If the loyalists were at odds with their Indian neighbors and erstwhile allies in the king's cause, Native Americans were equally divided among themselves. The Cherokees were divided into factions; older leaders such as Attakullakulla, fearing a repetition of the defeats of 1759–1761, favored accommodation with the whites, whereas younger chiefs like Dragging Canoe wished to drive the whites from their lands. Cherokee relations with the Creeks had been poor for many years and had been further strained by conflicting claims to territory ceded to the colonists in 1773. The Creeks, who were a confederacy of many peoples rather than a unified tribe, had internal divisions of their own. Some Creek towns supported the British, others the Americans, and many preferred to remain neutral. Furthermore, at the outbreak of the Revolution, the Creeks were at war with the Choctaws. Ironically, Stuart had rebuffed appeals by both parties for his help to negotiate an end to the war, believing that if the two nations remained at odds it would provide more security for the Southern colonies. When the Revolution began, Stuart quickly intervened and arranged a peace. But his efforts to unite all of the Southern tribes met with limited success, because Indian leaders, while cooperative when Stuart's advice served their policy, acted independently when they thought it best for their interests.[6]

Even more perplexing for British officials than questions concerning the role of Indians was the matter of the slaves. As with the Native Americans, a sharp difference of opinion existed over how slaves should be employed: some offered advice to the ministry recommending an active role for African Americans in suppressing the rebellion, and others urged the government not to meddle with the institution of slavery.

Among those favoring the use of armed slaves was an anonymous British writer who suggested that a British expedition to the southern provinces should be strengthened by enlisting "the Bravest and most Ingenious of the Black Slaves," who would readily "Join the King's Standard." A more comprehensive proposal submitted to Germain and Lord North, the king's chief minister, advised the creation of two battalions of 700 slaves each from the West Indies. Once these troops landed in the South, the writer predicted, there was "not a Slave in ten, but would desert to Such a Corps, a Circumstance I am well assured much more dreaded; & of more fatall Consequence to the Rebells than the loss of a Battle."[7]

Contradictory advice came from others such as Lord William Campbell, who advised General Gage not to employ slaves against the rebels. A group of British merchants agreed and, in October 1775, submitted a petition to the king expressing horror at the thought that slaves might be turned against their American masters. A British traveler in the colonies believed that any use of slaves against the rebels would do the government more harm than good, writing that the measure would put an end to disputes between rebels and loyalists and unite them against the British.[8]

The writer had made an accurate assessment of Southern colonists' views on slavery. Backcountry loyalists in South Carolina did not see slaves as potential allies in the royal cause. Most settlers in the interior, loyalist or Whig, saw slaves as valuable commodities crucial to upward economic mobility. Backcountry settlers struggled to "save a little Money . . . Wherewith to purchase Slaves." By the 1770s, demand for slaves in the backcountry had risen considerably. Although most of the purchasers were prosperous merchants, increasing numbers of "the middling & poorer sort" had begun buying small numbers of slaves on credit. There were an estimated 6,000 slaves in the backcountry when the Revolution began.[9]

Completely overlooked in the ministry's assessment of Southern affairs was the relationship between Native Americans and African Americans. It was not good, which was largely the result of decades of effort by British settlers fearful of both slaves and Indians to drive a wedge between the two groups. Laws prohibited Indian traders from taking blacks with them into Native American territory. Provincial officials paid Indians for every runaway slave they captured and returned alive, as well as for the scalps or heads of runaways killed by the Indians. Whites also portrayed each group to the other in an unfavorable light: slaves were told of the Indians' cruelty and savagery, while the Indians were told that blacks had brought the devastating smallpox to America. As outgoing South Carolina Governor James Glen told his successor, William Lyttelton, in 1758, "It has allways been the policy of this govert to creat an aversion in them [Indians] to Negroes." This policy was generally successful, though it did not prevent a limited amount of friendly interaction between African Americans and Native Americans.[10]

The complexity of the slave and Indian issues convinced the ministers to rely primarily on loyalist support for the coming Southern campaign; however, rumors of the various proposals for Indian attacks and arming slaves had circulated in London, where they came to the attention of Virginian Arthur Lee. Lee, a staunch supporter of the Revolutionary movement, sent this information to friends in America, and, in the aftermath of the Battles of Lexington and Concord, it produced an uproar in South Carolina. "If anything was designed to galvanize the phobia-ridden Low Country aristocracy into a united, anti-British stance, this was it," one historian has noted. "Abhorrence of Negro rule united all white men," another historian observes, and in a province where slaves outnumbered whites by an estimated 110,000 to 90,000, fears of slave insurrection were constant. Rebel leaders immediately appointed a committee to guard against such a threat. One of the first steps they took was to increase the strength of the nightly slave patrols, a measure approved by Lieutenant-Governor William Bull. Although Bull would later accept exile in England rather than acquiesce to rebel rule, he believed that action to keep the slaves under control was compatible with his duty as acting governor.[11]

Rebel officials also took prompt and brutal action against Thomas Jeremiah, a free black harbor pilot. Whig leaders charged Jeremiah with intending to incite a slave revolt, on the basis of the testimony of slaves. One of the accusers claimed that Jeremiah had discussed collecting arms "to fight against the Inhabitants of this Province," while another alleged that Jeremiah had told him a war was coming that would "help the poor Negroes." The rebels convicted Jeremiah in June 1775; he was hanged and then his body was burned. Governor Campbell considered the act nothing short of murder, but his intervention failed to sway the rebels. Aside from Campbell's protests, there are no indications that any of Charleston's loyalists criticized Jeremiah's execution.[12]

Rumors that John Stuart had received orders from General Gage "to Employ the Indians and to *Arm the negroes* for the Service of Government" forced the Indian superintendent to flee Charleston for his own safety. Stuart believed that Bull was responsible for circulating distorted information about the contents of a letter that the former had received from Gage. William Henry Drayton, a Whig leader, also accused Stuart of conspiring with the ministry to launch Indian attacks on South Carolina. Fearing the "Fury of a merciless and ungovernable Mob," Stuart fled first to Savannah, where subsequent harassment made him escape to safety in East Florida. After his departure, the rebels confined Stuart's wife and married daughter as hostages to prevent him from inciting an Indian war. Stuart's fellow loyalists either tacitly approved of the rebels' proceedings or dared not defend him, for they did nothing to assist him.[13]

The fates of Jeremiah and Stuart demonstrated the double-edged nature of any British plan to utilize Native Americans and slaves to help subdue South Carolina. Mere rumor of such plans had led to the death of one man and the flight of another, and had strengthened the unity and resolve of the Whigs. Even Henry Laurens, the most moderate of South Carolina's rebel leaders, remained horrified at the thought of British-instigated Indian wars and slave insurrections long after the initial turmoil had subsided. In February 1776 Laurens still expressed anger at the ministry's "Settled plan to involve us in all the horrible Scenes of foreign & domestic Butcheries (not War) . . . While Men of War & Troops are to attack us in front the Indians are to make inroads on our backs—Tories and Negro Slaves to rise in our Bowels."[14]

Laurens and other rebel leaders hoped that enough backcountry loyalists shared their resentment of Indians and slaves to make it possible to wean them from the king's cause. "The latent distrust of the slave seems to have been deliberately exploited by Southern patriots as a means of arousing animosity toward the British and of coercing those who were lukewarm or timid about breaking with England," Benjamin Quarles writes. Laurens used this issue as well as the Indians' ties to Britain in an attempt to convince Thomas Fletchall to accept rebel authority in South Carolina.[15]

Neither Fletchall nor his supporters were won over by Laurens's entreaties. If backcountry settlers disliked both Indians and slaves, they nonetheless reserved their greatest enmity for the lowcountry planter elite who dominated provincial politics. In the decades before the Revolution, planters in the assembly had refused to grant adequate representation to the backcountry, resisted the establishment of courts outside Charleston, and ignored frontier lawlessness that plagued those inhabiting the province's interior. These issues gave rise to a Regulator movement in the 1760s, which won some concessions from the provincial elite but did not satisfy all of the backcountry people's demands. When South Carolina planters embraced the Revolutionary cause in 1775, many backcountry settlers reacted with inherent suspicion, and in this respect the conflict between loyalists and Whigs "was a continuation and intensification of struggles that erupted during the Regulation."[16]

Many backcountry inhabitants, however, embraced loyalism out of political principle. This group included leaders such as Thomas Brown and Joseph Robinson, who denounced rebellion and believed that it was their duty to defend the legally established royal government against Whig usurpers.[17] Others in the backcountry held views that might best be described as localized and passive loyalism. Issues such as imperial taxation and the proper limits of the British parliament's authority were remote from their daily lives; stamp taxes and tea duties barely concerned them. The arguments of Whig radicals, therefore, did little to sway them, especially in view of the possible disruptions that a change in government might bring to their lives. When rebel officials in Charleston dispatched William Henry Drayton and the Reverends William Tennent and Oliver Hart in the summer of 1775 to persuade the backcountry people to support the Revolutionary cause, the effort failed. Drayton reported that Whig prospects in the backcountry bore "so unfavorable an appearance" that force would be required to overcome the loyalists there.[18]

Events in the backcountry, resulting from the animosity most inhabitants felt toward their Native American neighbors, soon gave Drayton the opportunity he sought to crush the loyalists. In late 1775, Drayton and other Whig leaders decided that a Cherokee war could be best prevented if the rebels kept the tribe supplied with the gunpowder and lead that had previously been provided by the British. Authorities in Charleston dispatched a wagon with a thousand pounds each of powder and lead for the Cherokees' winter hunt. Learning of the shipment, loyalist Richard Pearis circulated reports that the Whigs planned to arm the Cherokees and then unleash them on the loyalists. In response, Patrick Cunningham assembled about 150 loyalists, overpowered the escorting troops, and seized the wagonload of munitions on October 31. Some Cherokees were so enraged at the capture of their supplies that they considered taking revenge upon the loyalists.[19]

Both loyalists and rebels began mobilizing their supporters after Cunningham's seizure of the powder and lead. The loyalists besieged their Whig opponents in the town of Ninety Six for three days in November before both sides agreed to a treaty ending hostilities. On this occasion, the loyalists assembled the largest armed force they would put in the field at one time during the Revolution, some 1,900 men. Significantly, it was the fear that the rebels were cooperating with the Cherokees that induced so many men to turn out with the loyalists. Many neutral settlers and some erstwhile Whigs undoubtedly joined the loyalists on this occasion—backcountry attitudes toward the Indians were clearly as crucial as men's views on the political dispute with Britain in determining which side a man would take.[20]

Shortly after the Treaty of Ninety Six had been concluded, other parties of South Carolina Whig militia, assisted by detachments from North Carolina, claimed that they were not bound by the agreement and in the brief "Snow Campaign," forcibly disarmed the backcountry loyalists. About 150 of those who had taken prominent part in the seizure of the powder and siege of Ninety Six were arrested and sent to Charleston. Other loyalist leaders, including Brown and Robinson, fled to St. Augustine, in East Florida. Because some of the loyalists who were dispersed in the campaign were on Cherokee land, and several others were traders who dealt with the tribe, the rebels managed to remove any stigma from their attempt to supply arms to the Indians and achieved "a propaganda victory . . . by tapping deep-seated anti-tribal fears among the backcountry farmers." They succeeded in portraying themselves "as the opponents of alliance with the Cherokees," despite the fact that it was their effort to win the tribe's goodwill that had provoked the initial crisis.[21] Believing themselves to be secure under the terms of the Treaty of Ninety Six, the loyalists had been taken by surprise, deprived of their leaders and arms, and forced to submit to Whig rule. Military action had thus accomplished what persuasion had failed to achieve, neutralizing the backcountry loyalists until the British army finally arrived to assist them in 1780.

While the loyalists were being suppressed, John Stuart and his deputies, obeying orders from London, labored to restrain the Indians from taking any action against the Southern colonies until the tribes could act in unison with the aid of British troops. The Cherokees, however, soon demonstrated that, when they thought their interests were at stake, they would not await permission from British Indian agents before taking action. Infuriated by white encroachment on their lands, the Cherokees ignored Stuart's admonitions and launched attacks on South Carolina settlers in late June 1776.[22]

The Cherokee War proved disastrous for the tribe as well as for Britain's Southern Indian policy. Rebel militia from both Carolinas and Virginia responded with an invasion of Cherokee territory. Although there was little actual fighting, the Whigs burned every town they could reach, along with vast quantities of corn and other foodstuffs. Desperate to prevent disaster, Cherokee agent Alexander Cameron urged Stuart to bring the Creeks into the war to aid the Cherokees. Instead, the disasters suffered by the Cherokees convinced many Creeks that neutrality was the best policy they could pursue. Thus, the Cherokees' independent decision to go to war left the tribe defeated, deprived it of vast tracts of land in subsequent peace treaties, frightened the Creeks into passivity, and, as a result, entirely derailed British plans for coordinated operations with regular troops against the Southern colonies.[23]

The loyalists' response to the Cherokee War again demonstrated the animosity that existed between backcountry settlers, regardless of their political principles, and their Indian neighbors. The Whigs genuinely believed that Stuart had incited the attacks and gladly shared this opinion with the loyalist prisoners held in Charleston. Robert Cunningham, one of the leading advocates of the royal cause in Ninety Six District, "would not at first believe that the British Administration were so wicked as to Instigate the Savages to War against us." When he came to believe it was true, Cunningham and other imprisoned loyalist leaders saw no contradiction between their loyalty to the Crown and a willingness to defend the backcountry from the Cherokees. Defending their homes was as always their first priority, and British officials had not informed the loyalists that the Cherokees were now their allies. The prisoners therefore petitioned the Council of Safety for their release, which was granted. Cunningham and Richard Pearis both reported to Colonel Andrew Williamson's militia camp and volunteered for service. Although suspicious of Pearis, Williamson would have accepted Cunningham's services; however, the fact that other loyalists were actively supporting the Cherokees had "so much exasperated" Williamson's men that he did not dare employ Cunningham.[24]

As Williamson had already observed, however, not all loyalists put aside their differences with the rebels to cooperate against the Cherokees. Some loyalists, albeit a small number, were tired of rebel persecution and recognized that they had a common cause with their Indian neighbors. A few of these men, dressed and painted as Indians, were captured in skirmishes with raiding parties. Whig militia captured at least fifteen other white men in the Cherokee towns. David Fanning, of Raebern's Creek, serving a second stint in prison for loyalism, took advantage of the confusion caused by the Indian attacks and escaped to his home. There he found that "a number of my friends had already gone to the Indians" and others were willing to do so. Fanning assembled 25 men and joined a party of more than 200 Cherokee warriors on Reedy River. After unsuccessfully attacking a log fort nearby, Fanning left the Indians and went to North Carolina.[25]

Following the defeat of the Cherokees, the Whigs retained firm control in South Carolina until the British capture of Savannah, Georgia, in December 1778. Although Major General Benjamin Lincoln, the American commander in the Southern Department, afterward feared that the British would advance from upper Georgia into the South Carolina backcountry, unite with the Indians and loyalists, and take control of the interior districts, the British were too weak for such an ambitious undertaking. The British made no major effort to retake South Carolina until General Sir Henry Clinton, who in 1778 had been appointed commander in chief of the British army in America, launched a full-scale invasion of the state in 1780.[26]

In planning the capture of South Carolina, both Germain and Clinton chose to rely on the loyalists as their major source of assistance. Little mention was made of Native Americans in plans for the Carolina operations, and almost no attention was given to African Americans. As in 1775, British leaders found it simpler to incorporate loyalists into their plans than to deal with the complexities that would arise from efforts to employ slaves and Indians. Lieutenant General Charles, Earl Cornwallis, Clinton's second-in-command, recognized that any effort to use Native Americans would alienate many backcountry loyalists and chose not to call upon the Indians for aid.[27]

When Clinton landed his army in South Carolina in February 1780, he made no effort to encourage a loyalist uprising. Instead, he "avoided, as much as possible, every measure which might excite the loyal inhabitants to rise in favour of government, and thus bring danger and trouble upon themselves" while the king's troops were too busy operating against Charleston to provide assistance.[28]

After Charleston had fallen, events demonstrated to British leaders that their expectations of loyalist support in South Carolina had been sound. On May 24, "a whole company" of loyalists, armed and mounted, arrived in Charleston after a ride of a hundred miles to request ammunition "to secure themselves against the rebels' depredations." They were hardly alone. "From every Information I receive, and Numbers of the most violent Rebels hourly coming in to offer their Services, I have the strongest Reason to believe the general Disposition of the People to be not only friendly to Government, but forward to take up Arms in its Support," Clinton wrote Cornwallis on May 29. John Andre, Clinton's aide-de-camp, observed that the backcountry settlers were "very well disposed to take an active Part" on the British behalf. As of June 4, a Hessian officer estimated that more than 2,000 people had come to Charleston from outlying areas to volunteer their support for the royal cause.[29]

Clinton immediately set to work organizing a loyal militia to take advantage of this surge of support. In a handbill circulated soon after the town's capture, the British commander asked for "the helping hand of every man . . . to re-establish peace and good government." He stated that he expected men with families to serve in the militia of their home districts, whereas men without families should be willing to perform militia service with the British troops for as long as six months each year. To put the militia plan into action, on May 22 Clinton appointed Major Patrick Ferguson of the 71st Regiment to the post of Inspector of Militia in the Southern Department. Clinton described Ferguson as "a very zealous, active, intelligent officer." While the British commander made these arrangements, he sent various detachments of troops into the interior of South Carolina, which "were intended to awe the disaffected and receive their submissions, give spirits to the King's friends, and promote the arming of a trusty militia for the internal defense of the province." Internal defense was, in fact, the key role that both Clinton and Cornwallis envisioned for the loyal militia. The generals expected the militia both to keep the Whigs in check and to provide manpower when needed to support the regular troops. With the militia handling the task of pacification and domestic security, British regulars would be free to pursue operations in the field against the rebel armies without worrying about security in the army's rear.[30]

Clinton ordered Ferguson, "without loss of time, to form into Corps all the Young or unmarried Men of the Provinces of Georgia and the two Carolina's" to serve under Lord Cornwallis, who was to command in South Carolina when Clinton returned to New York. The men were to be organized into companies of fifty to a hundred men, which, when possible, were to be consolidated into battalions; otherwise, the companies would serve independently. Ferguson was to allow the men of each company to elect the lieutenant who would command them and to enforce discipline "with great Caution, so as not to disgust the Men, Or mortify unnecessarily their Love of Freedom." Additional measures intended "to Procure the general & hearty Concurrence of the Loyal Inhabitants" included limited terms of service (a maximum of six months on duty out of twelve) and assurance that the militiamen would not be "drawn into the regular Service without their Consent."[31]

Ferguson's efforts to organize an effective loyal militia immediately became mired in the internal politics of the British army, which delayed the organization and training of the men. Clinton and Cornwallis had been at odds since the spring of 1780, when the latter, who had been expecting to assume command of the army in America when the ministry accepted Clinton's resignation, learned that the government had rejected Clinton's request to resign and ordered him to continue as commander in chief. The fact that Ferguson had been appointed by Clinton was enough to make the earl distrust his inspector of militia. Cornwallis may also have hoped to see his protégé, Lieutenant Colonel Nisbet Balfour, receive the appointment.[32]

On the very day Clinton appointed Ferguson, Balfour called on the commander in chief and told him "that it was *generally* reported that Ferguson was violent tempered and treated his men with harshness." Balfour urged Clinton not to give Ferguson command of the militia. Clinton told Balfour he would give no credence to such rumors and attributed the remarks to the "infernal party" divisions prevailing in the army.[33]

Ferguson accompanied Balfour on the latter's march to Ninety Six in the interior of South Carolina. Because Balfour outranked Ferguson, he and Cornwallis then contrived to relegate Ferguson to the sidelines as soon as Clinton departed for New York at the beginning of June and took militia matters into their own hands. Cornwallis took the first step on June 2, writing Ferguson that although Clinton had notified him of Ferguson's appointment, the commander in chief had not given the earl any information regarding Ferguson's instructions. Therefore, Cornwallis said, he was "now busied on forming a Plan" to organize the militia, and "as soon as I have been able to compleat it I will transmit it to You, In the mean time I must desire that You will take no Steps in this business without receiving directions from me."[34]

In response to Cornwallis's letter, Ferguson promised to "pay the utmost implicit Obedience" to the order and take no further action relative to the militia. That same day, Balfour told Cornwallis that "Mr. Ferguson remains perfectly quiet, since he rec. your letters," though it still appeared that Ferguson was eager to organize a militia on the original plan formulated by Clinton.[35]

Cornwallis completed his own militia plan on June 4. It called for the division of loyalists into two classes. The first consisted of men older than forty, those with four or more children, owners of a hundred or more slaves, anyone who had served three years or more in a provincial or regular army unit, and the infirm. These men were to serve only within their home districts, except in cases of emergency. The second class included all other men older than eighteen, who were liable to serve any six out of twelve months in Georgia or the Carolinas, during which time they would receive the same pay and provisions as provincial troops.[36]

Balfour busied himself implementing this plan while Ferguson remained idle. On June 6, Balfour informed Cornwallis that he had selected a trustworthy person to raise a loyal association in the Orangeburgh area as a precursor to the militia. "As to the Militia arming to defend the country, I have not the smallest doubt of it, whenever you think it necessary." Balfour, however, also noted that it might be difficult to find "men of property, and consequence" to lead the militia.[37]

The lack of proper officers proved to be one of the greatest difficulties British officials faced in organizing a loyal militia in South Carolina. The most-qualified and influential men in the state had either joined the rebels or been banished several years earlier for their loyalty. Those who returned with Clinton's army had already received commissions in provincial units, such as the Florida Rangers and South Carolina Royalists, so they were not available to lead the militia. Cornwallis therefore chose "men with some property who had not been active for the Americans, but who had not resided long enough among their neighbors to have real influence." James Cary was typical of the militia officers Cornwallis appointed. Cary had been born in Virginia and had moved first to North Carolina and then to South Carolina in 1764, settling in Camden. An attorney and planter who owned 1,600 acres of land and forty-two slaves in 1780, Cary had taken the state oath abjuring his allegiance to George III but did not take an active part in the rebellion. Cornwallis appointed Cary major of militia in the Camden district. His performance in command, however, was poor, as was that of most other militia officers. Balfour stated that, though Cary was "a very good man," he was "credulous and imposed upon by the worst people in the district." Assessing the abilities of three other militia officers, Cornwallis described one as "a weak, well intentioned Man," another as "active & I believe well affected Man, but rather more intent on private plunder than the Kings Service," and a third as someone who "may be treated with civility, but not trusted," because of his former ties to the rebels.[38]

Despite the shortage of appropriate officers and Ferguson's forced inactivity, militia matters had "a promising appearance" by late June. The volunteers "equalled the wishes of their leaders, both as to numbers and professions of loyalty." Cornwallis informed Clinton on July 14 that the organization of the militia in "the lower districts" of the province was "in great forwardness."[39]

Two incidents involving the loyal militia in the summer of 1780, however, quickly destroyed most British officers' confidence in it. Colonel Mathew Floyd organized a militia battalion in the vicinity of the Tyger and Ennoree rivers, which received arms and ammunition from the British. The former rebel militia commander in that district, John Lisle, who had been noted "for his violent persecution of the loyalists," had fled the province, and later was captured and banished to the coastal islands. Taking advantage of the British offer of pardon, Lisle pledged his loyalty to the Crown, returned home, and was commissioned as Floyd's second-in-command. At the first opportunity, Lisle seized Floyd and led the entire battalion off to join the rebels. Lieutenant Colonel Banastre Tarleton of the British Legion declared that this affair "ruined all confidence between the regulars and militia."[40]

A second instance of militia treachery confirmed British officers' suspicions of the loyal militia. Colonel William Mills and a detachment of his battalion were assigned to escort more than a hundred sick soldiers of the 71st Regiment to Georgetown. As soon as Mills's force had marched a safe distance from the British camp, the militiamen mutinied, took their own officers prisoner, and carried them and the sick of the 71st to General Horatio Gates's American army. Cornwallis believed that Mills had not been careful enough in screening his men, and other officers thought that they could no longer trust the militia at all.[41]

Although the mutinous militiamen left no explanation for their actions, their reason for making a rapid shift in allegiance was primarily due to the approach of an American army under Gates. As Gates approached, he circulated a proclamation offering pardon to those who had joined the British if they would align themselves with the Americans. This incentive received added weight because Gates's army was believed to number more than 7,000 men—Gates himself thought this was the case until the eve of the Battle of Camden—and rumors circulated throughout South Carolina that Cornwallis, whose disease-reduced army could muster barely more than 2,000 men, would abandon his interior posts and retreat within the lines at Charleston, leaving the loyalists at the mercy of the Whigs. In view of the loyalists' weak or—in the case of Lisle—seditious leadership, the passive loyalism of many, and the prospect that Cornwallis's retreat or defeat would leave them vulnerable to imprisonment, banishment, confiscation of property, and other punishments they had seen the Whigs inflict on fellow loyalists during the past five years, it is not surprising that these men thought it wiser to shift allegiance to the apparent victor rather than risk the consequences of adhering to the royal cause in such circumstances. They could not have reasonably foreseen that Cornwallis would inflict a crushing defeat on Gates's larger army at Camden on August 16.

Such setbacks as the defections of Lisle's and Mills's militia notwithstanding, Cornwallis relied primarily on the militia, with a small contingent of provincials and British convalescents, to hold Camden when the British army marched to attack Gates. An additional 300 loyal militiamen accompanied the earl's army, forming part of the reserve on the British left flank during the Battle of Camden. The loyalists were thrown into the battle when the Delaware and Maryland Continentals attacked the British left, and they evidently performed adequately; though not singled out for praise after the battle, neither did they receive any criticism from British officers.[42]

By this time, Cornwallis had appointed Balfour commandant of Charleston and lifted the restraints that the two had imposed on Ferguson. Focusing his efforts in the western part of South Carolina, Ferguson made great progress in organizing the loyalists in the area surrounding Ninety Six. Even Cornwallis praised Ferguson for his "indefatigable exertions to put the Militia of that district into a respectable Situation" and for "the Success with which your Labour has been attended." Ferguson provided the energetic leadership the backcountry loyalists had lacked since 1775, which was crucial if they were to become an effective force.[43]

Ferguson's apparent success with the militia did not impress some officers, who believed that South Carolinians would be best employed as regulars in provincial corps rather than in the militia. Loyalist Evan McLaurin, major in the South Carolina Royalists, won the support of his commander, Alexander Innes, for a proposal to create a second provincial battalion. Writing in endorsement of McLaurin's plan, Innes told Cornwallis that every recruit in a provincial unit was "a usefull soldier gain'd to the King's Service and I am well convinced the Militia on their present plan will ever prove a useless disorderly, destructive banditti." Some British officers, such as Tarleton, agreed with Innes, though Tarleton believed that South Carolinians should be added to existing provincial units rather than organized into new battalions.[44]

Aware that many officers were losing confidence in the loyal militia, Ferguson found it necessary to defend the loyalists in a letter to Cornwallis. Ferguson insisted that several thousand South Carolinians were firmly attached to the British and that, with proper organization and discipline, they would prove a valuable asset. Conceding "that the Different bodys of Militia East of broad river" had "behaved so ill with the Army," Ferguson asserted that it was because those units "were form'd in a hurry, without the assistance of any officers of the Army to establish order & Discipline, employd immediately on Service, & no Scrutiny made into the Loyalty of the Officers or Men." In such circumstances, "it was of Course to be expected that a Mungrill Mob without any regularity or even organization, without fidelity without officers, without any previous preparation employd against the Enemy, would bring the name of Militia into discredit." The militia in Ninety Six District, in contrast, were loyal, disciplined, and well organized, Ferguson wrote. They lacked the military experience of their rebel counterparts, who had been serving actively for five years, but duty with the army, Ferguson believed, would give the loyal militia confidence and contribute to making them more effective soldiers.[45]

While Ferguson strove to create a reliable force of loyalists, Cornwallis had decided not to employ the Indians to support his army. During the siege of Charleston, Henry Clinton had received a visit from a Creek chief and had expressed regret that no Cherokees had come to see him, which indicated that he had planned to use the Indians in some capacity. Cornwallis, however, understood the loyalists' aversion to Indians and preferred not to employ them. On June 18, Lieutenant Colonel Thomas Brown, who since his flight from South Carolina in 1775 had risen to command of both the Florida Rangers and the garrison at Augusta, Georgia, as well as appointment to superintendent of the Creeks and Cherokees, sent Cornwallis a proposal to use both tribes. Brown wanted to assemble a large force of Indians to attack the rebel settlements in the Watauga region. Balfour discussed the plan in detail in a letter to Cornwallis several days later, noting that both Creeks and Cherokees wanted those settlers driven off. On June 28, Brown again urged Cornwallis to approve the attack, asserting that it would help "to secure the affections of our indian allies"; Brown also asked for funds to assist nearly 700 Indian families who were in a "distressed miserable condition."[46]

Cornwallis's reply must have shocked the superintendent. "I will in a few words tell you my Ideas & wishes in regard to the Indians," the earl stated. They were to be "kept in good humour by civil treatment & a proper distribution of such presents as are sent from England for that purpose, but I would on no Account employ them in any operations of War." He said the Indians' complaints regarding the Watauga settlements were too complex to be dealt with at present and also denied Brown's request for funds. There was no reason, Cornwallis declared, for "the Publick to be put to any considerable Expence" for the Indians' benefit. "If their Houses have been destroy'd, the Rebuilding an Indian Hut is no very expensive Affair, and I dare say they will get their usual Crops of Corn this Year," Cornwallis stated.[47]

The main reason for Cornwallis's decision to exclude the Indians from his operations was his recognition of the hostility between the loyalists and their native neighbors. Although Cornwallis left no written record of his thoughts on the subject, his subordinates, who were undoubtedly familiar with his opinion, stressed in their dealings with backcountry settlers that Indians were not acting with the British. When Richard Pearis accepted the surrender of rebels along the Saluda River on June 10, 1780, he included an article in the capitulation agreement promising "to defend the Inhabitants from the incursions of the Indians." Lieutenant Colonel Francis, Lord Rawdon, commanding the loyalist Volunteers of Ireland, found on reaching the Waxhaws on June 11 that the inhabitants "are apprehensive here, that they shall be troubled by the Catawba Indians." Rawdon assured them that the British would prevent the Indians from molesting them. Three months later Ferguson issued a "Declaration of Amnesty" to North Carolina rebels in which he emphasized this point. The people "were told [by the Whigs] that the Savages were to be solicited to Murder & lay waste, & that the British Troops were to assist them in desolating the Country," Ferguson wrote. He then emphasized that "the only Indians employ'd since the Invasion of Carolina are those of Catawbaw by the Rebels, & even the Cherokee Nation that followed the British Troops to Savannah River to revenge the burning of their Towns, were refused leave & sent back." Ferguson's intention, and Cornwallis's as well, was to win the confidence of the backcountry settlers by presenting the British as their protectors from Indian depredations.[48]

It was not long, however, before South Carolina felt the effects of Cornwallis's rejection of Indian assistance, and officials on the province's frontier began demanding that the earl send Indians to help them check rebel raiders. Some of these attackers came from the Watauga area, and McLaurin recommended a plan similar to Brown's. Unless the Indians attacked Watauga, "we shall not have either a quiet or an honest back Country," McLaurin asserted. "The Indians God knows are good for Little," he added, "but still they are a Bugbear & then would ly between the Province & the Overhill Settlements." By late September, even Balfour desired Native American help to secure the province's frontiers. He advised Cornwallis that the best method of ending rebel incursions "appears to me to be, the employing the Indians, to clear certain districts, where these people retreat to, & resort." Despite McLaurin's and Balfour's pleas, Cornwallis adhered firmly to his policy of keeping the Indians out of the struggle.[49]

Another problem Cornwallis faced was how to deal with the African Americans in the province, large numbers of whom had fled to the British army on its arrival in South Carolina. While the troops were preparing to sail from New York, Clinton had prepared various proclamations and regulations to be issued when he reached his destination. The general's original plan required all slaves who came to the army to provide their names and the names of their masters to civil officials. Those slaves belonging to rebel masters would then receive a certificate and be enrolled for service in noncombat roles; slaves belonging to loyalists would be returned to their owners. "All Negroes found without having such a Certificate . . . must be imprisoned; this will prevent the bad effects found at New York," Clinton declared. After Charleston's surrender, Clinton adopted a more lenient stance, yet he still hoped to "prevent the Confusion that would arise from a further desertion" of slaves to the British and suggested to Cornwallis that it would be best to put them "on abandoned Plantations, where they may subsist." Until he devised a better plan, Clinton authorized Cornwallis to "make such Arrangements as will discourage their joining us."[50]

Desiring more specific direction in this matter, Cornwallis asked Clinton for more information. "All I can do about Negroes is already directed to be done," Clinton replied. "But care must be taken that they are not ill treated—Something is now in Contemplation." The commander in chief, however, sent no further orders; Cornwallis appointed commissioners in Charleston "to arrange the differences which subsisted in Carolina concerning the negroes," a mandate that was vague at best. Neither he nor Clinton wished to create turmoil in the province by significantly altering the status of African Americans.[51]

Cornwallis accepted the presence of some blacks with his army and ordered that they wear badges "with the Number of the Regt. Or the Initial Letters of the Department that Employs them." Any African Americans lacking such a badge were to be flogged out of camp, while those who left the line of march to plunder would be immediately executed. Most of the blacks who accompanied the army served as officers' servants, pioneers, teamsters, and foragers, and Cornwallis was always concerned that there were too many African Americans with the army. In December 1780, for example, he informed Tarleton that he had seen the British Legion's convalescents at Winnsboro, "and there were rather more black attendants, both male and female, than I think you will like to see."[52]

Having rejected the use of slaves and Indians in a significant military role, Cornwallis soon saw his plan for pacifying South Carolina unravel with the destruction of its linchpin, the loyal militia. On October 8, rebels from the Watauga region, who might otherwise have been occupied with Brown and his Indians if the earl had accepted Brown's plan to attack the overmountain settlers, surrounded and annihilated nearly 1,000 loyalist militiamen at King's Mountain. Ferguson died leading his men in battle.

The cruelty the victors displayed during and after the battle had repercussions far beyond the field. The rebels shot down two men who were waving white flags and continued firing into the tight cluster of loyalists after the latter had thrown down their muskets. When they withdrew from King's Mountain after the battle, the overmountain men left more than 160 badly wounded loyalists untreated on the field.[53]

The first witnesses to the carnage at King's Mountain were relatives of loyal militiamen who had lived nearby. The day after the engagement, "the wives and children of the poor Tories came in, in great numbers," wrote James P. Collins, an American witness. "Their husbands, fathers, and brothers, lay dead in heaps, while others lay wounded or dying; a melancholy sight indeed!" Collins himself "could not help turning away from the scene . . . with horror, and though exulting in victory, could not refrain from shedding tears." When the loyalist family members returned home and reported what they had seen, the shock to their loyal neighbors must have been profound and discouraged many from further participation on the British side.[54]

For the prisoners the ordeal was far from over. On October 14, twelve Whig officers formed a tribunal "to try the Militia Prisoners Particularly those who had the most Influence in the country." Thirty men were condemned to death for alleged crimes, and the executions began in the evening. Nine men, including Lieutenant Colonel Mill, Captain Wilson, and Captain Chitwood, "fell a Sacrafice to their infamous Mock jury." The remaining twenty-one were reprieved. The next day, perhaps fearing that they, too, might soon be executed, some 100 prisoners made their escape during a march of more than thirty miles. Three more tried to escape on October 17, two succeeding and a third being wounded in the attempt. The wounded man was executed the following morning. Eventually, however, about 600 of the captives succeeded in escaping and returned to their homes. Their accounts of the treatment they and other loyalists had received further dampened the ardor of the backcountry inhabitants for the British cause.[55]

Lieutenant Colonel Robert Gray of the loyal militia recognized that King's Mountain and its aftermath sounded the death knell for British hopes of creating an effective loyalist force. The rebels' brutality, he noted, resulted in the loyalists "being overwhelmed with dismay," and they "became dejected & timid." The loss of Ferguson made it impossible to repair the damage. "Had Major Fergusson lived, the Militia would have been completely formed . . . the want of a man of his genius was soon severely felt," Gray wrote. Cornwallis never appointed a replacement for Ferguson, so, as in 1775, the loyalists were left defeated and leaderless. Ironically, Cornwallis's decision to reject Indian support to placate the loyalists allowed the rebels to concentrate against and destroy the earl's largest, most effective force of loyal militia. Although many loyalists would continue to serve, especially in the garrisons of British posts, until the evacuation of Charleston in December 1782, they would never again muster the numbers or perform the active service they had under Ferguson.[56]

It was not until late 1781, with most of South Carolina in American hands, that desperate British leaders decided to strengthen their forces by arming former slaves to assist in the defense of Charleston. When General Nathanael Greene marched his Continental Army toward Charleston in November, frightened South Carolina loyalists demanded that the town's defenses be strengthened, and in this atmosphere of panic "the most active Negroes were called to arms and enrolled." Many loyalists had sent an address to the new British commander at Charleston, General Alexander Leslie, pressing him to adopt this measure. The African American combat unit thus created, commonly referred to as the "Black Dragoons," was mounted and equipped for duty. Yet, while loyalists had at last come to accept the advantages that might derive from black soldiers, Americans were infuriated by the British use of armed blacks. Whigs referred to the Dragoons as "Affrican Banditty" and exulted whenever any of the black soldiers were killed in battle.[57]

The Black Dragoons were one of the most active British units in the last year of the war. They conducted patrols outside the Charleston lines, foraged for provisions, apprehended deserters, and performed garrison duty. Charles Cotesworth Pinckney wrote that the Black Dragoons "are daily committing the most horrible depredations and murder" in their forays. They fought alongside white loyalists in a skirmish with Francis Marion's men in August 1782 and on November 4 battled American troops under Tadeusz Kosciuszko. On December 8, just days before the evacuation of Charleston, the Black Dragoons conducted a foraging raid that brought a large quantity of badly needed livestock and provisions into the town.[58]

Some British officials and loyalists insisted that an even greater use of armed blacks could yet redeem British fortunes. The most ambitious proposal came from Lord Dunmore, the former royal governor of Virginia, who during a sojourn in Charleston, recommended purchasing 10,000 slaves from their masters, arming them, promising them freedom after the war, and then using this army to sweep the rebels from the South. But such a plan, though promising, was never put to the test, since in early 1782, after Cornwallis's surrender at Yorktown, parliament decided that no further offensive operations would be undertaken against the Americans.

If the loyalists who had taken refuge in Charleston had finally come to accept African American soldiers as allies, others who continued to resist in the backcountry had belatedly reached the same conclusion in regard to the Indians. By late 1781, some loyalists were cooperating with the Cherokees, and doing so with considerable effectiveness. Whig General Andrew Pickens led a rebel force into Cherokee territory at that time with disappointing results; he believed the foray would have succeeded, "had it not been for the Tories that went up under Col. Williams and others small parties that has since gon up." A rebel who had been captured by Williams's party and later escaped told Pickens that the loyalists had turned over their Whig prisoners to the Cherokees and that the Indians had executed twelve of them. Pickens feared that "unless some Spirited measures are taken and Immediately Carried into Execution against the Cherokees and Tories that are harboured in the nation—this part of the Country must be Evacuated for some time." Such fears were exaggerated, however, and Pickens later decisively defeated the Cherokees and their loyalist collaborators.[59]

The Revolutionary experience in South Carolina demonstrated that loyalists, Native Americans, and African American slaves were all willing to stand forth in support of the British cause. This was as the king's ministers had expected in 1775, but if they saw the larger picture clearly, they failed to notice the details that complicated any plan to regain control of the Southern provinces utilizing their three groups of supporters. The loyalists, though numerous, did not all act solely on the basis of political principle: many did, but others were passive and would withdraw their support when conditions jeopardized their safety, while still others were motivated by local issues and rivalries rather than a deep commitment to the royal cause. Their commitment and effectiveness depended heavily on their leaders' abilities to organize and motivate them, and the loss of the most capable leaders in 1775 through arrest and exile did much to impair their usefulness. The Cherokees, though potentially a valuable ally, proved less tractable than British leaders expected. Putting their own desire to preserve their lands ahead of their alliance with the British, they launched a war against the advice of Stuart that drove many loyalists, most of whom disliked Indians, to align themselves with the Whigs. The war resulted in a defeat so complete that the Cherokees contributed little to the British cause afterward, while making the Creeks reluctant to commit themselves to the British and risk the same fate. At the same time, the mere discussion of utilizing slaves to help subdue the Americans incited fears of slave insurrection that likewise alienated many loyalists, and along with the British-Indian alliance, provided valuable propaganda for the Whigs.

When the British army arrived in force in South Carolina in 1780, Cornwallis had come to recognize that he could not use slaves or Indians in a significant role without alienating many loyalists. Determined to create a strong loyal militia to secure the province from attack and maintain domestic order, he nevertheless wasted valuable time in army political squabbles, and when the militia was organized, with the exception of Ferguson and a few capable South Carolinians, it suffered from poor or indifferent leadership. Just as it appeared Ferguson's efforts might bring solid results, his militia was annihilated at King's Mountain, by Whigs who were left free to operate against it because Cornwallis chose not to utilize the Indians against them.

This circumstance highlights the dilemma that the British faced in South Carolina. In a time of unrest, Indians and slaves, in pursuit of their own interests, would not remain spectators. Opportunities for the former to protect their lands, and for the latter to seek freedom from bondage, were impossible to ignore. Even had the British not desired their assistance, slaves and Indians would naturally turn to them, simply because they were at war with the plantation owners and frontiersmen whom they considered enemies. If the British sought slave and Indian support, they alienated white loyalists; if they rejected it, they might find the Indians allied to the Whigs, who frequently courted them, and also lose the services of thousands of fugitive slaves who filled important noncombat positions in the army. Yet to make slaves and Indians partners in the effort to subdue the colonies meant, in effect, sparking a social revolution in order to suppress a political revolution.

Dimly aware of this, British political and military leaders focused their efforts on gaining loyalist support, while using slaves and Indians in more limited roles. Such half-measures were self-defeating, insofar as they were sufficient to inflame the Whigs and alienate many loyalists, but not enough to allow the military commanders to utilize fully every available resource to crush the rebellion permanently in South Carolina. Given the conservatism of Lord North, Lord George Germain, and other British leaders, who wanted only to restore the situation in the colonies to what it had been before 1765, this reluctance is understandable. They could not accept the policy advocated by Dunmore since 1775, which was to defeat the rebels, using any and every means available, and then sort out the situation once the war had been won. Nor did the ministry make any effort to unify slaves, Indians, and loyalists by explaining the necessity of cooperation to the latter and reassuring them that their interests would be protected after the war.

In a sense, British leaders envisioned loyalists, slaves, and Indians as three strands that, woven together into a rope, would bind South Carolina to the empire. But in fact each strand was itself composed of separate strands, some stronger than others, and no real effort was made to weave the strands together. In the end, when the loyalist strand, already frayed from friction with its slave and Indian counterparts and strained by five years of Whig persecution, broke at King's Mountain, the British effort to regain South Carolina, which began with such promise in May 1780, unraveled along with it.

Notes

1. Moses Kirkland to the Earl of Dartmouth, September 20, 1775, American Papers of the Second Earl of Dartmouth (microfilm, reel 14, no. 1526); Thomas Fletchall to Lord William Campbell, August 19, 1775, Dartmouth Papers (reel 13, no. 1446), David Library of the American Revolution; Lord William Campbell to Dartmouth, Dartmouth Papers, August 19, 1775 (reel 13, no. 1446); Dartmouth to General William Howe, September 15, 1775, Sir Guy Carleton Papers, vol. 1, no. 43 (microfilm), Library of Congress; Dartmouth to Howe, October 22, 1775, Carleton Papers, vol. 1, no. 68.

2. "Indian Agents," undated manuscript [1775], Dartmouth Papers, reel 3, no. 1210b.

3. Alan Valentine, *Lord North*, 2 vols. (Norman: University of Oklahoma Press, 1967), 1:375; John Brooke, *King George III* (New York: McGraw-Hill, 1972), p. 178.

4. Egerton Leigh to Lord Gower, January 15, 1775, in Jack P. Greene, "The Political Authorship of Sir Egerton Leigh," *South Carolina Historical Magazine* 75, no. 3 (July 1974): 146–48.

5. Tom Hatley, *The Dividing Paths: Cherokees and South Carolinians through the Revolutionary Era* (New York: Oxford University Press, 1995), pp. 119, 139–40, 180; Charles Woodmason, *The Carolina Backcountry on the Eve of the Revolution*, ed. Richard J. Hooker (Chapel Hill: University of North Carolina Press for the Institute of Early American History and Culture [IEAHC], 1953), pp. 93–94 [original emphasis]; Pierce Butler to unnamed, March 21, 1776, in Joseph Barnwell, ed., "Correspondence of Arthur Middleton," *South Carolina Historical and Genealogical Magazine* 27, no. 3 (July 1926): 140.

6. Colin G. Calloway, *The American Revolution in Indian Country: Crisis and Diversity in Native American Communities* (Cambridge: Cambridge University Press, 1995), pp. 44, 190–91; J. Leitch Wright, Jr., *Creeks and Seminoles* (Lincoln: University of Nebraska Press, 1986), pp. 3, 106, 113–14.

7. "Advantages of Lord Cornwallis's Expedition Going Rather to Chesapeak Bay than to the Carolinas" [1775]; "Campbell" to Lord George Germain, January 16,

1776; "Campbell" to Lord North, undated, enclosed in previous letter, Lord George Germain Papers, vol. 4, William L. Clements Library, University of Michigan.

8. Benjamin Quarles, *The Negro in the American Revolution* (Chapel Hill: University of North Carolina Press for the IEAHC, 1996), pp. 111–12; Winthrop D. Jordan, *White over Black: American Attitudes Toward the Negro, 1550–1812* (Chapel Hill: University of North Carolina Press for the IEAHC, 1968), p. 114.

9. "Remonstrance" of the South Carolina Regulators, November 1767, in Woodmason, *South Carolina Backcountry*, p. 226; Kenneth Morgan, "Slave Sales in Colonial Charleston," *English Historical Review* 113, no. 453 (September 1998): 917; Robert Olwell, *Masters, Slaves, and Subjects: The Culture of Power in the South Carolina Low Country, 1740–1790* (Ithaca, N.Y.: Cornell University Press, 1998), p. 31.

10. Wright, *Creeks and Seminoles*, p. 84, and *The Only Land They Knew: American Indians in the Old South* (Lincoln: University of Nebraska Press, 1999), p. 272; William S. Willis, "Divide and Rule: Red, White, and Black in the Southeast," *Journal of Negro History* 48, no. 3 (July 1963): 162, 165–66, 168–69.

11. Lewis Pinckney Jones, *The South Carolina Civil War of 1775* (Lexington, S.C.: Sandlapper Store, 1975), pp. 16–17; Jordan, *White over Black*, p. 114; John Richard Alden, "John Stuart Accuses William Bull," *William and Mary Quarterly*, 3rd ser., 2, no. 3 (July 1945): 318–19.

12. Lord William Campbell to Dartmouth, August 31, 1775, abstract, Dartmouth Papers, reel 13, no. 1467.

13. Alden, "Stuart Accuses William Bull," p. 118; J. Russell Snapp, *John Stuart and the Struggle for Empire on the Southern Frontier* (Baton Rouge: Louisiana State University Press, 1996), pp. 160–61, 172; John Stuart to Gage, July 9, 1775, Thomas Gage Papers, vol. 131, Clements Library.

14. Henry Laurens to William Manning, February 27, 1776, in David R. Chesnutt, ed., *The Papers of Henry Laurens*, 16 vols. (Columbia: University of South Carolina Press, 1988), 11:123–24.

15. Quarles, *Negro in the American Revolution*, p. 14; M. Foster Farley, "The South Carolina Negro in the American Revolution," *South Carolina Historical Magazine* 79, no. 2 (April 1979): 76.

16. Rachel N. Klein, *Unification of a Slave State: The Rise of the Planter Class in the South Carolina Backcountry, 1760–1808* (Chapel Hill: University of North Carolina Press for the IEAHC, 1990), p. 79.

17. Robert S. Lambert, *South Carolina Loyalists in the American Revolution* (Columbia: University of South Carolina Press, 1987), p. 39.

18. Keith Krawczynski, *William Henry Drayton: South Carolina Revolutionary Patriot* (Baton Rouge: Louisiana State University Press, 2001), p. 176.

19. Marvin L. Cann, "Prelude to War: The First Battle of Ninety Six, November 19–21, 1775," *South Carolina Historical Magazine* 79, no. 2 (April 1979): 76; James H. O'Donnell III, *Southern Indians in the American Revolution* (Knoxville: University of Tennessee Press, 1973), pp. 26–27.

20. Jones, *South Carolina Civil War*, 76; Cann, "Prelude to War," pp. 209–211; Hatley, *Dividing Paths*, p. 189.

21. Cann, "Prelude to War," pp. 212–13.

22. O'Donnell, *Southern Indians in the American Revolution*, pp. 37–42.

23. O'Donnell, *Southern Indians in the American Revolution*, pp. 46–49.

24. Henry Laurens to John Laurens, August 14, 1776, in Chesnutt, *Papers of Henry Laurens*, 11:231; Williamson to unnamed, July 22, 1776, in Robert W. Gibbes, ed., *Documentary History of the American Revolution in South Carolina*, 3 vols. (New York: D. Appleton, 1855–57), 2:27.

25. David Fanning, *Col. David Fanning's Narrative of his Exploits and Adventures as a Loyalist of North Carolina in the American Revolution*, ed. A. W. Savary (Toronto, 1908); Henry Laurens to John Laurens, August 14, 1776, in Chesnutt, *Paper of Henry Laurens*, 11:229, 231; Hatley, *Dividing Paths*, p. 195.

26. Benjamin Lincoln to Rawlins Lowndes, January 13, 1779, and February 4, 1779, Benjamin Lincoln Papers, microfilm, reel 3.

27. This assertion is based on an examination of the documents covering the planning for the campaign in the Germain Papers and Sir Henry Clinton Papers, Clements Library.

28. "Handbill Issued after the Surrender of Charles Town," in Banastre Tarleton, *A History of the Campaigns of 1780 and 1781, in the Southern Provinces of North America* (London: T. Cadell, 1787; repr., Spartanburg, S.C.: Reprint Co., 1967), p. 68.

29. "Diary Kept by Ensign Hartung," in "Hessian Reports and Accounts," Hessian Documents of the American Revolution, item Z, David Library; Clinton to Cornwallis, May 29, 1780, Cornwallis Papers, Public Record Office (U.K.) 30/11/2, no. 54 (hereafter PRO); Ferguson to Cornwallis, May 30, 1780, Cornwallis Papers, PRO 30/11/2, no. 58; Wilhelm von Wilmowsky to Baron von Jungkenn, June 4, 1780, in Bernhard Uhlendorf, ed., *The Siege of Charleston: With an Account of the Province of South Carolina: Diaries and Letters of Hessian Officers from the Von Jungkenn Papers in the William L. Clements Library* (Ann Arbor: University of Michigan Press, 1938), p. 419.

30. "Handbill Issued after the Surrender of Charles Town," in Tarleton, *History of the Campaigns,* pp. 69–70; "Instructions to Major Ferguson Inspector of Militia," May 22, 1780, Cornwallis Papers, PRO 30/11/2, no. 44; Sir Henry Clinton, *The American Rebellion; Sir Henry Clinton's Narrative of his Campaigns, 1775–1782,* ed. William B. Willcox (New Haven, Conn.: Yale University Press, 1954), pp. 175–76.

31. "Instructions to Major Ferguson Inspector of Militia," May 22, 1780, Cornwallis Papers, PRO 30/11/2, no. 44.

32. Franklin and Mary Wickwire, *Cornwallis: The American Adventure* (Boston: Houghton Mifflin, 1970), pp. 127–29.

33. Henry Clinton, "Sir Henry Clinton's 'Journal of the Siege of Charleston, 1780,'" in William T. Bulger, ed., *South Carolina Historical Magazine* 66, no. 3 (July 1965): 172 [original emphasis].

34. Cornwallis to Ferguson, June 2, 1780, Cornwallis Papers, PRO 30/11/77, no. 2.

35. Ferguson to Cornwallis, June 6, 1780, Cornwallis Papers, PRO 30/11/2, no. 92; Balfour to Cornwallis, June 6, 1780, Cornwallis Papers, PRO 30/11/2, no. 96.

36. "Part of a General Plan for Regulating the Province & forming a Militia," June 4, 1780, Cornwallis Papers, PRO 30/11/2, no. 86.

37. Balfour to Cornwallis, June 6, 1780, Cornwallis Papers, PRO 30/11/2, no. 96.

38. Robert S. Lambert, "A Loyalist Odyssey: James and Mary Cary in Exile, 1783–1804," *South Carolina Historical Magazine* 79, no. 3 (July 1978): 167–70; Balfour to Cornwallis, September 1, 1780, Cornwallis Papers, PRO 30/11/64, no. 1; Cornwallis to Captain DePeyster, August 31, 1780, Cornwallis Papers, PRO 30/11/79, no. 52.

39. Tarleton, *History of the Campaigns,* pp. 90–91; Cornwallis to Clinton, July 14, 1780, ibid., p. 118.

40. Tarleton, *History of the Campaigns,* p. 93; Lambert, *South Carolina Loyalists,* p. 128.

41. Tarleton, *History of the Campaigns,* p. 98; Cornwallis to Clinton, August 6, 1780, in ibid., p. 127; Lambert, *South Carolina Loyalists,* pp. 128–29.

42. Charles Bracelen Flood, *Rise and Fight Again: Perilous Times along the Road to Independence* (New York: Dodd, Mead, 1976), 313, 325, 331; Tarleton, *History of the Campaigns,* p. 104.

43. Cornwallis to Ferguson, August 5, 1780, Cornwallis Papers, PRO 30/11/79, no. 14.

44. Alexander Innes to Cornwallis, September 5, 1780, Cornwallis Papers, PRO 30/11/64, no. 29; Tarleton, *History of the Campaigns,* p. 98.

45. Ferguson to Cornwallis, August 29, 1780, Cornwallis Papers, PRO 30/11/63, no. 81.

46. Brown to Cornwallis, June 18, 1780; Balfour to Cornwallis, June 24, 1780; Brown to Cornwallis, June 28, 1780, Cornwallis Papers, PRO 30/11/2, nos. 166, 191, 208.

47. Cornwallis to Brown, July 17, 1780, Cornwallis Papers, PRO 30/11/78, no. 22.

48. "Terms of Capitulation," June 10, 1780, Cornwallis Papers, PRO 30/11/2, no. 133; Rawdon to Cornwallis, June 11, 1780, Cornwallis Papers, PRO 30/11/2, no. 123; "Declaration

of Amnesty to rebels," September 9, 1780, Cornwallis Papers, PRO 30/11/64, no. 62.

49. Evan McLaurin to Balfour, August 7, 1780, Thomas Addis Emmet Collection, no. 6589, New York Public Library; Balfour to Cornwallis, September 20, 1780, Cornwallis Papers, PRO 30/11/64, no. 83.

50. Clinton to Cornwallis, May 20, 1780, Cornwallis Papers, PRO 30/11/2, no. 38; Orders to Captain Russell, December 22, 1779, Cornwallis Papers, PRO 30/11/1, no. 33.

51. "Answers to Several Queries and Memorandums relative to the Command in Carolina," June 3, 1789, Cornwallis Papers, PRO 30/11/61, no. 7; Tarleton, *History of the Campaigns*, pp. 89–90.

52. "Lord Cornwallis's Orders 27th. Septr. 1780," in A. R. Newsome, ed., "A British Orderly Book, 1780–1781," *North Carolina Historical Review* 9, no. 3 (July 1932): 276, 280; Cornwallis to Tarleton, December 15, 1780, in Tarleton, *History of the Campaigns*, p. 206.

53. Flood, *Rise and Fight Again*, pp. 356–57.

54. James P. Collins, *Autobiography of a Revolutionary Soldier*, ed. John M. Roberts (North Stratford, N.H.: Ayer Company, [reprint ed.] 1989), pp. 52–53.

55. Anthony Allaire, Diary, entries for October 14, 15, 17, and 18, 1780, New Brunswick Museum, St. John.

56. Robert Gray, "Colonel Robert Gray's Observations on the War in Carolina," *South Carolina Historical and Genealogical Magazine* 11, no. 3 (July 1910): 144–45.

57. Christopher Ward, *The Delaware Continentals, 1776–1783* (Wilmington: Historical Society of Delaware, 1941), p. 130; Alexander Leslie to Henry Clinton, March 30, 1782, Sir Guy Carleton Papers; Joseph Lee Boyle, ed., "The Revolutionary War Diaries of Captain Walter Finney," *South Carolina Historical Magazine* 98, no. 2 (April 1997): 137.

58. Charles Cotesworth Pinckney to Arthur Middleton, August 13, 1782, in Barnwell, ed., "Correspondence of Arthur Middleton," 65; Francis Marion to John Mathews, August 30, 1782, "Genl. Marion's Report of the Affair at Wadboo," *South Carolina Historical and Genealogical Magazine* 17, no. 4 (October 1916): 176–77; Lieutenant General von Bose to Lieutenant General von Lossberg, November 18, 1782, "Reports of the War Under General von Lossberg," Hessian Documents of the American Revolution, Band V, Lage 15, David Library; Thomas Bee to John Mathews, December 9, 1782, Thomas Bee Papers, South Caroliniana Library, University of South Carolina, Columbia.

59. Andrew Pickens to Elijah Clarke, January 25, 1782, Thomas Addis Emmet Collection, no. 6670, New York Public Library; O'Donnell, *Southern Indians in the American Revolution*, pp. 126–27.

8

THE DILEMMAS OF ALLIANCE

The Oneida Indian Nation in the American Revolution

KARIM M. TIRO

More than any other episode in modern history, the American Revolution has served to define the distinct national identity of the Oneida people. When Oneidas tell the story of their participation in that war, they often dwell upon the experience of one woman, Polly Cooper. According to oral tradition, Cooper accompanied a contingent of Oneidas to Valley Forge. They carried large quantities of corn to feed the Continental Army in its hour of greatest distress. Cooper taught the grateful Americans how to prepare the corn but refused payment for her labors. Finally, at George Washington's insistence, Martha Washington took her to Philadelphia and bought Cooper a shawl, a hat, and a bonnet.[1]

The documentary record bears out some of the story's details but is silent in regard to others.[2] Nevertheless, the Cooper tradition conveys larger truths that are beyond question. As the story suggests, the Oneidas' wartime efforts were recognized by American officers, including Washington himself. The gift of corn—an item of sacred significance—signifies that the Oneidas' contribution to the patriot cause was of the highest magnitude. It was. Through combat, spying, and scouting, the Oneidas were indispensable to the survival of patriot communities on the New York and Pennsylvania frontiers. The Oneidas were arguably the United States' most important Native American allies. Their sacrifice was great as well. Hundreds of Oneidas suffered through privations and exposure to smallpox as wartime refugees after their villages and fields were burned as retribution for siding with the Americans. Before the war, there were perhaps a thousand Oneidas living in their homeland in present-day central New York. Disease, displacement, and other war-related traumas reduced that number to the low six hundreds.[3]

Yet even this alliance had its limits—limits that the patriots tested and sometimes exceeded. From the outset, the patriots were deeply ambivalent about the employment of Natives in war. Fearful white frontier communities and their defenders spoke of the prospect of Indian warfare in terms of "dread" and "Awe."[4] Thus, winning the assistance of Native Americans was greatly valued for reasons both defensive and offensive. Because the British enjoyed insurmountable advantages in the recruitment of Indians, however, patriots cultivated popular hatred of natives for propagandistic purposes. This was evident in the Declaration of Independence itself, with its histrionic condemnation of the king for his attempts "to bring on the inhabitants of our frontiers, the merciless Indian savages, whose known rule of warfare is an undistinguished destruction of all ages, sexes, and conditions." Appeals of this sort proved useful for recruiting white soldiers, particularly after the initial flush of Revolutionary enthusiasm had faded, but not for winning native help.

The Oneida-patriot alliance was also undermined by direct patriot assaults on Iroquois nations allied with Great Britain. The American Revolution had divided the Six Nations Iroquois confederacy, of which the Oneidas were a part. As a result, Iroquois warriors were faced with the disconcerting prospect of harming one another in the course of fighting someone else's war. Although enough hostile acts took place that some historians refer to the Revolution as an Iroquois civil war, most natives balked at taking the lives of their fellows.[5] Indeed, on many occasions, they attempted to mitigate the impact of the war on other Indians by negotiating prisoner exchanges and urging their white allies to exercise restraint vis-à-vis native foes. Like other Native Americans, the Oneidas experienced the American Revolution as a prolonged trial in which they constantly tried to balance contradictory imperatives. They had to protect the independence of their communities by assisting allies without killing kin or otherwise diminishing the native power on which their long-term interests depended. In other words, they behaved toward the United States as allies rather than subordinates. Although the Oneidas negotiated the vagaries of war quite effectively and served the patriots well, the Revolutionary War deepened preexisting antagonisms between whites and natives. This did not bode well for the Oneidas' ability to retain their homeland from the new nation that soon surrounded it.

When New England rebels issued an appeal for Iroquois support in the spring of 1775, the Oneidas replied with a declaration of neutrality that reflected the confederacy's initial official position. The New Englanders, sufficiently occupied by a war on a single front against a single foe, prudently declared themselves satisfied.[6] The Oneidas were content to buy time, as were most of the rest of the Iroquois. Neutrality had benefits recognized by all. The Six Nations had historically taken advantage of divisions among Europeans to protect their own autonomy. Because of their military prowess, diplomatic skill, and strategically crucial location, the Iroquois had effectively held the balance of power between the British and French until the end of the Seven Years' War. Because Iroquois political culture admitted scant central authority, factions favorable to one side or the other constantly threatened the equilibrium. Europeans faced a chronically volatile situation that required their attention and that sometimes felt more than a little like extortion. At a conference at Albany in 1775, a Six Nations spokesman put the patriots' goodwill to the test by requesting substantial trade and the return of two parcels of land that he claimed had been taken from them without compensation. On hearing their demands, the secretary to the patriot treaty commissioners observed privately, "It is plain to me that the Indians understand their game, which is to play into both hands."[7]

The Iroquois' game was more one of canny diplomacy than cynical ploy. They were making the best of a bad situation. Beneath the assertion of neutrality, members of the confederacy were truly at odds over how to proceed. Samuel Kirkland, the Presbyterian missionary to the Oneidas, reported after a March 1776 council involving the Oneidas and Cayugas, "Many of the Indians have observed to me that they never knew Debates so warm and Contentions so fierce to have happened between these two Brothers . . . since the Commencement of their Union."[8] Indeed, although the pendulum of fortune swung back and forth during the war, there was relatively little switching of sides by those who early on committed themselves firmly and freely to either the Crown or colonists. All could sustain a belief that their alliance best served the long-term interest of the confederacy, and they fought sincerely and effectively for their chosen side for the duration of the conflict.

To the extent that the concept of liberty made sense within a native cultural context, the Iroquois already enjoyed more of it than any British subject or American citizen ever would; the question was how to protect it. The Iroquois recognized they had a stake in the war's outcome, even if this was primarily a war among whites. But Iroquoia was large, and offered many different vantage points on what that outcome and its implication for natives would be. The westernmost nations, the Seneca and Cayuga, had witnessed some of the most violent manifestations of white aggression during Dunmore's War. This war, triggered in 1774 by competition over Ohio Valley lands, had pitted Virginians against Delawares, Shawnees, and Mingos, many of whom had Seneca and Cayuga relatives in Iroquoia. Many Senecas and Cayugas had been deeply frustrated by the Six Nations' collective decision to remain aloof from Dunmore's War. Now their lack of sympathy for the rebels was predictable, and calls for retribution became more difficult to resist. Besides, the presence of nearby Fort Niagara made the Crown's strength—and patronage—more palpable than the rebels' in western Iroquoia. Fort Niagara's personnel included an experienced cadre of Indian agents, many of whom spoke native languages.[9] There was little reason for the Indians there to question British officers' confident counsel that the Crown would prevail.

Pro-British sentiment among the easternmost Iroquois, the Mohawks, sprang from somewhat different sources. The Revolution presented the Mohawks with their last hope of slowing, arresting, or perhaps even reversing the white settlement around them. More than a century of contact with sharp-dealing white neighbors and speculators had left the Mohawks with little land left to lose and considerable hostility toward expansionist white settlers. Mohawk allegiance to the Crown had been cultivated and sustained by the Mohawk family of the late Sir William Johnson. Johnson had served as Britain's superintendent of Indian affairs for the Northern Department until his death in 1774. Joseph Brant, the brother of Johnson's Mohawk widow, traveled to Britain in 1776, where he was further impressed by the power and grandeur of the empire. Brant's influence extended to the Oneida town of Oquaga, where hundreds of Mohawks had emigrated over the previous decades as they were dispossessed of their homeland. Many Oquaga Oneidas followed the Mohawks into the British camp.[10] The Oquaga experience demonstrates that, although personal conscience was always the ultimate arbiter of behavior, allegiance was generally decided at the village, rather than the national, level. No nation was homogenous in its support of Crown or colonists. Among the Mohawks, many of those from Fort Hunter remained neutral throughout, and a peace party led by Great Tree existed among the Senecas. Then there were the Iroquois among the "Seven Nations" of the lower St. Lawrence Valley. Although no longer represented at confederacy councils, most of the Seven Nations Iroquois were Mohawks (but with a substantial number of Oneidas) who resided at Akwesasne and Kahnawake near Montreal. They maintained their autonomy from the Iroquois confederacy and had exhibited a consistent disinclination to take up arms in the wars of others. The American Revolution was no exception. Although they were officially allied with the British, their assistance was generally apathetic and some actively assisted the patriots.[11] The Onondagas also avoided taking clear sides early on, a strategy consistent with their geographical location at the heart of the confederacy. Their centrality made Onondaga the ceremonial capital of the confederacy, and often made the role of mediator incumbent upon them.

Why did the majority of Oneidas (and the Tuscaroras who resided among them) defy their fellow Iroquois and take up arms against the British? Historians have generally assumed that it was because, as Washington put it, Reverend Kirkland enjoyed "uncommon ascendancy" over the Indians to whom he had ministered since 1766. In fact, Kirkland's efforts to convert them to Christianity had reaped only modest gains. Although the Oneidas listened to Kirkland, they did not blindly follow him in matters of politics, diplomacy, and war any more than they did in matters of religion. Also present was James Dean, the U.S. agent and interpreter whose relationship with the Oneidas went back to the late 1750s, when he had moved to Oquaga at roughly the age of ten. As the Revolution approached, Kirkland and Dean were able to explain the complex and quickly evolving situation to the Oneidas in terms favorable to the rebels. Kirkland and Dean enabled the Oneidas to see beyond the "weak hearted" Tryon County militia and understand the patriots' true strength.

That they were biased was obvious, but the Oneidas could and did compare notes with other Iroquois on a regular basis. Perhaps most important to the forging and maintenance of an alliance, Kirkland and Dean conveyed to Congress the Oneidas' needs and dispositions toward the United States. By satisfying the former, Congress could hope to improve the latter.[12]

Oneida policy was fundamentally shaped by the fact that they occupied the eastern boundary of Indian country now that the Mohawks had been dispossessed. In early 1775, an Oneida spokesman told royal officials that they were "greatly alarmed at the endeavours of people to cross [the boundary] lately, and requested that they might be immediately prevented." Despite this request, the limits of Britain's ability to rein in frontier settlement had long been obvious, and dispossession was the likely consequence of the Oneidas' alienating their white neighbors. Moreover, "the Key of the Western Frontier"—the portage protected by Fort Stanwix— lay partially in Oneida territory.[13] As prospects of conflict grew, the Oneidas realized that they would have to come to terms with neighboring patriot communities. By way of an explanation to a British officer of his nation's alliance with the Americans, the Oneida sachem White Skin noted that "their People lived so near to the Rebels that they were constrained to a compliance."[14] The statement may have been made under duress, but as a description of extant power relations it was only a modest exaggeration. The Oneida chief Good Peter later put forth the same argument more positively when he recalled that "the love of peace, and the love of our land which gave us birth, supported our resolution" to back the United States.[15] According to the pension applications of warriors at Oriske—an Oneida village surrounded by colonial settlement—they mustered with the local militia in 1775 and reassured them that no Indian hostilities were imminent.[16]

Of course, when it came to solidifying those allegiances, a little patronage did not hurt. The patriot commissioners of Indian affairs noted ruefully that "the Enemy have a very capital advantage over us in their intercourse with the Indians as they have it in their power to afford them such ample supplies, and those in their interest are continually drawing Comparisons."[17] To nurture any latent support and secure active assistance, Congress loosened its purse strings and promised to keep its Indian allies supplied with gunpowder, provisions, and clothing. Diplomacy also carried a hefty price tag. Convening a treaty with the Six Nations in August of 1776, General Philip Schuyler noted, "The Consumption of provision and Rum is incredible. It equals that of an army of three thousand Men; altho' the Indians here are not above twelve hundred, including Men, Women, and Children."[18] The entertainment of small touring delegations of Indian allies proved a more cost-effective form of persuasion. Kirkland escorted a small contingent of Oneida warriors to New England and New Jersey in March 1777. The missionary had advised Schuyler to provide the Oneidas with "occular Demonstration" of "French gentlemen or French vessels."[19] Kirkland understood that the promise of an alliance with France gave the rebels crucial credibility in the eyes of many Oneidas. Oneida francophilia dated back to the seventeenth century, but its present incarnation was born largely of nostalgia for the era of imperial competition, and it was strong enough that British agents or their Iroquois supporters felt it necessary to deny stridently the existence of any such alliance.[20]

According to pastor (and soon-to-be Yale College president) Ezra Stiles, who met the touring Oneidas in Rhode Island, the native delegates also came "to inspect and report the Preparations & Strength of these States." At Boston they "were shewn the Fortresses & went on board . . . one of the American Men o' War. They desired to see the Canon discharged, & asked Capt Manly to fire one with Ball for Congress, two without Ball for G. Washington, & six without Ball for the Six Nations of Indians." Stiles reported that Rhode Island's "Assembly made an Entertainmt for them &c to amount of Expence 300 Dollars—among the rest a Gun or Musquet made in N. Engld exceedingly decorated worth 20 Dollars, tho' they gave 40 & presented it to the Chief Warrior."[21] On March 29, Washington informed the president of Congress that the six Oneidas had visited him at his headquarters, where "I shewed them every civility in my power and everything I thought material to excite in them an Idea of our strength and independence."[22]

These diplomatic efforts bred a modicum of camaraderie between the Oneidas, the diverse array of colonists gathered under the patriot banner, and their French allies. A New Jersey captain who spent time at an Oneida village in 1776 noted in his diary that Oneida warriors tutored Continental officers in "Ball, or what the Scott's call Golf." (He was actually referring to lacrosse.) Exhibitions of song and dance also brought natives and whites together to share in a recreational activity that transcended the language barrier, at least in part.[23] At a dance at a November 1777 council,

> One of the chiefs . . . took the commissioners, one at a time, by the hand, and danced them around the circle, then rubbing his hand about the grease and blacking of the pot, he blackened the face, first of General Schuyler, and then the other gentlemen, which excited much laughter.[24]

Claude Blanchard, the French commissary-general, recalled the visit of an Oneida-Kahnawake delegation to Rochambeau's fleet in Newport in 1780. He found their table manners satisfactory and commented that their dancing reminded him of French peasants pressing grapes in a vat.[25]

Such socializing promoted cohesiveness that was helpful during the trials of war. Those trials began in earnest in 1777, when Britain launched two expeditions south from Canada to rendezvous at Albany with forces based in New York City. If successful, New England would be cut off from the other colonies. Colonel Barry St. Leger marched straight into Iroquoia and laid siege to Fort Stanwix in early August. Seven hundred Tryon County militiamen under Brigadier General Nicholas Herkimer set out to relieve the fort, and sixty Oneidas were with them. The Mohawks and

British, with Seneca assistance, successfully ambushed the relief column at Oriskany Creek. An unknown number of Oneidas were among the 400 patriots who died in the ensuing battle.

The Oneida-patriot alliance survived this shock. The Oneidas' losses did not weaken their alliance with the patriots, and there is little evidence to suggest that the Indian participants in the battle were particularly penitent about the death of fellow Iroquois. Nevertheless, when the Iroquois exacted retribution for this battle, it was against property and white soldiers, not physically against other Iroquois. Tory Senecas made up for the loss of thirty-six warriors by clubbing to death some of their patriot prisoners. Oneidas and Mohawks sacked one another's villages at Oriske and Canajoharie—but they were already empty and their inhabitants were not pursued.[26] In fact, for the remainder of the war, Indians on opposite sides of the conflict generally avoided hostile encounters with one another. Events surrounding the Battle of Saratoga are one example of the Indians' rough balance of assistance to white allies and avoidance of native foes. In September, almost immediately after accepting a war belt from the Americans, the Oneidas, Tuscaroras, and Onondagas dispatched 150 warriors to join General Horatio Gates as the British marched a force of 7,000 men southward along the Champlain-Hudson corridor toward Albany. The patriot-allied Indians took prisoners and intercepted communications between British officers.[27] Of the Oneidas and the other patriot-allied Indians, John Hadcock recalled that his father, a Saratoga veteran, "always sayd they where Brave men and fought Like Bull dogs till Burgoine surrendert." Gates praised the Indians' "great service." Unlike Oriskany, however, the Battle of Saratoga itself did not pit Iroquois against Iroquois because, as one British soldier recalled, the British-allied Indians "ran off through the wood."[28]

Although the Oneidas' commitment to the United States remained strong, their willingness to serve was subject to some of the same limiting factors as the patriot militia. They were not professional fighters, and they would not serve if their home communities faced imminent danger. As for the prospects of an attack by other Indians, the Oneidas knew that whatever precedents for restraint existed were only that.[29] Although the Marquis de Lafayette boasted in March 1778 that "the love of the french blood mix'd with the love of some french *louis d'or* [i.e., money] have engag'd those indians to promise they would come with me," the Oneidas did not actually go anywhere until the French and Americans agreed to build a fort to protect their village. As the U.S. Indian commissioners observed, "It is not reasonable to suppose that they will march to the southward and leave their families defenceless."[30]

The approximately fifty Oneida warriors who finally left for Pennsylvania late that April proved themselves particularly useful adjuncts to the Continental Army during their brief service there. Prussian drillmaster Friedrich von Steuben valued them for their ability to "keep the Enemy Compact, prevent Desertion in our Troops, [and] make us Masters of Intelligence." By way of a European analogy, he noted "the Austrians always use the Croats (a kind of white Indians) for such Purposes and to so good Effect that the King of Prussia imitated them by enrolling a Body of Irregulars to Cover in like Manner his Army."[31] On May 30, the *Pennsylvania Gazette* accordingly reported that forty Oneidas had arrived in Trenton, New Jersey, "to scout near the lines, to check the unlawful commerce, too much carried on at present, between the country and the city."[32] But the Oneidas had come to fight as well. A week earlier, after the Battle of Barren Hill, the Oneidas' French commander had occasion to praise "their hability in firing."[33] The Oneidas' service yielded eleven officers' commissions at the ranks of captain and lieutenant. One Kahnawake Mohawk who served with them was made lieutenant colonel and a Tuscarora, lieutenant.

At the time the Americans had called up the Oneida warriors, they anticipated a major British offensive to the south. After it became clear that no such action would materialize, Washington suggested the Oneidas be sent home, with the request that they remain "in readiness to cooperate with us on any future occasion, that may present itself in advancing our mutual interest." In fact, the future occasion had already arrived. In a letter from Oneida dated three days earlier, James Dean related that "the Indians have been constantly ranging the Woods in quest of [a] party who fired upon their people." By the month of June it had become apparent to Congress that they faced "the commencement of an Indian war; which threatens with extensive devastation the frontiers of these United States."[34]

In mid-summer, Oneidas brought Schuyler first news of an assault on the frontier settlement of Wyoming.[35] In early November, the Oneidas passed along a crucial warning regarding a Tory-Indian raid that had yet to take place. An Onondaga had informed them that a large number of Indians and Tories had resolved to attack Cherry Valley. The warning went unheeded, and thirty-three persons were killed in the ensuing assault. The provenance of the Oneidas' Cherry Valley warning—the oral report of an Onondaga—indicates that the Oneidas' effectiveness as intelligence-gatherers lay not just in their scouting skills, but also in their relationships and contacts. Kinship ties enabled Oneida scouts to venture into hostile settlements. In one of the war's more daring feats of espionage, an Oneida known to whites as Deacon Thomas had concealed himself in the rafters of the council house at the Akwesasne Mohawk village in Canada while a British officer unfurled General Burgoyne's 1777 strategy. Deacon Thomas promptly relayed this intelligence to the patriots.[36] He continued to operate there and in other villages in the region with the consent and protection of friends and relatives until his controversial assassination by the British in 1780.[37]

The Iroquois recognized that volatile situations were more effectively managed when lines of communication with the opposing side remained open. Securing the better treatment or outright release of Iroquois prisoners was desirable. Thus, when a party of Seneca warriors arrived at Washington's headquarters to fulfill the terms of a prisoner exchange in June of

1778, Washington reported they were "attended by a few of our Oneida and Tuscarora friends, who were thought necessary to proceed with the truce." The Oneidas also assured the Cayugas that they had used "their Influence to relieve from close confinement some of their People."[38] In November 1778, the Oneidas reciprocated for earlier demonstrations of Kahnawake Mohawk goodwill by pleading successfully for the release of a Kahnawake warrior who had been captured by the patriots.[39] After the frontier raids of 1778, however, attention shifted from the fate of prisoners to preempting patriot retaliation on Iroquois communities. The first months of 1779 saw a flurry of diplomatic activity to this end. In January, the Oneidas claimed to have won the support of significant numbers of Onondagas, some of whom traveled to Oneida in April to surrender "a number of large Silver medals which had been given them by the agents of the King of Britain" as tokens of their support.[40] Two parties of Oneidas were dispatched to "the hostile tribes of the Six Nations." Upon their return, one Oneida with "a relation at Quiyoga [Cayuga] informed him the Quiyogas were determined to hold a conference with the Oneidas very soon."[41] Taking note of such proceedings, Sir Frederick Haldimand, Britain's supreme commander in North America, railed that "the perfidy of the Rebel Oneida Nation is come to that pitch that they even presume to debauch & invite the five nations to be of their sentiments & come over to them."[42]

Despite the overtures, Washington remained committed to striking those Iroquois nations he believed responsible for the devastating 1778 raids on Wyoming and Cherry Valley. He acknowledged that the only way the patriots could take Fort Niagara would be to have the Oneidas convince fellow Iroquois to betray it.[43] That was unlikely, and it was unclear whether the patriots could even find their way there through Iroquoia. In February 1779, seeking some general directions, Washington wrote Schuyler, "I have thought of no way more likely to gain this information, than from Mr. Deane or Mr. Kirkland to endeavour to get it from the Friendly Oneidas." He added that it should be obtained "in such a manner as not to give them any suspicions of the real design."[44] Colonel Goose van Schaik likewise professed ignorance of any planned attack when he met with Oneidas shortly before he carried out his orders to destroy the Onondagas' village in April 1779. This prompted the Oneidas afterward to ask him sarcastically whether "all this was done by design or mistake."[45] Although Van Schaik reported killing a dozen warriors and taking thirty-three prisoners, an Onondaga chief claimed that "some of the Young Women . . . [were] carried away for the use of their Soldiers & were afterwards put to death in a more shameful manner." Although there is no corroboration of this accusation, it is worth noting that New York Governor George Clinton had felt it necessary to issue a warning that, "although I have very little apprehension that any of the soldiers will so far forget their character as to attempt such a crime on the Indian women who may fall into their hands, yet it will be well to take measures to prevent such a stain upon our army." After Van Schaik's raid, most of the Onondagas fled to Niagara, where they received arms and encouragement to repay the favor. Nevertheless, about 130 sought refuge among the Oneidas, many among kin relations.[46]

Although the Oneidas raided Tory bases in 1779, the alliance slackened somewhat. They provided limited support to the much larger expedition against southern and western Iroquoia under General John Sullivan later that summer. Sullivan complained in September that only four Oneidas had assisted him in his effort "totally to extirpate" the pro-British Iroquois. Sullivan complained as well that those four were "totally unacquainted with every part of the country through which I have yet passed." Replying to Sullivan's complaint, a delegation consisting of one sachem and three warriors told him they had intended to send a hundred warriors but received word en route "that they were too late." The chief warrior present antagonized Sullivan further by requesting clemency for the Cayugas. The Oneida warriors claimed to "know there is a party of the Cayuga tribe who have ever wished to be at peace with their American brethren" under the leadership of Tegatleronwane, who was related to an Oneida sachem. They held out hopes for negotiation and "therefore request that you would not for the present destroy their cornfields."[47]

Sullivan proceeded anyway, but he might have done well to follow the Oneidas' advice. Indeed, the following year, a British officer noted with satisfaction that "we would not have had one third of the Six Nations in our interests at this time" if the patriots had exercised "more prudence & less severity." Although Sullivan had executed his orders competently, nothing he accomplished directly impaired the ability of hostile Iroquois to strike again. It only left them bitter and more dependent upon the British than ever.[48] Now operating out of Fort Niagara, British-Indian raids on New York's frontier began anew as soon as the spring thaw arrived. Their effect was no less devastating than in previous years. In June, the Oneidas received a warning from a pro-British Onondaga chief warrior recently at Niagara. The destruction of the principal Oneida town was regarded by the British and their Indian allies as a strategic necessity; the nation was to be taken captive. The Oneida chiefs informed the commanding officer at Fort Stanwix of their expectation of "a general Invasion" and the determination of the women, who had authority over village locations, "to move down into the Country and seek a place of safety among the Inhabitants of the United States." Their wishes were accommodated, because the Americans feared that more Oneidas would follow the others to Niagara if protection was not forthcoming.[49]

The raiders arrived before the Oneidas decamped, but instead of attacking the Oneidas unawares, as was the usual practice, they parleyed fruitlessly with Oneida representatives for two days. Although about 30 Oneidas joined the British, 400 took shelter in Fort Stanwix while their town was reduced to ashes, their crops destroyed, and their cattle driven away.[50]

Along with much of the population of the Mohawk Valley, they fled to Schenectady, only sixteen miles west of Albany, where the Mohawk River met the Hudson. Governor Clinton conceded that "Schenectady may now be said to become the limits of our western Frontier."[51]

Schenectady during wartime presented a bleak prospect. Everything except misery and fear were in short supply. Shortages hit the Oneidas particularly hard, and neither patriot nor Oneida interests were well-served by locals who took Oneida weapons in exchange for liquor. Proximity to the white population also facilitated the transmission of disease. Schuyler made repeated appeals to the Continental Congress on their behalf. He assured his superiors that

> As to Cloathing . . . if [the Oneidas'] whole Stock was collected, it would but tolerably cover an eight part of their number, and to add to their calamity, the small pox prevails with, and has already been fatal, to some of them, in this complication of distress, which beggars all description, I am overwhelmed with their lamentations.[52]

Schuyler also noted that, if "the dictates of humanity and a regard for the interest and honor of the United States" were not enough of a motivation for Congress, self-interest was:

> I fear their virtue will at last yield to a continuation of distress, which no human beings can endure, and that they will renounce an alliance which has exposed them to such variety of calamity, to form one with those who can amply supply every of their wants.[53]

General Pierre Van Cortlandt offered a similar assessment. Like Schuyler, he did not trust feelings of humanity or gratitude to carry the argument. He observed that "the Oneida's naked and precariously subsisted and threatning to go over the Enemy; the Effects of which will be severaly [severely] felt by the frontier Inhabitants."[54] The entreaties bore insufficient fruit, and only very slowly at that. The connection between the Americans and the Oneidas seemed about to break. Most Oneidas repaired to a spot north of the town and toward Saratoga, "in hopes to gain some subsistence by hunting" and where they might "more easily and plentifully be accommodated with fuel, which in their naked condition is an object of importance." They maintained what the Marquis de Chastellux described as "an assemblage of miserable huts in the woods, along the road to Albany."[55]

But the reasons for the Oneidas' flight to the outskirts of town had to do with more than mere subsistence. Initially they had been quartered in the town barracks, and the soldiers sent to live among the townspeople. This distance between the soldiers and Indians proved insufficient. In March of 1781, Schuyler reported that "Disagreeable Controversys have frequently arisen between the soldiery and the Indians . . . and one of the latter having lately been barbarously murdered and others Assaulted and dangerously wounded it became necessary to remove them to the neighboring woods."[56]

What had gone wrong since the amicable lacrosse lessons and dances? Part of the answer lies in the difference between common soldiers and their officers; the latter had been more thoroughly involved in those events. On Sullivan's expedition, the more plebeian attitude toward natives was manifested in toasts like "Civilization or death to the American savages" and the skinning of a dead Indian to make boot legs.[57] Moreover, although Schuyler and other officers now lamented the friction between natives and soldiers, they were also partially responsible for it. Gates had exploited the anti-Indian frenzy that followed the 1777 murder of Jane McCrea by Canadian Indians in the upper Hudson Valley to gain new recruits. Moreover, by employing natives to track and capture deserters—in short, as enforcers of military discipline—officers widened the breach between Indians and soldiers. When about thirty Continentals deserted Fort Stanwix in June 1780, a party of Oneida warriors was sent in pursuit. When sixteen of the deserters were overtaken, they opened fire upon their pursuers, who returned it, killing thirteen.[58] It was not the first incident of its kind. Regardless of whether fellow soldiers approved of the deserters' desperate measures, they could testify that the grievances that spurred them were very real. Washington acknowledged that "the want of pay and the necessary Cloathing, particularly Shirts, is assigned as the primary cause" of the 1780 escape.[59] From the common soldier's perspective, the natives who made them more secure also enforced their submission to harsh conditions.

For every reason that patriot soldiers valued their alliance with the Oneidas, they likewise feared and distrusted them. Dependency generated anxiety and, in turn, the anger that was vented in Schenectady. When Oneidas withdrew from a scouting party under his command in 1779, Lieutenant Thomas McClellan wrote his superior, "My Pen must fail to Describe to you the situation we wair in to See the Infernil Villins Deserting us in the Wide Wilderness, to See the Gloom that Set on the Braws of Each of our Brave Men."[60] If the Oneidas were the patriots' principal source of information on the enemy's movements, they instantly came under suspicion whenever patriot soldiers or settlements were surprised. In 1778, when a soldier who had left Fort Stanwix to catch a horse was scalped and killed, soldiers at the fort openly accused the natives of having countenanced the attack. It was the second such fatality in so many years. In response, a hundred Oneida and Tuscarora warriors appeared at the fort to reaffirm their allegiance to the Americans.[61]

The soldiers' concerns were not entirely without foundation. There was a price to be paid for the intelligence they needed, and the Oneidas maintained their end of the quid pro quo by allowing native opponents a modicum of freedom to act in the territory they controlled. In 1779, British Captain Walter Butler even asserted that "the Caghnawago [Kahnawake]

Indians who lately took the Prisoners at Fort Stanwix were not only with some Oneydas a little time before but were even directed by them where to make their Blow."[62] Although the truth of Butler's claim is impossible to ascertain, there is evidence that when native warriors on opposite sides encountered one another in the woods, they were more likely to parley than take prisoners—even when white soldiers were present.[63] That this courtesy extended beyond Iroquoian peoples to include Algonquians points to the development of a native identity that transcended older kin and confederate ones. As a British officer complained, "I have not white men sufficient to send after them, and I doe not think that Indians will doe anything to hunt those of their own Colour."[64]

The Oneidas, however, successfully kept the balance in the patriots' favor. In the summer of 1780, Senecas complained that Oneida scouts were altogether "too officious, & making Report to the Americans of every Tract [track] they discover." In October, the depredations of a British-Indian raiding party were limited by their interception by an Oneida scouting party. British commander Sir Frederick Haldimand complained to Lord George Germain that the Oneidas were "troublesome and treacherous to the last degree."[65]

In January 1781, Schuyler noted that "the enemy in small parties have already reappeared in Tryon County" and expressed his fear that "if the Oneidas should be driven to desperation by the hardships they endure, and join the enemy all beyond [Albany] will be one dreadful scene of desolation and slaughter."[66] Schuyler's sense of the Oneidas' crucial place in the defense of the frontier was now magnified by the fact that the patriot population of the Mohawk Valley was unwilling to unite in its own defense.[67] Colonel Abraham Wemple voiced a suspicion that "the Inhabitants along the Mohawk Rivers being all farmers, and a great many on our frontiers people not faithful to us[,] may immediately go and inform the Enemy of our weakness."[68]

The Oneidas continued to serve the Continental Army effectively through 1781. Haldimand complained that they "much impede our Scouts and Recruiting Parties, & are in many Respects very useful to the Rebels." The subsequent decline in their cooperation, however, only followed the lead of the white residents of the upper Hudson and Mohawk valleys, which was part of a larger trend.[69] War-weariness caused patriot unity and motivation to decay. By 1782, Dean's ability to mobilize Oneida scouting parties seemed to be flagging. On February 20, he penned an apologetic letter to Schuyler after a party of Indians he had engaged "declined the service & are gone to the Woods to hunt." It took multiple negotiations to convene another scouting party, only to have them turn back prematurely, ostensibly for want of acceptable snowshoes.[70]

Tensions between the Oneidas and the white civilians of Tryon County did not help the alliance. On May 1, 1782, Schuyler had to appeal publicly for calm amid rumors that an Oneida or Tuscarora warrior had killed some whites. Schuyler was assured by Deputy Quartermaster General Henry Glen "that he had full evidence that the Indian supposed to be concerned was not guilty of the fact." But the guilt or innocence of any particular Indian was beside the point to the would-be vigilantes; according to Schuyler, "the Inhabitants had threatened to put to death any of those Oneidas and Tuscaroras they might meet with." Exasperated, he reminded the public that

> It would be extreamly Imprudent & unjust to retaliate for any offence committed by an individual on others not Guilty, for the consequences would prove extreamly distressing as all those Indians might thereby be tempted to join the Enemy Increase their force, and thus still more distress the frontiers . . . casting an odious imputation on our national faith. I have therefore most earnestly to Intreat you to prevent any injury to them in their persons or property.[71]

Such conflict heralded trouble when the war would end, because the threat of Oneida defection would no longer serve as a check upon abuse. Nor would friction cease, for the approach of the war's end only revived competition for land. On September 9, 1782, a group of Oneidas and allied Indians complained to the commissioners of the subterfuges of "people who want to take away our Lands by Piece Meals." Referring to the success that one Colonel John Harper had in finding some compliant natives to sign a deed, they bluntly asserted, "If one two or three Sachems or Warriors should get into Liquor and make a sale of any part of our Lands the rest on finding it out will not agree to it and breach the agreement and it shall not stand."[72]

The bind in which the Oneidas found themselves is plainly evident in a February 1783 letter from a Continental officer, Pliny Moor, to his father. Moor began with a description of the patriots' arduous march to British-held Fort Oswego on the southern shore of Lake Ontario. The Oswego expedition had been an aggressive move to assert patriot control over both the lake and central and eastern Iroquoia. It ended in failure after the Oneida guide, Captain John Otaawighton, led them astray in the final hours of the nighttime approach. Moor seethed "that by the perfidy or Ignorance of one Savage guide (the former of which is more probable) the Continent is at more than a Thousand pounds Expence besides the loss of several good men a number of Toes frozen & a quantity of good health." Whatever suspicions Moor harbored were not sufficient to deprive Otaawighton of the land bounty due him as a continental officer. The remainder of Moor's letter, however, indicates precisely why the Oneidas might have considered early patriot control of the fort to be detrimental. During his service, Moor had been systematically reconnoitering Indian land and identified particular spots conducive for cultivation, mills, and trade. His letter indicated that he was already making arrangements to stake his claim.[73] It was clear that early United States dominance of the northern frontier would only hasten white settlement in Iroquoia.

Thus, even before peace was declared officially, the Oneidas were anxious to return to their burned-out villages. Kirkland's letters suggest the poverty to which they had been reduced. In 1784, he wrote of "the extreme scarcity of provision" at Oneida and reported subsisting mostly on "Strawberries, with now & then a little fish." Referring to the physical condition of the Oneidas the following year, he wrote that "the most of my people are degenerated as much as our paper currency depreciated in the time of war."[74] Nevertheless, some Oneidas remained optimistic. The trial was nearing its end, and having fought on the winning side, they even gloated to pro-British Iroquois over the apparent vindication of their position. At the Treaty of Fort Stanwix, in 1784, U.S. officials spoke to the rest of the Six Nations in harsh and disrespectful tones, but lauded "those nations who preserved their faith to them, and adhered to their cause, those, therefore, must be secured in full and free enjoyment of their possessions." Under such guarantees, the Oneidas should have been able to enjoy peace of mind that their land was safe and even contemplate the prospect of enhanced status among the Iroquois.[75]

The Oneidas' confidence was misplaced. The U.S. government had pledged its faith to its allies, but it did not exercise its authority over Indian affairs very vigorously. New York state was closer, hungry for revenue, and anxious to preempt Massachusetts's claim to Iroquoia. State officials, including Governor Clinton, had begun planning the Oneidas' expropriation before the war had ended. In 1783, the state appointed commissioners and instructed them to convince the Oneidas to exchange their land for some of the Senecas' further west.[76] The commissioners did not have the temerity to make such an offer, but New York was prepared to bring strong measures into operation, including threats to recognize illegal transactions such as Harper's unless the Oneidas ceded large swaths of territory. By 1788, the Oneidas' territory had been reduced from approximately 6 million acres to just 250,000.[77] To add insult to injury, during the late 1780s and 1790s, the dispossessed Oneidas watched in consternation as American relations with the Senecas and Cayugas warmed as part of an American initiative to isolate the western confederacy of Indians in Ohio. The Oneidas indignantly observed that "the promises made to us are disregarded, and we do not enjoy privileges equal to those who were your enemies."[78]

During the American Revolution, the Oneida nation fought to retain its independence and its territory. The Oneidas fought as allies but not subordinates; they usually refrained from actions that directly targeted their fellow Iroquois. By entering into an alliance with the war's eventual victor, the Oneida nation expected to share in its good fortune. Federal agent Timothy Pickering observed in 1792, however, that the "'consequences' of their attachment to us . . . have not been 'good' unless it is good for them to lose almost all their lands for a trifle."[79] Even during the war, it was clear that the patriots' treatment of the Oneidas was primarily a function of the power the Oneidas held. Facing a civilian population angered and distressed by the pressures of war, Continental officers trying to protect their Oneida allies found the most effective appeal for calm was not pointing out the Oneidas' past service, but rather threatening that the Oneidas might withdraw such service in the future. Once the war was over, the Oneidas' claim to rights and respect hung on little but gratitude for the "Blood and . . . brave men" who had been "lost in [the United States'] defence."[80] Such appeals made for nice speeches at official gatherings, but they did little to alter the final treaty texts and surveys. The Revolution had been fought to install governments that better reflected the people's will, and the will of the people was to expand onto native land.

Notes

I wish to thank Sarah Stuppi for her assistance in preparing this article for publication. Several passages were published earlier in "A 'Civil' War? Rethinking Iroquois Participation in the American Revolution," *Explorations in Early American Culture* 4 (2000): 148–65. They appear here courtesy of the Pennsylvania Historical Association.

1. Gloria Halbritter, "Oneida Traditions," in Jack Campisi and Laurence M. Hauptman, eds., *The Oneida Indian Experience: Two Perspectives* (Syracuse, N.Y.: Syracuse University Press, 1988), p. 145; <http://www.oneida-nation.net/pollycooper.html>. The Cooper story was also recounted by Amelia Cornelius at the "Oneida Journey" conference, Oneida, Wisconsin, June 1998.

2. In an April 7, 1778, letter to Marinus Willett, Louis de Tousard reported, "We are at present in plenty of Corn, which we received from the Indians them selves, who made a prohibition to receive any money for it, and every-day they carry Corn much more than we want for fitting our horses." Thomas Bailey Myers Collection, New York Public Library (hereafter NYPL).

3. Elisabeth Tooker, "The League of the Six Nations: Its History, Politics, and Ritual," in *Handbook of North American Indians*, vol. 15, *Northeast*, ed. Bruce G. Trigger (Washington, D.C.: Smithsonian Institution Press, 1978), p. 421; Samuel Kirkland, "A General Statement of the Six Nations of Indians Living within the United States," December 24, 1790, Samuel Kirkland Papers, Hamilton College Archives, Clinton, N.Y. (hereafter SKP).

4. Quoted in Max M. Mintz, *Gouverneur Morris and the American Revolution* (New Haven, Conn.: Yale University Press, 1973), p. 84.

5. Karim M. Tiro, "A 'Civil' War? Rethinking Iroquois Participation in the American Revolution," *Explorations in Early American Culture* 4 (2000): 148–65.

6. The appeal was so ill conceived that the Oneidas did them a great service by not passing it along. Provincial Congress of Massachusetts to Kirkland, April 4, 1775, in Peter Force, ed., *American Archives*, 9 vols. (Washington, D.C.: 1837–1853), 1:1349–50; Oneida declaration of neutrality, Samuel Kirkland Papers, 57, SKP; [Joseph Platt] Cooke to the Oneida Indians, July 1, 1775, 58a, SKP; James Sullivan, ed., *Minutes of the Albany Committee of Correspondence* (Albany: University of the State of New York, 1923), p. 96.

7. Anthony F. C. Wallace, "Origins of Iroquois Neutrality: The Grand Settlement of 1701," *Pennsylvania History* 24 (1957): 223–35; Jon W. Parmenter, "After the 'Mourning Wars': The Iroquois as Allies in Colonial American Campaigns, 1675–1760," in Stephen Carney and Daniel P. Barr, eds., *"The Only Way Open to Us": Warfare and Resistance in North American Indian History* (Washington, D.C.: United States Army Center for Military History, 2005); S. A. Harrison, ed., *Memoir of Lieut. Col. Tench Tilghman* (1876; repr., New York: New York Times, 1971), 88.

8. Samuel Kirkland to Philip Schuyler, March 12, 1776, r. 172, i. 153, 2:97, Papers of the Continental Congress, National Archives (hereafter PCC), Washington, D.C.

9. Abraham Yates to Clinton, January 9, 1779, in *Public Papers of George Clinton*, 10 vols. (New York and Albany: State of New York, 1899–1914), 4:478–80 (hereafter *PPGC*).

10. Colin G. Calloway, *The American Revolution in Indian Country: Crisis and Diversity in Native American Communities* (New York: Cambridge University Press, 1995), pp. 108–22.

11. James Duane to Philip Schuyler, May 25, 1778, *PPGC*, 3:356; Robert J. Surtees, "The Iroquois in Canada," in Francis Jennings, ed., *The History and Culture of Iroquois Diplomacy: An Interdisciplinary Guide to the Treaties of the Six Nations and Their League* (Syracuse, N.Y.: Syracuse University Press, 1985), pp. 68–72.

12. Christine Sternberg Patrick, "The Life and Times of Samuel Kirkland, 1741–1808: Missionary to the Oneida Indians, American Patriot, and Founder of Hamilton College" (Ph.D. diss., SUNY—Buffalo, 1993), pp. 109–110; Karim M. Tiro, "James Dean in Iroquoia," *New York History* 80 (1999): 391–422; David Levinson, "An Explanation for the Oneida-Colonist Alliance in the American Revolution," *Ethnohistory* 23 (1976): 265–89. On the morale of the Tryon County militia, see Philip Schuyler to the Committee of Tryon County, July 4, 1777, Schuyler Papers, box 1, folder 13, New York State Library, Albany, N.Y. (hereafter NYSL); Albany Committee to Tryon County Committee, July 15, 1777, in Maryly Barton Penrose, ed., *Mohawk Valley in the Revolution* (Franklin Park, N.J.: Liberty Bell Associates, 1978), pp. 121–24.

13. Proceedings of Guy Johnson with the Oneidas and Oughquageys, February 11, 1775, in E. B. O'Callaghan, ed., *Documents Relative to the Colonial History of the State of New York*, 15 vols. (Albany, N.Y.: Weed, Parsons, 1853–1887), 8:550–51 (hereafter *DHNY*); Pierre Van Cortlandt to the New York Delegates of the Continental Congress, January 17, 1781, in Jacob Judd, ed., *Correspondence of the Van Cortlandt Family of Cortlandt Manor, 1748–1800*, 4 vols. (Tarrytown, N.Y.: Sleepy Hollow Restorations, 1977–1981), 2:399.

14. Proceedings at two meetings with Guy Johnson, July 3–6, 1780, B119:96–99, Frederick Haldimand Papers, National Archives of Canada, Ottawa, Ontario (hereafter HP).

15. "Good Peter's Narrative of Several transactions respecting Indian Lands," Timothy Pickering Papers, 60:121–33, Massachusetts Historical Society, Boston (hereafter TPP).

16. Penrose, *Mohawk Valley in the Revolution*, pp. 19–21, 57; Sullivan, *Minutes*, pp. 167–68, 172.

17. Commissioners of Indian Affairs to Henry Laurens, January 12, 1778, in Maryly Penrose, comp., *Indian Affairs Papers, American Revolution* (Franklin Park, N.J.: Liberty Bell Associates, 1981), pp. 103–4 (hereafter *IAP*).

18. Quoted in Barbara Graymont, *The Iroquois* (New York: Chelsea House, 1988), p. 106.

19. Kirkland to Philip Schuyler, January 14–17, 1777, r. 173, i. 153, 3:63–69, PCC.

20. Kirkland to Schuyler, January 14–17, 1777; Washington to President of Congress, March 29, 1777, in John C. Fitzpatrick, ed., *The Writings of George Washington*, 39 vols. (Washington, D.C.: Government Printing Office, 1931–1944), 7:328–29 (hereafter *WW*); Washington to Schuyler, May 15, 1778, *WW*, 11:389–91.

21. Ezra Stiles, *The Literary Diary of Ezra Stiles*, 2 vols., ed. Franklin Bowditch Dexter (New York: Charles Scribner's Sons, 1901), 2:139–42.

22. Washington to President of Congress, March 29, 1777. Washington indicated the importance of such diplomatic encounters in a message to the Massachusetts legislature, September 28, 1775, *WW*, 3:525.

23. Joseph Bloomfield, *Citizen-Soldier: The Revolutionary War Journal of Joseph Bloomfield* (Newark, N.J.: New Jersey Historical Society, 1982), pp. 79, 90–93.

24. James Thacher, *Military Journal of the American Revolution* (1862; repr., New York: New York Times and Arno Press, 1969), pp. 115–16.

25. Claude Blanchard, *Guerre d'Amérique 1780–1783* (Paris: Librarie Militaire de J. Dumaine, 1881), p. 49; Count de Rochambeau, *Memoirs of the Marshall Count de Rochambeau* (New York: New York Times, 1971), p. 23; Howard C. Rice and Anne S. K. Brown, trans. and ed., *The American Campaigns of Rochambeau's Army, 1780, 1781, 1782, 1783*, 2 vols. (Princeton, N.J.: Princeton University Press, 1972), 1:121–23. On the fallout among British officers, see Père Huguet to Duncan Campbell, October 18, 1780, B111:239; and Mathews to Daniel Claus, October 19, 1780, B114:148, both HP.

26. Thomas S. Abler, *Chainbreaker: The Revolutionary War Memoirs of Governor Blacksnake* (Lincoln: University of Nebraska Press, 1989), p. 130; Daniel Claus to William Knox, November 11, 1777, in K. G. Davies, ed., *Documents of the American Revolution, 1770–1783,* 21 vols. (Shannon: Irish University Press, 1973–1981), 14:251 (hereafter *DAR*); Jelles Fonda to Commissioners of Indian Affairs, April 21, 1778, *IAP,* p. 134.

27. Graymont, *Iroquois,* 150; Joseph Lee Boyle, ed., "From Saratoga to Valley Forge: The Diary of Lt. Samuel Armstrong," *Pennsylvania Magazine of History and Biography* 121 (1997): 246–47; Henry Dearborn, *Revolutionary War Journals of Henry Dearborn, 1775–1783,* ed. Lloyd Brown and Howard Peckham (1939; repr., Freeport, N.Y.: Books for Libraries Press, 1969), p. 107.

28. Gates to Hancock [August] 12, 1777, 5:1059, Gates Papers, New York Historical Society, New York, N.Y. (hereafter GP); quoted in Graymont, *Iroquois,* p. 155.

29. Deane to Schuyler, May 25, 1778, *PPGC,* 3:356–58.

30. Lafayette to Laurens, March 20, 1778; George I. Denniston to George Clinton, April 2, 1778, *PPGC,* 3:118; "Extract from the Minutes of a Board of Commissioners of Indian Affairs for the Northern Department held at Albany," April 15, 1778, 7:85, GP. Washington to Schuyler, May 15, 1778, *WW,* 11:391.

31. Committee at Camp to Henry Laurens, March 2, 1778, in *Letters of Delegates to Congress,* 9:199–200.

32. *Pennsylvania Gazette,* May 30, 1778.

33. Tousard to unidentified correspondent, May 23, 1778, M247, r. 95, i. 78: 157–60, PCC; *Journals of Dearborn,* p. 121.

34. Washington to Schuyler, May 15, 1778, *WW,* 11:389–91; James Dean to [Schuyler?], May 12, 1778, Historical Society of Pennsylvania, Philadelphia; Extract from the minutes of the Board of War, June 11, 1778, 7:764, GP.

35. Schuyler to Clinton, July 20, 1778, *PPGC,* 3:565. The Oneidas could also sound the all clear. Peter Gansevoort to Caty Gansevoort, July 21, 1778, Gansevoort-Lansing Papers, NYPL (hereafter GLP).

36. Entries for May 28, July 30, and August 1, 1777, William Colbraith diary, Rosenbach Museum & Library, Philadelphia; Peter Gansevoort to Goose Van Schaik, June 1, 1777, GLP; Deposition of Frederick Helmer, July 17, 1777, in *Journal of the Provincial Congress,* p. 1007.

37. Duncan Campbell to Haldimand, July 22, 1779, B111:136; Haldimand to Campbell, July 26, 1779, B113:69; Campbell to Haldimand, July 30, 1779, B111:140, all HP.

38. James Dean to Philip Schuyler, January 18, 1779; Washington to the President of Congress, June 21, 1778, *WW,* 12:99.

39. Volkert P. Douw to Gansevoort, November 13, 1778, GLP.

40. Dean to Schuyler, April 1–10, 1779, r. 173, i. 153, 3:440–41, PCC.

41. Dean to Schuyler, April 1–10, 1779.

42. Haldimand to Campbell, April 8, 1779, B113:7 HP.

43. Washington to Schuyler, May 2, 1779, r. 169, i. 152, 7:287, PCC.

44. Washington to Schuyler, February 26, 1779, *WW,* 14:150.

45. Quoted in T. W. Egly, *Goose Van Schaick of Albany, 1736–1789* (n.p., 1993), pp. 60–65.

46. Goose Van Schaik, "Minutes and Proceedings of the Onandaga expedition," April 24, 1779, r. 187, i. 169, 5:259–63; Van Schaik, "A Return of Prisoners Taken and the Number Killed in the Onondaga Castle," April 21, 1779, r. 169, i. 152, 7:264, 305–6, both PCC; "Extract of a Speech Delivered . . . by the Principal Chiefs and Warriors of the Six Nations. . .," December 11, 1782, B102:228, HP; Anthony F. C. Wallace, *The Death and Rebirth of the Seneca* (New York: Alfred A. Knopf, 1969), p. 142; Calloway, *American Revolution,* p. 53; Van Schaik to Henry Glen, May 11, 1779, GLP.

47. Sullivan to Oneidas, September 1, 1779; Oneiga to Sullivan, September 1779, both in *Letters and Papers of Major-General John Sullivan,* ed. Otis G. Hammond (Concord: New Hampshire Historical Society, 1939), 3:114–16.

48. Quoted in Richard White, *The Middle Ground: Indians, Empires, and Republics in the Great Lakes Region, 1650–1815* (New York: Cambridge University Press, 1991), p. 406; Joseph R. Fischer, *A Well-Executed Failure: The Sullivan Campaign against the Iroquois, July–September 1779* (Columbia: University of South Carolina Press, 1997), pp. 192–97.

49. "A Speech of the Oneida Chiefs to Colo. Van Dyck," June 18, 1780, *PPGC*, 5:883–84; Volkert P. Douw to Schuyler, April 26, 1780, New York Historical Society; Van Schaik to Clinton, June 24, 1780, *PPGC*, 5:882

50. Van Dyck to Van Schaik, July 3, 1780, *PPGC*, 5:912–14; Guy Johnson to Germain, July 26, 1780, *DHNY*, 8:796–97; Schuyler to Lafayette, August 18, 1780; Van Schaik to Washington, July 29, 1780, both *WW*; Guy Johnson to Haldimand, August 11, 1780, B107:104–5, HP.

51. Quoted in Graymont, *Iroquois*, pp. 238–39.

52. Willett to Schuyler, September 28, 1780, Schuyler Papers, reel 17, NYPL (hereafter SP); Schuyler to Huntington, December 2, 1780, *IAP*, 265–67; "List of Necessary Clothing for 406 Indian Men Women & Children" r. 173, i. 153, 3:545; Schuyler to Samuel Huntington, January 18, 1781, r. 173, i. 153, 3:555; Richard Peters to Duane, April 20, 1781, r. 173, i. 153, 3:559; Schuyler to Pres. of Congress, December 26, 1780, r. 173, i. 153, 3:589, all PCC.

53. Schuyler to President of Congress, December 2, 1780, r. 173, i. 153, 3:551, PCC; Schuyler to Robert Morris, August 30, 1781, AU7002:8, Hanson Collection, NYSL.

54. Judd, *Van Cortlandt Family*, 2:400.

55. Marquis de Chastellux, *Travels in North America in the Years 1780, 1781, and 1782*, ed. and trans. Howard C. Rice, Jr. (Chapel Hill: University of North Carolina Press, 1963), p. 208.

56. Schuyler to Huntington, March 29, 1781, r. 173, i. 153, 3:547–49, PCC.

57. Frederick Cook, ed., *Journals of the Military Expedition of Major General John Sullivan* (Auburn, N.Y.: Knapp, Peck & Thomson, 1887), p. 8.

58. Washington to the President of Congress, June 20, 1780, *WW*, 19:36–37; Fraser to Haldimand, May 30, 1780, B127:137, HP; Charles Patrick Neimeyer, *America Goes to War: A Social History of the Continental Army* (New York: New York University Press, 1996), pp. 36–48; Washington to President of Congress, June 20, 1780, *WW*, 19:36–37; Abraham Hardenbergh, May 23, 1780, *WW*; Fraser to Haldimand, May 30, 1780, B127:137, HP.

59. Gansevoort to Washington, August 10, 1778, GLP; Washington to President of Congress, June 20, 1780, *WW*.

60. Thomas McClellan to Peter Gansevoort, March 14, 1779, GLP.

61. *Pennsylvania Gazette*, July 30, 1777; Robert Cochran to Gansevoort, September 18, 1778; Cochran to Gansevoort, September 28, 1778, all GLP.

62. Butler to John Butler, August 4, 1779, N105:126; for a similar, earlier claim involving the Kahnawakes and Oneidas, Fraser to Haldimand, July 29, 1779, B120:56, and "The Particulars of a Conference Held by a Deputation from Mr. Lorrimiers Scout with a Party of Oneidas," July 29, 1779, B120:62, all HP.

63. Tiro, "A 'Civil' War?" pp. 155–57, 162–63; Haldimand to Campbell, November 8, 1779, B113:101, HP; Haldimand to Claus, April 6, 1780, B114:103, both in HP. Van Dyck to Van Schaik, October 25, 1779, *PPGC*, 5:330; Richard Houghton to Haldimand, April 3, 1780, B111:188, HP; "The Particulars of a Conference," July 29, 1779, B120:62, HP; Fraser to Haldimand, September 10, 1779, B120:76, HP.

64. Campbell to Haldimand, July 6, 1780, B111:213, HP.

65. Fraser to Haldimand, June 1, 1780, B127:139, HP; Van Dyck to Van Schaik, July 3, 1780 *PPGC*, 5:912–14; Fraser to Haldimand, October 27, 1780, B127:184, HP; Haldimand to George Germain, October 25, 1780, *DAR*, 18:208–9.

66. Schuyler to Huntington, January 18, 1781, r. 173, i. 153, 3:555, PCC.

67. Abraham Wemple to Gansevoort, May 4, 1781, GLP. Willett to George Clinton, June 28, 1781, Marinus Willett Letterbook SC15705, NYSL.

68. Wemple to Gansevoort, November 1, 1781, GLP.

69. Haldimand to Powell, September 7, 1781; Campbell to Mathews, June 7, 1781, B112:56, HP; Anthony Ven Bergen to Gansevoort, October 14, 1781, GLP; Haldimand to Campbell, July 16, 1781, B113:213, HP.

70. Dean to Schuyler, February 20, 1782, box 13, SP.

71. Schuyler to the Inhabitants of the County of Tryon, May 1, 1782, BA9691:615, NYSL.

72. Speech by Oneidas, Tuscaroras, and "French Mohawks" to United States Commissioners, September 9, 1782, Huntington Library, San Marino, Calif., HM 11621; Franklin B. Hough, *Proceedings of the Commissioners for Indian Affairs* (Albany, N.Y.: Munsell, 1861), pp. 44, 73–74.

73. Pliny Moor to Noadiah Moor, February 21, 1783, Miscellaneous Mss. M, Ontario County Historical Society, Canandaigua, N.Y.

74. Walter Pilkington, ed., *The Journals of Samuel Kirkland* (Clinton, N.Y.: Hamilton College, 1980), p. 125; Kirkland to Jerusha Kirkland, September 10, 1785, 97b, SKP.

75. Conference with the Indians of the Six Nations, July 2, 1783, B119:184, HP; Graymont, *Iroquois*, p. 265; Neville B. Craig, *The Olden Time*, 2 vols. (1846; repr., Cincinnati: Robert Clarke, 1876), 2:425–26; Dean to Kirkland, July 11, 1785, 95aa, SKP.

76. "An Act for Indian Affairs," *Laws of the State of New York, Sixth Session*, chap. 48, March 25, 1783; Henry Glen, Peter Schuyler, and Cuyler to Clinton, August 29, 1783, A1823, New York State Archives, Albany, N.Y.

77. J. David Lehman, "The End of the Iroquois Mystique: The Oneida Land Cession Treaties of the 1780s," *William and Mary Quarterly*, 3rd ser., 47 (October 1990): 523–47; Tony Wonderley, "'Good Peter's Narrative of Several Transactions Respecting Indian Lands': An Oneida View of Dispossession, 1785–1788," *New York History* 84 (2003): 237–73; Barbara Graymont, "New York State Indian Policy after the Revolution," *New York History* 57 (1976): 438–74; William A. Starna, "'The United States will protect you': The Iroquois, New York, and the 1790 Nonintercourse Act," *New York History* 83 (2002): 5–33.

78. Speeches of the Oneida Chiefs to Israel Chapin, September 29, 1792, Chicago Historical Society, Chicago.

79. Pickering to Knox, May 2, 1792, 62:31, TPP.

80. Speeches of the Oneida Chiefs to Israel Chapin, September 29, 1792.

9

WIVES, CONCUBINES, AND COMMUNITY

Following the Army

HOLLY A. MAYER

In a "poor part of the Country" near Redding, Connecticut, which offered plenty of water and wood but too many Tories, Major General Israel Putnam planted his division of three Continental brigades for the winter of 1778–1779. General George Washington had ordered the division there to support local defense and secure forage. That February, Sergeant Major John H. Hawkins of Colonel Moses Hazen's 2nd Canadian Regiment described the winter encampment of his brigade. He wrote that it spread over a valley and hill and was "something like the City of Quebec" in that it had an "Upper and a Lower Town." The "Upper Town" consisted of the scattered lodgings of the field, staff, and other commissioned officers and their waiters, along with the public huts belonging to the commissary and quartermaster's departments, including those for the carpenters, shoemakers, tailors, the soap boiler, and the bake oven. In the "Lower Town," which had 116 huts built in regular lines, resided the noncommissioned officers and soldiers "with their Wives and Concubines." He concluded his tour of that military metropolis with the comment that the inhabitants "are like those to be found in other Towns, We have good and bad, rich and poor, black and white; we have Courts of Justice, which is opened almost daily[,] we have Statesmen, Politicians, [and] Doctors . . . Trades of various Kinds going on; and Camp Colourmen, whose Duty it is to keep clean the Streets, Lanes and Alleys in our City."[1]

The sergeant major's description provides evidence that the Continental Army was as much a social construction as a military organization. Various historians have analyzed aspects of that social structure.[2] They have provided much information on the economic and social rankings, as well as the race and ethnicity, of the soldiers. As they broke down the army according to social groups, however, they challenged traditional images of a cohesive military. That left the problem of explaining how the army held together for the eight years of war. Some authors rejected conclusions of ideological unity in favor of cohesion based on material interests or imposed by martial discipline. Others modified older interpretations to show that collective action was a paradoxical result of different groups interpreting and using Revolutionary ideology and rhetoric to serve their own ends. These authors have done much to explain the complexities of motivation, yet perhaps ultimately the reason for some soldiers was simpler than all of the above. Although many soldiers forsook the army to head home, for others the army became home, at least for a while. They were defending family and friends in a military community as well as in civilian ones.

Communities were at the heart of the Revolution in many ways. Individuals could not foment rebellion on their own; they had to get their neighbors involved. Communities, in turn, affected the breadth, depth, and effectiveness of the rebellion by how well they did—or did not—support their Revolutionaries. That applied to the establishment of the army as well. When resistance to the British government became armed rebellion, many men enlisted in the army (as in the militias) as part of coteries of family members and neighbors. They took part of their original social networks with them into the Continental Army regiments. Significantly for the army, some men included their wives and children. That was especially the case when they were driven from their homes by British occupation. These core groups and families helped create the regimental neighborhoods that made up the Continental Army's community. The military was thus more than formations of single men. It was also a society built upon personal connections. These social networks sustained the military even as they complicated its operations.

While the Continental Congress legislated the army into existence, and the army's commanding officers developed its structure, it was the people of the army—not just those who bore arms, but those who bore children and those who bore other burdens—who made it a community within the constraints of military maneuvers, regulations, and garrison guards. Over the eight years of war, these people had to live, not just fight. As the army became their livelihood, they maintained the army. Family followers also provided a measure of social stability that contributed to institutional continuity. Thus, they both directly and indirectly contributed to the mission of winning the War for Independence and establishing the United States of America.[3]

To win the war, the army had to survive. Followers of the army contributed directly to that survival by performing essential services in supplying the forces, nursing the men, and performing such housekeeping chores as washing clothes and cooking meals. Their endeavors, indeed their very existence, helped make the army, as Don Higginbotham described it, "a living, day-to-day symbol of the Revolution and emerging

American nationality." In creating and maintaining one army, difficult though that was throughout the war, the Revolutionaries showed that heterogeneity did not have to preclude unity. The people of the army did not put all regional and cultural distinctions aside. As seen elsewhere in increasingly diverse America, many still tended to form somewhat homogeneous groups, whether officially in state-affiliated regiments or unofficially in cultural or ethnic enclaves within regiments (especially in those that drew members from across state and regional lines). Yet they also demonstrated the fluidity of this society as they forged connections between the various groups and found that they could live and work together. Contemporaries and historians alike have explained that cohesion as a result of ideological bonds, esprit de corps, and bands of brothers.[4] But the development of community anchored by family life also explains it.

The focus of this essay is on the female part of the community: the wives and concubines who "went to town" by following the Continental Army. The principal emphasis is on those with the 2nd Continental Artillery and, particularly pertinent given Hawkins's comparison of the Redding encampment to Quebec, the 2nd Canadian Regiment. Some of the women in these units, like those with other regiments, followed because of ties of affection or for adventure or financial advantage, but others did so because they were fleeing the enemy. Many women with the 2nd Continental Artillery, for example, were refugees from the British-occupied New York City area, while many of those with the 2nd Canadian (as with the first) Regiment were refugees from loyalist Canada. The former group provides a picture of the "common" camp follower in that most of its members were British in ethnicity and Protestant in religion. The latter group offers another picture in that a considerable number of its members were French and Roman Catholic.

The 2nd Canadian Regiment provides a comparison, not a contrast, because, although the language and religion of these followers tended to isolate them somewhat from others and caused them to knit together more tightly, they also shared some common experiences as refugees and as camp inhabitants. Furthermore, "Congress's Own Regiment," as the 2nd Canadian was sometimes called, also recruited in the New England and Mid-Atlantic regions and thus included women more representative of the rebelling colonies' ethnic and Protestant foundations. Although there appear not to have been many, if any, free and slave African American women with these particular regiments, they can be found in other units of the Continental Army. These diverse women came from the various economic, social, and cultural strata of colonial North America, and their experiences with the army reflected the practices and prejudices of such groups.[5]

Some of the general practices and prejudices became clear at the onset of the war. Although General Washington and his subordinate commanders eventually admitted that they had to maintain some families so as to retain their men, they also tried numerous times and in various ways to dissuade women from following the army. This was because they saw women as adding to the expense and disorder of the conflict. It was also likely because of their struggle over defining and creating this force. Some thought of it as militia writ large, and women were not part of their vision of a proper militia. Rather, women were part of despised standing armies. Washington, however, wanted a regular army, though he wanted a new kind of army created out of temporary soldiers. This may have been why, unlike other practices, he did not want to adopt the British army's acceptance and use of women followers, a practice that marked a standing army manned by a permanent class of soldiers. But, as Washington came to find that he needed long-term soldiers, he came to accept the followers who helped root the men within the army. Followers, in turn, further promoted that acceptance through their labor.

Community Service

As initially unwelcome as most of the soldiers' wives were, and as problematic as some became, many were useful, for they helped maintain the health and welfare of the army. The army made the best of a tough situation—just as the women made the best of miserable circumstances—through the institution of services. The army needed women's labor, so the women supported the army as they worked to support themselves and their families. A few peddled goods, while others cooked and scrubbed as servants for officers and their wives. For instance, just before General Benedict Arnold deserted the American cause in September 1780, his aide, Lieutenant Colonel Richard Varick, wrote Colonel John Lamb of the 2nd Continental Artillery to ask whether he could recommend "a trusty industrious & decent Woman" to assist his housekeeper with the washing and other chores.[6]

The army found particular use for its female followers as washerwomen. The hiring, provisioning, and regulation of washerwomen rated frequent mentions in orderly books and letters. Officers in the 2nd Continental Artillery certainly dealt with them as it tried to meet both regimental and personal needs. Shortly before Varick wrote Lamb about domestic help for Arnold, Captain George Fleming asked his commander about keeping the widow of one of his soldiers on as a washerwoman. He thought it just compensation for both her and her husband's long service. He also asked whether he could certify another soldier's wife as a washerwoman to the company so that she could draw provisions. Again he justified his request by noting the soldier's excellent behavior and the justice in helping a good soldier support his wife. A few months later, Fleming realized that he had not properly established the full number of laundresses allowed him under the new system of supply. In November, he asked Lamb to increase the complement of his washerwomen (and increase provisions accordingly) to four, in line with the apparently accepted practice of "one Woman to Wash for ten." Followers registered as official washerwomen thus received provisions along with what they made through washing. Other followers could also charge for laundering. Some tried to overcharge, only to find that the price of their labor was regulated by the army. If they refused to comply with the restrictions, they could be prohibited from drawing rations and turned out of their regiments.[7]

Another important job was nursing. Soldiers nursed, but many times it was a matter of invalids caring for those more desperately wounded or sick. Because the army preferred not to detach able-bodied men from its lines, it looked to hire women from both the civilian and military communities. The hospital department advertised for and hired residents near its general hospitals in the areas of Boston, Albany, and Reading, Pennsylvania, as well as elsewhere. When not enough local or follower women volunteered, the army sometimes impressed the latter. That was especially the case in staffing regimental hospitals, the smaller facilities that stayed close to the troops. Although followers generally nursed their own men, they sometimes had to be induced to tend to others. Regimental commanders persuaded them by promising full rations and allowances for volunteers and threatening to withhold rations from those resisting the service. Resistance was understandable given the poor pay and harsh, even hazardous (more from disease than battle), conditions. As surgeons, surgeon's mates, and matrons ordered them around, the nurses labored to keep patients clean and fed and perform housekeeping chores. Women, however, not only tended the patients; sometimes they were the patients themselves because of accidents, illness, or complications of pregnancy and childbirth.[8] They suffered and survived along with their soldiers.

Community Command and Control

Even as the army's officers accepted and even welcomed some women, such acceptance was neither unregulated nor extended to all female followers. There was accommodation for those who helped and rejection of those who hurt the army. In the same month, June 1775, that the Continental Congress created the Continental Army, General Artemas Ward ordered that no lewd women be admitted into the encampments around Boston.[9] When Washington arrived at Cambridge in July, he generally ignored whatever women were flitting in and out of camp as he focused on shaping up the men. In fact, there may not have been many women with the colonial forces then. Most of the troops were militiamen who had hurried from home and expected to hurry back again; thus, their wives awaited them in the towns and villages of New England.

Only as summer gave way to fall, and then to winter, did more women appear in camp, heralded by the arrival of Martha Washington, Catharine Greene (wife of General Nathanael Greene), and other officers' wives. They encamped with their husbands outside Boston during the winter of 1775–1776. It was clear from the beginning that they were there as visitors, showing a feminine form of patriotism as they supported their husbands. They temporarily left the army when it marched from Boston but rejoined their spouses in New York in the spring and summer of 1776. When word came that the British were approaching, however, they were quickly packed off.[10]

It was not so easy to shoo off the women who solicited the soldiers. Although some people then and since thought of followers as prostitutes, the women selling themselves in New York City were generally not followers. They lived and worked in New York, and the soldiers went to them. Some of the men deliberately sought them out in the areas they frequented, while a few of the women returned the favor by visiting, whether by invitation or on their own initiative, in the soldiers' quarters. In May 1776, Colonel Alexander McDougall of the 1st New York tried to limit, if not eliminate, such intercourse by ordering that "No Woman of Ill Fame Shall be permitted to Come into the Barricks on pain of Being well Watred under a pump, and Every Officer or Soldier who shall Bring in Any Such woman will be tryd and Punished by a Court Martial."[11] McDougall feared the prostitutes' bedfellows of disorder and disease.

Some prostitutes did follow the army, just as some followers did become prostitutes. Washington worried about "bad women from Philadelphia" infiltrating his lines in the summer of 1777 and continued to worry about others elsewhere throughout the war.[12] Yet most followers were not prostitutes, and the army ensured that by checking their reputations and connections to the soldiers at various times.

The army counted the women and children and examined their relationships with the men as it attempted to help the families that sustained its soldiers. It registered those eligible to remain with the troops and obtain rations and other support. The army was rarely flush with supplies—indeed, it was too often the reverse. Thus, it could only provision followers with a legitimate family connection and an acceptable reason for being with the army. Returns (reports listing troop numbers and status) that note the numbers of women are rather rare, and those noting actual names are rarer still. One of the earliest known general returns that indicates a number of women was drawn up in December 1777. That "Account of Rations drawn by the Infantry of ye Standing Army" records 400 allotted for women. Because it lists rations rather than specifically women, it may indicate that there were 400 women (or a combination of women and children, with the children generally receiving half-rations) with the almost 15,000 noncommissioned officers and privates in the infantry at Valley Forge.[13] After 1780, by which time the army and its supply system were more organized, the returns were more frequent and specific.

On January 2, 1780, Sergeant Major Hawkins recorded in the 2nd Canadian Regiment's orderly book that "No Provision is to be allowed to any Woman or Women whatever, but such as may be ordered by the Commanding Officer of the Regiment; nor is any Woman or Women whatever to be admitted or harboured in Camp, except by Leave obtained from the Commanding Officer of the Regiment, for which the Commanding Officers of Companies will be responsible." They were at Morristown, and it was a lean, mean time. The army had to weed out unrelated personnel to eke out its food stores.[14] Yet it did not exclude all women and children, just those not part of an official military family.

At the end of the year, on November 17, at West Point, the 2nd Continental Artillery asked companies to prepare returns of the women and children who were drawing provisions and to distinguish between those who were married and those who were not. In August of the following year, the army at "Cinksing" asked that returns of the women (and children) in camp note those who had husbands, and then list the husbands' names and whether they were in this division of the army. The 2nd Continental Artillery quickly complied. The regiment also ordered counts of its women in May and December of 1782. And on January 24, 1783, in the "Return of the number of Women and Children in the several regiments and Corps stationed at, and in the vicinity of West Point and New Windsor, that drew Rations under the late Regulation," the 2nd Artillery Regiment recorded that it had twenty-two women and twenty-eight children with it.[15]

The army's attempts to keep records of the disbursement of rations provides an indication of how many women were with the army and how much they were a part of it. The evidence indicates that the numbers of these followers varied greatly between regiments and even from company to company within the regiments. A December 1777 return for the main army at Valley Forge indicated there was approximately one woman to forty-four enlisted men. A return for the main army at New Windsor in January 1783 suggested an average of one woman per every twenty-six enlisted men. Over those years, "the average ratios may have been within the range of one to thirty and one to thirty-five." Some companies may not have had female followers at the beginning of the war, but that "had changed by 1783 when the average was two women for each company with the main army."[16] The symbiotic relationship between the army and its followers had matured.

Although the women in that relationship supported the army, they also troubled it. When the Continental Army accepted followers and put them on the ration rolls, it expected them to accept its authority. Washington and his officers always saw the women as encumbrances to military order and movement, but they also calculated that, as long as the women followed orders, ill effects on army action could be minimized while positive contributions could be maximized. When he started organizing the army in Cambridge in 1775, Washington commanded that regimental adjutants communicate all general orders to their officers and soldiers and record the commands in orderly books. There were to be no pleas of ignorance for noncompliance. Women would have heard the recitation of orders when the soldiers did or heard them from their men. When too many women paid too little heed, however, Washington made it clear that they had to follow the rules if they were going to continue following their soldiers. At Verplanck's Point on September 8, 1782, Washington declared, "As there are many orders for checking irregularities with which the women, as followers of the army, ought to be acquainted, the ser[g]eants of the companies to which the women belong, are to communicate all orders of that nature to them, and are to be responsible for neglecting so to do."[17] As retainers to a camp—meaning dependent family members, servants, and volunteers belonging to the army—women were "subject to orders, according to the rules and discipline of war" in accordance with Article 23, Section XIII, in the 1776 American Articles of War. By military law and practice they were at least partially, if not fully, integrated into the army.

Followers dealt with that integration within the military's organization and operations in a number of ways. In doing so, they contributed to and illustrated some of the social tensions within the military community. When they obeyed, they not only maintained order, but also reinforced the community's structure of law and command. When they disregarded or outright disobeyed orders, they challenged the hierarchical authority established by the Articles of War. The army responded by continuing to assert its authority, but not always to the fullest extent granted by the articles (as when it banished women guilty of fomenting desertion rather than hanging them).

Most women obeyed the commands regulating their conduct. One of the most common of orders directed when, where, and how they were to move with the troops. In general, they were to stay with the baggage and off the wagons. Other common orders regulated the work that they did for the army and the payment for such work. Then there were the orders promising dire punishment for plundering and other forms of stealing. For instance, on March 25, 1780, Colonel Hazen rapped his regiment's knuckles by repeating a standing order from November 12, 1778. He strictly forbade "all Bartering, Buying or selling any article of Clothing, Merchandize goods, or Effects of any kind, name or Nature soever, by the Non Commisd officers or soldiers, otherwise than meat, Drink and other Food, of such species, and in such Quantities as may be Necessary for the Immediate Nurishment of the Human Body, on pain of being severely punished for Disobediance of Orders." Only if a commissioned officer had given permission could they do any of the above. He added that as of April 1, "any Non-commissioned officer or soldier, or woman of the Regiment, on whome or with whome, may be found any Articles of Commerce, Manufactories, Marchandize Goods, or Effects whatever, not any part of his or their Regimentals, or Clothing Received from the Public, without Leave of the Commanding officer of the Company, or some other Commissioned officer of the Regt. All such Articles shall not only be forfeited . . . but all and every such persons shall be Tried by a Court Martial, not only for Disobedience of Orders, but on lawfull Grounded suspicion of theft, and punished accordingly." He knew his people were trying to offset scarcity, but he expected more from those who had overcome adversity before.[18]

Adversity in the form of interpersonal relations, however, was particularly tricky. There were conflicts due to close quarters, sensitivities over status, and prickly personalities. Officers' quarrels at times escalated to duels or disputes before courts-martial. The quarrels of soldiers and followers sometimes exploded into slugging matches. As his regiment settled in at "Pracaness" in early July 1780, Hazen ordered regimental courts-martial to determine the causes and consequences of a camp fight that had occurred a few days before the regiment left Ramapough. The fight had started among the regiment's women.

At the first trial, on July 6, the court passed judgment on "the Complaint of Serjt. Major M'Lachlan against Margaret Batten, a Follower of the Army." The court found her guilty on all charges and sentenced her "to leave the Regiment within the Space of Forty-eight Hours, and not return under Penalty of receiving 25 Lashes and be drummed out of the Regiment."[19] The orderly book record did not note what the charges were, but the account of a succeeding court-martial implied what they must have been: disruptive behavior and, perhaps, assault. Apparently Sergeant Major Hawkins deemed the events and participants noteworthy, for he made a lengthy transcription in the orderly book. His recital reveals how social tensions at times tore at the Continental Army's community and undermined military order.

Hawkins noted that a new court assembled a few days after Batten's conviction to consider charges against Sergeant Major Colin McLachlan, Mrs. McLachlan, Mrs. McLane, and John Batten. The charges appear to have been brought because Mrs. Batten's conviction had not fully lanced the festering boil of community and command disorder. McLachlan had confined Private Batten "for threatening him after he had read the Sentence of the Court-Martial concerning his Wife's Conduct." Yet the sergeant major also found himself confined for misuse of authority and lack of respect for rank (both his own—by escalating a female fight—and an officer's). Captain John Carlile charged McLachlan with "promoting a Quarrel in Camp begun by two Women, and striking a soldier of his Company when he had it in his Power to confine him" and, more important, for insolence to the captain when Carlile took action to end the fight. McLachlan pleaded not guilty to all charges except that of striking the soldier.[20]

Captain Carlile deposed that, just before the regiment left Ramapough, there was a great disturbance that drew a crowd. The captain, among others, ran to determine the cause and found it in his own company. He saw McLachlan and his wife fighting with a soldier, so he stepped in to stop it. Carlile said that he grabbed the stick that the woman was swinging at the soldier and then struck the soldier and the woman with it. That separated the combatants, but then McLachlan swore impertinently to his face, "that for Capt. Carlile's striking the Woman before mentioned, that he would the first Opportunity shoot Margaret Batten, who he intimated had occasioned the Quarrel." After hearing that account versus those of McLachlan and his defense witnesses, the court determined that McLachlan was not guilty of any of the charges except that of striking the soldier. Furthermore, the court believed McLachlan was justified in striking the soldier and so acquitted him of that too.[21] This dismissal of a noncommissioned officer's impertinence to a junior officer was striking, given that William Mason was sentenced—though, with a recommendation of leniency—by the same court to 100 lashes for cursing a general officer in the presence of several officers. Yet the court may have been taking into account McLachlan's long service and what could be interpreted as a manly defense of his wife.

In deciding McLachlan's case, the court also heard the evidence against the women. Major James R. Reid swore that he heard Mrs. McLane uttering threats when they were at Ramapough. He recalled asking her whom she resented so much to threaten and McLane's answer "that Mrs. Batten had abused her, and she intended to take the first Opportunity to revenge herself." She stalked off and apparently started fighting with Batten. Reid testified that he then saw Mrs. McLachlan, who had been at a brook some distance away, immediately head into the noisy brawl. Some time thereafter, Reid saw Sergeant Major McLachlan moving in that direction, "as he thought to quell the Fray, which was immediately after effected by the Interposition of Capt. Carlile and some other Officers."[22]

Quartermaster Sergeant John Jones swore that the sergeant major "was with him at his Tent when the Fray began amongst the Women." When some soldiers told them that the women were fighting, McLachlan and he walked over and there saw Batten and the women quarreling. Although the account is not clear about how the fight escalated, it appears that Private Batten had gotten involved in the quarrel between his wife and the Mistresses McLane and McLachlan. Then "the Serjeant-Major's Wife said something to Batten, and Batten immediately struck her, then the Serjt. Majr. struck Batten, and Batten returned the Blow, and knocked the Serjt. Major down, and struck him several Blows after he was down." After Jones managed to part them, McLachlan ordered his wife away. She went, and the fray ended.[23]

Just as the court had acquitted McLachlan for striking Batten, it acquitted Batten of threatening McLachlan. It also acquitted Mrs. McLachlan and Mrs. McLane, concluding that the charges against them were not supported. The court released all the prisoners from confinement and ordered them back to duty. This was an extreme example of what Washington and others deplored about having women in camp. Some did, obviously, undermine good order. Yet, notably, Hazen's regiment reasserted discipline by banishing only the one person it thought to be the root of the trouble and essentially using a court-martial as a means to clean out lingering grievances and restore order in the community.

Community Cohesion .

Legally and socially, the army's encampments and garrisons were rustic communities with inhabitants who were at once provincial and continental. Although all of the military's people were essentially nationalistic in that they fought and labored for the independence of the United States, some were provincial in that they limited their association and assimilation into a continental American culture, whereas others welcomed the exposure to different peoples and ideas. Yet, willing or not, the mingling of these men and women whose local and national experiences varied widely helped produce a kind of continental American culture that was eroding colonial sensibilities.

The French Canadians' experiences differed somewhat in comparison to the experiences of other members of the military community in terms of their refugee status, religion, and language, but not in regard to social rank and camp life. They became refugees because they chose to fight for an independence that might also extend to the Canadian provinces. In late 1775 and early 1776, James Livingston and Moses Hazen organized the 1st and 2nd Canadian Regiments, respectively. The Massachusetts-born Hazen had served with colonial forces and then as a lieutenant in the British army's 44th Regiment in the Seven Years' War. After the war, he moved to Canada, married a Catholic woman, and became a prominent landowner. Hazen waffled about joining the American cause, but, once he made his decision, he recruited some of his French Canadian neighbors to form the regiment that deployed around Montreal, St. John, and Chambly. When the American forces had to withdraw in June 1776, Hazen and his more than 200 soldiers—and some of their families—retreated with them.[24]

When their provinces remained loyal to the British Crown, the Canadians became outcasts. The ostracism may not have meant a complete severance from the members of their families and communities who remained, but it was certainly deepened by the actions of the seventh bishop of Quebec, Joseph Olivier Briand. When American forces marched on Montreal and Quebec in the late months of 1775, Briand commanded Canadian Catholics to remain loyal to the British government that had offered them religious and political rights in the Quebec Act of 1774. He followed that by telling his priests to refuse the sacraments to colonial sympathizers and threatened excommunication to all who joined the Continental Army.[25] They thus had to suffer spiritually as well as materially in choosing one cause and community over others.

As the French Canadians marched out of Canada and into the rebelling colonies, the rough English of many and their Catholicism continued to set them apart. Moreover, they faced the antipathy of some people in the lower thirteen colonies who opposed the Quebec Act. Some New Englanders denounced George III as "the Pope of Canada," as well as the "Fool of England," but they had to subdue their antipapal sentiments when the

Continental Congress appealed to the inhabitants of Quebec to join the cause and then again when not only some Catholic French Canadians, but also the French, joined. Even so, some Continental soldiers continued to see them as aliens rather than allies. Sergeant Major Hawkins, a man from supposedly tolerant Pennsylvania and the senior noncommissioned officer of the 2nd Canadian Regiment for most of the war, showed a hint of that prejudice. Perhaps he had had a particularly trying time with the French Canadians when he jotted in his journal, "I am unacquainted with the People or Language of the Country, as well as their Mode of Religion, and should chuse ever to be so." Later he calmed down or reconsidered, for he crossed out the comment and, echoing Hazen's sentiments, praised the unity and dutifulness of the regiment.[26]

Because of the cultural differences and the regiment's demographics, many of the refugee soldiers experienced a measure of isolation. Although the Canadian soldiers were the longest-serving core of the regiment, the additional soldiers recruited from New England and the Mid-Atlantic states came to outnumber them. Furthermore, the few French Canadian officers were junior officers.[27] (Hazen and his lieutenant colonel, Edward Antill, volunteered from Canada, but they were not French Canadians.) Nevertheless, the isolation was somewhat ameliorated by the fact that most of the refugees congregated in their own companies and some had their families with them.

A man's military position affected his and his family's options and treatment during the war. The sergeants and soldiers of the Continental Army usually, though not always, came from the lower orders of society. Most were native sons, but many were immigrants. Besides the French Canadians, there were Scots-Irish, Irish, and Germans, among others, in the ranks. The families of most enlisted men, like those of most of the officers, stayed home. If a problem arose there, a man could request a hardship furlough to go handle it. If denied, he had to let his family deal with it or, as a few did, desert. Because the latter decision was detrimental to military readiness and discipline, some commanders came to acknowledge that allowing families to become followers was the lesser of two evils. Washington himself admitted in January 1783, with particular reference to the New York regiments, which could have included the 2nd Continental Artillery with its numerous New Yorkers with families who had fled British occupation, that the army had to provide for such dependents "or lose by Desertion, perhaps to the Enemy, some of the oldest and best Soldiers in the Service."[28] Thus families followed soldiers, and the army accommodated them, because of the exigencies of war.

Senior officers generally came from the upper and middle strata of American society, and their wives were accorded the courtesies and comforts of their husbands' ranks when they visited. Junior officers were a more varied lot in age as well as social and military rank. That, in turn, had an impact on the reception of their wives in camp. The treatment of most officers' relatives tended to vary according to whether they were short-term visitors providing solace and gaiety in a winter garrison or longer-term residents who required quarters and comforts themselves. Because officers more readily received furloughs than their soldiers in the winter months, they generally left their families at home and saw them there when possible rather than trouble with arrangements for them in camp. Officers also had the option of resigning if family or business matters demanded their return home.[29]

A few of the officers of the 2nd Continental Artillery did extend their furloughs or resign due to family problems, but the regiment's colonel, John Lamb, a merchant who had been a leader of the New York Sons of Liberty, persevered in juggling regimental and family demands. Like the families of many of his soldiers, Lamb's wife and daughters became refugees when the British occupied New York City and some of its environs in 1776. Lamb, like many other officers, preferred them to lodge with friends or in rented houses rather than following the army. Fortunately, one of his junior officers, Captain Robert Walker, offered the use of his house in Stratford, Connecticut. Lamb moved his family there by February 1777 and, a few months later, settled them into rented lodgings in Southington, a town north of New Haven that was celebrated for supposedly not having a single Tory. Lamb moved his family again early in 1779, but by October 1782, when Baron Ludwig von Closen of the French army noted seeing Lamb's "pretty young girls" there, the family was again in Southington. In light of the time Lamb spent away from camp and the energy he expended in getting them settled, his wife and daughters might have been less of a distraction if they had become camp followers. Walker, too, absented himself from his army duties so as to put his personal affairs in order. After his marriage in the spring of 1779, he took a short leave from his army duties so as to escort his new wife from "Redbook" (possibly Red Hook, New York) to Stratford.[30]

In contrast to his colonel and fellow captain, Andrew Moodie had his wife live in camp with him for a while. While Lamb had the resources and connections through which to seek alternatives and Walker was fortunate in that he still had his Connecticut home, Moodie had neither good fortune nor connections. He had joined then-captain John Lamb's Company of Artillery as a second lieutenant in June 1775 and served with it at Quebec that December, where he was taken prisoner. Upon his release, he rejoined what was then the 2nd Continental Artillery as a captain in 1777 and served until the army started to disband in June 1783. When the British occupied New York City, it is likely that Moodie lost his home. He may or may not have been married at that time, but he certainly was in 1781, and his wife (and possibly a daughter) was with him and apparently causing some problems by interfering in how he managed his command. Lieutenant Henry Williams was so disgusted with the "eternal discord" in the company and being "commanded by Mrs. Moodie & not him" that he asked Lamb for a transfer that June.[31] Even though Mrs. Moodie caused discord and the possible loss of Lieutenant Williams, her husband probably stayed with the army because it accepted his family. The company kept its captain.

The Canadian officers and their families also paid a heavy price to fight for independence. General John Sullivan ordered the destruction of Hazen's property so that it could not be used by the British; thus Charlotte de la Saussaye Hazen lost her home. She may not have been with her husband throughout the war, but she was with him near the end, when Hazen made his headquarters at Pompton, New Jersey, in late October 1782.[32]

Some families, such as Captain Clement Gosselin's, did not suffer exile, possibly because they had strong extended families to care for them, but they endured long separations. Others, such as Captain Antoine Paulin's family, paid a price similar to the Hazens'. In January 1837, Theotist Paulin, an infirm widow from Champlain, New York, recounted their ordeals when she applied for benefits under the 1836 Pension Act, which offered some relief to qualified widows. As was the case for many of the veterans and dependents providing recollections in their applications, Madam Paulin no longer remembered all the details, but she still provided a vivid account. She said that when the war began between the colonies and Canada, at the time the American army entered Canada, she lived with her husband in St. Denis Parish. Her husband joined the American forces that fall and went to Quebec. He did not return until the following spring, at which time he packed up his wife and their four children and, leaving behind his land, house, other buildings, and all the property he could not carry, took them to St. John, where they embarked in a boat and went to Crown Point and then on to Albany. Paulin said that she "continued near her husband through the war, [and] she generally laid with him in the Barracks [wherever his company was garrisoned] in the winter." She noted that "in the summers when her husband was in active service she lived with her children generally away from her husband."[33]

Alexander Ferriol, who had mustered as a fifer into the company commanded by his father, Lieutenant Alexander Ferriole, in 1776, substantiated Paulin's story. He stated that he had lived in a parish adjoining that of the Paulins before the war and that he, the captain, and other Canadian refugees settled at Champlain after the war. Ferriol swore that Paulin lived "with her husband in the Baracks in the winters during the war."[34]

Proving marriage was a vital element in these pension claims just as it had been to receive rations during the war. In the process of proving that they had been wives, not concubines, the widows and their witnesses provided evidence of religious and wedding practices, the ages of soldiers and followers, and both Anglicization (Americanization) of names and families along with continuance of older cultural, communal ties. Theotist Paulin, for instance, provided a copy of an extract from the Register of Acts of Baptisms, Marriages, and Burials of St. Antoine Parish, district of Montreal, which stated that the seventeen-year-old Theotist had been married to the thirty-year-old Antoine on January 12, 1767, within the Roman Catholic Church.[35] This indicates that Madame Paulin was approximately twenty-six years old when she became a refugee and follower of the army. She was also at the time, as noted above, a mother of four.

Theotist Blow, who identified herself as the daughter of the late Captain Paulin, provided more details on the family and community ties that distinguished the French Canadians during and after the war when she supported Sally Robenet Chartier's application in 1837. Blow remembered that near the end of the war her father's family and other Canadian families lived at Fishkill, New York, a key defensive and staging area for Continental and militia units. Her family had lived near Lieutenant Gilmort and thus she was well acquainted with "Sally Robenet," who had been the daughter of Mrs. Gilmort by her first husband. Indeed, the two girls had spent most of their childhoods with the army, for Blow said she had been about twelve years old at the end of the war and that Sally was three or four years older. She remembered neighbors saying that Robenet had married John Chartier, but she neither witnessed the marriage nor recalled the year. She did, however, remember that Sally lived with Chartier as his wife and was called his wife and that they lived together "before the families of the Canadian Refugee Officers and soldiers left Fish Kill & went to West Point."[36]

Former private John Chartier started receiving a pension in 1818. When he reapplied in compliance with the 1820 act, which required veterans to show more evidence of poverty, the laborer, then sixty-three, confirmed his need and that of his supposedly forty-five-year-old wife as well as a teenage son and daughter. He died in 1832, and five years later his widow applied for assistance under the 1836 act.[37] Their applications, like others, show that people were not always rigorous record keepers, and thus determining dates and ages was often a matter of approximation. Even so, here is another example of a wide age gap between husband and wife. This French Canadian soldier had married the teenage daughter of another such soldier after a camp courtship.

The explanations about Sally Chartier's marriage and name reveal more of the culture of the refugees, as well as how they handled the challenges of life in the army and America. Mrs. Chartier testified that she had married John Chartier on May 13, 1783. She distinctly remembered that it was months before her husband's discharge and that it was "by the Revd father Francis Vall[?]y a Catholic Priest at a place called the Highlands in the State of Newyork, the troops then being stationed at Pompton in said State of Newyork; and she lived with the said John Chatier as his wife until the time of his death" in Massena, New York. She also informed the court that she had had eight children with her husband, two of whom still lived. Her sister, Polly Chartier, backed her up by swearing that she saw Father Francis Vally marry her sister to Chartier in the spring of 1783 at the Highlands.[38]

Enoch Woodbridge, justice of the peace in Addison County, Vermont, declared that he had known the Chartier families for more than forty years. He stated that both women had long been acknowledged by their community as the wives of their respective veterans, despite no written proof. He explained the lack by noting that the widows were still Catholics and that there was no chance "of obtaining from any Catholic Church, the record of their marriages; or from any place in the State of New York, as it is well understood, there is not even yet any law in the State of New York requiring marriages to be recorded." Furthermore, he believed that the priests who married them were "traveling ministers attending on Hazen's Regt. most of whom [the soldiers] were Refugees."[39]

Alexander Ferriol told the Clinton County, New York, commissioner of deeds that he had retreated from Canada with John Chartier in 1776 and had served with him through the war. He "became acquainted with Sally Robinet or Robinson in 1776 when she was about seven or eight years old, her Father was also a Reffugee, having married a French woman in Canada & was a sergant in . . . Hazens Regiment." So the father had been an English colonist who, like Hazen, had moved north and married a French Canadian. His daughter confirmed those French Catholic Canadian ties in her own marriage partner. Ferriol deposed that Chartier had married "Sally Robenet or Robinsan, while a soldier as aforesaid early in the spring of 1783 at Fishkill in the state of New York, by a Roman priest of the name of Vally, and but a few months before the discharge of the said John Chartier & the other Reffugees together with this deponent, which took place at New Windsor the last of June 1783." He said he was present at the marriage and continued to know the Chartiers after the war.[40]

When William Slade of the House of Representatives, acting as a conduit for applications, sent on Ferriol's deposition to J. L. Edwards Esquire, Commissioner of Pensions, in June 1837, he added his own conclusions. He believed the declaration proved "the marriage of Sally Chartier . . . and also her age at the time of her marriage, which was 14 or 15—an age not uncommon for the marriage of Canadian french girls. The testimony in the case of Polly Chartier, to whom you have granted a pension, shows how a Roman Catholic priest came to be with the army at the time these marriages took place."[41]

In October 1837, Basil Nadeau of Champlain swore that he had served as a sergeant in Captain Olivie's company of Hazen's regiment until discharged in June 1783 (though a regimental roll noted that he deserted in March 1780). He had been "well acquainted" with Private Chartier of Paulin's company and with "Sergeant Robinet (so called in french) or Robinson in English who served in Capt Leberts Company in Coll. Hazens Regiment." He had known Robinson's family before they retreated from Canada. He also noted, providing evidence of the practice of soldiers' widows marrying other soldiers, that "Sergeant Robinson was dead at the time of [his daughter's] marriage and his widow was married to Lieutenant Gilmart." He stated that while the regiment was at Pompton, he and others "obtained leave to go to Fish Kill in the State of New York to see a Roman catholic Prest, who had come to visit the Canadian families or the families of the Officers & soldiers—who then resided at Fish Kill." Nadeau said that he saw the priest marry John Chartier and Sally Robinson and that he thought the bride was about fifteen or sixteen years old. He believed the marriage was solemnized in late April or early May, which he remembered as the time when he had had leave to visit that priest. He remembered the marriage taking place about a mile out from the Fishkill barracks, at a farmer's house where the priest was staying. Afterward, Nadeau returned to Pompton, from which the regiment marched to Newburgh, where the soldiers were discharged. Nadeau, Chartier, and other Canadians then went to West Point, where they drew provisions and remained for a while.[42]

Alexander Chartier (he noted he was otherwise called Carter) testified to the legitimacy of his parents' marriage in February 1837. He then testified in July 1838 that his French grandmother always called his mother Mary, as did his father when speaking French. When his father spoke English, however, he called his wife Sally. Sally Chartier confirmed that her Christian name was Mary Therese but that in English she was called Sally. Ferriol also addressed the name problem in another deposition that year. He said that "when she resided with English people she was called Sally, her father being an American called his daughter Sally at the same time her mother called her Thesen." He added that he knew several females who were called Therese in French but Sally in English. Julius Hubbell, the commissioner of deeds in Champlain, responded to Commissioner Edwards's questions over the marriage date, Sally's age, and her name, in the same manner. He reiterated that she was old enough to be Chartier's wife at the end of the war and that her two names were the result of having an English father and then coming to live among the "English."[43]

There were no questions over Polly Chartier's name, but she too had to battle for benefits. Fortunately, her husband, Peter, had already provided her with the ammunition of his own pension. In both 1818 and 1820, he had proven that he had served in Hazen's regiment through such battles as Brandywine, Monmouth, and Yorktown and been honorably discharged. In 1820, the seventy-one-year-old veteran declared that he was a laborer who was unable to work and that, beyond his pension, he depended on his friends for help, for he had only his fifty-seven-year-old wife at home. He died at Vergennes, Vermont, in December 1829 or 1830 or June 1832.[44]

The two old widows, sisters and sisters-in-law, must have appeared before the Addison County, Vermont, court together, for Polly Chartier presented her application the same day that her sister, Sally, did, on February 22, 1837. Both had prepared for the event by having family witnesses swear statements as to their identities and marriages two days beforehand. Sally's son Alexander and Polly's son James (who, like Alexander, had accepted the Anglicization to Carter) supported their mothers. And, as Polly had done for her sister, so her sister did for her: on February 20, the seventy-year-old Sally Chartier swore to a justice of the peace that she saw

Polly and Peter Chartier married by the Reverend Father Defarm, a Roman Catholic priest, at the Highlands in the late fall of 1779 or 1780. She stated that Peter had been a soldier at the time. She believed there were no records of the marriage in New York and that the priest was long dead, for he had been an aged man at the time of the marriage.[45]

Polly Chartier originally stated that she was eighty-three or eighty-four, an age that, like her sister's name, resulted in questions because of the discrepancy between her own and her husband's accounts. In trying to clarify the issue the following May, she recounted more of her history. She said that she was about thirteen years old when she "was brought out of Canada with my fathers family in the year 1776." Her father had been James Robinson, who, she believed, had been a sergeant major in Hazen's regiment and had died at Crown Point on the retreat from Canada. She said that she had been married at about twenty (a date-age disjunction, for she had earlier claimed that she married Peter Chartier "on or about the 15th day of November 1779 or 1780 but she believes it was 1780") by a "Mr. Deferm," a priest, near Fishkill. To explain her memory lapses and lack of written documentation, she noted that she was "a woman of no learning & cannot read nor write & have been many years infirm in health."[46] The latter may have been related to age, but the former was further evidence of her social rank.

Alexander Ferriol, who apparently made a career out of supporting pension applications, confirmed the Chartier's marriage and, in doing so, further disclosed how the refugees contrived to meet social and religious needs. He said that he had been present in the spring of 1780 when Peter Chartier and Polly Robinson "agreed before a witness to live together as man and wife until they should be able to find some Roman Catholic Prist to solemnize their marriage. That this occurred at or near Fishkill. That subsequently in the spring of 1782 about three miles from the baracks at Fishkile this deponant was present when the marriage between [them] was solemnized by a Mr Ferm or Farm a Roman Catholic Priest who came from Philadelphia to visit the Canadian Roman Catholics of the Regiment."[47] Establishing a common-law marriage before there could be a religious wedding was the field-expedient method to legitimize their relationship.

In 1851, three of Polly Chartier's children (Joseph Chartier, Sally Alden, and Fanny Yaltow) claimed that she had not received all of her pension before she died in May 1850 and tried to get the arrears. That appears not to have succeeded, nor apparently did the 1849 attempt by Peter and James Chartier, both of whom were "very poor," to get pensions based on their own "service." Their application, however, sheds more light on camp life, as well as the hardships faced by some soldiers' families long after the war. Polly Chartier had deposed that, after she married Peter, she gave birth to her son Peter at West Point on July 5, 1778, and then James at Fishkill on May 13, 1781. Besides providing evidence that followers were bearing and raising children in camp, this deposition also reveals another

discrepancy over the date of her marriage and/or the state of her (and Ferriol's) memory. It is possible that she had her first child before marriage.
Yet legitimate or not, their births while their parents were with the army
would not have garnered them a pension. Their mother, however, argued
that, "after the birth of my said sons, they were both enrolled or enlisted
by their Father & attached to the service of the United States & enrolled in
the said Captain Oliviere's Company, and I distincly recollect that after
their enrollment or enlistment as aforesaid, they, or their father for them,
regularly drew their rations as soldiers until the close of the war, which I
now believe was somewhere about two years." Because she had heard that
other boys so enrolled had received pensions and lands, she thought her
sons were entitled to the same.[48] They were not entitled. They may have
been "enrolled"—that is, noted on a regimental roll—for the partial rations sometimes provided children, but that was not enlistment.

The Chartier children were not the only offspring to file for their parents' or, in the Constantine case, their grandparents' pensions. Nicholas
Constantine, who died in 1840, had received a pension. His widow, who
died in 1845, apparently had not. Eighty-one-year-old Charlotte Constantine applied for benefits in October 1841. In June 1843, Julius Hubbell,
Clinton County's commissioner of deeds, asked Commissioner of Pensions Edwards why the evidence presented was not enough to establish
marriage and thus the pension. Perhaps Edwards was just being especially
cautious, for there had been some fraudulent claims from French Canadians.[49] Nevertheless, Charlotte Constantine and then her five grandchildren (asking for arrears) and their advocates pushed on and, in doing so,
revealed more about the French Canadian part of the military community.

Alexander Ferriol deposed in March 1846 that he had attended the
Constantine marriage at Schenectady in the winter of 1779. The marriage
had taken place in "the common barrack room," and was conducted by
his father, Lieutenant Alexander "Ferrial" of William Satterlee's company,
in Hazen's regiment. That October, eighty-five-year-old Mary Louisa La Fond,
of Point Au Meule, Canada East, who said that "her maiden name was Mary
Louisa Chartier (sometimes familiarly termed Lozelle)," noted that she herself
was "a pensioner of the United States as the widow of Simon La Fond, who
was a Revolutionary Soldier," and that she remembered well the marriage of
her deceased sister Charlotte. She said the marriage took place at the barracks
in Schenectady in November or December of 1778. Lieutenant "Ferriall" performed the ceremony, for "both parties were Roman Catholics; and there was
no priest of that persuasion there at that time."[50]

Despite minor discrepancies in the dates, they confirmed Charlotte
Constantine's earlier 1841 statement that Captain or Lieutenant "Fer-
niall" had married her to Nicholas Constantine in February 1779 at the
"Schenactady Barracks." The widow Mary Cayeaux also had corroborated
her story, saying that she had retreated from Canada with Charlotte
Chartier in 1775 and then in the winter of 1779 saw her married to

Nicholas Constantine by "Captain Ferniall." Cayeaux continued that "Ferniall" had married several of the Canadian refugees that winter, among them herself to her late husband Joseph Cayeaux."[51]

Former private Ferriol had confirmed that account in 1841. He said that "the Canadian families that lay at the Schenactada Barracks in the winter of 1779—[ha]d no other language than the French, n[o]r could they understand any other—that they were composed of old & young people of both sexes, most of them retreated from Canada together, the young Men principally as soldiers, some became soldiers after they came out.—some of the Girls were too young to be married when they first came out—some were married before they came out." He added that when "his Father performed the rites of matrimony for Nicholas Constantine & Charlote Chartier, there was no Chaplain to the French troops." Nor, he believed, had there ever been one. While "there might have been English & Dutch Clergymen in the City at the time," he never saw them at the barracks; "besides the French Canadians were all Catholicks." Ferriol avowed that he could name many of the people present when the Constantines, "as well as Madam Cayeaux & Madam Defoe were married, but they are all dead." He could not think of another person still living "who was present when this claimant was married as aforesaid, except the two above named and himself." Ferriol also noted that "it was customary, during the War, for the officers among the French Canadians, to perform the rites of Matrimony." He had a sister married at West Point by an officer, and he seemed to remember another soldier married at Fishkill by Captain Paulin. Furthermore, although a Catholic priest came from Philadelphia to Fishkill and stayed a short while in 1781, he could not recall "of hearing of or seeing any other one during the war, in this state."[52]

Not all French Canadian soldiers married the widows, sisters, and daughters of their countrymen in camp. Assignments, as well as the availability of women, affected the formation of relationships. Peter Blanchard, for instance, married an American. Blanchard (as Piere) enlisted at Albany in 1776 and served as a private to the end of the war, though when the regiment disbanded he was in Rhode Island, where, as the regiment's former adjutant, Benjamin Mooers, testified in 1818, he was serving as "a waiter with some of the French officers." Blanchard later added that he had been "detached under Count Rochambeau and the Marquis De Lafayette."[53] While serving these allies, he courted a local woman.

Blanchard died in 1823, and his seventy-eight-year-old widow applied for a pension in September 1836. Martha Blanchard, who said that her husband had acted as an interpreter for the French army in 1782, declared that the minister Joseph S[n]ors had married the couple that June at Providence. Basil Nadeau supported her by saying he had served as "bridesman" at their marriage. Blanchard also remembered living in a small house at the northern end of the town while the troops occupied the college. Her first child, William, was born at Coventry, Rhode Island, on May

3, 1783, and shortly thereafter her husband left the army.[54] Ultimately, the family settled near other veterans of the regiment in Clinton County.

Like her French Canadian sisters-in-marriage, Blanchard had to have recognized authorities confirm that she married her soldier before the war ended. These authorities did so not only because they believed her story, but also because of their perceptions of the people who joined and followed the army's ranks. Mooers deposed in January 1837 that he believed the Blanchards did not keep a record of the marriage for "they were both ignorant and I believe neither of them knew how to write or read." Apparently to confirm that, he pointed out that Peter had been a Catholic Canadian, though he implied Martha was Protestant by noting she was born in Rhode Island. Another official concluded, "It is not at all probable that any record of her marriage was ever made, as persons of her *caste* are not very particular in such matters." Yet it was not that people of that ethnic or economic group were not particular in such things; it was that unsettled churches and ministers on top of the disruptions caused by revolution and war confounded record keeping. Elizabeth Heaton, an unlettered old washerwoman, and her advocate Henry Muhlenberg attributed the lack of a church record documenting her 1776 Reading, Pennsylvania, marriage to James to their having been married by an itinerant minister of the German Reformed Church.[55]

War and military service made getting married and maintaining family life a challenge, but obviously not impossible. Propinquity played a major part in the formation of families and the military community. Living alongside people from different backgrounds, some soldiers and followers wed and created families across the cultural divisions. Others preferred to marry those who shared their religious beliefs, cultural backgrounds, and wartime experiences. One resulting pattern, for the French Canadians, was that of marriages between older soldiers to much younger, teenaged, sisters and daughters of other soldiers (marriages to older women and widows were underrepresented in records because so many were dead by the time Congress legislated pensions). Furthermore, although Livingston's regiment had an official Catholic chaplain for some time, Hazen's did not. His people did what other soldiers (and civilians) did when without a minister: they established a procedure for common-law marriage and then had a religious wedding when they could. Marriage provided both a legitimate sexual outlet and family stability for the soldiers. It also offered more support for these women as they switched from children's (as the daughters of soldiers) to wives' rations. Such marriages also established ties of affection that supported company camaraderie and regimental authority.

The French Canadians were not the only married members of Hazen's regiment, but they left some of the most substantial records of marriage and life during the war, perhaps because of their refugee experiences and struggles against ethnic and religious biases. Other widows of the regiment's soldiers applied for pensions, but they did not tend to explain where they remained or what they did during the war years. This suggests that they stayed home. Their applications thus tend to support a traditional image of the war: men marching off and women shouldering the burdens on the home front. In contrast to the followers, when the stay-at-home women married soldiers, they did not marry the army. This meant that their soldier spouses shuttled between communities as they tried to fulfill their obligations in both or, in some cases, ended up neglecting, or deserting, one or the other. Mary Dick provided insights into how a serving soldier could establish a family away from the army.

Mary Dick, eighty, widow of Jacob Dick, a private turned shoemaker, applied for a pension in Baltimore in 1840. She said that she had been married at the Bethelehem Church in York County, Pennsylvania, on November 24, 1782. She also gave two statements about the births of the couple's eleven children: one suggests that one or more may have been born before the wedding; the other says that the first came in 1782 (month not specified). A corroborator, Stephen Freeland, seventy-three, said that he recalled the time of the marriage because Jacob Dick returned from "revolutionary service," as he remembered Dick explaining, "expressely to get married after which time he left his wife and returned to his service."[56] This suggests that the couple married either right before or directly after she gave birth. Because Private Dick enlisted from Pennsylvania, he may have come from that area and had courted Mary before leaving. Another possibility is that they met when the regiment garrisoned at Lancaster (with detachments at York and elsewhere) to guard prisoners of war for most of 1782. The regiment marched to northern New Jersey and New York the same month the couple wed. In establishing a family as they did, Jacob and Mary Dick sustained each other and linked army camp and home front.

Abigail Stanley Roberts, who had been married to the fifer William Roberts (died 1797), said nothing about accompanying him during his service from 1777 through 1781. When the eighty-eight-year-old widow stood before a Hartford judge in November 1838, she stated that she had married William at the Congregational Church in Coventry, Connecticut, on October 28, 1772. Although there was no record of her following him in the army, the birthdates of two of her children—Seth, in September 1778, and Isaac, in January 1781, who died that March—were during their father's enlistment.[57] Extramarital relations while the husband was away in service were not unheard of, but the likelihood is that either William had furloughs to visit home or his wife visited him in camp.

These women had to prove that they were married to their soldiers before the war ended. The immediate purpose of the demand for evidence was the federal government's attempt to avoid fraud, but the result is glimpses into the women's war, the effects marriage and military service had on each other, and the diversity of the army's community.

Conclusion

Pension applications record memories that are detailed enough to provide insight into camp life and, occasionally, home life during the Revolution. There are limits to what they reveal, however, because thousands of veterans and their wives died prior to the passage of the pension acts. It was not until 1818 that Congress granted service pensions to Continental Army veterans, and Congress did not grant such pensions to militias and state troops until 1832. It was not until 1836 that Congress passed an act that allowed some veterans' widows, provided they had married before their spouses had left the army, to apply for what essentially would have been their husband's pensions under the 1832 act. Later acts extended the benefits to women married after their husbands' service.[58] The fact that the women could apply only decades after the war means that their accounts, and those of their witnesses, while vivid, were those of distant memories into which fallacies or fiction may have crept.

Orderly books, rosters, letters, and journals written during the war by those with the army offer more immediacy, but the women's presence is revealed all too rarely within them. They tend to emerge more often when they were deemed problems than when they were not. This indicates that they were generally seen as an unremarkable, meaning not unusual, part of the military community. The army accepted them because of the services they provided and the desire for stability and security they represented. The 2nd Continental Artillery accommodated its followers because so many of them were refugees from the British-occupied New York City area, and, as they washed, cooked, and nursed, these followers reminded soldiers and officers of homes and independency not only threatened but lost. They had to win to regain or improve what they once had.

The records of the French Canadians who were with the Continental Army indicate that, in supporting the War for American Independence, many lost much if not all of what they had in Canada. They trundled their families into the camps and garrisons of the American army where, for the next eight years, they created a distinct community within the greater military society. They maintained their language, religion, and customs as they became the longest-serving core of one of the most cohesive units within the army. That fellowship continued after the war when many accepted the bounty lands offered them in New York (and, in turn, Vermont) and settled together in communities near the Canadian border. Yet there are also indications of assimilation into the broader society and culture of the new United States. The Anglicization of names both during and after the war provides evidence of that. Furthermore, their applications for Revolutionary War pensions indicates that the French Canadians generally shared the social status or condition of many of the other soldiers and followers. Some too, like other veterans and their families, suffered from disabilities and impoverishment that led them to apply for pensions because they needed, as well as deserved, them.

Wives and concubines, along with their children, were part of the Continental Army's community from its inception in 1775 to its dissolution in 1783. They were as diverse in origins, religion, ethnicity, and class as the soldiers. That diversity, along with the added gender issues the women's presence raised, challenged and strengthened the military community's cohesion. Although women and children added to the provisioning problems and contributed to camp disorder, the army accommodated them because it found that it needed the women. By following their soldiers into the army, women helped keep them there by making the military a social institution, in other words a home, to many, especially the refugees. The soldiers and followers made it a viable working community as they maintained families in the camps over the course of the war. Ultimately, by attending to the soldiers, followers served American independence by helping to sustain the morale and cohesion of the army.

Notes

I thank the David Library of the American Revolution, the Library Company of Philadelphia, and the Historical Society of Pennsylvania for their much-appreciated research support.

1. Mark V. Kwasny, *Washington's Partisan War, 1775–1783* (Kent, Ohio: Kent State University Press, 1996), p. 230; John H. Hawkins, February 11, 1779, Journal, 1779–1781, Historical Society of Pennsylvania, Philadelphia.

2. Gregory T. Knouff, *The Soldiers' Revolution: Pennsylvanians in Arms and the Forging of Early American Identity* (University Park: Pennsylvania State University Press, 2004); James Kirby Martin and Mark Edward Lender, *A Respectable Army: The Military Origins of the Republic, 1763–1789* (Arlington Heights, Ill.: Harlan Davidson, 1982); Charles Patrick Neimeyer, *America Goes to War: A Social History of the Continental Army* (New York: New York University Press, 1996); John P. Resch, *Suffering Soldiers: Revolutionary War Veterans, Moral Sentiment, and Political Culture in the Early Republic* (Amherst: University of Massachusetts Press, 1999); Charles Royster, *A Revolutionary People at War: The Continental Army and American Character, 1775–1783* (1979; New York: W. W. Norton, 1981); John Shy, *A People Numerous and Armed: Reflections on the Military Struggle for American Independence*, rev. ed. (Ann Arbor: University of Michigan Press/Ann Arbor Paperbacks, 1990).

3. Holly A. Mayer, *Belonging to the Army: Camp Followers and Community during the American Revolution* (Columbia: University of South Carolina Press, 1996). Women's contributions are more broadly addressed in a number of works, including Linda K. Kerber's *Women of the Republic: Intellect and Ideology in Revolutionary America* (Chapel Hill: University of North Carolina Press, 1980), and Mary Beth Norton's *Liberty's Daughters: The Revolutionary Experience of American Women, 1750–1800* (Boston: Little, Brown, 1980).

4. Don Higginbotham, *War and Society in Revolutionary America: The Wider Dimensions of Conflict* (Columbia: University of South Carolina Press, 1988), p. 98. Higginbotham also discusses how Washington tried to foster common bonds in the army, in *George Washington: Uniting a Nation* (Lanham, Md.: Rowman & Littlefield, 2002), pp. 29–35.

5. Records of women in Constance B. Schulz, "Daughters of Liberty: The History of Women in the Revolutionary War Pension Records," *Prologue* (Fall 1984): 139–53. John C. Dann and John Harriman, "The Revolution Remembered—By the Ladies,"

American Magazine and Historical Chronicle 3, no. 2 (Autumn–Winter 1987–1988): 68–83. A good example is the Sarah Osborn pension memoir, in John C. Dann, ed., *The Revolution Remembered: Eyewitness Accounts of the War for Independence* (Chicago: University of Chicago Press, 1980), pp. 240–50.

6. Lieutenant Colonel Richard Varick to Lamb, Headquarters Rob[inson] House, September 14, 1780, in John Lamb Papers, The New-York Historical Society (microfilm), reel 2; noted in Mayer, *Belonging to the Army,* p. 139.

7. Fleming to Lamb, September 1, 1780, and November 19, 1780, in John Lamb Papers (microfilm), reel 2; and as noted in Mayer, *Belonging to the Army,* pp. 140–41.

8. Mayer, *Belonging to the Army,* pp. 221–23, 142–43, 134.

9. Walter Hart Blumenthal, *Women Camp Followers of the American Revolution* (Philadelphia: George MacManus, 1952), p. 59.

10. Mayer, *Belonging to the Army,* pp. 15, 147.

11. Isaac Bangs, New York, April 25, 1776, in *Journal of Lieutenant Isaac Bangs, April 1 to July 29, 1776* (1890; repr., New York: Arno Press, 1968), pp. 29–31; Headquarters New York City, May 7, 1776, Orderly Book, Col. Alexander McDougall's 1st New York Regiment, March 25–June 15, 1776, The New-York Historical Society's Collection of Early American Orderly Books (microfilm), David Library of the American Revolution.

12. General Orders, Headquarters at Derby, August 24, 1777, in John C. Fitzpatrick, ed., *The Writings of George Washington from the Original Manuscript Sources, 1745–1799,* 39 vols. (Washington, D.C.: Government Printing Office, 1931–1944), 9:129–30.

13. John Rees, "'. . . the multitude of women,' An Examination of the Numbers of Female Camp Followers with the Continental Army," pt. 1 of 3, *Brigade Dispatch* 23 (Autumn 1992): 5.

14. John H. Hawkins, Camp near Morristown, January 2, 1780, in Orderly Book, no. 1, January 1–April 23, 1780, 2nd Canadian Regiment, Historical Society of Pennsylvania, Philadelphia.

15. Mayer, *Belonging to the Army,* pp. 129; Rees, "'. . . the multitude of women,'" pt. 3 of 3 (Spring 1993): 2.

16. Rees, "'. . . the multitude of women,'" pt. 3, p. 3.

17. Mayer, *Belonging to the Army,* pp. 34, 248; Verplanck's Point, September 8, 1782, in Fitzpatrick, *Writings of Washington,* 25:139.

18. Mayer, *Belonging to the Army,* pp. 135–42; Regimental Orders, Headquarters, Camp, March 25, 1780, in Hawkins, Orderly Book, no. 1, and as quoted from the Papers of Moses Hazen, 1780 (Orderly Book, January 1–April 27), in The Peter Force Collection, ser. 8D, vol. 68 (microfilm), in Manuscript Division, Library of Congress.

19. John H. Hawkins, Headquarters, July 7, 1780, in Orderly Book, no. 2, April 23–July 26, 1780, 2nd Canadian Regiment, Historical Society of Pennsylvania, Philadelphia.

20. Hawkins, Headquarters, July 8/9, 1780, Orderly Book 2. McLachlan was called a sergeant major here, but payrolls and rosters record him as a sergeant.

21. Ibid.

22. Ibid. Rosters for Carlile's company list a fifer by the name of Thomas McLane or McLean or McClean. There were also pension applications by the widows of Colin McLachlan and John Batten (Battin), but they appear to have been subsequent wives, for they married the veterans after the war.

23. Ibid.

24. Allen Everest, *Moses Hazen and the Canadian Refugees in the American Revolution* (Syracuse, N.Y.: Syracuse University Press, 1976), pp. 12–23, 33–36, 38–43.

25. "Joseph Olivier Briand," *Catholic Encyclopedia,* vol. 2 (1907), online edition (ed. K. Knight, 2003), <http://www.newadvent.org/cathen/02778b.htm> (accessed January 30, 2004). Father Louis Eustace Lotbinière, chaplain of Livingston's regiment, had congressional, but not church, sanction; James E. Newell, "A Brief Account of Religion and the Revolutionary War Chaplaincy: Part 1" (1995),

<http://www.continentalline.org/articles/9504/950404.htm> (accessed January 30, 2004), and Charles H. Metzger, "Chaplains in the American Revolution," *Catholic Historical Review* 31 (April 1945): 35–36.

26. Francis D. Cogliano, *No King, No Popery: Anti-Catholicism in Revolutionary New England* (Westport, Conn.: Greenwood Press, 1995), pp. 49, 60–65. Hawkins, Journal, undated entry; it followed a count of the members of the regiment with particular mention of the number of officers and soldiers in the "French" companies.

27. Authorized a thousand, the regiment probably reached its maximum in the spring of 1778 with more than 700 men. Return of the Names, Rank, and Dates of Commissions of the Officers in the Regiment of Foot commanded by Col. Moses Hazen, Camp near West Point, November 2, 1780, listed forty-two officers, of whom sixteen, including Hazen, Antill, and Major Joseph Torrey, were listed as volunteers from Canada. The return is in Additional Miscl. Records, film 4, reel 132 (no. 0255), *Revolutionary War Rolls, 1775–1783*, record group 93, National Archives (microfilm), David Library.

28. Washington to Morris, January 29, 1783, in Fitzpatrick, *Writings of Washington*, 26:78–80. On the 2nd Continental Artillery, see Robert K. Wright, Jr., *The Continental Army* (Washington, D.C.: Center of Military History, 1983), pp. 102, 337.

29. Mayer, *Belonging to the Army*, pp. 56–57.

30. Ibid., pp. 145–46.

31. Francis B. Heitman, *Historical Register of Officers of the Continental Army during the War of the Revolution, April, 1775, to December, 1783* (1914; repr., Baltimore: Genealogical Publishing, 1982), pp. 397, 565; Mayer, *Belonging to the Army*, pp. 135, 146; Williams to Lamb, Fort Harkimer, August 1, 1781, John Lamb Papers (microfilm), reel 2.

32. Everest, *Moses Hazen*, pp. 43, 103.

33. Theotist Paulin's (common variation was Paulint) pension application of January 17, 1837, is filed under her husband's name on microfilm reel 1891 in the *Revolutionary War Pension and Bounty-Land-Warrant Application Files* (hereafter noted as *Revolutionary War Pension Files*), part of *Record Group 15, Records of the Veterans Administration*, National Archives (microfilm), David Library. A 1778 letter from Gosselin to his wife is noted in Everest, *Moses Hazen*, p. 64. Gosselin may have visited his family when he was spying in Canada in the winter of 1778–1779 (Hawkins noted Gosselin's return in his journal on June 7, [1779]).

34. Feriol (usually Ferriole or Ferriol), deposition, January 17, 1837, in Paulin application file.

35. Paulin pension file.

36. Theotist Blow, affidavit, November 6, 1837, in Sally Chartier pension application file, filed under John Mary Chartier, microfilm reel 524, in *Revolutionary War Pension Files*. Gilmort was probably Francis Gilmot.

37. John Mary Chartier application file. John Chartier is the Anglicized version of Jean Marie Chartie found in the Pay Roll of an Independent Company Command. by Captain Antoine Paulint in the Service of the United States of America and Annexed to Col. Moses Hazens Regiment, August 1778, and A Roll of Captn. Antoine Paulint Independent Company in the Service of the United States of America and annexed to Colo. Moses Hazens Regiment, Septr. 13th 1778—Engaged until the Conquest of Canada, film 4, reel 131, in *Revolutionary War Rolls*.

38. Sally Chartier, deposition, February 22, 1837, Addison County, Vermont; Polly Chartier, affidavit, February 20, 1837, in John Chartier pension file. Hazen's regiment had a Protestant minister for some time, but there were claims that a Father De la Valinière also served. He may have been the Vally mentioned here, but he is not registered as an official chaplain. Metzger, "Chaplains in the American Revolution," p. 52.

39. E. D. Woodbridge to William Slade, Vergennes, [month illegible] 22, 1837, in John Chartier pension file.

40. Alexander Fernial (Ferriol), statement, June 9, 1837, in John Chartier pension file.

41. Slade to Edwards, Middlebury, Vermont, June 20, 1837, in John Chartier pension file.

42. Basil Nadeau of Champlain, Clinton County, New York, affidavit, October 18, 1837, in John Chartier file. "Copy of a Caption made upon a Regimental List or Roll made out in 1783 by Benjamin Mooers Lieut. And adjutant thereof—Copied for the use of the Secretary of Treasury of the United States—Names of Persons in the Congress own Regiment Co-manded by Colonel Moses Hazen Brigadier General by Brevet, in the service of the United States 1782," film 4, reel 132, in *Revolutionary War Rolls*, notes Nadeau's desertion, but it is possible that he returned—though two 1782 rosters do not list him.

43. Alexander Chartier (Carter), affidavit, February 20, 1837, and testimony, July 14, 1838; Alexander [Ferriol], affidavit, 1838; letter, Hubbell to Edwards, undated, all in John Chartier pension file.

44. Peter Chartier pension application file, reel 524, in *Revolutionary War Pension Files*.

45. James Chartier (Carter) and Sally Chartier, statements to E. D. Woodridge, February 20, 1837, in Peter Chartier pension application file.

46. Polly Chartier, declaration in court, Middlebury, Addison County, February 22, 1837; Polly Chartier, declaration to Justice of Peace Philip Tucker, Addison County, May 2, 1837, both in Peter Chartier pension file.

47. Alexander Ferriol of Chazy, Clinton County, statement, May 1, 1837, in Peter Chartier pension file. In another case, in December 1842, Ferriol stated that he never saw any register recording the marriages he witnessed. Affadavit of Alexander "Fernioll" of Chazy, December 15, 1842, to Henry C. Dickinson, Judge of Clinton County courts, in Constantine pension file.

48. Henry Weed, power of attorney to act for Chartier children, August 25, 1851; E. D. and F. E. Woodbridge to James L. Edwards, Commissioner of Pensions, Vergennes, June 12, 1849; Polly Chartier, deposition, [1849], all in Peter Chartier pension file.

49. Guertin (grandchildrens' surname) application, Clinton County, October 8, 1846; Charlotte Constantine of Plattsburgh, Clinton County, declaration before Court of Common Pleas, October 5, 1841; Hubbell to Edwards, Chazy, New York, September 18, 1842, June 27, 1843, all in Nicholas Constantinau (Constantinan) and Charlotte Constantine pension file, reel 631, in *Revolutionary War Pension Files*. A note in this file points to the John Gauley File for the official report into frauds by Canadian refugees.

50. Alexander "Ferrial" of Chazy, deposition before Clinton County clerk, March 20, 1846; Mary Louisa La Fond of Point Au Meule Canada East, deposition to Charles Burnard, Justice of the Peace of Clinton County, October 6, 1846, both in Constantine pension file.

51. Charlotte Constantine, declaration, October 5, 1841; Mary Cayeaux, statement to Julius Hubbell, September 4, 1841, both in Constantine pension file.

52. Alexander "Fernioll," depositions to Julius C. Hubbell, October 6 and December 8, 1841, in Constantine pension file. Ferriol himself had probably been between eleven and twelve when he first mustered in as a fifer in 1776.

53. Peter Blanchard of Chazy, Clinton County, New York, depositions before Court of Common Pleas, March 31, 1818, and October 3, 1820; Benjamin Mooers, deposition, April 1818, all in Peter and Martha Blanchard pension file, reel 264, in *Revolutionary War Pension Files*.

54. Martha Blanchard of Chazy, statement before the court, September 14, 1836; Basil Nadeau of Chazy, sworn statement, March 4, 1837, both in Blanchard pension file.

55. Mooers, deposition, January 1837; J. Douglas Woodward of Plattsburg to Dudley Farlin, House of Representatives, January 6, 1837, both in Blanchard pension file. Elizabeth Heaton, application August 4, 1836; Hen[ry Augustus Philip] Muhlenberg to J. L. Edwards, Commissioner of Pensions, Reading, August 25, 1836, both in James and Elizabeth Heaton pension file, reel 1245, in *Revolutionary War Pension Files*.

56. Mary Dick, declaration before Justice of Peace Henry Kidd, Baltimore County, January 24, 1840, declarations before Orphans Court of Baltimore County, March 25, 1840, and May 12, 1841; Stephen Freeland, statement before Justice of Peace William Dorsey, Baltimore County, February 3, 1840, both in Mary (and Jacob) Dick pension file, reel 809, in *Revolutionary War Pension Files*.

57. Abigail Roberts of East Hartford, declaration, November 28, 1838, in William and Abigail Roberts pension file, reel 2060, in *Revolutionary War Pension Files*.

58. "Pension Legislation," in *Revolutionary War Pension and Bounty-Land-Warrant Application Files* (Washington, D.C.: National Archives and Records Service, 1974), pp. 2–3.

10

"WE BEAR THE YOKE WITH A RELUCTANT IMPATIENCE"

The War for Independence and Virginia's Displaced Women

JOAN R. GUNDERSEN

My Mind has long been distresst by the present troubles, the Measures that have been adopted, & the consequences they would inevitably draw after them —private Misfortunes we must, & ought to bear, with humility & resignation, —but when Evils are brought on us by wrong measures, & by Persons whom we think have no great right to impose them—then (in my opinion) they become more insuportable & we bear the Yoke with a reluctant impatience.

When Elizabeth Feilde wrote these words to Maria Carter Armistead, her friend had already become one of the War for Independence's refugees.[1] British foraging raids on Virginia's Eastern Shore had led the Armisteads to leave their Gloucester County home. The tables were soon turned, and, as Feilde became a refugee, she found that she had a much heavier "Yoke" to bear than her friend Maria. Maria and her husband were supporters of the Revolution, and their moves were all within Virginia. Elizabeth Feilde, however, would follow her loyalist husband, the Reverend Thomas Feilde, into exile in New York, later returning to England as a widow.[2] These two friends, divided by independence, were among the thousands of Virginian women who found themselves uprooted from their homes and their lives by the political and military events of the Revolution. A closer look at these women, and the events that precipitated their uprootings, reveals not a simple process of victimization, but rather a pattern of choice tied to women's political identity. In a world where some events might be beyond their control, women continued to weigh options and make choices framed by their race, class, and politics.[3] Women displaced by the War for Independence were not passive victims traumatized by events, but active participants whose decisions affected the course of the war.

As alternating waves of political and military action washed across Virginia during the Revolution, they produced thousands of refugees. On Virginia's expansive western frontier, there was almost continuous upheaval creating successive streams of refugees, both Indian and white, beginning in 1774 and continuing into the 1790s. The trans-Appalachian frontier claimed by Virginia was inhabited by a patchwork of peoples—multiple Indian tribes, French settlements recently brought into the British Empire, and a growing number of new settlers. Alliances shifted, and attacks could be carried out by mixed groups of Indians and whites or by more homogenous groups. The war soon turned most inhabitants into refugees, abandoning scattered farms or small villages for fortified towns, or blockhouses. The disruption in settlers' farming and the destruction of Indian fields and corn supplies meant that everyone suffered from a "want of Subsistence" and settlers were likely to flee.[4]

At the opposite edge of the state, the tidewater rivers and bays that had played an important role in the economic development of Virginia were an open channel for raids both by the British and privateers. Those waters also provided routes of escape for slaves seeking the freedom promised by the British. Troop movements provided a current that uprooted women and complicated their struggle to maintain families and livelihoods. Well before Virginia's delegates in the Continental Congress voted to approve the Declaration of Independence, several thousand residents of the port towns of Norfolk and Portsmouth had been swept from their home by the ebb and flow of military action by the British lieutenant governor, Lord Dunmore, and responses by Virginia militias. The same currents of political necessity that led the Continental Congress to house British and German prisoners of war in Virginia deposited their wives and families in the state. British raids in 1779, 1780, and 1781 and the maneuvers leading to Yorktown uprooted many more women. Questions of loyalty could displace a family at any time, especially as the Virginia government began taking prominent loyalists into custody and as local committees of safety disciplined men and women deemed unsupportive of the Revolution.[5] By taking a careful look at these displacement events, the patterns of experience hint at the ways in which women's displacement involved conscious political decisions. In this, as in so many other areas of women's experience, women were actors as well as victims.

Becoming a refugee often was a choice. Leaving the immediate scene of a battle was prudent for any civilian, as the war offered enough instances of soldiers in other venues raping or plundering women living along the route of march. Frontier campaigns in Virginia were lethal to women, so the prudent there had plenty of cause for flight. Although in the settled regions of the state, there were surprisingly few documented cases of soldiers of either army physically assaulting civilians, the well-publicized cases elsewhere, especially New Jersey and Pennsylvania, meant that Virginians were aware of the risk. Virginia's most notorious case involved British soldiers injuring the hands of a woman in Suffolk as they ripped off her rings.[6] That Virginians made as much of this case as they did suggests they had little else they could publicize.

When Norfolk burned early in the war, the British dismantled most of the homes in York while preparing for the siege at Yorktown, or American troops burned a Cherokee village, those who lost their homes had little choice other than moving, but it is striking how fast women reappeared even when their houses no longer existed. Their choice was to be on home ground, even if that ground was now bare. The desire to stay on home ground led women to pick and choose when to leave. In the face of a major British invasion in 1781, Carter Braxton gave a higher priority to keeping his wife Elizabeth and their large family in their West Point, Virginia, house than he did to calling out the militia to guard the town. As he wrote to Governor Jefferson, "It will subject the few People in the little Village to much disquiet and Insult and oblige my Family to remove in quest of a House which at this time is not to be had." Braxton went on to say that he and nine other well-armed men were already in West Point and could turn out quickly. It is not clear what he thought ten men (or fifty militiamen) could really do against a raid in force. Braxton's position was probably strengthened by the refusal of his wife Elizabeth to uproot their large family. Elizabeth Corbin Braxton was the daughter of a prominent loyalist and probably thought she had little to fear from the British, despite the fact her husband had signed the Declaration of Independence.[7] In most cases during the war, rather than fleeing from *all* armies, Virginia women responded to the advance of *specific* armies. While eight-month-pregnant Maria Carter Armistead fled her Gloucester home because she feared the possibility of raids launched from the British ships foraging for supplies on the Eastern Shore, her loyalist neighbors, including the Feildes, stayed at home.[8] Similarly, on the frontier, Indian women understood that they were much more at risk from an American force than those led by the British.

Once the Virginia legislature suspended clergy salaries and required a loyalty oath of Anglican clerics, the Feildes needed to make a choice, for Thomas Feilde was not willing to take the new oath. Some clergy who refused the oath remained quietly living on the glebe in their parishes, especially those who had married in Virginia. Although that path seems to have had some attraction for Feilde, both he and his wife were from Britain, and thus without kin to provide some protection and support. When Thomas decided to leave for New York, Elizabeth went along. Her political sentiments were loyalist, and there were no property or family ties to keep her.[9] Though many other loyalist women made the same choice Elizabeth Feilde did, others persisted in Virginia despite prosecution of men in their family and confiscation of land. Much depended on how neighbors perceived the politics of the woman. Elizabeth had no reason to stay because the Feildes apparently had no other land to protect. They had lived on the parish glebe lands.

The case of Mary Willing Byrd can help to illustrate the politically charged atmosphere surrounding decisions to stay or go. For Byrd, the war was definitely a civil war, with prominent family members on both sides. More than once, events pushed her to the edge of political abysses. She responded with calculated moves designed to preserve her family holdings and resist becoming a refugee. Like Elizabeth Feilde, Mary Byrd was not born in Virginia. A member of a prominent family in Philadelphia, Mary Willing had married the even-more-prominent William Byrd III of Virginia soon after his first wife died.[10] When William Byrd committed suicide at the beginning of 1777, his wife was faced with large debts and the need to protect his estate for her children.[11] William had been known to sympathize with the British. His son by his first marriage held a commission in the British army. Mary's own family included both leading rebels and loyalists. Benedict Arnold had married her cousin, and the brother of her sister's husband was another British officer. Mary herself claimed to be a "virtuous citizen" and a "friend of her Country" who had dutifully supplied a substitute soldier to the American forces, but her neighbors remained suspicious.[12]

On three occasions, the British chose to land at Westover, the Byrd plantation. Each time they damaged the plantation and enlisted her slaves, but each time she "received them according to my idea with propriety."[13] Her decision to stay put was based on calculations that, although the British might stable their horses in her nursery, her family ties would shield her and her children from physical harm and her home from total destruction. If she had fled, the British troops might well have been less restrained about damaging her property. The presence of the British also provided opportunities for Byrd and her children to send letters to family members with the invaders, an act that was technically corresponding with the enemy. These actions became very public when a British officer, Lieutenant Charles Hare (and the brother of Mary's brother-in-law) was detained by Americans despite a flag of truce. He was trying to arrange the return of some of her slaves and compensation for others taken by the British. Because the British usually only made the offer to return slaves to loyalists, the Virginia government had forbidden such returns. The Americans investigated Byrd for treason, and she narrowly escaped punishment.[14] In her fight to clear her name, Byrd cashed in every connection she had to the Virginia elite.

The Early Refugees

By the end of 1776, Virginia had already experienced major dislocations along the coast and the frontier. In fact, the frontier became a battleground before the War for Independence officially started. A series of skirmishes had raised tensions along the frontier to the breaking point between 1770 and 1774. White settlers rushed to safety in the East. In

1774, Lord Dunmore led a militia expedition against the Shawnee, who were unable to enlist other tribes in their cause. After inflicting some damage on the Virginia militia, the Shawnee sued for peace, the price of which was a major land cession. In 1776 the Cherokee, encouraged by Iroquois, Shawnee, and Delaware emissaries, declared war on the Americans. Not all Cherokee women supported going to war in 1776, and some women insisted on showing their neutrality by aiding the American militias when the Americans launched a major counterattack and invaded the Cherokee homeland. The women's actions took real courage, in light of the militias' notorious inability to distinguish friend from foe. The militia destroyed most of the Overhill Cherokee towns and negotiated a major cession of Cherokee lands. Those who refused to sue for peace emigrated to the Chickamauga area and continued fighting. By July 1777, the Cherokee had officially returned to neutrality, but their towns remained tempting targets. Cherokee women knew that their choices were political, and they continued to cut an independent path throughout the war years. They paid a high price for this independence. The crops destroyed belonged to women and town life was centered around women's kin. As the Cherokee dispersed, women lost their community support and a portion of their power.[15]

A closer look at the choices made by Norfolk women illustrates that, even under the most difficult of situations, Cherokee women were not the only ones making politically charged decisions. With the war tearing the Norfolk community apart, women still relied on the informal networks of kin and friendship to provide support. Containing 6,000 people and about 1,300 houses, Norfolk was Virginia's largest city and the busiest port in the South. The city was an important hub for trade among Virginia, Great Britain, and the West Indies, gathering tobacco, wheat, and corn not only from Virginia, but also Maryland and North Carolina. The forested areas south of the city supplied the port's need for lumber, tar, turpentine, and pitch. The hogs and cattle that foraged in the Great Dismal Swamp provided a source of meat for Norfolk and its ships. Although a number of the most prosperous merchants built plantations in the adjoining countryside and commuted to their businesses in the city, these merchants also built substantial houses in town. Norfolk was filled with brick homes. Its brick Anglican church, many inns, warehouses, and shops gave it a comfortably prosperous appearance.[16]

Scots merchants, especially those with ties to Glasgow firms, played an important role in Norfolk. Many had lived in the colonies for years and had developed tight-knit family clusters through marriage, a number of them to local women. Members of the Scottish community were active in politics and had represented Norfolk in the House of Burgesses, and served as aldermen, mayor, and justices of the peace. Although some incidents, such as the smallpox inoculation riot of 1768, revealed tensions between native Virginians and the Scots, until 1774 the community seemed to act as one. Throughout the protests associated with the Stamp Act and

Townsend Duties, Norfolk seemed united in the support of the protests. In less than two years' time, however, that community fabric unraveled nearly completely.[17]

The year 1775 began with relative unity. Virginia's lieutenant governor, Lord Dunmore, was basking in the glow of his successful campaign against the Shawnee, and he still had the trust of Virginia leaders. In May 1775, however, he dissolved the Virginia House of Burgesses because they had voted to hold a day of fasting in response to the closing of Boston's port. As before, American resistance to parliamentary acts took the form of trade boycotts. The Norfolk community seemed solidly committed to the Association, which ended importation of British goods on November 1, 1774, and specified the end of all exports on August 10, 1775.[18] If enforced effectively, this would destroy Norfolk's economy, and, as merchants began to try to find ways around the Association, fracture lines appeared in town. When committees of safety began rooting out dissent all over Virginia, Norfolk's population swelled with people preparing to leave Virginia. Lord Dunmore's decision to remove the powder stored in the magazine in Williamsburg on April 21, 1775, touched off a crisis that mobilized militias. As a mob searched for Attorney General John Randolph (who had supported Dunmore), rumors circulated that his daughter had been the governor's mistress. That the tales were false makes even more evident that their purpose was to discredit the family. They literally inscribed politics onto the daughter's body by making it the symbolic site of disloyalty. It is not surprising that conservative leaders sent their families from town, away from the reach of mobs and the damage such rumors could wreak. Lord Dunmore sent his own wife and children to safety aboard the HMS *Fowey* at Yorktown and fortified the governor's palace. As the situation seemingly calmed, his family returned briefly, but on May 12 the Dunmores, accompanied by Captain Edward Foy and his wife, boarded the HMS *Magdalen,* which had been waiting for them at Queen's Creek. Dunmore transferred to the *Fowey,* but Lady Dunmore and the children left Virginia on the *Magdalen* on June 29, as refugees.[19]

The next six months made Norfolk both a source of and haven for refugees. During the summer, the leaders of the Virginia Convention built an armed force. Shippers from Norfolk began bringing in cargoes of arms. Governor Dunmore fumed aboard ship until reinforcements arrived from East Florida in September; then he acted. British ships raided and foraged along the coast and on the Eastern Shore, thus precipitating Maria Carter Armistead's flight. The Americans tried desperately to prevent loyalists from supplying Dunmore and the refugees packed on British ships. Although Americans were able to capture the British tender the *Otter,* which had run aground off Portsmouth in a hurricane, Dunmore was able to launch numerous successful amphibious raids, destroying more than seventy cannon, including twenty near Norfolk, and seizing the printing press of John Hunter Holt, whose Norfolk-based *Virginia Gazette or Norfolk*

Intelligencer had ridiculed the British. In late October, after Virginia militias drove back British troops in Portsmouth, Dunmore escalated the situation. On November 7, he issued a proclamation offering freedom to African American slaves who joined the British, and one week later, during the night of November 14, the British occupied positions at the Great Bridge. Two days later, the British marched into Norfolk and occupied the town. Dunmore insisted that inhabitants swear an oath of allegiance and wear an identifying red cloth strip. His troops, including the recently recruited regiment of escaped slaves, searched for militiamen in hiding and looted as they went. They also dismantled thirty-two structures to build fortifications.[20]

The British became concerned at the increased number of American troops massing near the Great Bridge and sent a force of regulars and loyalists to push them back on December 9, 1775. Outnumbered, the British attack failed, and they abandoned their fort and boarded ship. Loyalists crowded on board commercial and navy vessels. The Americans occupied Norfolk on December 14. A new war of nerves ensued. The Americans would parade in view of the British ships and fire small arms toward the ships. The British, in turn, threatened to turn their ships' guns on the town. Something had to give. The British needed supplies; the American position was too exposed and was tying up resources. On December 30, the British issued an ultimatum; the next day they fired on the parading Americans. The British sent troops ashore, and, while exchanging fire with the Americans, burned some buildings along the waterfront. Considering Norfolk a loyalist haven, the American troops decided to complete the job and burned and looted their way through the town for the next three days. Drunk on liquor from looted stores, the troops went on a binge of destruction that made no distinction between the property of friend or foe. When it was over, the Americans had destroyed 863 buildings and the British were responsible for destroying another 51 (including 32 razed to build fortifications earlier). In follow-up skirmishes and during the American withdrawal in February, the British destroyed 3 more buildings and the Americans another 416. In all of Norfolk, only about a dozen buildings remained.[21]

And where were the women—loyalist, patriot, and neutral—during these chaotic months of occupation and counter-occupation? Many were still in the city. During the British occupation of Norfolk, the local Committee of Safety restricted civilian travel through the lines to limit opportunities for the British to gather information, but many American supporters left before the British officially occupied the city. In October, one correspondent commented that American supporters "have abandoned this town; most of the houses and shops are empty."[22] Often they had sought refuge with family living outside the town. Many loyalist men moved their belongings to ships and slept on board, leaving their families onshore at home. William Forsayth, for example, was a Scot shoemaker who had arrived in Norfolk about 1773 and married there in 1775. He "quitted his residence when Lord Dunmore & the Troops left," placing his goods on a schooner he owned. His wife Penelope does not seem to have been with him, but she may have been among the many women and children who jammed aboard the British ships after the British defeat at Great Bridge in December. Supplies were scarce, and, amid overcrowding, diseases spread rapidly. When Dunmore requested permission for women (such as Penelope) and their children to land, the American commander allowed it only if they did not return to the ships and promised to provide no intelligence to the British. Penelope Forsayth apparently returned to Norfolk while her husband remained on shipboard, eventually leaving with Dunmore.[23] Robert Shedden's wife and children definitely left Dunmore's fleet. Mrs. Shedden's father, who was smuggling needed supplies for the Americans, was able to secure permission for her and the children to go stay in Portsmouth. Robert accompanied them despite a warning and was arrested.[24] Some Americans apparently returned to Norfolk once the British left, thus increasing the chaotic comings and goings and making the town a confusing blend of loyalties.

The confusion over whether women should stay or leave Norfolk reflected community ties and ambivalence about the role of women in politics. Many people had trouble seeing women as political and therefore affected by the shifting status of Norfolk. Women were also reluctant to leave. This was their community. It was filled with family and friends who should be willing to support and protect their "own" women and children. The women themselves saw little to fear from armies made up of their close relations and neighbors, and some of the women were supporters of the resistance to Britain. Events soon made clear, however, that a woman's presence in the area had political dimensions. It really did not matter whether a woman sent food to her husband on board a British ship because she was caring for her spouse or because she was trying to aid the British. The result was the same. Family news could include valuable military information that the other side—British or American—was eager to acquire. The situation made women's actions political.

As the destructive events of New Year's Day unfolded, many of the women in Norfolk took their families and huddled at the edge of town, trying to stay out of the way.[25] Others stayed put. Mary Webley, for example, was at home with her disabled husband and family, when, "while suckling her Child the youngest of three now dependent on her, had her leg broken by a Cannon Ball from the Liverpool Man of War."[26] On January 3 after two days of looting and destruction by American troops, Sarah Smith was out wandering the town. When she returned from the wharf to her house, where she was storing five or six casks of butter and a sixty-gallon cask of rum that Captain Finney and Lieutenant Howe of the American troops had taken from Mr. Greenwood's store, she found the destruction had reached her block, for her neighbor's house was burning. Over the course of the three-day burning spree she doled out liquor and butter, arguing with various militia officers over who was entitled to claim the looted goods. She also scolded soldiers tearing down a fence. The troops, although clearly out of control, were less interested in killing than looting. Smith later claimed that another officer had told her that they had accepted two dollars from a man to delay burning his house until he had removed his wife and family. Eventually the American officers ordered Smith's property be burned too.[27] Both Webley and Smith appear to have been American supporters. Webley petitioned for aid in 1776 when only those who sided with the Revolution had a hope of success. Literate and propertied, Smith obviously did not fear the American troops. During the American occupation she had struck a deal with the American commanders to store confiscated loyalist goods. She continued to negotiate and argue with leaders as the town went up in flames around her.

Obviously, after the January fires, many women had little choice but to leave the ruins of the city, but a number of others simply crowded into the some 400 remaining buildings in the city. Mary Ross's tavern, which survived the fires, undoubtedly sheltered some of the homeless. Sarah Taylor, who lost more than £187 of personal property in the fires, may have moved in with Mary Taylor, whose house survived. The houses of Joyce Edwards, Mary Williamson, Ann Wineto, Aphia Wonycott, and Eliza Haneford still stood after the January burning, and as single women they may have sheltered friends or relations. Some loyalist women, cut off from friends and family, became fugitives. The wife of the Reverend John Agnew hid in the swamps (a traditional hideout for outlaw groups) for three years before connecting with British troops. Her husband had joined the loyalist forces raised by Dunmore as a chaplain.[28] Those women who had thought that their own support for the Revolution and family ties to the patriots would protect them, however, found their trust had been misplaced. For, when the Americans withdrew from Norfolk on February 3, their properties were among those razed.[29]

By February 3, when Americans began destroying the remaining houses, many women had already left Norfolk in wagons supplied by the Americans. It was winter, however, and some had nowhere to go. Mary Webley, for example, pleaded the following October that "She hath at present no Ways or Means to procure Shelter or acquire Subsistance for herself and miserable little children, her Husband and Self having had all of their Effects totally destroyed in the Flames of Norfolk." Such refugees camped in tents in the backcountry or lived in shanties.[30] For some "drawn from their peaceful Habitations into the Woods without Bead or Raiment, at a most inclement Season," the hardships proved fatal.[31]

Whether loyalist, Revolutionary, or neutral, the displaced women of Norfolk had to scramble to survive. William and Rebecca Aitchison lost their elegant Norfolk home in the January fires. They had other properties, however, and moved first to the estate in Princess Anne County and then to one in Northampton. Aitchison, however, had associated himself publicly with Dunmore, and his country neighbors made them very unwelcome. Blocked from moving to a property in North Carolina, Aitchison died in December 1776 while an American prisoner. Rebecca Aitchison's brother Jacob Ellegood had fought for the British at Great Bridge and was later captured while escorting some women and their families to the Eastern Shore. He was imprisoned for more than five years. Rebecca's brother-in-law, James Parker, was a business partner with William Aitchison and was also captured and imprisoned. Unlike Ellegood, he escaped and left Virginia in 1776. The widowed Rebecca, her sister Margaret Parker, and their combined families crowded together into a cottage smaller and less elegant than either had occupied in Norfolk. To survive for the next six years, these elite, urban women turned to domestic manufacture of cloth, dairying, and poultry-keeping, with the help of their children. This was an abrupt change for the women and their daughters, and it prevented the girls "from improving themselves by reading, writing, keeping polite company, etc.," but Margaret was "thankful for such an Asylum [when] many of the poor inhabitants of Norfolk are greatly distressed for any house at all."[32] These sisters were not the only refugee women to band together to survive the war as refugees, and, like female survivors in most wars, they demonstrated resiliency and ingenuity in the way they survived.

Women's choices of where to go once Norfolk had been razed were further limited by the decision of the American leaders to evacuate Portsmouth, which they thought a loyalist hotbed. Just across the river from Norfolk, Portsmouth would have been a natural haven for displaced Norfolk women. General Charles Lee and other American leaders were sure that Portsmouth's women and children were acting as British spies. It was hard not to suspect someone such as Ann Roberts, whose husband, Humphrey, was a Portsmouth merchant who had moved his goods on board ship in December 1775. A Virginia native, Ann Roberts remained in Portsmouth. There were enough examples from nearby counties of passing information to the British to give credence to such suspicions. For example, the committees of safety in Isle of Wight and Nansemond counties found Mary Eason, Betsy Hunter, and Martha Wilkinson guilty of allowing information to be passed to Lord Dunmore. In Hunter's case, she had revealed troop positions in a letter to her mother and brother (who had joined a loyalist regiment) in Norfolk in 1775.[33]

The patriot leaders ordered an evacuation of Portsmouth and much of the surrounding county. The officials also ordered the destruction of all livestock to prevent it falling into British hands and demanded that all able-bodied, loyalist-owned male slaves older than sixteen be turned over to authorities. The original deadline for evacuation was early February, but there was such uproar that the evacuation was not implemented until April 10. To fully implement the order would require relocating more than 20,000 people. The Americans set aside £1,000 to pay for transport wagons to carry the women and children as well as their beds and cooking utensils (but no other furniture or goods). Local protests, however, resulted in only a partial evacuation. A committee of Princess Anne patriots was allowed to investigate and clear neighbors in the countryside who had supported the Americans or remained neutral. In the end, those country folk who had supported the British and all city folk were forced to leave. Ann Roberts retired to the family's Northampton property. Everyone's livestock and small boats were to be removed. The evacuation was not permanent, and Roberts was among the many who returned to the city as the British threat faded. In fact, she managed to prevent confiscation of their property and remained in possession of it after the war, despite British raids on the town in 1779 and 1780 that saw the town partially burned.[34] The repeated vulnerability of these port towns prolonged displacements and slowed rebuilding. For the women who lived there, it must have been exhausting as they responded to repeated threats, invasions, and disruptions to life.

Rebecca Ellegood Aitchison's and Margaret Ellegood Parker's sister-in-law, Mary Ellegood, weathered the war years on the family's estate, Rose Hill, in Princess Anne County. Although she was spared her sister-in-laws' fates of being burned out, Mary Ellegood was turned into a refugee when Virginia seized her husband's estate after the Americans captured him in December 1775. The evacuation order for Portsmouth and Princess Anne County ensured she could not seek shelter with friends nearby. As her husband later noted, despite being "plundered of every thing, . . . [Mary] made a shift to get the better [i.e., she was able to replace the goods]." In June 1776, she petitioned the Virginia legislature for an allowance of her husband's estate. Relief finally came when the legislature passed an act granting the wives and children of loyalists the equivalent of a dower right in the sequestered property. She was thus assigned use of her husband's plantations and one-third of the moveable property. Mary Ellegood was expected to pay taxes and the costs of her husband's incarceration from that share. Her hardships were increased by the death of two of her five children while her husband was a prisoner. In August of 1781, Jacob Ellegood was allowed to go to New York, but his family stayed behind. The French navy seized the supplies of meat and bread he left for his wife's support in 1781, and she depended on money he sent for support. Unlike her sisters-in-law, her neighbors were more supportive and she was treated "with great Civility & attention."[35] Her sisters had gone to a family-owned farm that had not been a primary residence. Thus, they were viewed as strangers in the area. Ellegood remained in a community filled with family and friends who knew her well.

Despite obvious hardships, many women were determined to return to the burned-out town as soon as possible. They found their way back to Norfolk, where they built lean-tos on their former property or lived in surviving outbuildings. Only about fifteen houses had been rebuilt, when young Jenny Steuart wrote in 1779, "Nobody could conceive that did not see it [Norfolk] how much it is altered. It shocks me exceedingly when ever I see it. There are a great many small huts built up in it. The inhabitants cannot be happy anywhere else." Jenny, a former resident of Norfolk, lived in the country with Rebecca Aitchison and Margaret Parker. Mrs. Parker had noted at the beginning of that year that her cousins, "greatly distressed for a tolerable house" as refugees living at Kemps, were talking about building in Norfolk that spring. British raids on the town delayed their plans. Visitors were still describing the town as a scene of "Ruin and Devastation" in 1785.[36]

The Declaration of Independence in July 1776 was almost an anticlimax for the several thousand uprooted Virginia women who had already felt the direct impact of war. Many married women had for all practical purposes becomes heads of households in the absence of their husbands, and patriot committees, especially in Princess Anne County, distinguished between women who cooperated with the emerging patriot governments (either by maintaining neutrality or positive action) and those who did not. After independence, the political stakes became even higher. The Virginia Assembly resolved that British merchants had until February 10, 1777, to leave the commonwealth or swear allegiance to the new government. All males older than sixteen were to swear allegiance by October 10 or be disarmed, disenfranchised, and barred from using the courts for commercial transactions. By the end of 1777, loyalist debts had been "sequestered" so that payments went to the Virginia government. Another wave of men flowed from Virginia. Their wives had a choice. Some, such as Margaret Goodrich, stayed, living on a portion of her husband's sequestered estate; others, such as Elizabeth Feilde, left.[37]

African American Women

The African American inhabitants of Westover and Norfolk experienced the war for independence very differently than did Mary Byrd or Margaret Goodrich. Those enslaved by loyalists could be displaced because of the politics of the family they served and not through their own choice. Slave labor was a valuable commodity that each party (including the slaves themselves) tried to control. Rumors of British intentions to declare a general emancipation encouraged those enslaved to offer help to Governor Dunmore or to escape to British ships throughout the summer of 1775.[38] As the British navy and privateers foraged along the Virginia coast, slaves escaped to join them. At first the British returned these blacks to the whites that claimed them. By October 1775, British raiding increased and Dunmore put his ships under a commander who refused to return slaves. The loss of slave labor hurt the patriots while providing the British with useful hands. In November, Governor Dunmore issued his famous offer of freedom to those enslaved Africans who escaped and joined British service, provided that their owners supported the rebellion. More than a thousand slaves soon took advantage of Dunmore's offer. Every time the British returned to Virginia or raided its coast, more followed, including many of those from Westover.[39] In fact, part of the reason Mary Byrd was investigated for treason was her attempt to recover forty-nine Westover slaves who had left the plantation with Benedict Arnold.[40] The Americans likewise sought to control African American labor. When they confiscated the property of loyalists, such as John Goodrich, the Americans also confiscated his slaves (including two older women, Sarah, age fifty-five, and Phillis, who was sixty-five) and sent them to labor in Virginia lead mines. This not only transferred the benefit of the labor to the American cause, but also worked a serious hardship on the Goodrich family. Margaret Goodrich found it nearly impossible to hire even one slave to help her farm. When she did hire labor, "the said Slaves either from inclination or seduction have so frequently absconded from their duty as to leave her Crop in a condition which precludes all hope of its being sufficient to supply the wants of her family."[41]

The labor of enslaved women was a valuable commodity during the war. Enslaved women produced a good proportion of home-manufactured cloth.[42] Women provided much of the labor for planting, hoeing, pinching suckers, and deworming tobacco crops. When the owner of a foundry making arms for the Americans specifically sought to hire women in 1781 "to answer the purposes for which women are wanted," he pointed out that having women to cook and wash allowed the men to have more time to spend on the job. South Carolina refugee Nicholas Everleigh brought two families of seven each, including young children, to Virginia in 1780, hoping to rent their labor, but shortages of food and clothing forced him to sell the slaves to a Virginian eager for the labor. The presence of children and the fact that he referred to families is strong evidence that the group included women and that he assumed women's labor would be valued.[43] The absence or presence of African American women and the labor they could provide was a war issue, and it is not surprising that British raiders would sweep up all the slaves in sight to remove them from American hands. Americans complained that the British were "stealing our Negroes," but Captain Thomas Graves noted in his ship logs that he dealt with slave "Refugees," whom he sent to places where the British needed laborers.[44] African American women sought to convert themselves from the status of property to persons by fleeing slavery. Both British and Americans officials, however, saw these displaced women in terms of the labor they could supply.

Family groups, not just able-bodied men, sought freedom within British lines.[45] African American women found their way to freedom by different routes, but usually in the company of others, especially kin. Sue, a slave claimed by patriot John Cooper, joined her husband, enslaved by loyalist Andrew Sprewle, in March 1776 on board a schooner owned by Sprewle. Sprewle refused to return her to Cooper because he feared that her husband would not stay without her. The British recognized that other enslaved couples might feel the same. Thus, although the British offer of freedom was only for able-bodied men who were willing to bear arms, they also sheltered the women, children, and infirm who arrived. In fact, of the roughly 1,100 slaves who took advantage of Dunmore's offer, about 300 were enlisted in the regiment organized for them. The rest, not considered suitable for enlistment, were used for civilian labor. Women and children made up a majority of these laborers. Unfortunately for all of those who sought freedom by joining Dunmore, smallpox ravaged the British ships. When Dunmore withdrew from Virginia in July 1776, Americans were appalled by the evidence of mass death they found at the former British base at Gwynne's Island. Both Sue and the loyalist whose ship had harbored her were among those who succumbed to disease there.[46]

Records compiled by the British in New York at the end of the war provide glimpses of the African American women who fled to British lines and survived British service and disease to the end of the war. About 3,000 African Americans were registered by the British and transported to Nova Scotia, Europe, or other colonies. Approximately 300 Virginia women were among the 3,000. The British recognized the service of half of the Virginia women by awarding them prized certificates of freedom. At least one-quarter of the women had escaped with children. At the time of the escape, most of these children were quite young. Several of the women were either pregnant or carrying infants in arms when they left for the British lines. For example, Alice Tankard left her master, Scarborough Tankard, in 1778, the same year her daughter was born. Dolly and Charles Dixon escaped with four children, ranging from six to eleven years old; a fifth child was born the year they left Norfolk. Because many of the women listed in the registers had escaped four to seven years earlier—and in light of the high risks of infant and child mortality—the women listed as having no children old enough to have escaped probably included mothers whose children had died. Once they had reached freedom, many of these women had established families. Sixty-one of the Virginia women on the British transport lists were traveling with children born free behind British lines. Mary Stratton, from the Eastern Shore of Virginia, for example, had escaped with her four-year-old daughter, Rose, in 1779. By the time she took transport to Nova Scotia with eight-year-old Rose, she also had two more children, two-year-old Johnny and four-month-old Peggy.[47]

Throughout the war, slave women continued to risk flight to freedom if an opportunity presented itself. "Risk" is the operative word. Mortality among African Americans in the British camps was very high, and there was always the risk that they could find themselves in American hands again and be reenslaved. Other enslaved women judged the risks too great and rejected leaving. There are accounts of slaves refusing to go with British troops. Of the several hundred slaves owned by the Burwell family at the time of the Revolution, only one, Sally Dennis, definitely joined the British, despite the fact that they had good opportunities to do so, especially in the spring of 1781, when Cornwallis occupied the area around

Kings Mill.[48] For many slaves, escape meant taking a boat and avoiding American ships to reach the British fleet. Two women and seven men, for example, were caught in an open boat in December 1776 while trying to make their way to Norfolk. Americans threatened, but apparently did not actually follow through, to file charges of theft (a capital offense) against slaves caught escaping in boats belonging to whites.[49] The records kept by Captain Thomas Graves of HMS *Savage* in late March and early April of 1781 during a raiding expedition of several ships up the Chesapeake reveal nearly daily arrivals of groups of escaping slaves. Seventeen of George Washington's slaves reached the *Savage,* most of them apparently having escaped together on a twenty-four-foot boat owned by Washington. Three young women—Deborah (age sixteen), Esther (eighteen), and Lucy (twenty)—were among their number. The group had some very nervous moments when Lund Washington, George's nephew, who managed the plantation, arrived under flag of truce with provisions to try to recover the slaves. The British refused.[50]

Women who joined the British were more likely to have left with a British raiding or foraging party. In such cases, large groups of slaves at a plantation might attach themselves to the raiders. For example, in August 1781, fifty slaves from one plantation left with a British raiding party about twenty miles from Richmond.[51] Unfortunately, they were soon reenslaved when American privateers captured the British ship transporting them. Major General Alexander Leslie's invasion and occupation of Portsmouth in 1780 triggered a wave of escapes from slavery. When Leslie withdrew, however, Americans recovered a number of African Americans left behind. The Americans claimed the labor of those whose owners were loyalists; the others were returned to their masters. Among those who left with General Leslie were Celia and Hester, whose master, Money Godwin of Norfolk, had joined Leslie's fleet and "gave them permission to do the same." The vessel they served on, however, was captured as an American prize and the two women, along with another former Godwin slave, were returned to slavery as part of the "property" seized as a prize of war.[52]

British Invasions, 1779–1781

Predictably, the Collier raid in 1779, General Leslie's arrival in 1780, and the British military maneuvers in Virginia in 1781 resulted in major dislocations of white and black women. Sir George Collier arrived on May 8, 1779, with twenty-eight ships led by the HMS *Raisonable,* a sixty-four-gun ship, and 1,800 soldiers. With the *Raisonable* blockading Hampton, the other ships moved up the Elizabeth River. The force surprised and overpowered the Americans at Fort Nelson and quickly occupied Portsmouth. After two weeks of plundering, during which Suffolk was destroyed, Collier withdrew, taking ninety loyalists with him. Half were women and children. In addition 518 slaves sought safety with the British.[53] Collier's raid produced some refugees moving to stay out of the reach of the troops, but most Americans seem to have decided that, though their property was at risk, their persons were not. The fact that Americans made much of a woman whose hands were injured when some of Collier's soldiers tore off her rings suggests that they could find no more severe case of injury to use for propaganda purposes. Thus, it made sense for women to stay and try to preserve their property. Only when there was no possibility of staying at home—such as the burning of Suffolk—did the raid produce refugees seeking aid. The wife and children of Captain George Blackwell, who were left homeless by Collier, for example, had so few resources that the Virginia Executive Council relieved them of county taxes.[54]

The Collier raid was still fresh in women's minds when General Leslie invaded Virginia in October of 1780. The pattern was repeated. Guided by Norfolk-area Tories, Leslie landed his 2,200 troops at Portsmouth, Newport News, and Hampton. They threatened Williamsburg, but withdrew in mid-November, leaving behind several hundred escaped slaves for lack of room on his ships. Five weeks later, General Benedict Arnold, now commanding British troops, arrived, landing 800 men at Westover (home of his kinswoman Mary Byrd). Arnold reached Richmond on January 5, 1781. From this point until the siege of Yorktown began that fall, the British were able to move troops at will around Piedmont and Tidewater, Virginia, and British naval vessels and privateers raided along the coasts and bays. Cornwallis arrived in May, bringing the total British forces to 7,000. Portsmouth was once again in British hands and its residents "almost famished for want of Bread."[55] Cornwallis soon realized he was not going to catch Lafayette, so the British general retired toward the coast, where he found orders waiting to assume a defensive position and settled in to fortify Yorktown and Gloucester. By August 30, Cornwallis was trapped as the French fleet helped Washington complete a rapid move southward. The formal siege of Yorktown began September 28. The town took cannon barrage after barrage before Cornwallis met to negotiate surrender terms on October 18, 1781.

The military action in Virginia throughout 1781 created a constant stream of displaced women, some trying to avoid British troops, some made homeless, and some trying to reach British lines. In this chaotic scene, it was hard to know where safety lay. Refugees began returning to Petersburg as soon as the British left the first time, only to be surprised when they returned.[56] Leaders distracted by the need to move their own families to safety also complicated the Virginia response. St. George Tucker took time out to move his wife and their week-old son to a safer location before returning to help neighbor Theodorick Bland evacuate. Governor Thomas Jefferson sent his wife Martha and their children, including a daughter only a few weeks old, to Tuckahoe while he stayed to supervise removal of records. As the wife of a signer of the Declaration of Independence and the governor's wife, Martha Wayles Jefferson would have been a prime catch for the British. Jefferson caught up with his family at 1 a.m. on January

5, escorted them another eight miles and then returned to Westham to supervise the evacuation of the government. Jefferson checked on his family on the sixth and then returned to his official duties. In light of Jefferson's efforts to fulfill his duties to both family and Virginia, it is little wonder he was frustrated with John Tyler. Tyler refused to gather with other government leaders until "my little domestic affairs are brought into order again" after being "obliged to retire to a more secure situation with their Families."[57]

Martha Jefferson's travels and troubles were not over. She moved multiple times, trying to stay close to her husband and out of reach of the British. In the midst of these constant comings and goings, tragedy struck. Lucy Elizabeth Jefferson, aged four and a half months, died on April 15. There was little time to mourn. Two weeks later, the family was again on the move, but having trouble because the quartermaster had requisitioned all the canoes in the area and sent them down river with grain for the troops. When Richmond proved too vulnerable as a capital, and the government moved temporarily to Charlottesville, Martha returned home, serving as hostess to several of the legislators. Jefferson's term of governor was over and he returned home. The Jeffersons were about to serve breakfast to their guests when on June 4, Banastre Tarleton's troops swept into the area. Martha and the children quickly packed and were sent down the mountain in a carriage. The legislators rode off to warn the town, and Jefferson packed up papers and left by horseback through the woods ten minutes ahead of the British. He hoped to lead the troops away from his family. The Jeffersons were reunited at Colonel Cole's home, where they ate, and then continued to Colonel Hugh Rose's plantation in Amherst County the next day. Jefferson left them there, rode back to Monticello, then returned to escort his family from the Roses' to Poplar Forest in Bedford County, the plantation Martha had inherited from her father.[58]

When more than 7,000 British, loyalist, and German soldiers descended on tiny Yorktown, residents were overwhelmed. Camp followers, loyalists, and escaping slaves, who continued to seek refuge behind British lines, swelled the population of the town. As loyalist Jacob Ellegood reported "almost every house in York is pulled down, poor Mrs. Riddle I feel for her I was quarter'd at her house while I stay'd in York, her distress and many more must be horrid, that country for many miles round must be ruin'd." It is not clear whether Riddle was there or whether her empty house had been commandeered, but once the British left, she faced a ruined town and house. The dislocation grew after surrender, for the Americans began moving the prisoners of war inland as rapidly as they could. Half of those able to travel went to Winchester and the other half to Frederick Town in Maryland, but about 1,700 remained in Gloucester, too sick to move. About 250 loyalists and escaped slaves (including Sally Dennis, from the Burwell plantation and Deborah from George Washington's estate) used a loophole in the terms of surrender to pack on the British sloop *Bonetta* and thus escape to New York. By the time the British offered transportation to Nova Scotia, Deborah had married Harry Squash, a slave of an artillery officer. Polly, Deborah, and Harry all went to Nova Scotia. Others were not so lucky, as freedom proved temporary for many of the escaped slaves who had reached British lines. Virginians like Washington searched among slaves recaptured at the surrender of Yorktown for escaped slaves Lucy and Esther. They had been received as refugees in April on board the *Savage*. Washington reclaimed both women and returned them to his plantations.[59]

Camp Followers and Prisoners of War

British, German, and American troops all traveled with women camp followers, many of whom were wives of soldiers, and some of whom held regularly paid positions with the troops. Other women accompanied male civilian support personnel such as sutlers, carpenters, and smiths. They provided necessary support services—including cooking, washing, and nursing—that today are performed by specialized units within the armed forces. These women traveled with the baggage, and their presence was a part of the logistical challenges facing any eighteenth-century army on the move. While officers' wives were less likely to travel continuously with troops, many joined their husbands between campaigns. Although many gave up the conveniences of their homes, their social class and resources meant that their experiences were very different from those of women following enlisted men. Although their contemporaries did not refer to officers' wives as camp followers, all that separated these women from that label was their class. Camp followers were as racially and ethnically diverse as the soldiers they accompanied. They also had choices. For women in officer's families, the choices were not as stark. Many had homes where they could remain, or relatives with whom they could stay, but were intent on avoiding years of separation and living as dependents in the homes of relations.[60] Even on campaign, they could choose to stay close to the troops or find lodging in more comfortable areas. On several occasions, the British tried to get women to remain in cities where they had encampments while troops were on maneuvers. Enlisted men's kin had fewer resources and often no home or means of support away from their male kin. If left behind, as happened to the families of German soldiers when their units were sent south in 1781, the women could come close to starvation and be forced into prostitution to support themselves.[61] In 1777, when Williamsburg was a collecting point for American troops, impoverished camp followers so filled the town that a panicked Bruton Parish vestry and wardens petitioned the General Assembly to ensure that these poor would not be counted as residents and thus have a claim on the parish for relief.[62] When their menfolk became prisoners of war, many of the women chose to stay with the troops and went into captivity with them.

The surrender of British and German troops after the Battle of Saratoga in 1777 eventually affected Virginia. The new nation suddenly had several thousand prisoners to feed, house, and prevent from escaping to British lines. Among the prisoners were several hundred women. In early 1779, the "Convention Army" (as the Saratoga prisoners were called) arrived in the Charlottesville, Virginia, area. It had been a long trip. The women with them had walked from Canada to Saratoga, carrying their possessions in huge baskets on their backs. When the convention prisoners were first marched to Boston, the women picked up their baskets and marched along. Boston, however, was just a temporary stop. The 4,145 men faced a long winter march from Cambridge, Massachusetts, to Virginia without proper clothing. General von Riedesel, the ranking German officer among the prisoners, turned to the women camp followers among his troops to better supply his men. The women were ordered to cut off the long skirts on the men's coats to get cloth to patch their uniforms. Holding special inspections, the commanders then praised the women for the neatest patches. Riedesel paid the women to knit caps and mittens. When the Convention Army left for Virginia, the women finally got to ride on some of the 384 wagons accompanying the troops. Once in Virginia, the enlisted men and lower-ranking officers built barracks near Ivy Creek, where the prisoners were allowed to supplement rations by gardening. The women shared these basic accommodations.[63]

The senior officers rented homes in Albemarle County, near Charlottesville. The ranking British officer, William Phillips, rented Blenheim from Edward Carter. By the time Baron von Riedesel arrived, British officers had secured most of the limited stock of available housing. Riedesel rented Phillip Mazzei's home, Colle, where his wife and three children soon joined him. After a journey of more than 700 miles in an open coach, the baroness arrived to the smell of rotted meat improperly preserved on the Mazzei estate. Mazzei was busy preparing to move to Europe and sold all his furniture at auction. The Riedesel's built their own house on the property, where they and the British officers soon became a part of the local social life, including dining with Thomas Jefferson, who sold the Riedesels a pianoforte so the baroness could have an instrument to play. Jefferson even granted the Riedesel's special permission to travel to Virginia's hot springs spas in Louisa, Berkley, and Augusta counties. While the baroness was at Berkley Springs in September, she received word that the family had been given permission to return to the British in New York under parole. Leaving immediately, they stopped in Bethlehem, Pennsylvania, for six weeks while the very pregnant baroness nursed her children through the whooping cough. By early 1780 they were in New York.[64]

The German troops, however, remained in Virginia, where conditions deteriorated. The enlisted men's wives and daughters were not worrying about finding a pianoforte or entertaining guests. They were working as day laborers, washing, cooking, and struggling on limited rations in the barracks. The winter of 1779–1780 was very severe, with prolonged spells below freezing throughout December and January. There was still snow on the ground in Hanover County in April. The harvest that year was inadequate. By 1780 Virginia could not clothe and feed its own troops, much less several thousand prisoners of war and their dependents. Apparently both men and women among the prisoners were hiring out their labor in hopes of supplementing supplies. When Generals Leslie and Arnold arrived in late winter, the Americans feared the British troops would free the prisoners and add them to the British ranks. Thus, in November, Governor Jefferson struggled to find wagons "to lighten the inconveniences which will attend their removal" and gave orders that an accounting be made of the money owed "to soldiers, women, &c. about to remove" so that their pay could be sent to them.[65] Because, except for invalids, the prisoners would walk, the wagons were for their gear, their wives, and their families. The Americans moved 800 British prisoners to Fort Frederick, Maryland, but moved the 1,500 German captives and their dependents only to Winchester, in Virginia, where they were "in a distressed situation for want of covering and food" and so were quickly returned to the Albemarle County barracks. That spring, supplies remained very short and, with the militia called out to deal with the invasion, farms were shorthanded. In response, the Americans allowed the German prisoners to hire out to farmers, who would serve as security and feed them.[66] Presumably, German women were already working for pay because they were technically not prisoners.

Conclusion

As raids intensified along the coast, the frontier war also heated up. In 1779, a new wave of settlers flowed into Kentucky reoccupying abandoned forts and adding new ones. As the British renewed their raids on coastal Virginia, sending new waves of refugees in 1780, they also launched raids from Detroit against settlements in Kentucky, thus taking advantage of the fact that Virginia commander George Rogers Clark was concentrating on the far west of Illinois. The British took more than 350 prisoners from Ruddle's and Martin's Stations, including many women and children. Clark's response was to destroy the Shawnee town of Chillicothe and their corn supplies, forcing the residents to become refugees. Other frontiersmen under Colonel John Sevier launched a preemptive strike in December 1780 against the Cherokee, destroying Chota and ten other settlements, including more than a thousand homes and 50,000 bushels of corn. The result was that a good portion of the Cherokee nation became refugees again, and many women and children had to depend on supplies from the British to survive the winter. Most of the destruction occurred after a delegation of Cherokee led by Nancy Ward tried to sue for peace. "With the prisoners, perhaps twenty Women and children, some Horses, and Goods," Sevier hastened back to his base. The twenty actually included seventeen prisoners, mostly women and children, and Nancy Ward and her family. The latter were technically refugees, not prisoners. With homes destroyed, there was no reason to stay. An ally of the Americans, Ward now expected "be maintained by the publick."[67]

Between 1779 and 1781 the backcountry of Virginia was hit by waves of refugees from both the east and the west as the conflict moved to the Southern states. With supplies short everywhere, hunger was very real for uprooted women in a state that had no governmental systems in place to deal with them. Refugees were forced to rely on friends and family. The tangled cousinry of Virginia genealogy now proved an asset. The bonds of community, stretched and frayed by a civil war, nonetheless were crucial factors in women's decision making. Loyalist women pooled resources and lived together; African American women took their children with them as they escaped and often escaped with others from their same plantation; women seeking refuge relied on bonds of friendship and kin to find a haven. How dire one's circumstances were depended greatly on class. Martha Jefferson was uprooted multiple times, but each time she settled on another Jefferson-owned property. En route, she could count on the hospitality of friends. The house might be small or inconvenient, but she always had a refuge. Rebecca Aitchison, like Martha Jefferson, had other property to turn to when her home in Norfolk burned. It was crowded, and she had to do unaccustomed work, but she had a refuge. Baroness von Riedesel, like the other elite women, had options and her income and status assured her of a residence. By contrast, Nancy Ward, though she might be a leader of her people, was forced to become a dependent of the state after the destruction of her town. Women from the middle and yeoman classes might find themselves truly homeless. With a shortage of tents, the Americans could not even guarantee that level of shelter. In 1781, the British could offer little more to those who sought their protection. In fact, they turned many of the escaped slaves out of Yorktown, forcing them into the no-man's-land between armies and eventually into the hands of Americans.

Throughout the war, women assessed their options. Those who uprooted themselves were clearly identified with one side or another and felt threatened. They understood their lives had a political dimension. Those who returned quickly to an area or remained even when given an opportunity to flee had also clearly made a choice. Mrs. Agnew and Elizabeth Feilde, wives of Tory clergy, were themselves supporters of the British. Feilde left with her husband, but Agnew hid in the swamps until she could join her husband. Left behind by her loyalist husband, Rebecca Aitchison lived quietly, obeying the new government throughout the war and retaining her property. Although Aitchison left after the war to reunite with her husband in Nova Scotia, others (including Ann Roberts) never reunited with their husbands and remained in Virginia.[68] When an enslaved woman chose to flee, she thought she was making a permanent choice to leave. The fact that, tragically, for women like Lucy and Esther from Washington's plantations, their escape from slavery to freedom proved temporary does not erase the intentionality of their original escape.

The scale of uprooting in Virginia during the Revolution was huge. If even a third of Norfolk's population was female, the burning of the town left 2,000 women homeless. The evacuation of Portsmouth and the surrounding countryside disrupted the lives of at least another 10,000. In view of the number of escaped slaves reported in Dunmore's forces and transported by the British at the end of the war, at least 2,000 more (and possibly as many as 12,000) of Virginia's women uprooted themselves by escaping slavery.[69] Using conservative formulas, it is safe to estimate at least another 100–200 women accompanied prisoners of war to Virginia. To this number we must add those loyalists who left Virginia, the entire Indian villages left homeless, and the frontier settlers who fled to the safety of a fortification or more settled area. The personal was political for Virginia women during the war. They made their basic life decisions in a politicized context of civil war, which was grudgingly recognized by male leaders. Their labor was a valuable commodity that made leaders care what women decided. Officials made few accommodations to the masses of displaced women struggling to survive in Virginia. Policymakers' only efforts were providing compensation for homes destroyed in Norfolk and occasional relief to a petitioner, supplying some wagons for women traveling with prisoners of war, and passing legislation designed to allow women to retain a dower claim on confiscated loyalist property (and thus to have a home and subsistence).

There were certainly constraints affecting women's choices, and Virginians only reluctantly recognized the political nature of women's actions. Ideology dictated a dependent role for women incompatible with the reality of Virginia women's lives. The result was an ambiguity that cloaked the political implications raised by displaced women during the war but that could never quite erase it. Thus, only traces were left for modern women's historians to follow. By using Virginia as a case study, it is possible to recover the political dimension of women's lives and the extent to which even women traditionally characterized as dependent or helpless refugees were actively involved in determining their lives. There has long been a tendency to focus northward, to Boston and New York, for the story of the first years of the war for independence. Looking southward, however, balances the story. Small skirmishes could result in major destruction, as the residents of Norfolk learned in 1776. The fact that Virginia was faced with almost 20,000 people displaced by the conflict before July 1776 could not help but shape perceptions that there was no turning back on the road to independence. Historians will be well served by looking more closely at the war's impact on civilians, especially women and children, if they wish to understand how the battle for people's hearts and minds was won.

Notes

1. E[lizabeth] Feilde to [Mrs. Maria Carter Armistead], June 3, 1776, Armistead-Cocke Papers, Swem Library, College of William and Mary.

2. John E. Selby, *The Revolution in Virginia, 1775–1783* (Williamsburg, Va.: Colonial Williamsburg Foundation, 1988), p. 177; Hugh Edward Edgerton, ed., *The Royal Commission on the Losses and Services of American Loyalists, 1783–1785 Being the Notes of Mr. Daniel Parker Coke, M.P., One of the Commissioners During That Period* (New York: Burt Franklin, 1914), p. 268.

3. Traditional passive interpretations are found in Mary Beth Norton, *Liberty's Daughters: The Revolutionary Experience of American Women, 1750–1800* (Boston: Little, Brown, 1980), pp. 206–12; Cynthia A. Kierner, *Southern Women in Revolution, 1776–1800: Personal and Political Narratives* (Columbia: University of South Carolina Press, 1998), p. 4; and Elaine Forman Crane, *A Dependent People: Newport, Rhode Island, in the Revolutionary Era* (New York: Fordham University Press, 1985), pp. 92, 122–23, 158–59. Even Linda Kerber, who tends to credit women with more agency, portrayed women refugees as so traumatized by the experience that they embraced the cult of domesticity after the war. Linda K. Kerber, *Women of the Republic: Intellect and Ideology in Revolutionary America* (Chapel Hill: University of North Carolina Press for the Institute of Early American History and Culture, 1980), p. 47.

4. John Montgomery to Thomas Jefferson, New Orleans, January 8, 1781; John Todd to Thomas Jefferson, Lexington, January 24, 1781; Arthur Campbell to Thomas Jefferson, Washington County, January 27, 1781, all in Julian P. Boyd, Lyman H. Butterfield, and Mina R. Bryan, eds., *The Papers of Thomas Jefferson,* (Princeton, N.J.: Princeton University Press, 1950–), 4:319–20, 422, 457.

5. Selby, *Revolution in Virginia,* passim.

6. Adele Hast, *Loyalism in Revolutionary Virginia: The Norfolk Area and the Eastern Shore* (Ann Arbor: UMI Research Press, 1979 and 1982), p. 99; Selby, *Revolution in Virginia,* pp. 206–7.

7. Carter Braxton to Thomas Jefferson, May 16, 1781, in Boyd, Butterfield, and Bryan, *Jefferson,* 5:656–57; Alonzo Thomas Dill, "Braxton, Carter," *American National Biography Online* (New York: Oxford University Press, for the American Council of Learned Societies, 2000), <http://www.anb.org/articles/02/02-00040.html> (accessed April 7, 2004).

8. Hast, *Loyalism,* pp. 34, 67. Elizabeth Fielde inquired about her friend's pregnancy several times. E[lizabeth] Feilde to [Maria Carter Armistead], [January] 3, 1776, and E[lizabeth] Feilde to [Maria Armistead], February 8, 1776, Armistead-Cocke Papers.

9. Edgerton, *Royal Commission,* p. 268; Otto Lohrenz, "The Advantage of Rank and Status: Thomas Price, a Loyalist Parson of Revolutionary Virginia," *Historian* 60 (1998): 561.

10. Julia Cherry Spruill, *Women's Life and Work in the Southern Colonies* (New York: Norton, 1972), pp. 170–71.

11. Louis B. Wright, *The First Gentlemen of Virginia* (Charlottesville: University Press of Virginia, 1964), p. 327.

12. Mary Willing Byrd to [Thomas Nelson], Westover, August 10, 1781, in Boyd, Butterfield, and Bryan, *Jefferson,* 6:703–4.

13. Mary Willing Byrd to Thomas Jefferson, Westover, February 23, 1781, in Boyd, Butterfield, and Bryan, *Jefferson,* 4:689–90. Boyd reprinted the letter from Benson J. Lossing, ed., *American Historical Record* 2 (1783), pp. 4667–69.

14. Mary Willing Byrd to Sir Guy Carleton, Westover, June 5, 1783, in Boyd, Butterfield, and Bryan, *Jefferson,* 6:704–5. See Boyd, Butterfield, and Bryan, *Jefferson,* 5:671–81; Thomas Jefferson to Mary Willing Byrd, in council, March 1, 1781; Mary Willing Byrd to [Thomas Nelson], Westover, August 10, 1781, both in Boyd, Butterfield, and Bryan, *Jefferson,* 5:31–32, 6:703–4; Selby, *Revolution in Virginia,* p. 268.

15. Jack M. Sosin, *The Revolutionary Frontier, 1763–1783* (New York: Holt, Rinehart and Winston, 1967), pp. 89–91; Theda Perdue, *Cherokee Women: Gender and Culture Change, 1700–1835* (Lincoln: University of Nebraska Press, 1998), pp. 106–8.

16. Brent Tarter, "'An Infant Borough Entirely Supported by Commerce': The Great Fire of 1776 and the Rebuilding of Norfolk," *Virginia Cavalcade* 28 (1978): 56–57; Hast, *Loyalism,* pp. 9–11.

17. Hast, *Loyalism,* pp. 10–11

18. Selby, *Revolution in Virginia,* pp. 17–18; David Ammerman, *In the Common Cause: American Response to the Coercive Acts of 1774* (New York: W. W. Norton, 1974), pp. 30–38; Hast, *Loyalism,* pp. 15–25.

19. Woody Holton, *Forced Founders: Indians, Debtors, Slaves, and the Making of the American Revolution in Virginia* (Chapel Hill: University of North Carolina Press for the Omohundro Institute of Early American History and Culture, 1999), pp. 148–53. Selby, *Revolution in Virginia,* pp. 1–5, 41–45, 47; James Parker to Charles Steuart, May 6, June 12, and June 27, 1775, *Magazine of History* 3 (1906): 158–59.

20. Selby, *Revolution in Virginia,* pp. 58–59, 62–65, 81–84; Hast, *Loyalism,* pp. 46, 52; Robert McCluer Calhoun, *The Loyalists in Revolutionary America, 1760–1781* (New York: Harcout, Brace and Jovanovich, 1965), p. 462; extract of a letter from Norfolk, in Virginia, October 28, 1775, printed in the *Morning Chronicle and London Advertiser,* December 28, 1775, in Margaret Wheeler Willard, *Letters on the American Revolution, 1774–1776* (Princeton, N.J.: Houghton Mifflin, 1925), pp. 221–22.

21. Selby, *Revolution in Virginia,* pp. 81–84; extract of a letter from a Midshipman, December 9, printed in *Lloyd's Evening Post and British Chronicle,* March 4–6, 1776, in Willard, *Letters,* pp. 234–39; Hast, *Loyalism,* pp. 55–57; Tarter, "Norfolk," pp. 53–57.

22. Extract of a letter from a Gentleman at Norfolk, in Virginia, to his Friend in Aberdeen, October 20, 1775, printed in *Lloyd's Evening Post and British Chronicle,* in Willard, *Letters,* p. 218.

23. Claim of Penelope D'Ende', widow of William Forsayth, March 20, 1784, in Edgerton, *Royal Commission,* p. 111.

24. Hast, *Loyalism,* pp. 48–50, 80.

25. Hast, *Loyalism,* p. 45, 57; Calhoun, *Loyalists,* p. 464; Selby, *Revolution in Virginia,* p. 68.

26. Mary Webley Petition to Virginia General Assembly, October 11, 1776, Norfolk Borough, reel 213, Library of Virginia.

27. Commissioners Report, Deposition of Sarah Smith, no. 19. The investigation by special commissioners was so damaging to the Americans that it was suppressed for fifty years before publication.

28. Selby, *Revolution in Virginia,* pp. 206–7.

29. Commissioners Appointed by the Act of the General Assembly, October 10, 1777, Schedule of Claims entered for Losses Sustained; George Kelly Affidavit, December 11, 1787, Commissioners File, Library of Virginia; Edgerton, *Royal Commission,* pp. 92–94.

30. Extract of a letter from Norfolk, in Virginia, February 20, 1776, printed in *Lloyd's Evening Post and British Chronicle,* April 15–17, 1776, in Willard, *Letters,* pp. 262–63.

31. Virginia General Assembly, Legislative Petitions, Norfolk Borough, 1776–1811, December 17, 1776, reel 213, Library of Virginia.

32. Mrs. [Margaret] Parker to Charles Steuart, January 3, 1779, Princess Anne, in "Letters" *Magazine of History* 3 (April 1906): 214–15; Hast, *Loyalism,* pp. 73–74, 82–83, 129; Lieutenant Colonel Ellegood Testimony on William Atchison Claim, June 25, 1785, in Edgerton, *Royal Commission,* pp. 390–91.

33. Hast, *Loyalism,* p. 30.

34. Hast, *Loyalism,* pp. 5, 62–66, 131; Humphrey Roberts Claim, June 13, 1785, in Edgerton, *Royal Commission,* pp. 385–86; Selby, *Revolution in Virginia,* p. 204.

35. Jacob Ellegood Claim, February 4, 1784, in Edgerton, *Royal Commission,* pp. 70–71; Jacob Ellegood to Charles Steuart, October 16, 1781, New York, in "Letters," *Magazine of History* 3 (April 1906): 215–16; ibid., March 23, 1782, p. 217.

36. Selby, *Revolution in Virginia,* pp. 206–7; Jenny Steuart to Charles Steuart, November 1779; Mrs. Parker to Charles Steuart, January 3, 1779, Princess Anne, both in "Letters," *Magazine of History* 3 (April 1906): 215, 214–15; Tarter, "Norfolk," p. 57.

37. Selby, *Revolution in Virginia,* pp. 149, 155–56. Hast, *Loyalism,* pp. 48–50; Petition of

Margaret Goodrich to the General Assembly, October 23, 1778, RG 78, box 175, folder 1, Nansemond County, Library of Virginia microfilm; Petition of Dorothy Goodrich to General Assembly, May 26, 1779, Miscellaneous Petitions, Library of Virginia, microfilm.

38. Holton, *Forced Founders*, pp. 152–55.

39. Hast, *Loyalism*, p. 46; extract of a letter from Norfolk, in Virginia, October 28, 1775, printed in the *Morning Chronicle and London Advertiser*, December 28, 1775, in Willard, *Letters*, pp. 221–22; Holly A. Mayer, *Belonging to the Army: Camp Followers and Community during the American Revolution* (Columbia: University of South Carolina Press, 1996), p. 165; Calhoun, *Loyalists*, p. 462.

40. Mary Willing Byrd to [Governor Thomas Nelson], Westover, August 10, 1781, in Boyd, Butterfield, and Bryan, *Jefferson*, 6:703–4; Boyd, Butterfield, and Bryan, *Jefferson*, 5:680–81.

41. Petition of Margaret Goodrich to the General Assembly, October 23, 1778, RG 78, box 175, folder 1, Library of Virginia, Nansemond County microfilm.

42. Joan R. Gundersen, *"To Be Useful to the World": Women in Revolutionary America, 1740–1790* (New York: Twayne, 1996), p. 64; Thomas Randolph to Mrs. Randolph, November 16, 1776, Tucker-Coleman Papers, Swem Library, College of William and Mary.

43. George Mutter to Thomas Jefferson, War Office, January 24, 1781; Nicholas Everleigh to Thomas Jefferson, Mecklenburg Co., November 25, 1780, both in Boyd, Butterfield, and Bryan, *Jefferson*, 4:438–39, 152.

44. Thomas Gaskins to Thomas Jefferson, Northumberland, April 13, 1781, in Boyd, Butterfield, and Bryan, *Jefferson*, 5:430; Fritz Hirschfield, "'Burnt All Their Houses': The Log of the HMS *Savage* during a Raid up the Potomac River, Spring 1781," *Virginia Magazine of History and Biography* 99 (1991): 522–24.

45. Benjamin Quarles, *The Negro in the American Revolution* (Chapel Hill: University of North Carolina Press for the Institute of Early American History and Culture, 1961), pp. 19–32.

46. Petition of John Cooper to Virginia General Assembly, May 31, 1777, RG #78, box 181, folder 2, Library of Virginia, Norfolk County microfilm; Selby, *Revolution in Virginia*, pp. 104, 125; Calhoun, *Loyalists*, p. 462; Quarles, *Negro*, pp. 171–72.

47. Graham Russell Hodges, ed., *The Black Loyalist Directory: African Americans in Exile after the American Revolution* (New York: Garland, 1996). For the specific cases of the Dixons, Tankard, and Stratton, see pp. 30, 104, and 190.

48. Lorena Walsh, *From Calabar to Carter's Grove: The History of a Virginia Slave Community* (Charlottesville: University Press of Virginia, 1997), pp. 251, 311.

49. Quarles, *Negro*, pp. 26, 27n.

50. Hirschfield, "HMS *Savage*," pp. 522–24. George Washington to Lund Washington, April 30, 1781, in the George Washington Papers at the Library of Congress, letterbook 2, ser. 3h, Varick Transcripts, American Memory on-line. A footnote in the Fitzpatrick edition of Washington's writings cites a document listing the losses from the raid, identifying it as coming from the Toner Transcripts. It lists the slaves who left and the fact that a boat with a twenty-four-foot keel also was taken. The on-line version uses the Fitzpatrick work as its source of a transcription and annotation. John C. Fitzpatrick, ed., *The Writings of George Washington from the Original Manuscript Sources, 1745–1799*, 39 vols. (Washington, D.C.: Government Printing Office, 1931–1944), 22:14–15.

51. Mayer, *Belonging to the Army*, p. 166.

52. Thomas Jefferson to Horatio Gates, November 19, 1780; Virginia Delegates in Congress to Thomas Jefferson, Philadelphia, January [23], 1781; Thomas Jefferson to Thomas Newton, February 3, 1781, all in Boyd, Butterfield, and Bryan, *Jefferson*, 4:127, 436, 521.

53. Selby, *Revolution in Virginia*, pp. 204–7.

54. Thomas Jones to Thomas Jefferson, March 30, 1781, in Boyd, Butterfield, and Bryan, *Jefferson*, 5:295.

55. Selby, *Revolution in Virginia*, pp. 216–17, 221, 223; Thomas Jefferson to Thomas Sim Lee, January 30, 1780; William Peachey to Thomas Jefferson, Richmond, March

31, 1781; Thomas Jefferson to Philip Mazzei, Williamsburg, April 4, 1780, all in Boyd, Butterfield, and Bryan, *Jefferson,* 3:279–80, 5:305, 3:341–43.

56. Selby, *Revolution in Virginia,* pp. 265, 269, 272–74; Hirschfield, "HMS *Savage,*" p. 515, passim; Richard Bush, "Raids on the Potomac, March–April, 1781," *Northern Neck of Virginia Historical Magazine* 45 (1995):1518–23.

57. Diary of Arnold's Invasion and Notes on Subsequent Events in 1781, the 1796? version; John Tyler to Thomas Jefferson, Charles City, February 3, 1781, both in Boyd, Butterfield, and Bryan, *Jefferson,* 5:258–59, 4:522–23.

58. Boyd, Butterfield, and Bryan, *Jefferson,* 4:261; Diary of Arnold's Invasion and Notes on Subsequent Events in 1781, the 1796? version; Thomas Jefferson to David Jameson, April 16, 1781; Volling Stark to Thomas Jefferson, Fairfield, April 30, 1781, all in Boyd, Butterfield, and Bryan, *Jefferson,* 5:258–59, 468–69, 579–80; Selby, *Revolution in Virginia,* pp. 275–80; 1816 Version of the Diary and Notes of 1781; Deposition of Christopher Hudson respecting Tarleton's Raid in June 1781, July 26, 1805, both in Selby, *Revolution in Virginia,* pp. 265, 277.

59. Jacob Ellegood to Charles Steuart, October 16, 1781, New York, in "Letters," *Magazine of History* 3 (April 1906): 216–17; Selby, *Revolution in Virginia,* p. 311. *Register,* p. 172, 16. Fitzpatrick, *The Writings of George Washington,* 22:14–15.

60. Baroness Frederika von Riedesel, who came to Virginia in 1779 with the Convention Army prisoners of war, fits this description.

61. Mayer, *Belonging to the Army,* passim; Louise Hall Tharp, *The Baroness and the General* (Boston: Little, Brown, 1962), p. 357.

62. Petition of the Church Wardens and Vestry of Bruton Parish to the General Assembly, May 20, 1777, York County Petitions, box 260, folder 9, Library of Virginia.

63. Tharp, *Baroness,* pp. 254, 268, 290–91; Selby, *Revolution in Virginia,* pp. 218, 220.

64. Tharp, *Baroness,* pp. 312–17, 335; Thomas Jefferson to Riedesel [July 1779]; Riedesel to Thomas Jefferson, New York, March 30, 1780, both in Boyd, Butterfield, and Bryan, *Jefferson,* 3:59–60, 338.

65. Riedesel to Thomas Jefferson, New York, March 30, 1780; letter in council, Thomas Jefferson to James Wood, November 16, 1780, both in Boyd, Butterfield, and Bryan, *Jefferson,* 3:338, 4:16; Selby, *Revolution in Virginia,* pp. 197, 218, 220, 245.

66. Thomas Jefferson to James Wood, Richmond, January 12, 1781; Francis Taylor to Thomas Jefferson, Winchester, May 5, 1781, both in Boyd, Butterfield, and Bryan, *Jefferson,* 4:347, 5:607.

67. Selby, *Revolution in Virginia,* pp. 198–203; Arthur Campbell to Thomas Jefferson, Washington County, January 15, 1781; Arthur Campbell to Thomas Jefferson, Washington County, January 27, 1781; Joseph Martin to Thomas Jefferson, February 7, 1781; Arthur Campbell to Thomas Jefferson, Washington, March 28, 1781; William Christian to Thomas Jefferson, Montgomery County, April 10, 1781; John Floyd to Thomas Jefferson, April 16, 1781; Arthur Campbell to Thomas Jefferson, Washington, April 25, 1781; Thomas Jefferson to Arthur Campbell, Richmond, February 17, 1781, all in Boyd, Butterfield, and Bryan, *Jefferson,* 4:359–62, 457, 551–52, 5:267–68, 395–96, 465–68, 552–53, 4:634.

68. Hast, *Loyalism,* p. 131.

69. My low estimate is a simple rounding up to the nearest thousand of the numbers of women among the slaves with Dunmore in 1776 and among those resettled in Nova Scotia after the war. Thomas Jefferson estimated that 30,000 of Virginia's slaves escaped during the war. Historians have thought his estimate an exaggeration, but the numbers are not unreasonable. Women were about 40 percent of both the Dunmore and Nova Scotia groups. I applied that percentage to the Jefferson figure to get an upper estimate. The Jefferson comment is found in Holton, *Forced Founders,* p. 219. Cassandra Pybus has recently questioned Jefferson's numbers as much too high. Cassandra Pybus, "Jefferson's Faulty Math: The Question of Slave Defections in the American Revolution," *William and Mary Quarterly,* 3rd ser., 62 (April 2005): 243–64.

HISTORIOGRAPHIC ESSAY

11

CHANGING MEANINGS OF THE AMERICAN REVOLUTION

An Overview, 1789–2006

JOHN RESCH AND

WALTER SARGENT

The American Revolutionary War has challenged every generation of historians to describe and interpret the essential meanings of the struggle for independence. During the time of the Revolution itself, the understandings of the conflict were hotly contested. The Revolution was simultaneously a war for political independence, a revolution for social reform, a struggle for emancipation, a civil war over political power, and a war for survival. Thousands of volumes have been published on the American Revolution since the founding era. This essay will offer a brief synopsis of the major contours of the various schools of thought with emphasis on the current directions of American Revolutionary history.

In 1789, just six years after the Treaty of Paris, David Ramsay published one of the first comprehensive accounts of the war, *The History of the American Revolution*. In it, he offered a slightly less partisan account than the fiery wartime pamphlets but largely reinforced the justifications for the war. Ramsay's work is an example of the early "Whig History"—the inevitable progress toward a democratic and constitutional society. By reminding readers of how all Americans had shared in the hardships of the war for independence, Ramsay contributed to a sense of national unity at the time when the U.S. Constitution was just being implemented.[1] Mercy Otis Warren, the first woman to write on the Revolution, published a multivolume history in 1805 that also validated the American independence movement as a beacon of "liberty, righteousness, and truth."[2]

For the first postwar generation, whom Joyce Appleby has labeled "the inheritors," the claim to the mantle of the Founders was a valuable and hard-fought prize for both Republicans and

Federalists because they presented competing visions of America.[3] As a consequence the literature consisted primarily of biographies of such icons as George Washington. By the time of the passing of the last Founders, American poets and writers began to single out and honor the heroism of the soldiers of the Revolution.[4] Ralph Waldo Emerson's "Concord Hymn" (1837) and Henry Wadsworth Longfellow's "Midnight Ride of Paul Revere" (1860) memorialized the "embattled farmer" who left his plow in the fields to defend his liberty by firing the "shot heard round the world." Historians, however, did not include ordinary soldiers in their narratives of the Revolution despite journals, correspondence, and memoirs by officers and men that contained rich descriptions of their experiences during the war and their views of the character of the Revolution.

During the 1830s, in the midst of American expansionism, George Bancroft produced a multivolume history that celebrated the democratic spirit born of the Revolution and reaffirmed the greatness and destiny of America.[5] Bancroft's treatment of the Revolution was less an attempt at analysis than a nationalistic narrative intended to swell patriotic pride. Despite its savagery and heavy cost in lives on both sides, the Civil War was viewed by victorious Northerners as the conclusion of the Revolution and as affirmation of a particular vision of America, eloquently expressed by Lincoln as an experiment in self-government dedicated to liberty. By the time of the centennial, in 1876, historians celebrated America's progression from its idealized birth in Revolution through nationhood.

As America emerged as a great industrial power in the late nineteenth century, however, concerns emerged that the Revolutionary ideas of equality and liberty were failing. During the Progressive era at the turn-of-the-twentieth century, social critics such as Carl Becker portrayed the Revolution as the first salvo in an ongoing battle for social justice fueled by class conflict, which he claimed was one of its central features. Becker's study of the Revolution in New York argued that the contest was as much over "who should rule at home" as independence from Britain. In 1913, historian Charles Beard added to this view by arguing that the leaders of the Revolutionary movement sought to promote foremost their own economic advantages rather than "liberty and justice for all." Beard's thesis is that the Founders orchestrated the writing of the U.S. Constitution to protect their political and property rights and enhance the fortunes of the elite faction who had managed to steer the Revolution. Beard's thesis sparked the "Progressive School" and shaped historiography for several succeeding generations of twentieth-century historians. Reinforcing Beard's view, historian J. Franklin Jameson emphasized the potential for social revolution during the War for Independence. He wrote that the Revolution was like "a stream that overflowed its banks to spread across the land" but that a conservative elite turned back its egalitarian and democratic impulses.[6] These interpretations of the Revolution constituted a clarion call for social reformers to renew efforts for creating a just society. As in earlier periods, the Revolution was interpreted for its use in addressing issues facing the nation.

An alternate school of historians working during the years between the world wars remained focused on intellectual issues and reinterpreted the Revolution as a constitutional squabble and a policy battle between the British government and colonial political leaders. Historians such as Charles MacLean Andrews stressed the cultural affinity between Americans and their British forbearers, characterizing the split as akin to a family fight. These historians are known as the "Imperial School," and one of their intentions was to highlight the solidarity of the Anglo-American tradition.[7]

Following World War II, the majority of historians pursued new interpretations of the Revolution. In so doing they rejected the view of the Revolution as an Imperial feud and especially the Progressive School's materialist thesis of class conflict and the Revolution as a means to sustain elite power. By then, Beard's calculations had been systematically scrutinized and his thesis had gradually succumbed to critics in the face of increasingly persuasive analyses of contrary evidence. In the context of the Cold War, historians of the 1950s like Louis Hartz, Daniel Boorstin, Robert E. Brown, John Alden, and Edmund Morgan found a broad consensus on the liberal traditions of democracy and freedom among colonial and Revolutionary Americans. These works generally agreed on the democratic and egalitarian character of colonial Americans, and they characterized the Revolution as a popular defense of traditional rights against tyranny and oppression. In this view, the archetypal citizen-soldier reemerged as a nobly inspired defender of liberty and republican principles rather than a contestant for power in a conflict-ridden society. These historians, labeled the "Consensus School," depicted the revolutionaries not as radicals but as conservatives who were simply defending the existing social order and existing American traditions of liberty.[8]

In the 1960s, Bernard Bailyn carried the notion of popular consensus into the realm of ideology. Bailyn argued that Americans' view of their relationship with Britain was shaped by neoclassical republican ideology. Bailyn studied the torrent of Revolutionary-era pamphlets and observed that they drew on radical and libertarian English traditions, such that ordinary readers were motivated by fear of losing their constitutional rights and their property to an increasingly tyrannical aristocratic ministry. In his extraordinary study, *The Ideological Origins of the American Revolution*, Bailyn concluded that republican ideology was at the core of Americans' belief system. A critical difference between Bailyn's republican synthesis and the Consensus position of the 1950s might be described as follows: whereas the Consensus School historians saw democratic impulses originating almost organically in the soil and toil of independent-minded American farmers, the republican thesis posited that the formation of American Revolutionary notions arose out Americans' adoption of British republican and libertarian traditions, which collided with British imperial policy following the Peace of Paris of 1763.[9]

Following Bailyn's lead, scholars confirmed that Revolutionary-era Americans were indeed informed by republican ideologies and motivated to fight for independence by their growing fears of British tyranny. Studies of republicanism became a cottage industry throughout the 1970s and 1980s, as historians explored the rhetoric and content of private communications and public print of the era, expanding the weight of evidence to support their proposition that classical republicanism and civic humanism had widely permeated political thinking in the colonies by the mid-eighteenth century.[10] In this interpretive framework, the Revolutionary soldier was still assumed to have been the yeoman farmer Emerson idealized a century before. The focus on shared political-ideological values in the republican synthesis overshadowed class tensions, African American roles in the war, women's contributions and experiences of the war, and the engagement of Native Americans in the struggle for America.

Rather than focusing on ideology, many young American historians turned their attention to the lives of ordinary people and their communities.[11] Following the lead of European social historians, in particular the "Annales School," they brought a new sensitivity to the conflicts in America over social justice and adopted new methodologies in their historical practices. Jesse Lemisch and Alfred Young provided models of social history from the "bottom up" in their respective studies of ordinary sailors and a shoemaker who did extraordinary things during the War for Independence.[12] Destiny gave way to contingencies produced by the actions of individual men and women in the midst of the Revolution.

John Shy and Richard Kohn began to consider the Revolutionary War not simply as a history of battles and campaigns, but as a new window through which historians could gain a unique view of society and the complexities of the Revolution.[13] The home front and ordinary soldiers became topics worthy of historians' labors. Shy astutely pointed out that the experience of living through the Revolution touched virtually every American; some 25,000 families lost a son or husband. Topics of the "new" military history expanded to include the characteristics of America's rank-and-file soldiers, their families and towns, the operations of local government, relations between the military and civil institutions, the effects of the war on women, the role of race and slavery, the decisions and roles of native peoples, and the attitudes and values of members of colonial society, to name but a few of the new areas of inquiry. Bringing social science skills to bear, Richard Buel, Jr., contributed a model study on the institutional and economic complexities of Connecticut's mobilization during the Revolution. Wayne Carp explored the reluctance of civil officials support the army adequately, a critique never entertained in traditional nationalist narratives. Ronald Hoffman and Peter Albert assembled and edited a wide-ranging collection of essays on various facets of America's armies, displaying the broad perspectives of the emerging "new" military history. Harold Selesky demonstrated a comprehensive approach to the integral involvement of the larger society in war in his 1990 study of colonial Connecticut. In *War and Society in Revolutionary America: The Wider Dimensions of Conflict,* Don Higginbotham summed up a range of new perspectives for historians, many of which are addressed in this volume.[14]

Historians began applying social science methodologies to analyze social conditions and behaviors through a close examination of a specific locale or subject, in a practice called "microhistory."[15] Robert A. Gross employed this approach to reconstruct the workings of society in Revolutionary-era Concord, Massachusetts. He found that the war stressed relationships in that community, and he penned the oft-repeated phrase that the war became "a poor man's fight."[16] Using similar techniques, Mark Lender, James Kirby Martin, Edward Papenfuse, Gregory Stiverson, and John Sellers produced a series of influential studies of specific groups of soldiers. These close studies of the ordinary rank-and-file soldiers, based on empirical demographic and economic data, revealed that many Revolutionary recruits were young, landless, and poor, a finding that deromanticized the image of the embattled farmer and indirectly critiqued the presumption that America was the cradle of egalitarian democracy. Their findings reinvigorated the Progressive School's claims of class division and conflict.[17]

The findings of Gross, Lender, Martin, Stiverson, and Papenfuse spawned a historiographical debate about the character of America's armies. Charles Royster's book, *A Revolutionary People at War: The Continental Army and American Character,* delved further into character and motivations of American soldiers during the war and found that their economic status was not necessarily determinative of their army service.[18] On the other hand, Charles Neimeyer recapitulated the economic thesis of Lender et al. in his 1996 publication, *America Goes to War: A Social History of the Continental Army.*[19] Meanwhile, John Resch and Mark Kwasny, among others, have presented contrary findings on the status of America's soldiers. Both statistical and qualitative analyses suggest that, at least in some sections of the country, the common soldier was quite representative of colonial society. Moreover, Kwasny defends the utility of the citizen-soldier militias despite a historical tradition of dismissal of their competence and importance. Wayne Bodle's study of the army at Valley Forge highlights the difficulties encountered and the commitment of American soldiers.[20] New work from Charles Neimeyer, John Resch, and Walter Sargent that appears in *War and Society in the American Revolution* furthers recent inquiry into the characterizations of America's Revolutionary soldiers.

Challenging the republican synthesis of Bailyn et al., Steve Rosswurm employed social history methods and class analysis in *Arms, Country, and Class: The Philadelphia Militia and "Lower Orders" in the American Revolution,* a work that reinvigorated Carl Becker's claim that the Revolution was indeed a struggle over who would rule at home.[21] Woody Holton more recently has argued, in *Forced Founders,* that class tensions in Virginia pushed the Tidewater elite to embrace the Revolution.[22] Following this line of inquiry, Michael McDonnell explored the class dimensions of military service in Virginia society in an important article on mobilization in Virginia.[23] McDonnell's contribution in the present volume furthers and refines our understanding of class tensions in Revolutionary Virginia, and Wayne Lee illuminates social divisions in the backcountry. James Peicuch also addresses social tensions in his essay, which explores the uneasy and shifting alliances among backcountry loyalists, Indians, and slaves.

Modern scholarship on African Americans owes a significant debt to Benjamin Quarles. His pathbreaking 1961 work, *The Negro in the American Revolution,* introduced to the civil-rights generation the hitherto little-recognized contributions of African Americans in the War for Independence. Philip Foner expanded on Quarles's work for a bicentennial publication, and Sidney and Emma N. Kaplan contributed an invaluable addition to the scholarship with *The Black Presence in the Era of the American Revolution.* More recently, Sylvia Frey and Gary Nash have built on Quarles's and Foner's works by emphasizing the actions of African Americans seeking to maximize their own opportunities for freedom during the Revolutionary era. Gregory T. Knouff has added "whiteness" to the explanations of racial and class conflicts that shaped the Revolution and American culture. In the present volume, Judith Van Buskirk contributes a sophisticated analysis of race and memory in Revolutionary-era New York.[24]

Prior to the 1970s, there was little note of women in school texts or academic histories for American history in general, and historians' treatment of the American Revolution was no different. The one exception, Elizabeth Ellet's *Women of the American Revolution,* published in 1849, was the most cited reference for over a century—because it was virtually alone in the field. According to Linda Kerber, Ellet's portrayals of women in the Revolution reflect more of the "sensitivity and sentiment" of the romantic era in which Ellet lived than they do of the gritty experiences of the Revolutionary-era women.[25]

In 1947, Elizabeth Cometti's concise article in the *New England Quarterly* shifted the inquiry about women in the Revolution from a few exceptional, romanticized images to profile the activities of many ordinary women. Cometti had the temerity to suggest that, although women "generally remained at home ministering to the needs of their households," they nonetheless were involved in a variety of significant roles, many of which extended beyond their homes into the public arena of the war effort.[26] In reframing our perspective of the Revolution beyond the battlefield, she anticipated the broadened historical agenda that came into full bloom with the next generation of social historians.

In 1980, two works set the benchmark for modern Revolutionary women's history: Mary Beth Norton's *Liberty's Daughters* and Linda Kerber's *Women of the Republic.* Norton expanded on the themes of women's activism and autonomy by locating women's roles across a broad social spectrum during the Revolutionary era, emphasizing that the Revolution was "a civil war with profound consequences for the entire population."[27] Joy Day Buel and Richard Buel, Jr., focused on a Connecticut family to demonstrate the centrality of women to any comprehensive discussion of the Revolution.[28] Joan Gundersen and Holly Mayer have continued their work on women's lives and the meaning of gender with contributions of new work to this volume, examining the experiences of displaced women and examining closely the activities and contributions of "camp followers," respectively.[29]

Traditional histories of the American Revolution largely relegated Native Americans to the margins, generally dismissed as British mercenaries who employed especially vicious tactics. Native American studies took off with the explosion of social history in the 1970s, and two early studies of Native Americans in the Revolution include James O'Donnell's study of Southern Indians and Barbara Graymont's study of the Iroquois. Gregory E. Dowd's book, *A Spirited Resistance: The North American Indian Struggle for Unity, 1745–1815,* explored the Native American perspective, presaging the direction of modern scholarship. Colin Calloway published a valuable survey of the engagement and aims of Native Americans from Maine to Georgia in his 1995 publication, *Revolution in Indian Country.* Max Mintz illuminated the predispositions of American policies toward the Iroquois in his *Seeds Of Empire: The American Revolutionary Conquest of the Iroquois,* in 1999.[30] Karim Tiro furthers the explorations of Native Americans with a subtle analysis of the Oneida in his contribution to the present volume.

The outpouring of scholarship in recent decades indicates the vitality of the field of American Revolution studies. The influence of social history has opened the door to exciting new questions and illuminating analyses. The scope of study, as this volume indicates, now reaches every geographic region from the hills of New Hampshire to the metropolis of New York City, across the South, and throughout Indian country. The studies of real lives lived in the time of America's Revolution now embrace not only the traditional heroes, but all of the peoples who made America.

Notes

1. David Ramsay, *The History of the American Revolution in Two Volumes,* ed. Lester H. Cohen (Indianapolis: Liberty Classics, 1989). Gordon S. Wood characterizes the early Whig histories as justifications for America's resort to war, "Rhetoric and Reality in the American Revolution," *William and Mary Quarterly,* 3rd ser., 23 (January 1966): 3–32.

2. Mercy Otis Warren, *History of the Rise, Progress, and Termination of the American Revolution. Interspersed with Biographical, Political and Moral Observations, by Mrs. Mercy Warren,* 3 vols. (Boston: Printed by Manning and Loring, for E. Larkin, No. 47, Cornhill, 1805): 3:455. For discussion on Warren's efforts, see Rosemarie Zagarri, *A Woman's Dilemma: Mercy Otis Warren and the American Revolution* (Wheeling, Ill.: Harlan Davidson, 1995).

3. Joyce Appleby, *Inheriting the Revolution: The First Generation of Americans* (Cambridge, Mass.: Belknap Press, 2000).

4. Alfred F. Young, *The Shoemaker and the Tea Party: Memory and the American Revolution* (Boston: Beacon Press, 1999); David Waldstreicher, *In the Midst of Perpetual Fetes: The Making of American Nationalism, 1776–1820* (Chapel Hill: University of North Carolina Press for the Omohundro Institute of Early American History and Culture, 1997). For an example of nineteenth-century biographies, see Parson Mason L. Weems, *A History of the Life and Death, Virtues and Exploits, of General George Washington* (Georgetown, D.C., 1800).

5. George Bancroft, *History of the United States,* 3 vols. (Boston, 1834–1840).

6. Carl Becker, *The History of Political Parties in the Province of New York, 1760–1776* (Madison: University of Wisconsin Press, 1909); Charles Beard, *An Economic Interpretation of the Constitution of the United States* (New York: Macmillan, 1913); John Franklin Jameson, *The American Revolution Considered as a Social Movement* (Princeton, N.J.: Princeton University Press, 1926). See Forrest McDonald, "Colliding with the Past," *Reviews in American History* 25, no. 1 (March 1997): 13–18.

7. See such "Imperial School" historians as Herbert Levi Osgood, *The American Colonies in the Eighteenth Century,* 4 vols. (New York: Columbia University Press, 1924); George Louis Beer, *The Commercial Policy of England toward the American Colonies* (New York: Columbia College, 1893); Charles McLean Andrews, *The Colonial Background of the American Revolution* (New Haven, Conn.: Yale University Press, 1924).

8. For example, Louis Hartz, *The Liberal Tradition in America: An Interpretation of American Political Thought since the Revolution* (New York: Harcourt Brace, 1955); Daniel J. Boorstin, *The Genius of American Politics* (Chicago: University of Chicago Press, 1953); Robert E. Brown, *Middle-Class Democracy and the Revolution in Massachusetts, 1691–1780* (Ithaca, N.Y.: Cornell University Press, 1955); John Richard Alden, *The American Revolution, 1775–1783* (New York: Harper & Row, 1954); Edmund Morgan, *The Birth of the Republic, 1763–1789* (Chicago: University of Chicago Press, 1956).

9. See Bernard Bailyn, ed., *Pamphlets of the American Revolution, 1750–1776* (Cambridge, Mass.: Belknap Press of Harvard University Press, 1965), *The Ideological Origins of the American Revolution* (Cambridge, Mass.: Belknap Press of Harvard University Press, 1967), and "The Central Themes of the American Revolution," in Stephen Kurtz and James H. Hutson, eds., *Essays on the American Revolution* (Chapel Hill: University of North Carolina Press, 1973).

10. See Robert Shalhope, "Republicanism and Early American History," *William and Mary Quarterly,* 3rd ser., 39 (April 1982): 334–56; Pauline Maier, *From Resistance to Revolution: Colonial Radicals and the Development of American Opposition to Britain, 1765–1776* (New York: Vintage Books 1974); and Gordon Wood, *Creation of the American Republic, 1776–1787* (Chapel Hill: University of North Carolina Press, 1969), and *The Radicalism of the American Revolution* (New York: Vintage Books, 1991).

11. The American practitioners of social history are indebted to European scholars such as Marc Bloch and Fernand Braudel, of the Annales School. These historians sought to broaden the scope of academic history through a conception of *l'histoire totale* that linked history with the social sciences. That linkage led to new approaches to access the histories of ordinary lives rather than the traditional concentration on "great men," high politics, and wars. See J. H. Hexter, "Fernand Braudel and the *Monde Braudellien,*" *Journal of Modern History* 44 (December 1972): 480–539.

12. Jesse Lemisch, "The American Revolution Seen from the Bottom Up," in Barton Bernstein, ed., *Towards a New Past* (New York: Random House, 1968); Alfred Young, "George Robert Twelves Hewes (1742–1840): A Boston Shoemaker and the Memory of the American Revolution," *William and Mary Quarterly,* 3rd ser., 38 (October 1981): 561–623.

13. John Shy, "A New Look at Colonial Militia," *William and Mary Quarterly,* 3rd ser., 20 (April 1963): 175–85, and *A People Numerous and Armed,* rev. ed. (Ann Arbor: University of Michigan Press, 1990); Richard H. Kohn, *Eagle and Sword: The Federalists and the Creation of the Military Establishment in America, 1783–1802* (New York: Free Press, 1975), and "The Social History of the American Soldier: A Review and a Prospectus for Research," *American Historical Review* 86 (1981): 553–67.

14. Buel, Richard, Jr., *Dear Liberty: Connecticut's Mobilization for the Revolutionary War* (Middletown, Conn.: Wesleyan University Press, 1980); E. Wayne Carp, *To Starve an Army at Pleasure: Continental Army Administration and American Political Culture* (Chapel Hill: University of North Carolina Press, 1984); Ronald Hoffman and Peter J. Albert, eds., *Arms and Independence: The Military Character of the American Revolution* (Charlottesville: University Press of Virginia, 1984); Don Higginbotham, *War and Society in Revolutionary America: The Wider Dimensions of Conflict* (Columbia, S.C.: University of South Carolina Press, 1988); Harold E. Selesky, *War and Society in Colonial Connecticut* (New Haven, Conn.: Yale University Press, 1990).

15. Richard D. Brown, "Microhistory and the Post-Modern Challenge," *Journal of the Early Republic* 23 (Spring 2003): 1–20.

16. Robert A. Gross, *The Minutemen and Their World* (New York: Hill and Wang, 1976), 147. Gross offers numerous observations that render the statement above somewhat ambiguous during the course of his discussion on the military efforts of the Concord people. For example, on the following page Gross notes that "the military burden was widely shared in the years when demands for manpower were at their height" (148). Models of microhistories in early American historiography include Philip J. Greven, Jr., *Four Generations: Population, Land, and Family in Colonial Andover, Massachusetts* (Ithaca, N.Y.: Cornell University Press, 1970); Kenneth Lockridge, *A New England Town: The First Hundred Years, Dedham, Massachusetts, 1636–1736* (New York: W. W. Norton, 1970).

17. Mark E. Lender, "The Social Structure of the New Jersey Brigade: The Continental Line as an American Standing Army," in Peter Karsten, ed., *The Military in America: From the Colonial Era to the Present* (New York: Macmillan, 1980); Edward C. Papenfuse and Gregory A. Stiverson, "General Smallwood's Recruits: The Peacetime Career of the Revolutionary War Private," *William and Mary Quarterly*, 3rd ser., 30 (January 1973): 117–32; John R. Sellers, *The Common Soldier in the American Revolution* (Colorado Springs, Colo.: United States Air Force Academy, 1976); James Kirby Martin and Mark E. Lender, *A Respectable Army: The Military Origins of the Republic, 1763–1789* (Arlington Heights, Ill.: Harlan Davidson, 1982).

18. Charles Royster, *A Revolutionary People at War: The Continental Army and American Character, 1775–1783* (Chapel Hill: University of North Carolina Press, 1979).

19. Charles Neimeyer, *America Goes to War: A Social History of the Continental Army* (New York : New York University Press, 1996).

20. John Resch, *Suffering Soldiers: Revolutionary War Veterans, Moral Sentiment, and Political Culture in the Early Republic* (Amherst: University of Massachusetts Press, 1999); Mark V. Kwasny, *Washington's Partisan War, 1775–1783* (Kent, Ohio: Kent State University Press, 1996); Wayne K. Bodle, *The Valley Forge Winter: Civilians and Soldiers in War* (University Park: Pennsylvania State University Press, 2002); Walter L. Sargent, "The Continental Soldier," in Keith Krawczynski, ed., *History in Dispute: The American Revolution* (Detroit: St. James Press, 2003).

21. Steven Rosswurm, *Arms, Country, and Class: The Philadelphia Militia and "Lower Sort" during the American Revolution, 1775–1783* (New Brunswick, N.J.: Rutgers University Press, 1987).

22. Woody Holton, *Forced Founders: Indians, Debtors, Slaves, and the Making of the American Revolution in Virginia* (Chapel Hill: University of North Carolina Press, 1999).

23. Michael McDonnell, "Popular Mobilization and Political Culture in Revolutionary Virginia: The Failure of the Minutemen and the Revolution from Below," *Journal of American History* 85, no. 3 (December 1998): 946–81.

24. Benjamin Quarles, *The Negro in the American Revolution* (Chapel Hill: University of North Carolina Press for the Institute of Early American History and Culture, 1996); Philip S. Foner, *Blacks in the American Revolution* (Westport, Conn.: Greenwood Press, 1975); Sidney Kaplan and Emma N. Kaplan, *The Black Presence in the Era of the American Revolution, 1770–1800* (Greenwich, Conn.: New York Graphic Society, 1973); Sylvia R. Frey, *Water from the Rock: Black Resistance in a Revolutionary Age* (Princeton, N.J.: Princeton University Press, 1991); Gary B. Nash, *Race and Revolution* (Madison,

Wis.: Madison House Publishers, 1990); Duncan J. MacLeod, *Slavery, Race and the American Revolution* (New York: Cambridge University Press, 1974); Peter Wood, "'The Dream Deferred': Black Freedom Struggles on the Eve of White Independence," in Gary Y. Okihiro, ed., *In Resistance: Studies in African, Caribbean, and Afro-American History* (Amherst: University of Massachusetts Press, 1986), 161–87; Gregory T. Knouff, *The Soldiers' Revolution: Pennsylvanians in Arms and the Forging of Early American Identity* (University Park: Pennsylvania State University Press, 2004); Judith Van Buskirk, "Crossing the Lines: African Americans in the New York City Region during the British Occupation, 1776–1783," *Explorations in Early American Culture: Pennsylvania History* 65 (1998): 74–100.

25. Linda K. Kerber, "'History Can Do It No Justice': Women and the Reinterpretation of the American Revolution," in Ronald Hoffman and Peter J. Albert, eds., *Women in the Age of the American Revolution* (Charlottesville: University Press of Virginia, 1989), 25.

26. Elizabeth Cometti, "Women in the American Revolution," *New England Quarterly* 20, no. 3 (September 1947): 329, 332–44.

27. Cometti, "Women in the American Revolution," 329–46; Linda K. Kerber, *Women of the Republic: Intellect and Ideology in Revolutionary America* (Chapel Hill: University of North Carolina Press, 1980); Mary Beth Norton, *Liberty's Daughters: The Revolutionary Experience of American Women, 1750–1800* (New York: Harper Collins, 1980). See also Barbara Clark Smith, "Food Rioters and the American Revolution," *William and Mary Quarterly*, 3rd ser., 51 (January 1994): 3–38.

28. Joy Day Buel and Richard Buel, Jr., *The Way of Duty: A Woman and Her Family in Revolutionary America: The Diary of Mary Gold Silliman* (New York: W. W. Norton, 1984).

29. Prior publications include Joan R. Gunderson, *To Be Useful to the World: Women in Revolutionary America, 1740–1790* (New York: Twayne, 1996); Holly A. Mayer, *Belonging to the Army: Camp Followers and Community during the American Revolution* (Columbia: University of South Carolina Press, 1996).

30. James H. O'Donnell III, *Southern Indians in the American Revolution* (Knoxville: University of Tennessee Press, 1973); Barbara Graymont, *The Iroquois in the American Revolution* (Syracuse, N.Y.: Syracuse University Press, 1972); Gregory E. Dowd, *A Spirited Resistance: The North American Indian Struggle for Unity, 1745–1815* (Baltimore: Johns Hopkins University Press, 1992); Colin G. Calloway, *The American Revolution in Indian Country: Crisis and Diversity in Native American Communities* (New York: Cambridge University Press, 1995); Max M. Mintz, *Seeds of Empire: The American Revolutionary Conquest of The Iroquois* (New York: New York University Press, 1999).

LIST OF CONTRIBUTORS

Joan R. Gundersen, Founding Professor Emeritus of History at California State University—San Marcos, is currently a research scholar in women's studies at the University of Pittsburgh. She has published more than twenty scholarly articles and five books, mostly in the fields of early American women's history, history of Anglicanism, and legal history. Her *"To Be Useful to the World": Women in Revolutionary America, 1740–1790* (New York: Twayne Publishing, 1996) was named an "Academic Book of the Year" in 1997 by the library journal, *Choice,* and a second edition was published in August 2006 by the University of North Carolina Press.

Wayne E. Lee is an associate professor of history at the University of North Carolina—Chapel Hill. His primary research interests are in early modern military history, in particular the relationship between culture, violence, and warfare. He also regularly participates with multidisciplinary archaeological projects, including in Greece, Albania, and Virginia. His major related publications are *Crowds and Soldiers in Revolutionary North Carolina: The Culture of Violence in Riot and War* (Gainesville: University Press of Florida, 2001); "Fortify, Fight, or Flee: Tuscarora and Cherokee Defensive Warfare and Military Culture Adaptation," *Journal of Military History* 68 (2004): 713–70; "Early American Ways of War: A New Reconnaissance, 1600–1815," *Historical Journal* 44 (2001): 269–89; and "From Gentility to Atrocity: The Continental Army's Ways of War," *Army History* 62 (Winter 2006): 4–19.

Holly A. Mayer is an associate professor of history at Duquesne University, in Pittsburgh, Pennsylvania. Her primary focus in scholarship is the American Revolution, particularly cultural issues and civil-military affairs during the War for Independence. She is the author of *Belonging to the Army: Camp Followers and Community during the American Revolution* (Columbia: University of South Carolina Press, 1996), and, with David E. Shi, editor of *For the Record: A Documentary History of America,* rev. 2nd ed. (New York:

W. W. Norton, 2004). She has also contributed essays to a number of anthologies and journals, most recently "From Forts to Families: Following the Army into Western Pennsylvania, 1758–1766," *Pennsylvania Magazine of History and Biography* (January 2006): 5–43.

Michael A. McDonnell lectures in the Department of History at the University of Sydney, Australia. He has published articles on the American Revolution in the *Journal of American History,* the *William and Mary Quarterly,* the *Journal of American Studies,* and the *Australasian Journal of American Studies.* His most recent publications include "Class War?: Class Struggles during the American Revolution in Virginia," *William and Mary Quarterly* 63, no. 2 (April 2006): 305–44, and *The Politics of War: Race, Class, and Conflict in Revolutionary Virginia* (Chapel Hill, N.C.: University of North Carolina Press for the Omohundro Institute of Early American History and Culture Series, 2007). His current research focuses on Indian, French, and Métis communities in the Great Lakes region.

Charles Neimeyer is presently the executive director of Regent University's Washington, D.C., campus and a professor in the Robertson School of Government, where he teaches courses on National Security Affairs. His recent publications include an article for *Newport History,* published in fall 2004, entitled "Rhode Island Goes to War, 1776–1778." He is also the author of *America Goes to War: A Social History of the Continental Army, 1775–1783* (New York: New York University Press, 1996).

Jim Piecuch, assistant professor of history at Kennesaw State University in Kennesaw, Georgia, received his Ph.D. from the College of William and Mary. He is the author of several articles, including "Empowering the People: The Stamp Act in New Hampshire," *Historical New Hampshire* 49, no. 4 (1994): 229–65; "'Of Great Importance Both to Civil & Religious Welfare': The Portsmouth Social Library, 1750–1786," *Historical New Hampshire* 57, nos. 3–4 (2002): 67–84; and "Washington and the Specter of Cromwell," in *George Washington: Foundations of Presidential Leadership and Character,* ed. Ethan Fishman et al. (New York: Praeger, 2001). He is also the author of *The Battle of Camden: A Documentary History* (Charleston, S.C.: The History Press, 2006), and is a member of the editorial board of the *Encyclopedia of North American Colonial Warfare,* ed. Spencer Tucker (Santa Barbara, Calif.: ABC-CLIO, forthcoming).

John Resch is professor of history at the University of New Hampshire—Manchester. He is author of *Suffering Soldiers: Revolutionary War Veterans, Moral Sentiment, and Political Culture in the Early Republic* (Amherst: University of Massachusetts Press, 1999). He is editor in chief of *Americans at War: Society, Culture, and the Homefront,* 4 vols. (New York: Macmillan Reference USA, 2005). His is also the author of several articles and book chapters, including "Poverty, Patriarchy, and Old Age: Analysis of the House-holds of Revolutionary War Veterans, 1820–1830," in *Old Age in Pre-Industrial Society,* ed. Susannah R. Ottaway, L. A. Botelho, and Katharine Kittridge (Westport, Conn.: Greenwood Press, 2002). He is currently conducting research for a book, *Peterborough, New Hampshire: A Study of the Market Revolution, 1790–1860.*

Walter Sargent is assistant professor of history at the University of Maine at Farmington. His publications include "Massachusetts Mobilization," in *Boatner's Encyclopedia of the American Revolution,* rev. ed. (New York: Charles Scribners' Sons, 2006), and "The Continental Soldier," in *History in Dispute: The American Revolution,* ed. Keith Krawczynski (Detroit: Gale, 2003). He is also currently revising his doctoral dissertation, "Answering the Call to Arms: The Social Composition of the Revolutionary Soldiers of Massachusetts, 1775–1783" (Minnesota, 2004), for publication.

John Shy is professor of history emeritus at the University of Michigan. He has taught and worked in the fields of early American history and the history of war. His published work includes *Toward Lexington: The Role of the British Army in the Coming of the American Revolution* (Princeton, N.J.: Princeton University Press, 1965), *A People Numerous and Armed: Reflections on the Military Struggle for American Independence* (Ann Arbor: University of Michigan Press, 1976; rev. ed. 1990), and "Jomini," in *Makers of Modern Strategy,* ed. P. Paret (Princeton, N.J.: Princeton University Press, 1986).

Karim M. Tiro is assistant professor of history at Xavier University. He is coeditor, with Cesare Marino, of *Along the Hudson and Mohawk: The 1790 Journey of Count Paolo Andreani* (Philadelphia: University of Pennsylvania Press, 2006). His articles have appeared in *American Quarterly, New York History,* and elsewhere. He is presently working on a book-length study of the Oneida Indian Nation from the Revolution through 1850.

Judith L. Van Buskirk is an associate professor of history at SUNY—Cortland. She is the author of *Generous Enemies: Patriots and Loyalists in Revolutionary New York* (Philadelphia: University of Pennsylvania Press, 2002), as well as articles on Revolutionary-era topics.

INDEX